RICHARD BRYA[...]rsity of Reading and wa[...] the same university for [...]logy of south-west Irela[...]phy at the Polytechnic [...]t at Eastern Washingto[...]waii. He has extensive field experience of Norway, southern Ireland, north-west Scotland and southern England. His main academic interests are in the geomorphology and biogeography of the Quaternary period. He has contributed several research papers in these fields and is the author of *Physical Geography* (W. H. Allen).

DICK KNOWLES graduated in geography from the University of Cambridge and was later awarded an MA from the University of Nottingham for research in urban morphology. He worked for some years as Head of the Geography Department at Rickmansworth Grammar School, and has also worked as an extra-mural tutor for the University of London, tutor-counsellor for the Open University and visiting lecturer at the University of South Carolina. He is now a senior lecturer in geography at the Polytechnic of North London. He is the author of a number of publications including the *O-Level Passbook: Geography*, *Model Answers in Geography*, *Geography Reference Library Book*, and the *Geography* and *Regional Geography* cards in the Key Facts Series (Intercontinental Book Productions), *General Geography* and *The Regional Geography of Africa* (Oxford University Press), and, as co-author, *Europe in Maps Vols. I and II* (Longman), *North America in Maps* (Longman), and *Economic and Social Geography* (W. H. Allen).

JOHN WAREING gained his first degree in geography from the University of Leeds and an MSc degree in Geography and a Diploma in Education from the University of London. He worked as an editor for a firm of cartographers before entering teaching as a master at St. Marylebone Grammar School, and is now a principal lecturer in geography at the Polytechnic of North London. He has published a number of research papers in the field of migration studies and is co-author of *Economic and Social Geography* (W. H. Allen).

GCE A-Level Passbooks

BIOLOGY, H. Rapson, B.Sc.

CHEMISTRY, J. E. Chandler, B.Sc.
and R. J. Wilkinson, Ph.D.

PHYSICS, J. R. Garrood, M.A., Ph.D.

PURE MATHEMATICS, R. A. Parsons, B.Sc.
and A. G. Dawson, B.Sc.

GCE A-Level Passbook
Geography

R. Bryant, B.A., Ph.D.
R. Knowles, M.A.
and
J. Wareing, B.A., M.Sc.

Published by Intercontinental Book Productions
in conjunction with Seymour Press Ltd.
Distributed by Seymour Press Ltd.,
334 Brixton Road, London, SW9 7AG

This book is sold subject to the condition that it shall not, by way of trade or otherwise, be lent, re-sold, hired out, or otherwise circulated without the publisher's prior consent in any form of binding or cover other than that in which it is published and without a similar condition including this condition being imposed on the subsequent purchaser

Published 1980 by Intercontinental Book Productions,
Berkshire House, Queen Street, Maidenhead, Berks, SL6 1NF
in conjunction with Seymour Press Ltd.

1st edition, 1st impression 8.80.0
Copyright © 1980 Intercontinental Book Productions
Made and printed by C. Nicholls & Company Ltd
ISBN 0 85047 928 2

Contents

Introduction, 7
1 The Earth–Atmosphere System, 9
2 Atmospheric Moisture, 18
3 Circulation Patterns, 26
4 Weather Systems, 36
5 Climates, 44
6 Rocks and Relief, 59
7 Slopes, 71
8 Rivers, 81
9 The Work of Ice, 92
10 Wind Action, 102
11 Coastlines, 107
12 Soils, 117
13 Ecosystems, 128
14 Major Natural Habitats, 142
15 Environment and Man, 152
16 Population Patterns, 161
17 World Population Growth, 170
18 Population Dynamics, 181
19 Population Composition, 194
20 The Geography of Economic Activity, 202
21 Transport and the Adjustment of Space, 209

Contents (cont)

22 The Geography of Agriculture, 224

23 Physical Resources: Minerals and Energy Sources, 236

24 The Location of Manufacturing Industry, 244

25 Theories of Economic Location, 257

26 The Geography of Economic Development, 267

27 Rural Settlement, 276

28 Urban Relationships, 285

29 Urban Morphology, 293

30 City and Region, 306

Further Reading, 314

Index, 316

Introduction

This book has been written as a revision aid for students preparing for the A-Level examination in Geography. Its content is based on a close study of the syllabuses of the various Examination Boards, and therefore reflects the range of geographical topics which A-Level students are currently required to study. A few topics which appear on the syllabus of just one or two Examination Boards are not included, but the book does cover the essential core material common to all Boards.

The A-level syllabuses of the various Boards are very wide-ranging and cover a great deal of material. Students will be well aware of this point. In writing this book the main problem has been the limitations imposed by its format which has precluded the treatment of topics in depth. It has not been possible to provide more than a concise outline of most topics. However, for a book which is basically a revision aid, this may be seen as a virtue by students. It does mean, of course, that the book should be used in conjunction with class-notes and the more specialized texts which are listed at the end of the book. Students are also recommended to supplement the material contained here with their own information derived from field-work and map-study. The examiners give a great deal of credit for evidence of personal observation and the collection of original case material. The book contains no regional geography as such. At present most syllabuses require that students should be able to provide regional examples of the topics which are studied systematically in both physical and human geography, but considerable freedom is usually given in the actual choice of regions. A close study of one or two countries from the developed and developing world is advised in order to provide the necessary regional examples. However, be sure to check the exact requirements specified by your Examination Board.

In the section of the book dealing with physical geography, the view is taken that the subject is essentially concerned with the natural environment as a whole, in which its main component parts, namely the atmosphere, landforms, soils, plants and animals, are closely linked by flows of mass and energy. A systems approach, backed up by flow diagrams, is employed to explain these important inter-relationships. In the chapters on the atmosphere, particular attention is paid to the dynamics of the general circulation as the essential link between meteorological processes and climatology; the review of geomorphology emphasizes a process-response approach rather than cyclic or historical thinking; soils and biogeography are treated in the belief that a knowledge of ecosystem functioning is necessary for an understanding of the geographical distribution of organisms. The sections on physical geography should be seen as an essential part of the study of the relationship between environment and human activity which is described in later chapters.

Various aspects of both social and economic geography are brought together in the second half of the book. The chapters dealing with population geography examine influences on density and distribution, the processes of population change, and the ways in which those processes affect population composition. The chapters dealing with economic geography focus on the major areas of activity and discuss the factors which affect their operation and location. Various approaches to the study are discussed, and the role and importance of transport is stressed as a space-adjusting technique binding the world economy together. The major sectors of economic activity—agriculture, mining and manufacturing—are examined, and various theoretical approaches to their study are discussed. The processes of economic development and some of the problems arising from imbalances in levels of economic development are also examined. Finally, in the chapters on settlement geography, emphasis is firmly placed on urban settlements, although the relationships between town and country are emphasized throughout.

It is hoped that from a study of the book the student will become aware of the complex system of relationships that exist between man and environment. In many ways an appreciation of the overall unity of the subject is more important than a detailed knowledge of its individual parts.

Acknowledgement

Thanks are due to Elizabeth Dawlings who drew all the maps and diagrams included in the book.

Chapter 1
The Earth-Atmosphere System

Physical geography is concerned with the study of the natural environment as it affects man. Although this definition could be taken to embrace everything from the subatomic to the astronomic level, the primary interest is in the visible environment, and particularly in the explanation of its spatial aspects. In this context, the main components of the subject matter include primarily: the landsurface, its waters and soil, the atmosphere and oceans, and the biosphere. Although often treated as discrete entities, all are closely linked by continuous exchanges of mass and energy, and all are part of an integrated system which can be called the Earth-Atmosphere system (Fig. 1). Within this framework, one can also identify major subsystems in which the links are particularly strong; for example, the hydrological system or cycle, where the mass transfer of water is the obvious link, and the plant-soil system (Chap. 12), where nutrient exchange is a fundamental feature. If we define a **system** as a set of objects or attributes (that is, characteristics of an object, such as size or shape) linked in some discernible relationship, then this concept is very useful in physical geography in providing a means of describing and understanding complex phenomena. One convenient way of illustrating the operation of systems is to use **flow diagrams**, and several examples are employed in various parts of the book (e.g. Figs. 2 and 49).

Energy sources and transfers

The Earth-Atmosphere system needs continuing inputs of energy in order to operate, since without energy the world would have no motion or life. There are two basic sources of this energy; the sun, and the interior of the Earth. Solar energy is received and transformed in a complex series of energy transfers, especially in the atmosphere, and these are described below (Fig. 2). The interior of the Earth provides radioactive energy, derived from the time of the formation of the planet. It is the driving force behind crustal movement and uplift, which result in the major landforms of the world (Chap. 6). In addition, there are two fundamental forces which, although not energy sources in themselves, influence the passage of energy in the natural environment. The mass of

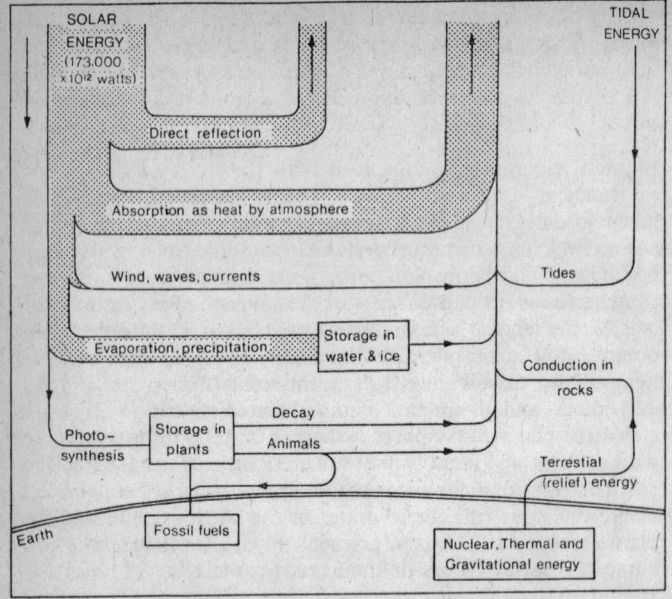

Figure 1. Energy flow in the Earth-Atmosphere system

the Earth sets up the force of **gravity**, and because of its influence many natural systems can be regarded as **cascading** systems, especially those on land, since the main transfers of mass and energy are downhill. Opposing gravity is the force of **friction**, which slows down and would finally prevent all motion in the Earth-Atmosphere system were it not for fresh inputs of energy from the sun or the interior of the Earth.

The energy in the natural environment exists in a variety of forms and it is important to be aware of these in order to understand some of the basic processes encountered in the study of physical geography. **Radiation** is the prime means of transfer of energy from the sun, and is achieved through the transmission of electromagnetic waves. All objects give off some radiant energy at various wavelengths, including the visible (light) and infrared sections. **Heat** is another form of energy of paramount significance; it will flow from one object to another if they have different temperatures. The transfer of heat is affected by one or more of the processes of radiation, the main method in the atmosphere, of **conduction**, transfer by contact, important in the rocks and soil, and of **convection**, the transfer of heat in fluids and gases and of prime significance in the oceans as well as in the atmosphere. The transfer of heat may involve not only a change of temperature (**sensible heat**) but a change of state (e.g. solid to liquid) involving hidden or **latent heat**. The effect of this is well illustrated in the case of atmospheric moisture (Chap. 2).

Potential energy and kinetic energy are both forms of the energy of motion. **Potential energy** is possessed by a body by virtue of its position. Thus, an object some distance above the ground has more gravitational potential energy than an object at ground level. If released, the potential energy will be converted to **kinetic energy** (the energy possessed by a body by virtue of its motion) as the object accelerates towards the Earth. Rivers are a good example of the conversion of potential energy into kinetic energy. The atmosphere contains a great deal of kinetic energy in its winds; this is dissipated by friction at the ground surface. Finally, **chemical energy** is the energy used or released in chemical reactions. One of the most important of these reactions in the natural environment is the process of photosynthesis in plants (Chap. 13). Other forms of energy, such as nuclear, electric, and magnetic, are of little direct concern here. The most obvious form of electric energy encountered in the natural environment is that of lightning in thunderstorms. Magnetic energy is of interest in the very high atmosphere at the edge of space.

The atmospheric energy balance

The atmosphere, taken as an entity, is a good example of an open system, as it receives both mass and energy from outside its boundaries. The heat and light or **insolation** from the sun accounts for the bulk of the energy; that received from the Earth is largely reflected energy. Mass also crosses in and out of the system, mainly in the form of water as part of the hydrological cycle (Fig. 3). Although the atmosphere is constantly receiving solar energy, by and large it is not getting any hotter. There clearly exists a balance in which the amount of energy coming in is balanced by equal loss; in other words the system is in general equilibrium. In figure 2, a flowline relation diagram depicts the main energy exchanges in the atmosphere. The incoming insolation arrives in different wavelengths, and is therefore subject to varying diversions by the atmosphere

If we assume for convenience that 100 units of radiant energy are available at the top of the atmosphere, then less than half (47) actually gets through to the Earth. Much of the rest (36 units) is returned to space by various forms of scattering and reflection, constituting the Earth's **albedo**. Another 17 units are absorbed by gases in the atmosphere, especially oxygen and ozone at high levels, and carbon dioxide and water vapour in the lower atmosphere; this absorption leads to a rise in the temperature of the air. The energy received by the Earth is re-radiated back into the atmosphere at much longer wavelengths. Some is lost directly to space, but a great deal of the rest is absorbed, especially by the clouds. In turn, the atmosphere reflects much of this heat back again, setting up a continuous exchange of energy with the ground. In this process there is a net gain to the atmosphere of about 14 units. Significant gains accrue to the atmosphere in latent heat transfer, and there is also a small amount gained by conduction.

One of the most significant aspects of this energy budget is that the atmosphere is largely heated from below. The atmosphere either

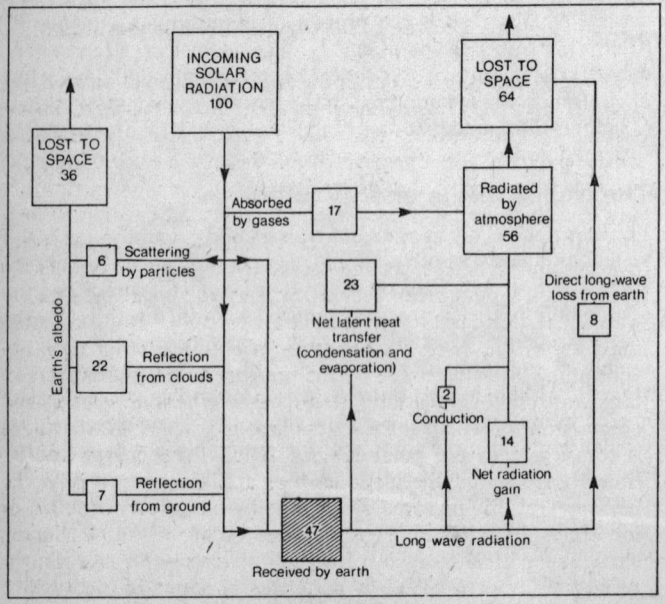

Figure 2. The atmospheric energy balance

reflects or lets through much of the incoming shortwave radiation, but traps the bulk of the outgoing longwave energy, and by this means the atmosphere is warmed. The term **greenhouse effect** aptly describes the situation.

Because the lower layers of the atmosphere are the most dense, they are best able to absorb the longwave radiation from the Earth. Hence temperatures generally drop with height, this being referred to as a **lapse rate**. It is possible to recognize distinct temperature layers in the atmosphere, the lowest three of which are the most important. The first 10 to 15 km form the troposphere, in which the average lapse rate is about 6·4°C/km. Nearly all the weather processes that materially affect us take place within this zone. At the top of the troposphere there is a reversal or inversion of the temperature gradient, appropriately known as the **tropopause**. This acts as a ceiling to weather generated in the troposphere. Above this occurs the **stratosphere** in which temperatures increase with height, especially in the upper layers above 30 km, because of the concentration of ozone at these levels. Temperature zones at even higher levels are much more difficult to define because of the thinness of the atmosphere.

Substantial variations occur in the amount of insolation received over the globe, and the outline given above presents only a general picture. These differences are fundamentally a result of **latitude**, which controls the intensity of insolation. Even taking into account the continuous summer daylight of the polar regions, in any year, high latitudes receive considerably less insolation than low latitudes. Put another way, the equatorial areas have a positive heat budget, whereas the poles have a negative budget. In theory, this should mean that tropical areas should get steadily warmer, and the Arctic and Antarctic even colder. But such is not the case, as the mean temperatures of both areas remain fairly constant. This is explained by the presence in the atmosphere of large horizontal circulation systems, namely the wind systems and ocean currents, whereby the excess heat received at low latitudes is transferred to the polar regions. Thus, solar energy and its transference round the globe as heat and kinetic energy is the fundamental driving force behind the **general circulation** of the atmosphere (Chap. 3), and hence of weather and climate. Recognizing that solar insolation is so crucial to the Earth-Atmosphere system, there is much recent scientific evidence to support the contention that long-term changes cause major shifts in climatic zones.

The global hydrological cycle

There are several important pathways of matter within the Earth-Atmosphere system, including rock erosion and deposition, and various nutrient systems (Chap. 12). However, the passage of **water**, in its vapour, liquid and solid states, is unique in that it forms a significant component of nearly all parts of the system, and thereby plays a major link role in the study of physical geography. As we have seen, the flow of water is intimately linked with the transfer of energy in the system, since large amounts of sensible and latent heat are circulated by atmospheric moisture and by ocean waters, and kinetic energy is transported by rivers and glaciers.

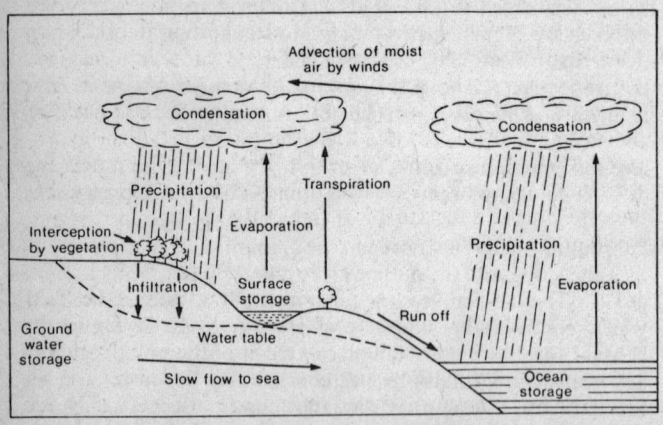

Figure 3. The global hydrological cycle or system

The main pathways and storages of water are schematically represented in Figure 3. Water in the oceans evaporates under the influence of solar radiation, and the resulting water vapour, some of it in the form of clouds, is transported to the land areas by atmospheric circulation. The solar energy expended in bringing water to this elevated position is considerable, although some of the latent heat required in evaporation is returned to the atmosphere in condensation when clouds are formed. The fall of precipitation over the land converts potential energy to kinetic energy, but much of this is dissipated by friction due to air resistance, and only a fraction remains as potential energy on the land to be used in geomorphological systems. Some of the precipitation reaching the land is intercepted by vegetation; some infiltrates the soil;

some percolates down to the ground water system and flows underground towards the sea; and the remainder flows as run-off, mainly in rivers. Evaporation from the land and transpiration from plants returns some of the moisture back to the atmosphere to be recycled.

In addition to its circulation patterns, the hydrological cycle also embodies a number of reservoirs or **storages**. Surprisingly large inequalities exist in the global amounts stored. The oceans contain 93% of the total; glaciers about 2%; and terrestrial waters constitute 5%, of which the vast majority is groundwater storage. Only a fraction therefore is held on or near the surface in the soil, yet this very small quantity sustains all life on land. An even smaller amount (0.001%) is held in the atmosphere as water vapour. However, these figures belie the fact that only a small part of the ocean waters enters the circulation system at any one time, whereas the atmospheric moisture has a very short residence time and is being continually transformed. A great deal of the circulating moisture does not enter into the **terrestrial** part of the hydrological cycle at all: nearly 80% of global precipitation falls over the oceans and, in terms of annual flux of mass and energy, the atmosphere/ocean subsystem is therefore the most important part of the world's climatic system.

The role of the **oceans** is a crucial yet neglected part of the study of the Earth-Atmosphere system. The two fluid layers in the system, the atmosphere and the oceans, complement each other in determining the energy flow round the Earth's surface. The atmosphere has little ability to resist stresses and moves easily and rapidly, whereas the oceans move only slowly in response to changes in force applied by the winds. The total mass of the oceans is about 280 times that of the atmosphere, and their heat capacity is nearly 1,200 times greater. These differences in mechanical and thermal inertia mean that the atmosphere imposes quick fluctuations of temperature from day to day and season to season, whereas the oceans suppress great swings of temperature. The comparison has been well made between the atmosphere as the fast spender in the global heat budget, and the oceans as the banker with huge assets in reserve.

Changes in the system

From a wide variety of evidence, it is well known that the present-day pattern of activity in the Earth-Atmosphere system has been substantially different in the past. This applies to all the major realms, including the planet's climate, geomorphology, hydrology, soils, and biogeography. Past changes in the system have left their mark in many respects on today's landscapes and it is important to bear in mind that when describing and explaining modern day features, many of them are **relict**. In other words, it takes a long time for many parts of the present-day Earth-Atmosphere system to adjust to new conditions of energy input; **time** is an important factor in physical geography, especially when considering landforms and the distribution of plants and animals.

Although there are many immediate causes of natural change in the environment, most of them are related ultimately to geological changes induced by activity in the interior of the Earth, or to climatic change. Large-scale changes have occurred in the past in the position and shape of the Earth's ocean and land areas. The mechanisms involved in these movements, which still continue today, are reviewed in Chapter 6. Climatic change (Chap. 5) occurs on many different spatial and temporal scales. In the geological past, a change of climate in any one area may have been brought about by continental drift rather than by changes in the atmosphere. But modern research has shown that, on a shorter time-scale, climatic changes affecting the whole globe are the result of shifts in atmospheric circulation caused by fluctuations in the amount and distribution of insolation received by the Earth.

This idea is embraced in the **Milankovitch curve**, put forward in the 1930s as an explanation of long-term climatic change, including glacials and interglacials. The curve is a calculation of radiation input for various parts of the Earth, taking account of the Earth's changing attitude to the sun in three respects: in the shape of its elliptical orbit; in the relation of the seasons to the orbit; and in its angle of tilt – at present $23\frac{1}{2}°$. Although Milankovitch's ideas were out of favour for many years, in the last decade a great deal of radiometrically-dated evidence from ocean cores has shown that the timing of cold and warm phases in the past agrees with the Milankovitch curve. Thus it seems that the receipt of solar energy by the Earth-Atmosphere system has fluctuated regularly in the past, sufficiently to have acted as the 'pacemaker of the Ice Ages'. However, taking a geological timescale, the *initiation* of Ice Ages such as that of the Quaternary period only comes about under certain combinations of continental position in relation to the poles; for instance, Antarctica is at present sited at the

South Pole. The causes of short-term climatic change, as in the historical past (Chap. 5), are less certain, and may result from a variety of causes.

Finally, it must be stressed that many of the important recent changes in the Earth-Atmosphere system have nothing to do with natural causes, but have been brought about by man's activities. This may even apply to recent climatic change: it has been suggested that the general warming trend in the last hundred years has occurred because of the output of carbon dioxide into the atmosphere by industrial processes. A review of man as an agent of change in natural processes is given in Chapter 15.

Summary

The Earth-Atmosphere system is supplied with energy from the sun and from the interior of the Earth. This energy is transferred in several ways within the natural environment, and is affected by gravity and friction. The atmosphere is largely heated from below by re-radiated energy. The transference of heat in the atmosphere around the globe is the driving force behind the general circulation. Mass is also cycled in the Earth-Atmosphere system, the most important pathway being that of water, which plays a crucial role in nearly all parts of the natural environment. Long-term changes in the system are induced by tectonic activity or climatic change and, more recently, also by man.

Chapter 2
Atmospheric Moisture

As part of the global hydrological cycle (Fig. 3), moisture is continually entering the atmosphere by evaporation and transpiration, and leaving it in the form of precipitation. The amount of moisture that any part of the atmosphere can hold at any one time (**saturation limit**) depends on temperature: cold air can hold very little moisture in absolute terms, and much more moisture can be evaporated into warm air before it becomes saturated. Several expressions are used for describing the amount of moisture in the air. **Absolute humidity** is the mass or weight of water vapour per unit volume of air, in grams per cubic centimetre; however, as a body of air rises or sinks it undergoes volume changes, and its absolute humidity is thus not a constant figure. Meteorologists make use of the term **specific humidity**, the ratio of the weight of water vapour to the weight of the air, since this figure remains constant whatever the volume changes, unless water is actually added to or lost from the body of air. Another expression useful to the geographer is **relative humidity**, which is the ratio of the actual amount of water in the air to the maximum amount the air could hold at that temperature, stated as a percentage. For example, air which contains only half the amount of moisture needed to saturate it has a relative humidity of 50%. This figure applies whatever the absolute or specific humidity of the air: an air mass with a temperature of 25°C and a relative humidity of 50% is carrying far more moisture than one with a temperature of 5°C and a relative humidity of 100%. Or, to put this another way, the relative humidity of an air mass will alter automatically with temperature: quite commonly, even with no actual moisture changes, the relative humidity during the day changes quite markedly, being lowest around midday when temperatures are highest.

Evaporation and condensation

Moisture exists in all three states of matter in the atmosphere, as vapour, liquid, or solid; changes from one to the other are known as phase changes, and significant amounts of energy are involved in accomplishing these changes. In the process of **evaporation**, 600 calories of latent heat are required to change one gram of water from a liquid to a vapour state; the effect of this on one kilogram of air is to cool it by 2.5°C. Normally such a heat loss would be quickly compensated by conduction and radiation. In the reverse process of condensation, latent heat is released into the atmosphere, causing a slight rise in temperature. The main exchanges are summarized in figure 4.

Three principal factors favour **evaporation**. First, the initial humidity of the air: the drier the air (low relative humidity), the greater the potential evaporation from water surfaces. Second,

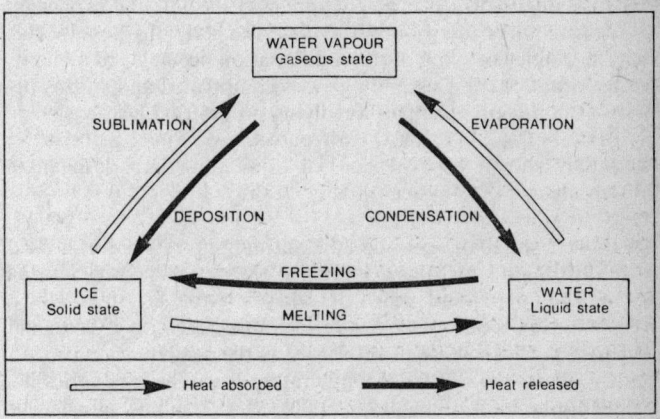

Figure 4. Moisture phase changes and latent heat exchanges

heat is needed to maintain evaporation, and the rate of evaporation will be proportionally higher depending on the warmth of the water surface and the air immediately above it. Third, wind force can be a significant factor, especially in turbulent conditions, where saturated air is continually replaced by fresh air. In general, the greater the wind strength, the more effective evaporation is likely to be.

Condensation occurs either when enough water is evaporated into the air mass for it to reach saturation point or, alternatively, when the temperature drops sufficiently to achieve the same result. The second method is the more common. However, condensation occurs only with the utmost difficulty in the pure air which exists in the higher layers of the atmosphere. A basic requirement is some tiny particle or nucleus on which the water vapour can condense. In the lower atmosphere this is normally no problem, since abundant **condensation nuclei** exist, principally common salt derived from the sea, and dust particles.

Adiabatic processes

Bodies of air frequently move from one level to another in the atmosphere for a variety of reasons, including convectional heating of the ground below, orographic uplift, turbulence in the airflow, and uplift at frontal surfaces (Chap. 4). Rising air expands because of the decrease of pressure with height; the expansion process requires energy, and therefore the body of air cools. This is responsible for much of the condensation occurring at all levels in the atmosphere. Descending air is compressed and warms up. These temperature changes, involving no external heat-exchange but accomplished within the air parcel, are termed **adiabatic**, and they should be distinguished from non-adiabatic changes which involve the physical mixing of air.

In dry air, adiabatic cooling and warming takes place at a fixed rate of 10°C/km, and this is known as the **dry adiabatic lapse rate**. The **saturated adiabatic lapse rate**, for air in which condensation is occurring, has lower values, between 4°C/km and 9°C/km, because latent heat released in the condensation process partly offsets the adiabatic temperature loss. The rate varies because the amount of latent heat released will be much greater for warm saturated air than for cold saturated air. Adiabatic lapse rates should not be confused with the normal or **environmental lapse rate** of the atmosphere (page 13); the adiabatic rates apply only when air is actually moving up or down. In Figure 5, we can see the effects of the adiabatic process on a small parcel of rising air with a temperature near the ground of 20°C and a **dewpoint** (saturation limit) temperature of 10°C. The air cools first at the dry adiabatic rate, and then at the saturated rate in the cloud. The air continues to rise until it reaches the same temperature, and therefore the same density, as its surroundings (the environmental lapse rate). A notable example of the operation of adiabatic processes is provided by the **Föhn** (European Alps) and **Chinook** (Alberta) winds, which rise on the windward, rainy side of the mountains at the saturated adiabatic rate, but then, having lost most of their moisture, descend at the much greater dry rate, bringing hot dry air to the valleys.

A distinction needs to be made between stable air, which will only rise when it is forced to, for instance over a mountain, but will sink once the original cause of uplift has ceased, and unstable air, which continues to rise spontaneously. Air is defined as **unstable** if the environmental lapse rate exceeds the dry adiabatic lapse rate, as is the case in figure 5, where the air on rising immediately becomes warmer and lighter than its surroundings and therefore continues to rise. This kind of instability tends to occur on very hot days when the ground layers of air are considerably heated; if the air is moist enough, strong vertical cloud development is likely. On the other hand, **stable** air conditions exist when the environmental air has a lapse rate less than both the dry and saturated adiabatic rates. In this case, if air is displaced upwards, it immediately becomes cooler and denser than its surrounding and will sink groundwards again.

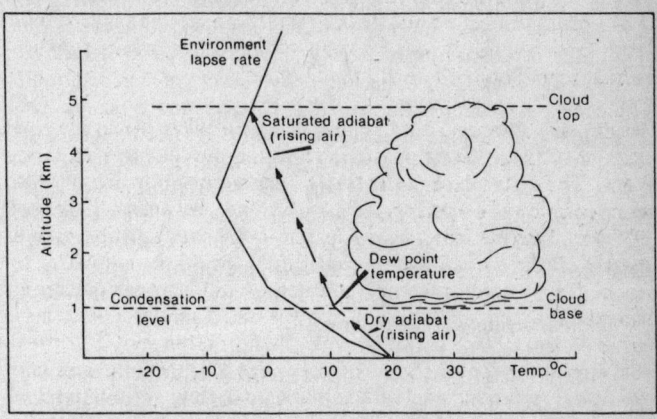

Figure 5. *The spontaneous rise of unstable air*

Conditional stability exists when the environmental lapse rate lies between the two adiabatic rates. The air is stable as long as it remains dry but, should it become saturated, then on rising at the saturated rate it would eventually become warmer than the environment air and hence unstable.

Clouds and fog

Clouds are a visible manifestation of condensation in the atmosphere. There is a great profusion of cloud forms, but one can draw a distinction between **stratiform** clouds, which have a layer-like appearance, and **cumuliform** clouds, which are heaped or massive in shape. Two related factors are important in determining cloud shape, that of air stability and the mode of uplift. In unstable conditions, the dominant form of uplift is convection, and this is primarily responsible for the vertically-developed cumuliform clouds. Stratiform types, on the other hand, tend to be the product of stable air conditions, in which turbulence is the principal cloud-forming mechanism. Frontal uplift gives rise to a variety of clouds, depending on the type of front and the stability of the air (Chap. 4). Similarly, clouds formed by orographic uplift can be either stratiform or cumuliform, depending on the stability of the air.

The internationally accepted classification of cloud types is that contained in the *Cloud Atlas of the World Meteorological Organization*. Four main cloud 'families' are recognized, embracing ten cloud *genera*, and an impression of these is given in figure 6. The **high clouds** are composed largely of ice-crystals, and include the wispy cirrus and the mackerel-sky effect of cirrocumulus. The prefix alto- defines the **middle clouds**, and these are generally found at heights of between 3 and 6 km. The **low clouds** are often indicative of dull weather: stratus, for instance, is a dense low-lying cloud, and in the form of stratonimbus indicates the presence of precipitation. These first three families all fall into the broad stratiform category. The fourth family, **clouds with vertical development**, are clearly cumuliform, reflecting in their shape something of the upcurrents within them. Cumulus is the familiar white woolpack cloud.

Fog is cloud that forms close to the groud. There are three principal types, each indicative of different ways in which cooling takes place. **Radiation fog** is caused by radiation cooling of the land at night; in turn, the ground chills the adjacent air layers by conduction. This type of fog tends to be common in calm conditions under clear skies in late autumn and early winter. **Advection fog** forms when moist air is blown (advected) over a cool surface and is chilled by contact. Typically this occurs over sea areas in early summer, creating a sea fog. **Steam fog** is generally much more localized than the other two types, and develops where cold air blows over much warmer waters. Evaporation from the water body quickly saturates the cold air and the resulting condensation is seen as steam. The best examples occur in polar areas, where very cold air blows off ice-covered land over relatively warm seas. All three types of fog are rapidly dispersed or lifted by turbulence.

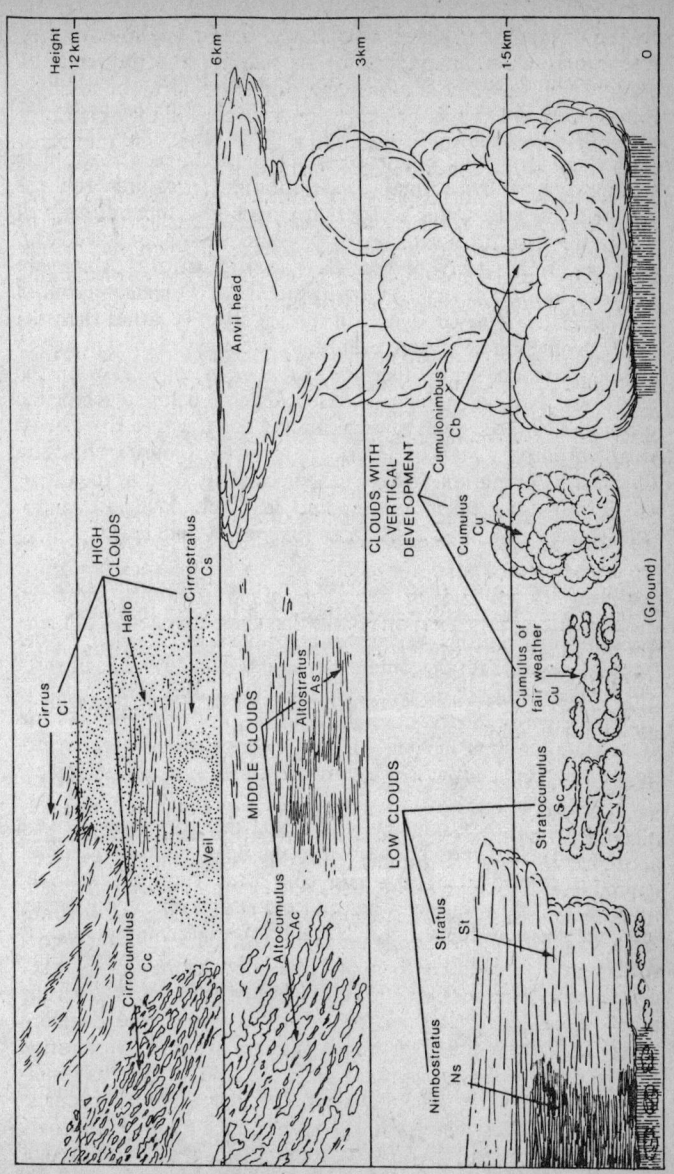

Figure 6. The ten principal cloud types, grouped into 'families'

Precipitation

Not all clouds give rise to precipitation, and it is important to realize that there is a difference between the tiny droplets that make up clouds and the much larger drops that fall as rain. The process of producing raindrops is not simply a case of droplets getting bigger by normal condensation. It requires the co-existence of both water and ice in clouds at temperatures well below freezing. The water exists in unfrozen super-cooled form because of the rarity of special **freezing nuclei** which are required to form ice crystals. In this situation, the water vapour in the cloud tends to condense on the ice crystals rather than the water droplets. The crystals eventually become sizeable enough to fall and coalesce with other crystals to form snowflakes on the way down. Normally, they melt into raindrops before reaching the ground. This process of rainmaking is known as the **Bergeron mechanism**, after the Norwegian meteorologist who first outlined its operation. It has been successfully used as the theoretical basis for artificial rain-making in which clouds are seeded with dry ice or similar substances (pages 154 and 228).

Clouds which are too warm, with no freezing nuclei, will not produce rain by this process. However, it is likely that there may be other mechanisms, especially in tropical areas, where it has been observed that rain comes from clouds which have great vertical development but do not reach the temperature levels required by the Bergeron theory. Possible raindrop-producing mechanisms in these situations include condensation on extra-large hygroscopic nuclei, and growth by electrical attraction between droplets.

Hail is of a rather different origin from the rain, snow, or sleet (partially melted snow) described in the Bergeron theory. A hailstone is composed of alternate concentric rings of clear and opaque ice, and is formed when an ice crystal is repeatedly carried up and down in the vertical currents of a large cumulonimbus cloud. Freezing and partial melting may occur several times before the pellet is large enough to escape from the cloud.

Thunderstorms

Thunderstorms develop when unstable conditions extend to great heights, and this allows powerful updraughts to develop within cumulonimbus clouds. Within a storm there may be several convective cells, each of which goes through a life-cycle. In the

developing stage, the initial updraught, formed in response to convection, is considerably accelerated by the energy released as condensation occurs. The great strength of the updraught initially prevents rain from falling. In the **mature stage**, heavy rain accompanied by thunder and lightning occurs, and the top of the cloud spreads out under the tropopause in a characteristic anvil shape. The storm passes into the **dissipating stage** as the supply of moisture in the cell is gradually exhausted. Downdraughts become predominant, spreading out below the cloud and preventing any further convective instability in the immediate vicinity. **Lightning** occurs in thunderstorms to relieve the electrical tension between oppositely-charged areas within the cloud, or between the cloud and the ground. Broadly speaking, the upper part of the cloud is positively charged, and the lower part negatively, except for a small positively-charged region around the rain area. **Thunder** occurs because lightning heats the immediate air to very high temperatures, causing rapid expansion and vibration of the air column, which is heard as thunder.

Summary

Of the various expressions used to describe atmospheric moisture amounts, relative humidity is the most common, although it can be a misleading quantity. Evaporation and condensation processes are basic to many meteorological phenomena. The vertical movement of air causes adiabatic changes of temperature, and the relation between the dry and saturated adiabatic lapse rates and the environmental lapse rate is fundamental in determining stability conditions. The many types of cloud form are all composed of tiny condensed water droplets, whereas precipitation drops are much bigger. The Bergeron mechanism accounts for most of the precipitation of middle and high latitudes, including that in thunderstorms.

Chapter 3
Circulation Patterns

Horizontal air movement or **wind** occurs on many scales, from small eddies to major circum-planetary wind systems, and also tends to be much more powerful than the local vertical motion described in the last chapter. The basic impulsion to air movement is provided by the inequalities in the atmospheric energy budget (Chap. 1). Variable heating sets up variations in pressure, and this becomes one of the basic forces governing air movement. Once air is in motion, other factors come into play, including: Coriolis force, the deflection caused by the Earth's rotation; centripetal force, which acts around circulatory pressure systems; and the frictional force exerted by the Earth's surface.

Forces governing winds

Pressure is normally measured in millibars, spatial variations of pressure being depicted on maps by **isobars**, lines connecting places having the same barometric pressure. The gradual change of pressure between different areas is known as the barometric slope or the pressure gradient. As on a contour map, the closer the isobars, the greater the gradient. The **pressure gradient force** always acts down the pressure gradient, attempting to cause the general movement of air away from high-pressure towards low-pressure areas. This ought to mean that winds will blow at right angles to the isobars, but in practice this is hardly ever so because of the influence of the other forces: in fact winds tend to flow more nearly parallel to the isobars.

Coriolis force is named after the French physicist Coriolis, who in the 19th century formalized the concept of the Earth's deflecting force. This causes an apparent deflection of moving air to the right in the northern hemisphere and to the left in the southern, whatever the original direction. The phenomenon affects all freely moving objects, including ocean currents and projectiles. Although its effects seem real enough to anyone on the ground, the force is sometimes called 'apparent', because, if viewed from outer space, objects moving across the face of the Earth would appear to travel in a straight line, while the Earth rotates beneath them. To the observer on the ground, the

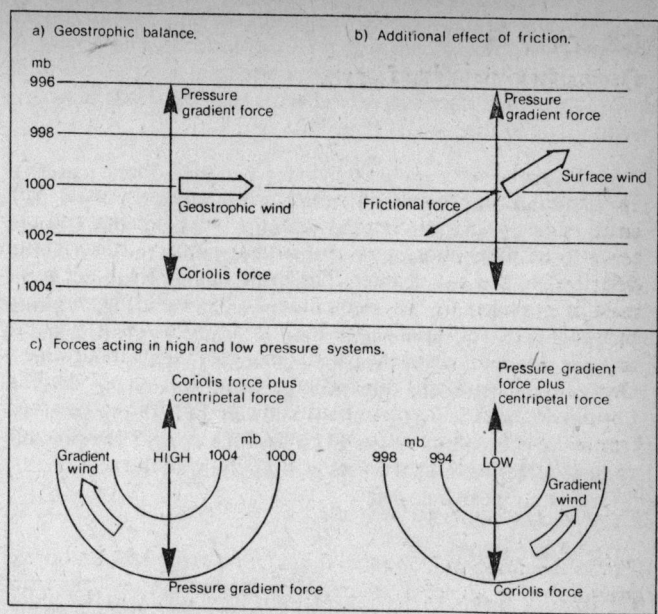

Figure 7. Forces governing air motion

deflecting force varies with the speed of the moving air and with latitude: the faster the wind, the more ground it covers in a given time, and the greater the effect of rotation can be. Near the equator, where the Earth's surface is spinning in a plane almost parallel to the axis of rotation, the Coriolis force is very slight, but it has marked effects in higher latitudes.

Wind directions adopt a condition of equilibrium or balance between various forces, the most important of which is the **strophic balance** that exists between the pressure gradient and Coriolis forces. In the free atmosphere, above the level of flow affected by surface topography, the flow of wind parallel to the isobars indicates that the two forces are exactly balanced (Fig. 7a). This sort of air motion is known as the **geostrophic wind**. A qualitative expression of the geostrophic situation is **Buys Ballot's Law**, which states that if one stands with one's back to the wind, then in the northern hemisphere low pressure always lies to the left, and high pressure to the right. The reverse applies in the southern hemisphere. In the lowest parts of the atmosphere, the frictional drag exerted by the ground lessens the speed of the wind and in doing so weakens the Coriolis force. This allows the pressure gradient to assert its greater strength, and thus the usual situation on a surface synoptic chart is that the winds blow at a slight angle to the isobars (Fig. 7b).

Centripetal force applies to winds when the isobaric pattern is markedly curved. The fact that air is following a curved path means that in addition to the pressure gradient and Coriolis forces, a third force is acting centripetally, pulling the air inwards. Wind which is in balance with these three forces is known as the gradient wind. Motion around a low-pressure area (Fig. 7c), anti-clockwise in the northern hemisphere, is termed **cyclonic**, and in this case the result of the centripetal force is to make the Coriolis force weaker than the pressure gradient force: the wind is subgeostrophic. The **anticyclonic** flow in the high-pressure case is supergeostrophic, since the Coriolis force exceeds the pressure gradient force. Frictional forces will apply in both these cases if the winds are near the surface.

Upper air motion

The study of airflow in the upper troposphere is vital to the understanding of many surface weather patterns, for depressions and anticyclones are essentially three-dimensional phenomena. Broadly speaking, wind speeds tend to increase with altitude because of lower air densities and the lessening of frictional effects. Pressure patterns, and hence wind patterns, also tend to be simpler higher up than those at surface level. Another feature is that pressure patterns visible at the surface do not always persist into the upper air, and hence wind directions may change direction with altitude. For instance, cold anticyclones, which at ground level are often characterized by intense high pressure, seldom persist beyond 2 km in altitude and are replaced by relatively warm air with lower pressure than surrounding regions.

Such changes in pressure distribution with height are largely related to changes of temperature. The basic principles involved are illustrated in figure 8, where two adjacent columns of air in the troposphere are depicted. At ground level the pressure exerted by the two is the same, but important changes ensue if column A is warmer and therefore less dense than B in the troposphere. For any level in the columns, for instance at 2 km, there is a greater pressure of air still above this level in column A than in column B.

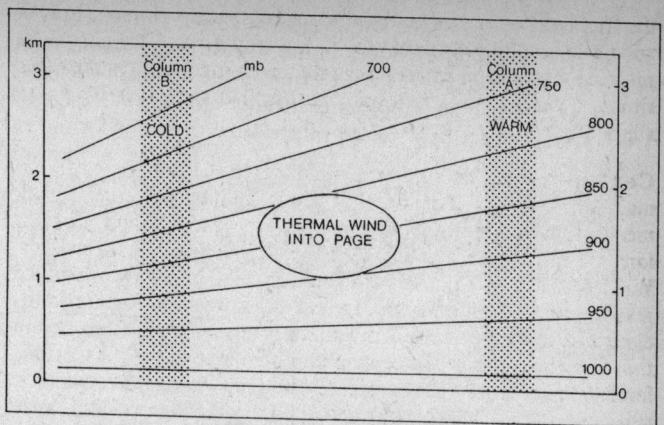

Figure 8. The principle of thermal winds

Thus a pressure gradient from A to B gradually develops and intensifies with height, where none existed at the surface. The resultant geostrophic wind, blowing at right angles to the pressure gradient because of Coriolis force (into the page), is known as a **thermal wind** since it derives from temperature contrasts in the atmosphere. In the northern hemisphere, cold air always lies to the left of the thermal wind when viewed downwind, and to the right in the southern hemisphere. Applying this on a global scale, the decrease in temperature from equator to poles results in upper air winds that are predominantly westerly in both hemispheres.

Concentrated bands of rapid air movement in the upper troposphere are termed **jet streams**. They are in reality intense thermal winds, being associated with latitudes where the poleward temperature gradient is particularly strong. Two such zones occur in each hemisphere: a subtropical jet stream at about 30° of latitude, and a polar front jet stream (Fig. 11).

The flow of the geostrophic winds around the globe is rarely exactly parallel with latitude, but usually occurs in huge meandering paths called **Rossby waves**. These have an important bearing on surface weather patterns; for instance, the waving of the fronts that we commonly see on weather charts is closely linked to them. Variations in the Rossby waves are described in terms of a zonal index which is a measure of the strength of the upper air flow. In a fairly **average index** situation (Fig. 9), three to six

Rossby waves encircle the atmosphere in amplitudes covering 15° to 20° of latitude. The troughs in the waves reach towards lower latitudes and this is where jet streams are at their strongest. Although the pattern migrates eastwards around the globe, the troughs and ridges may persist in preferred positions for several weeks at a time, guiding the track of the passing depressions beneath them. In a **high index** period, the waves may be hardly recognizable. The upper westerly air flow is strong, and its effect on the surface weather is a tendency to be mild and windy in mid-latitudes. In contrast, in a **low index** period, the Rossby

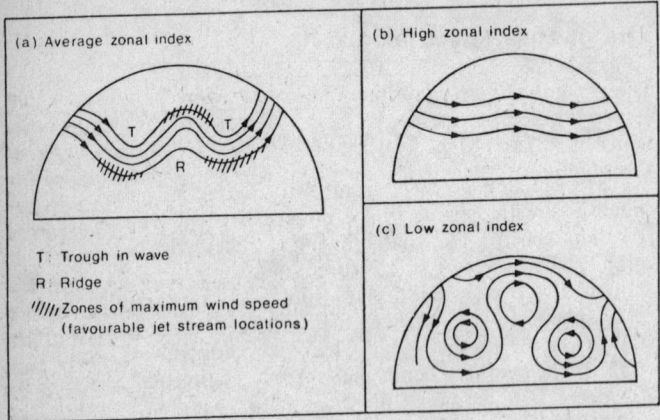

Figure 9. *Variations in the Rossby wave flow*

wave pattern breaks down into large cells which allow meridional flow of air. Strong incursions of cold air can move equatorwards, allowing cold anticyclones to develop, whereas in other places there is a poleward movement of warm air. In that they are a good guide to trends in surface weather, the study of Rossby waves is of considerable help to weather forecasters.

Convergence and divergence

When the geostrophic wave pattern is weak or has broken down, the upper and surface air patterns are often connected by large-scale but slow vertical motions of air. These are set up as part of a system of air inflow or convergence and outflow or divergence at different levels. In a surface low-pressure system, the pressure gradient sets up a net inflow of air, with the wind blowing at a slight angle to the isobars (Fig. 15). However, if the low pressure is to persist, then the influx of air needs to be relieved by a vertical ascent of air. In turn, the vertical motion is itself accompanied by outward divergence at high level. Similarly, in a surface high-pressure system (Fig. 15), there is divergence of air at low levels which is maintained by convergence higher up. This type of air motion may persist over several days, and goes some way towards explaining why many anticyclones, characterized by descending and therefore warming air, are relatively cloudless, whereas in low-pressure regions the ascent of air is liable to give cloud and bad weather.

The general circulation

The general principles outlined above can now be illustrated in respect of the planetary or general circulation of the atmosphere. Much new knowledge has been added to our understanding of this subject in recent years through the information supplied by satellites about conditions in the upper troposphere. In its simplest form, the general circulation should operate like a gigantic heat engine and produce, in vertical cross-section, a single cell circulation in each hemisphere, in which there is rising air at the equator, high-level outflow towards the poles, and a return surface flow in the opposite direction. Taking into account the Earth's rotation, the upper flow should be predominantly westerly and, with the additional effects of friction, the surface flow should be slightly south of easterly; but several important factors disguise this pattern. Perhaps the most significant is that the interchange of heat between equator and poles does not take place only in a vertical sense, but is also accomplished in a horizontal sense, particularly in middle latitudes, where large masses of air penetrate north and south past each other in upper air waves and surface frontal patterns. This means in effect that frontal systems are a major force in the maintenance of the general circulation and not mere appendages to it.

A modern cross-sectional representation of the general circulation (Fig. 10) shows that a thermally-driven cell (**Hadley cell**) operates in low latitudes; this gives surface winds with an easterly component (trade winds). However, polewards of 30° the picture becomes more complicated and is characterized by the horizontal mixing of contrasting air masses. The position and strength of the polar front between these air masses varies considerably. In polar areas there is some weak subsidence of dense, cold air. This model

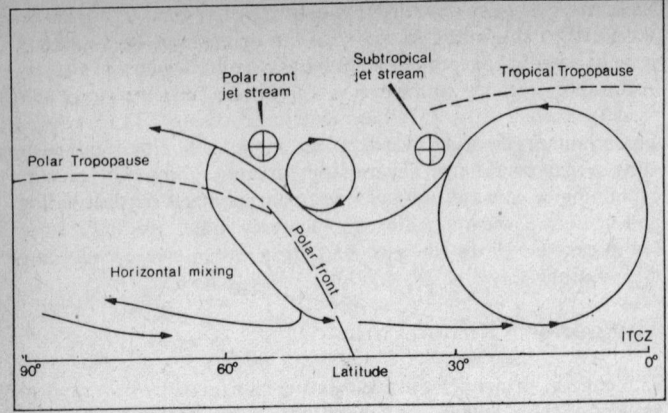

Figure 10. Cross-sectional model of the general circulation

is only an average picture; in plan view, variations to the air flow are caused by the distribution of oceans and continents, topographic barriers, and differences between the northern and southern hemispheres.

Planetary wind belts

Broadly speaking, all the major wind systems around the globe are predominantly zonal or latitudinal in character, especially the upper winds. The surface wind pattern (Fig. 11) is dominated by two wind belts in each hemisphere. One of these is the **trade-wind** belt, which covers nearly half the surface of the globe, between latitudes 30° N and S. The permanency of the subtropical high-pressure zones has an important bearing on the constancy of these winds. The two trade-wind systems converge towards each other in the equatorial low-pressure trough. With the annual migration of the trough with the overhead sun, the trade winds sometimes cross into their opposite hemisphere, giving a narrow zone of **equatorial westerlies**: the south-west monsoon of Asia is an exaggerated version of these winds. The second major surface wind belt in each hemisphere is the **mid-latitude westerlies**, which develop out of the poleward sides of the subtropical high-pressure cells. The westerlies of the southern hemisphere are the stronger and more persistent, as there is minimal interference from land masses, in contrast to the northern hemisphere. Polewards of the westerlies, high-latitude areas are generally regarded as being in the regime of the **polar easterlies**, but in the Arctic, where the polar high-pressure area is only a winter phenomenon, these winds tend to be seasonal. In Antarctica, easterly winds appear to be more reliable.

Important zones of surface convergence and divergence exist in the general circulation. The most important regions of divergence on the globe are the two subtropical high-pressure zones. These

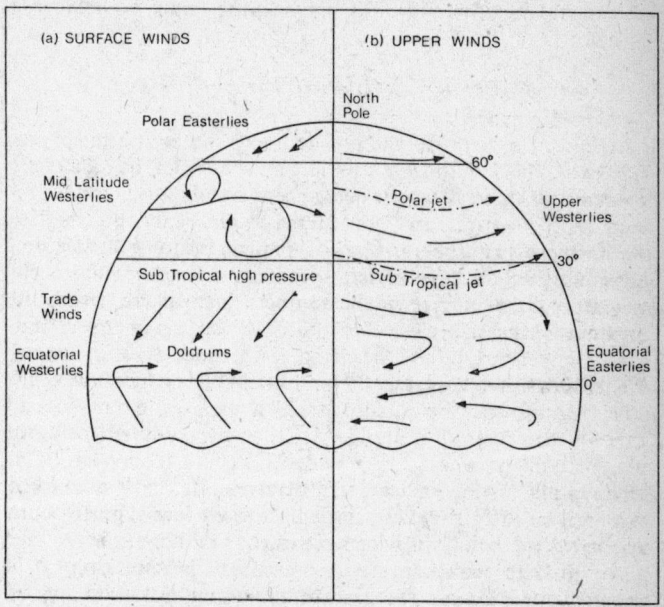

Figure 11. Surface and upper air planetary wind belts

are areas of relatively calm winds, sometimes given the name 'horse latitudes'. Three major zones of net convergence encircle the globe. Two of these are the **polar front zones** of each hemisphere, between the westerlies and polar easterlies. The third lies in the equatorial trough between the inblowing trade winds and is termed the **inter-tropical convergence zone**. It is rather a variable feature, being easily recognizable only where there are noticeable temperature and humidity contrasts in the two converging trade winds; elsewhere calm doldrums may exist.

The upper air general circulation is characterized all year by **upper westerlies**, from about 15° of latitude almost to the poles. These flow in each hemisphere as a large **circumpolar vortex**, incorporating both the Rossby waves and the two jet stream belts referred to earlier in the chapter. In low latitudes there is a much narrower belt of **upper easterlies**, whose extension again depends on the seasonal migration of the equatorial trough. With the July monsoon in India these winds reach as far as about 20° N, and are accompanied by a marked tropical jet stream, but at other times of the year the upper easterlies are limited.

Influence of the Earth's surface

The differences between the northern and southern hemispheres in the wind belts outlined above largely arise from the differences in land area. The southern hemisphere circulation is more uniform, more vigorous, and less affected by seasonal contrasts than the northern hemisphere. Marked summer heating of Asia and Africa north of the equator sets up monsoonal effects which occur only to a minor degree in the southern hemisphere, where the conservative heating characteristics of the oceans impose a tempering influence. On the other hand, the great coldness of Antarctica ensures that a strong thermal gradient between the south polar regions and the equator drives a vigorous circulation all year.

The world's major **mountain chains** also have a marked influence on the general circulation. At lower levels, north-south orientated topographic barriers obstruct zonal flow, as in the case of the Rockies, which effectively prevent the penetration of west coast maritime air into the continental interior. East-west aligned mountains inhibit meridional flow: the Himalayas, for instance, form an extremely effective barrier to the northward movement of the summer monsoon. High mountains also interfere with the upper air flow. The best studied example is again the Rockies, which cause the upper westerlies to contract (high pressure) on their western side, but expand vertically (low pressure) on their lee side. The latter then becomes one of the favoured locations of a Rossby wave trough, which encourages high-level cold air to move southwards over the continental interior of North America in summer, helping to counteract the development of any large monsoonal effect in the continent. By analogy, similar reasoning can be applied to the Andes and South America.

The general circulation gives context to many weather phenomena, and those most commonly encountered are described in the next chapter. Equally, it is also the starting point for the explanation of large scale climates outlined in Chapter 5.

Summary

Impulsion to winds is created by pressure gradients, but they are also affected by friction, the Earth's rotation, and centripetal force. Upper geostrophic winds, responding to pressure differences caused by large-scale thermal gradients in the atmosphere, contain Rossby waves and jet-streams in middle latitudes. Under certain conditions, upper and surface wind systems are linked by convergence and divergence. In the general global circulation both vertical and horizontal interchange of air masses takes place. The planetary wind systems are dominated by trade winds and westerlies at the surface, and by westerlies at high level. Complications are imposed by differences in amounts of land and sea in the northern and southern hemispheres, and by large-scale topographic barriers.

Chapter 4
Weather Systems

Although all areas of the world experience meso-scale weather systems occasionally, mid-latitude regions lying in the westerlies belt, including the British Isles, can be said to be characterized by them. Here, description of the weather is formulated in terms of air masses, fronts, depressions and anticyclones.

Air masses

Large bodies of air whose physical properties, particularly those of temperature and humidity, are more or less uniform over considerable areas, are referred to as air masses. Since the lower layers of the atmosphere acquire these properties via the Earth's surface (Chap. 1), it is possible to recognize **air mass source regions** in which air masses pick up their distinctive features. These source regions are areas where the Earth's surface is fairly uniform, such as oceans, deserts, or large ice- and snow-covered areas. In addition, they are also regions of relative calm in the general circulation where homogeneous air mass characteristics can develop. Although air masses can become considerably modified as they travel, it is usual to describe the main types in terms of their region of origin.

The principal air masses which affect the British Isles are depicted in figure 12. There are two major groups, **Polar** (*P*) and **Tropical** (*T*) air masses. The Polar Front represents the fluctuating boundary between these two types. The Polar air masses actually originate in cool-temperate regions rather than the polar areas themselves. Two additional groups are sometimes encountered, Arctic (*A*) and Equatorial (*E*) air masses, which occasionally migrate well beyond their source regions. Each of these major groups may further be described on the basis of their humidity characteristics as either **maritime** (*m*) or **continental** (*c*). In the northern hemisphere, Polar continental (*Pc*) air masses have their source regions over central Canada and Siberia, and air masses emanating from here are extremely cold and very dry, bringing some of the coldest weather experienced by the British Isles. Polar maritime (*Pm*) air masses originate over the northern ocean areas, and are essentially cool and moist, and unstable in their lower layers. They are frequent visitors to the British Isles, bringing dull rainy conditions. The subtropical high-pressure centres over oceans act as source regions for Tropical maritime (*Tm*) air masses; these are typically warm, moist and unstable, especially in summer. Tropical continental (*Tc*) air masses originate over warm desert areas, such as the Sahara and, not unexpectedly, they are hot, dry and unstable, although too deficient in moisture to cause cloud development.

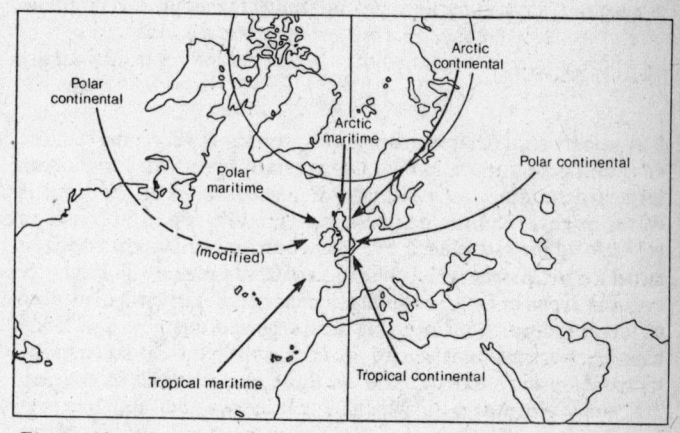

Figure 12. Principal air masses affecting the British Isles

Air masses move away from source areas in accordance with the pattern of the general circulation, and their basic characteristics may change in two ways: either by internal modification, for example by subsidence, bringing about adiabatic changes (Chap. 2), or by the external influence of the surfaces over which they are passing. The end-result is to produce **secondary air masses**. One typical example is Polar continental air originating from the high-latitude interior of North America. This frequently travels westwards across the Atlantic towards the British Isles, increasing in temperature and moisture content in its lower layers, and being transformed into a *Pm*-type air mass.

The concept of air masses works very well for practical weather explanation in mid-latitude zones, but is more difficult to apply in equatorial regions, where air mass contrasts are less well marked.

Fronts

Where air masses of different characteristics are in juxtaposition, broad **mixing zones** occur which are called fronts. These are commonly represented on weather maps as single lines, but the associated weather may cover an area several hundred kilometres wide. Frontal zones also have considerable vertical extent, reaching right up to the tropopause. The colder (denser) of the two air masses forms a wedge underlying the warmer air mass, as in figure 13. Conventionally, the slope of a frontal zone is much exaggerated in a diagram, and in reality the slope is very small, often less than 1°, hence an observer may well see the symptoms of an approaching front many hours before the surface front actually reaches him.

The weather associated with moving fronts is very variable; the common denominator is that it is generally unsettled. Two factors largely determine the weather experienced: whether the front is warm or cold, and the degree of activity. Where a front passes in which cold air is replaced by warmer air, it is a **warm front**; a **cold front** passes when the cold air comes second. The activity on both types of front is mainly dependent on the vertical motion of air in the warm air mass. If the air here is unstable and rising rapidly, the resultant active front is called an **ana-front** by meteorologists. **Kata-fronts** are those characterized by the general sinking of warm air which suppresses weather activity.

The **ana-type of warm front** (Fig. 13) is by far the most common in Britain. The rising motion in the warm air mass often proceeds at different rates at different levels, and this, together with varying relative humidity, produces a multilayered effect rather than one solid mass of cloud. As the front approaches, normally at an average speed of about 50 km/hr, the typical cloud sequence will be: cumulus and stratocumulus in the cold air mass well ahead of the front, dying out as it approaches; isolated cirrus in the warm air above the front, gradually increasing and merging into cirrostratus; then a thickening and lowering of these clouds to altostratus, obscuring the sun and giving precipitation. Near the surface front nimbostratus predominates, giving persistent rather than heavy rain. **Frontal fog** may form in the cold air mass near the frontal zone as this moisture condenses. The precipitation behind the frontal zone usually comes from stratocumulus clouds but gradually dies out, being replaced by unsettled weather. The changes of temperature as the front passes may be of

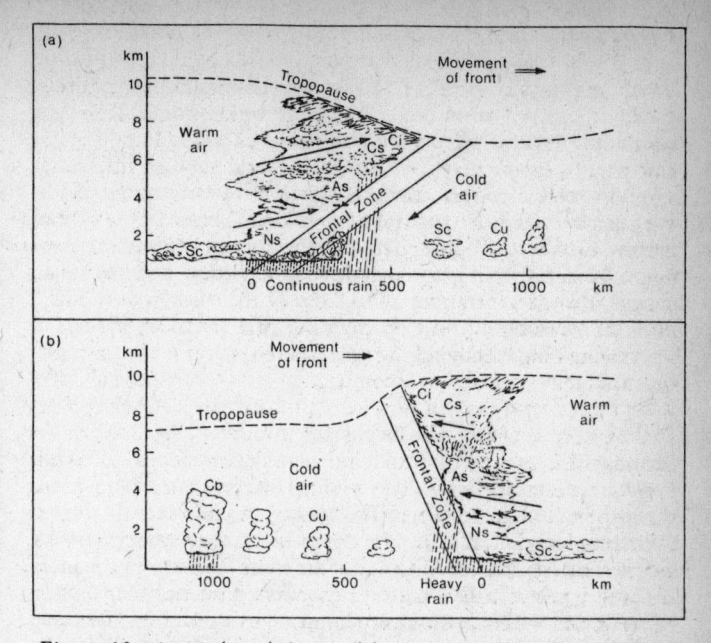

Figure 13. Active (ana-) fronts: (a) warm, and (b) cold

the order of 4° to 5°C over a period of one or two hours. Pressure levels, which would have been falling steadily as the front approached, recover slowly. The wind usually veers (clock-wise) on the passage of the front.

On **kata-warm fronts**, the downward motion of the air in the warm air mass restricts the development of medium and high-level clouds. Changes in temperature, pressure and winds occur in similar fashion to those for an ana-front, although they are usually much smaller in amplitude.

Cold fronts over Britain tend to include both ana- and kata-types. In the *active* type (Fig. 13) the distribution of clouds and precipitation is very similar to an ana-warm front, but in reverse. The most important difference is that the frontal slope is two to three times greater, so the cloud belt passes more quickly. There is typically a rather abrupt change in the weather, from the heavy rain of nimbus clouds at the front itself to bright showery weather in the cold air mass. The *inactive* variety is dominated by thick stratus clouds. The front passes through almost unnoticed with only gradual changes in temperature, pressure, wind, and precipitation amounts.

Depressions and occlusions

The majority of fronts occur in association with areas of low pressure known as **frontal depressions**. These have a typical life cycle of 4 to 7 days. The initiation (cyclogenesis) of these depressions depends on the upper air situation and relates to convergence and divergence (Chap. 3). In the Rossby wave pattern, acceleration and deceleration of air and the polar jet stream are continually taking place as the waves meander equatorwards and polewards. In conjunction with these speed changes there is compensatory air flow across the isobars, causing convergence in some places and divergence in others (Fig. 14). This is sufficient to generate and maintain moving cyclones and anticyclones at surface level underneath. Divergence tends to occur downstream of a trough in the Rossby waves, and this is the favoured location for the development of surface depressions. Conversely, strong convergence of air takes place downstream of the ridges in the Rossby pattern. The waving on the polar front at lower levels within a surface depression is caused by the rapid increase in wind shear (change of speed and direction) with height. This takes a spiral-like form and causes the front to twist itself into wave patterns.

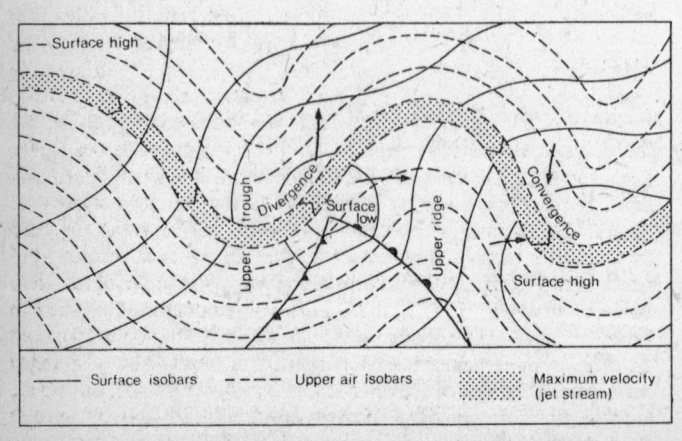

Figure 14. A frontal depression in relation to upper air flow

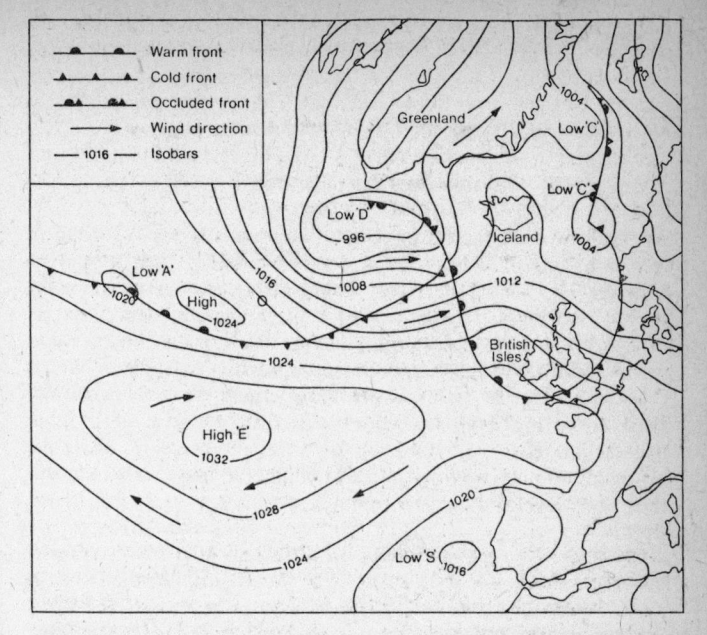

Figure 15. North Atlantic synoptic chart, 8 July 1979

Frontal depressions in various stages of development are shown in Figure 15. The first sign of a developing depression at surface level comes with the formation of a **wave distortion** on the polar front (e.g. Low 'A'). The apex of the wave becomes the centre of the low pressure area, and warm air becomes trapped in the **warm sector** between the cold air in front and behind. At this stage, with the depression moving eastwards in the westerlies, an observer on the ground would experience the warm front/cold front sequence of weather described earlier. In the majority of frontal depressions which reach the warm sector stage the cold front travels faster than the warm, overtaking and wedging beneath it, first of all near the centre of the low and then progressively further outwards. This is the process of **occlusion**, as seen in Low 'D', in which the warm sector is raised aloft and the two cold air masses meet beneath it. A new front is nearly always formed here, since the two cold air masses, originally the same, have been modified in different ways. If the second cold air mass is warmer than the first then we have a warm occlusion; a cold occlusion occurs if the second mass is colder. Occlusions reaching the British Isles tend to be of the warm type in winter, and cold in summer. In either case, since we have the original cold and warm fronts raised up in addition to the new surface front, they give rise to some of the wettest frontal weather. The system begins to decay when the occlusion is complete; the frontal contrasts become weaker and the depression fills up. This latter process will be rapid if another depression moves into the area.

As illustrated in figure 15, frontal depressions rarely occur in isolation, but in series known as **depression families**. This complex waving of the polar front can give spells of unsettled weather lasting a week or more. The sequence is eventually terminated when the polar front, having been pushed further and further south with each successive depression, is replaced by an extensive wedge of high pressure (low zonal index). **Secondary depressions** commonly occur within the circulation of the main depression. They may form at the point of occlusion, or as the result of renewed waving on the trailing cold front, in which case they may develop into new main depressions.

It needs to be stressed that not all depressions are frontal. Shallow **thermal lows** may develop at a wide variety of scales because of local overheating of the Earth's surface; **lee** or **orographic depressions** may form on the downwind side of mountains because of divergence of the airstream; tropical depressions, variously known as **hurricanes**, cyclones or thyphoons, are a feature of subtropical areas, originating where sea surface temperatures are greater than 27°C. All depressions share in common the characteristic of rising air, which in most cases inevitably leads to cloud and precipitation.

Anticyclones

In contrast to depressions, anticyclones usually cover a wider area, they tend to be more persistent, and they are slower moving. In the northern hemisphere they have a clockwise circulation of winds (high 'E', Fig. 15). The high pressure in an anticyclone is the result of cold dense air somewhere in the vertical column and, on the basis of where this cold air occurs, can be classified into warm and cold types. In **cold anticyclones**, the cold air is confined to the lower parts of the atmosphere, and is chilled by contact with the Earth's cold surface in winter. The great seasonal anticyclones which develop over Siberia and Canada are of this type. **Warm anticyclones** are characterized by relatively warm air in the lower parts of the troposphere, and the excess of pressure arises from the coldness of air in the upper troposphere and lower stratosphere. The permanent subtropical anticyclones are of this type. Some of the summer anticyclones which affect Britain originate as ridges of warm air which encroach northwards when a low zonal index situation prevails.

The subsidence of air in all anticyclones imposes generally calm weather conditions, with stable air. However, although most anticyclones passing over Britain are of the warm type, the weather varies considerably with the air mass and time of year. Summer anticyclonic spells are usually fine, but in winter, when moist *Pm* air is present, continuous stratus cloud may persist, trapped beneath an inversion formed in the subsiding air above. Other, drier winter anticyclones give clear skies and low temperatures, leading to frosts. Some of these anticyclones may be little more than ridges of high pressure between passing depressions, but others may be much longer lasting, developing when the upper air flow breaks down into a cellular pattern. A **blocking situation** may be created in which the surface anticyclone blocks the passage of surface depressions, steering them well to the north or south. Such a situation developed over Britain in the long hot summer of 1976. Similarly, in the notable winter of 1962–3 a blocking anticyclone centred to the north of the British Isles persisted for several weeks, bringing easterly winds and extremely low temperatures.

Summary

Air masses can be classified according to the temperature and humidity characteristics of their source region. Many of those affecting the British Isles have been modified during their passage. The mixing of air masses on the polar front creates warm and cold surface fronts which give rise to typical weather sequences. Most frontal systems are associated with depressions which are initiated by divergent flow in the upper air. Occlusions develop on many frontal systems. Anticyclones are characterized by cold dense air somewhere in their vertical structure, and this leads to subsidence and generally calm weather.

Chapter 5
Climates

In describing the climate, or average state of the weather, of any area, we need to consider not only the statistical record of the various climatic elements, such as temperature, precipitation and winds, but also the dynamic background to the figures. Explanation is as important as description in climatology. For large-scale climates, the general circulation provides the essential background for the characteristics of each climatic zone. For local climates, small-scale weather systems are set up by detailed geographical features in certain places at times when the general circulation is slack.

Classification of climates

Despite the seemingly endless variety of climates, patterns of weather repeat themselves in various parts of the world where the essential governing factors are similar. In attempting to categorize these similarities, most climatic classifications make use of temperature and precipitation data. However, there are two problems: first, the availability of data is very uneven throughout the world, and second, what values or boundaries are meaningful? In order to overcome these difficulties, many classifications have zones which are based on the *effects* of climate, such as natural vegetation boundaries. Investigations have been carried out to determine what temperature and rainfall amounts control the boundaries at certain places, and these figures have then been extrapolated for apparently similar boundaries in the rest of the world. Examples of this type of classification include those by W. Köppen and A. A. Miller. However, the difficulty with all effect-type classifications is that the so-called effects are rarely the result of climate alone. For instance vegetation is also a function of soils, past climates, and man.

Another approach is to base classification on the *causes* of climate. The main difficulty here is to ensure that the causes are fully understood. Inevitably, these genetic classifications use less precise boundaries than 'effect' classifications, but this is perhaps a much more realistic approach to the real world. Recently, as more has become known of the workings of the atmosphere, new

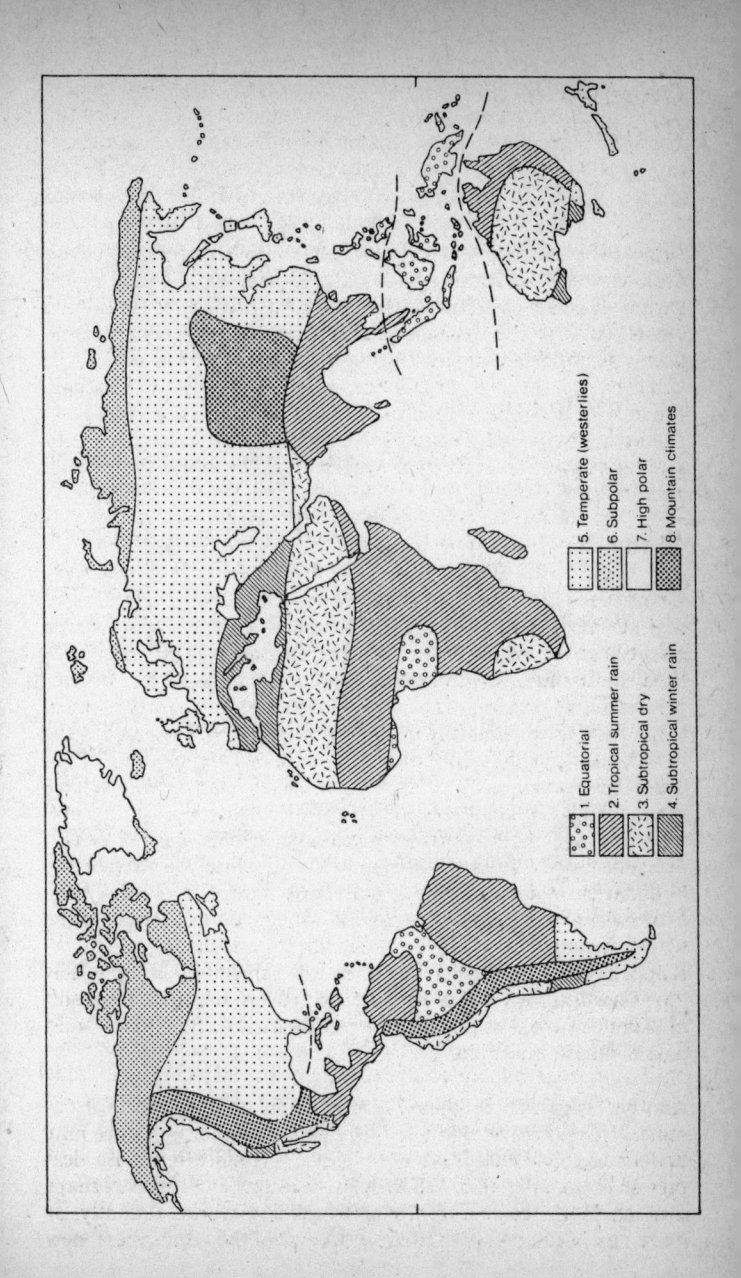
1. Equatorial
2. Tropical summer rain
3. Subtropical dry
4. Subtropical winter rain
5. Temperate (westerlies)
6. Subpolar
7. High polar
8. Mountain climates

attempts have been made to use genetic classifications. Some have been based on air mass types, but probably the most fruitful approach is simply to use the major features of the general circulation as a basis for division. This is the approach followed in this chapter, based on the categories suggested by H. Flohn. It builds directly on the information about the dynamics of the general circulation and its causes that has been outlined in previous chapters. Seven major zones are recognized, as depicted on a world map (Fig. 16). The eighth category shown on the map, mountain climates, recognizes that smaller-scale factors are paramount here, and these are considered later under 'local climate'.

World climatic zones

1. Equatorial rain zone Climates here are dominated by the influence of the equatorial trough, in which winds are generally weak and variable. In some areas, such as parts of Zaïre and Amazon basins, the daily pattern of weather-change, with heavy convectional rain each afternoon, is more regular than any seasonal rhythm. Temperatures around 30°C and relative humidities over 60 per cent are normal during most of the day; only at night, which is sometimes labelled 'the winter of the tropics', is there a significant temperature drop.

This classic daily rhythm does not apply to all areas all of the year, since the dominance of the equatorial trough varies with seasonal migration. Coastal West Africa, for instance, has a definite rainier season as the trough and the associated intertropical convergence zone (ITCZ) pass northwards in June. The same applies to Indonesia and surrounding countries, where the large changes in the position of the ITCZ create two distinctly wetter periods, one in June and the other in September.

2. Tropical summer rain zone The circulation basis is that the weather of the equatorial trough prevails in summer but trade-wind conditions are in evidence in winter. The poleward migration of the trough in summer in both hemispheres brings weather similar to that experienced by the equatorial rain zone. This season usually begins and ends with heavy thunderstorms associated with the passing ITCZ. The term **monsoon** can be loosely applied to the arrival of these rains in most parts of the zone. In Africa, the south-west monsoon in June affects a large tract of country stretching from the savanna lands of West Africa eastwards to Ethiopia. Similarly in the southern part of Africa, summer rain associated with the equatorial trough reaches the veldt country in December and January. These summer rains provide a refreshing contrast to the dry conditions of winter. In this season, trade winds blow from an easterly quarter, often having crossed hot deserts, and inevitably bring dessicating conditions. In northern Nigeria, the *Harmattan* is a strong version of the trade wind and, although it may relieve the humid atmosphere of the coast, it is most unwelcome in the north of the country. In complete contrast, on the eastern sides of Africa and South America the winter trade winds blow onshore having crossed large tracts of ocean. Thus the winter season is not one of drought, but of moist conditions, and there is in effect no real dry season in places such as Malagasy, northern Queensland, eastern Brazil, and the Caribbean Islands.

The **Indian sub-continent** experiences, in dynamic terms, an exaggerated version of the tropical summer rain type, but with marked seasonal contrasts. The primary circulation features (Fig. 17) show that in winter westerlies dominate the upper air flow, with a jet-stream just south of the Himalayas steering winter depressions and precipitation into northern India. Surface winds over the rest of India are generally from the north, developing from air subsiding beneath the westerlies. In spring and early summer thermal low pressure develops over north-east India, but the rapid advance of the summer monsoon from the south does not occur until the jet stream has switched to the north of the

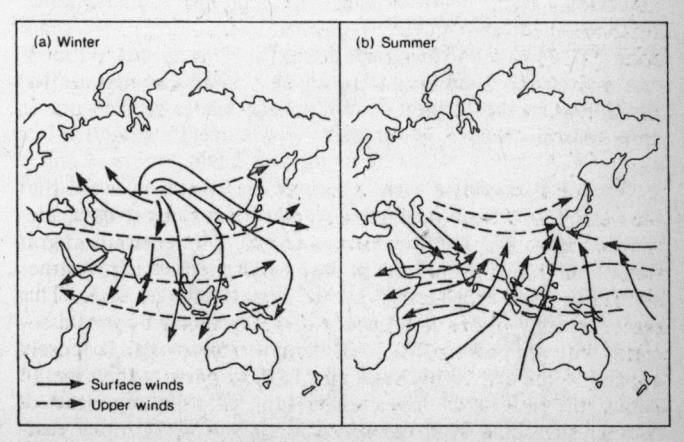

Figure 17. Circulation features in the Indian monsoon region

Himalayas and a pattern of upper easterly winds has been established. The equatorial trough then migrates to reach southern India in early June and the Himalayas by mid-July, and dominates the weather of the subcontinent until September/October. The climate of the region can thus be summarized as having four distinct seasons: a relatively cool period from mid-December to March; a very hot, dry period in April and May; a cooler wet period during the monsoon; and a warmer period from October to December during the retreat of the monsoon, accompanied by cyclonic rain.

3. Subtropical dry zone The climate of large areas of the globe between 20° and 30° of latitude is controlled all year round by dry trade-wind air originating from the subtropical high-pressure cells. Such regions include all the **hot deserts** of the world. The subsiding anticyclonic circulation makes rainfall very rare in these areas but there are perhaps only a few places where no rain falls at all; intermittent disturbances in the trade winds or in encroaching westerly air masses in winter bring occasional precipitation to most localities. With so few clouds temperatures reach considerable extremes, with daily maxima up to 50°C not uncommon. On the western sea margins of many of the major deserts upwelling cold currents cool the adjacent air, giving clammy and often foggy conditions. However, rainfall amounts still remain very low as the moist air is usually only shallow and replaced above by the more characteristic subsiding air of the subtropical belt.

4. Subtropical winter rain zone In relatively small areas on the western side of all the continents, the general circulation alternates between the drought conditions of the desert trade winds in summer and the variable weather of the temperate westerlies belt in winter. This type of climate is unique in having its dry season in summer and its rainy season in winter. The best known and by far the largest in area of this type of climate is the **Mediterranean basin**. Here, the size of the area and its complex coastline creates many local variations on the general pattern. Passing depressions in winter draw in very cold winds from the north, such as the *mistral* of the Rhône corridor, or warm winds from the south, like the *sirocco* of North Africa. In general the eastern Mediterranean has a more extreme climate than the west. Elsewhere, a similar but simpler pattern of weather recurs in the Cape Region of South Africa, California and Oregon, central Chile, and south-west Australia. Mean summer temperatures lie between 20° and 28°C, and around 6° to 10°C in winter, above the lower limit for plant growth. Rainfall amounts in winter are largest on the poleward side of these regions, closest to the main depression tracks.

5. Temperate westerlies zone Middle latitudes come under the influence of the circulation of the westerlies wind belt for most of the year. As seen in the last chapter, both tropical and polar air masses are brought into this wind system, whose interchange along the polar front plays a major role in the weather of the whole zone. Truly temperate conditions, in the sense of being mild and equable, are found only on coastal locations on the western margins of continents; elsewhere there are quite large extremes of warmth and cold. Two types of temperate climate are usually recognized: **maritime**, as experienced by the western sides of continents, and **continental**, characteristic of mid-latitude Eurasia and North America. The east coasts of the continents are to some extent intermediate between the two types; temperature contrasts are greater than on west coasts, but they have a more varied climate than continental interiors. However, the whole zone has in common a great variety of weather, and many parts have in addition the dubious quality of unreliability

The maritime climate of **north-west Europe** (Fig. 18) is controlled in terms of pressure by the gradient between the Azores high and the Icelandic low, with the addition in winter of the Siberian high. In winter, when the influence of the Azores high is

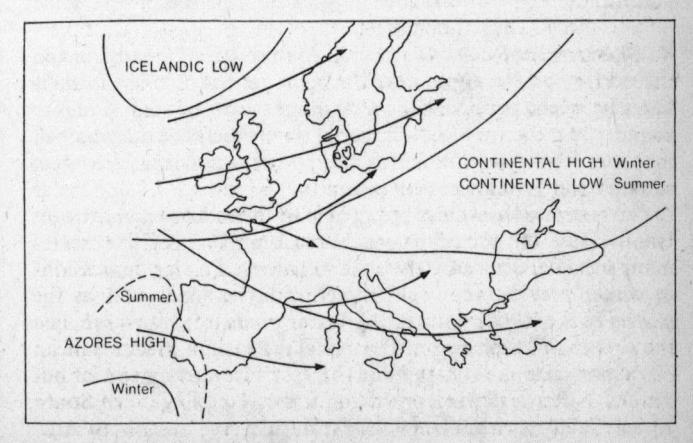

Figure 18. Pressure belts and depression tracks in Europe

at its weakest, the average strength of the westerlies is about twice that in summer, when weather changes are less marked. The warmth of the Gulf Stream ensures that mean winter temperatures are generally above 0°C, this situation persisting in Norway as far north as 70° latitude. In summer, mean temperatures in maritime Europe lie between 15° and 16°C. There is no dry season, although the month of maximum precipitation varies, being in winter in western Britain and other Atlantic situations, but in summer in south-east England and throughout central and eastern Europe. The most marked precipitation differences, however, are created by the effects of relief.

The transition eastwards from a maritime to a continental climate through **Eurasia** is gradual, and westerly depressions penetrate well into the heart of the continent, particularly in summer. The westerlies influence is weakest in winter, for although the upper airflow is still dominated by westerlies, the surface Siberian anticyclone is very persistent, giving extremely low temperatures. Further east still, in China and Japan, westerly winds again play a prominent role all year. Depressions regenerate in the lee of the Tibetan plateau, bringing precipitation to southern China and Japan in winter and to the whole of China at other times of the year.

A broadly similar pattern of temperate climates can be recognized in North America but here, in contrast to Eurasia, major topographic boundaries are aligned north-south, and this creates some unique effects. The temperate climate of the continent is effectively restricted by the Rockies to coastal Alaska, British Columbia and the north-west Pacific States. On the other hand, in the interior and east of the continent the lack of east-west mountains allows the free interchange of hot and cold air masses over the whole of the zone from the Gulf of Mexico to the tundra margins. This situation can bring winter temperatures as low as $-10°C$ to the Gulf coast, and moist sweltering heat to the east coast and Great Lakes region in summer. Nevertheless, the whole region remains under the influence of the zonal westerlies all year, and major depression tracks trend west-east across the continent, many originating in Texas and Alberta. Another major region of cyclonic activity lies off the coast of New England in winter, where polar air masses passing over the Labrador Current meet warm air from the south. However, the prevailing westerly airflow prevents the oceanic influence from being very strong on the Atlantic coasts of America, in contrast to Europe.

In the **southern hemisphere**, temperate westerlies climates lie between 40° and 45° S in Chile, Tasmania and New Zealand. These small land areas lie just to the north of the main active polar front zone in the hemisphere and receive rainfall at all seasons.

6. Subpolar zone Although the influence of the westerlies is still felt, in this zone the effects of the polar and northern continental anticyclones increasingly dominate the weather at higher latitudes. The seasons become emphasized by the great differences between summer and winter daylight hours. A continental variety of this climate is found in Siberia and Arctic Canada, where the main characteristics are a great seasonal range of temperature, extremely severe winters, and a small annual precipitation concentrated in the short summer. Areas in Siberia experience some of the coldest winter temperatures recorded in the northern hemisphere ($-78°C$ in the Lena valley). Permafrost is found throughout most of this part of Canada and Siberia, the summers not being sufficiently long to thaw out the frozen ground beyond a metre or so.

Iceland, southern Greenland and most of Alaska experience a maritime climate in which the temperature extremes of the continental interiors are not experienced. Instead, a rather damp and cold regime persists all year round. Low summer temperatures of the order of 10°C and strong winds from varying directions create an almost treeless landscape, although the ground flora can be quite rich. Winter temperatures are usually below freezing point, and the considerable snow amounts nourish glaciers in the higher mountains surrounding the North Atlantic and Pacific oceans.

7. High polar zone The three largest areas of ice in the world, Antarctica, Greenland, and the Arctic Ocean, differ from the subpolar zone by lying entirely within easterly zonal circulation all year, having fewer depressions and lower average temperatures. Most of this zone has surprisingly little snowfall, the maximum amounts falling around the periphery of the two land ice sheets, Antarctica and Greenland. Summer temperatures rarely rise above freezing: so much latent heat is required in melting that temperatures are inhibited from rising any higher. In winter, the average monthly temperatures fall to $-30°C$ in the Arctic Ocean near the North Pole, to $-45°C$ in central Greenland, and to

−70°C in Antarctica. These conditions occur under the influence of intense cold anticyclones which develop in the polar regions during the long winter night.

Local climate

Relief effects give rise to probably the most significant local variations to the major patterns of climate just outlined. Precipitation, temperature, pressure and air flow are all affected, so much so that large mountain regions can be regarded as having a unique climatic type, a mosaic of local climates.

Not only do temperatures drop with height, but **aspect** can have an important bearing on temperatures in any area of accentuated relief. In the Alps, large mountain valleys running east-west are well noted for having a south-facing side receiving large amounts of insolation and a north-facing side which may be in constant shadow all winter. In the United States in areas of low rainfall a different pattern results: thick forests grow on shaded north-facing slopes, but scrub and cactus on heated south-facing slopes. It is worth stressing that although aspect differences play an important role in local climate in many parts of the world, the effects vary considerably (page 227).

Orographic precipitation effects are also universal, provided that the air has sufficient moisture. The uplift of air caused by relief tends to reinforce whatever other rain-giving mechanism may be in operation, and even stable air may be induced to part with some moisture. A rainfall map will confirm that the windward side of hills and mountains have much heavier amounts than the lee sides, where marked rain-shadow areas may exist.

Airflow is affected by high relief, both on a broad scale (Chap. 3), and also locally: the lee sides of mountains are generally considerably calmer than windward sides and summit areas. In some cases, a *Föhn* effect (page 20) may also be produced. In addition to these direct mechanical influences, elevated areas can create special **mountain and valley winds** (Fig. 19). During the day, warm air tends to blow up the valley in response to the heating of air in contact with the upper slopes of the valley and the surrounding upland. Such winds are termed **anabatic.** At night the situation reverses: the upper slopes cool more quickly and dense cold air drains down towards the valley bottoms. This night-time or **katabatic** wind is generally stronger

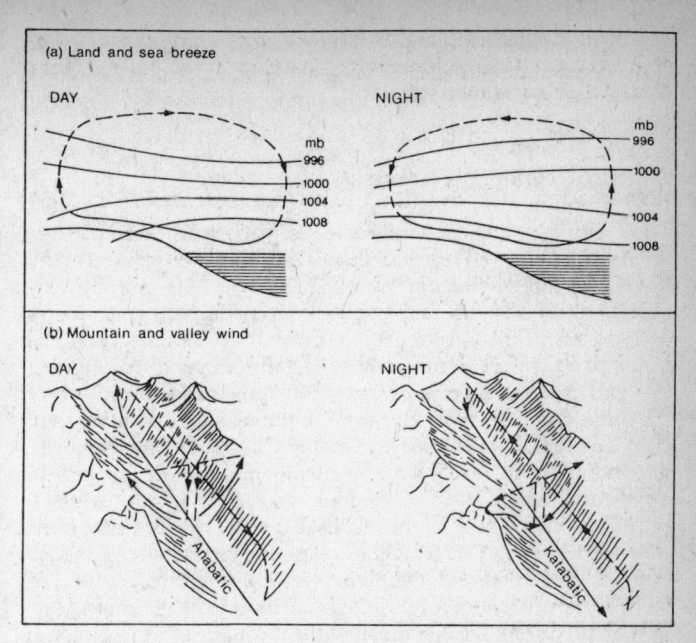

Figure 19. Examples of local wind circulations

than its day-time counterpart and has more noticeable effects. It can lead to the development of severe frosts, especially in **frost hollows**, low-lying ground where this happens frequently. Even minor differences of relief can produce frost-hollow effects, as in sheltered valleys of south-east England, or small hollows in fields and gardens.

The effect of **water bodies** on local climate reinforces the moderating effect of the oceans in general. Coastal areas tend to have the smallest range of temperature. On the other hand, they frequently suffer from fog: in summer this is of the advection type, whereas in autumn and winter fog often occurs because of the cooling of moist sea air as it moves inland. On warm days coastlines may experience a **land-and-sea breeze** mechanism, which is caused by expansion of the air column over the land tilting the local pressure gradient landwards near the ground surface and seawards higher up (Fig. 19). The net result is a small circulatory system in which a sea breeze blows landward during the day. At night the air over the sea is warmer, and an offshore land-breeze results. In middle latitudes the Coriolis effect causes these breezes to be deflected so that by late afternoon it blows nearly parallel to the shore. Similar features can be observed around lakes.

Climate near the ground

The type of ground an area possesses, particularly whether it is vegetated or not, and the character of the vegetation, creates many interesting micro-climatic variations. These may not be very significant in absolute terms but are very important to man's detailed use of the lowermost two metres of the atmosphere. The outstanding feature of this layer is its daily temperature range. At one extreme, **bare rock** or brick and stone surfaces may warm up considerably in sunshine, more so if they are dark rather than light in colour. Some of this heat is stored and re-radiated at night, maintaining a relatively warm air temperature. A dry or **sandy soil**, containing a good deal of air, also heats up very strongly during the day, but at night this heat is quickly lost. Conversely, on a **wet soil**, surface temperatures show the least diurnal range because of the high water content. Wet soils are usually also cold soils, kept cool by evaporation. **Snow** represents the coldest surface of all: during the day much of the incoming solar radiation is reflected away, and at night heat loss by long-wave radiation proceeds rapidly and very low minimum temperatures may be recorded just above the snow surface. Such variations in climate caused by ground type become less apparent under windy conditions or where the ground is covered by vegetation.

All **vegetation** protects the underlying surface to some extent from the temperature extremes that can be observed over open ground. Much depends on whether the vegetation is horizontally structured, as in a forest, or vertically structured, as in the case of most cereal crops. The latter type allows higher temperatures to develop during the day within the vegetation space. In a grass sward, day temperatures are kept comparatively low by evapotranspiration, and at night the moist stagnant air between the grass stalks is additionally cooled by radiation. Thus low temperatures and frost are especially likely over grassy surfaces, and in long grass, heavy **dew** is common.

Forests produce well-marked temperature stratification. The radiating surface is transferred in effect from the ground to the canopy, so the highest and greatest ranges of temperature occur here, as long as the forest is in leaf. In contrast, temperatures inside the forest are generally lower by day but warmer by night compared with areas outside. The amount of light and heat getting through to the forest floor will depend considerably on the type of trees: in a tropical forest ground conditions will be much darker than in a coniferous type. Forests generally show marked humidity increases compared with open ground; this is partly a result of moisture from the trees, and partly a function of the lack of evapotranspiration loss within the forest because of lower temperatures and wind velocities. Air movement is slight in forests, and quite large variations in outside wind velocity have little effect within a thick forest. However, one of the side effects of wind-speed reduction is the increased possibility of frosts in clearings. In all, the micro-climate within a forest tends to be cooler, calmer, and more humid than that outside.

Urban climate

Large towns and cities create climates no less distinctive than those of forests or mountain valleys. As within forests, urban structures tend to reduce wind speeds to lower values than those recorded in open country. The effect varies according to street pattern: the wind channels down grid-iron streets, such as those of New York, but is more dissipated in the irregular urban morphology of London. Unlike forests, cities tend to have lower humidities than their surroundings: the general absence of vegetation

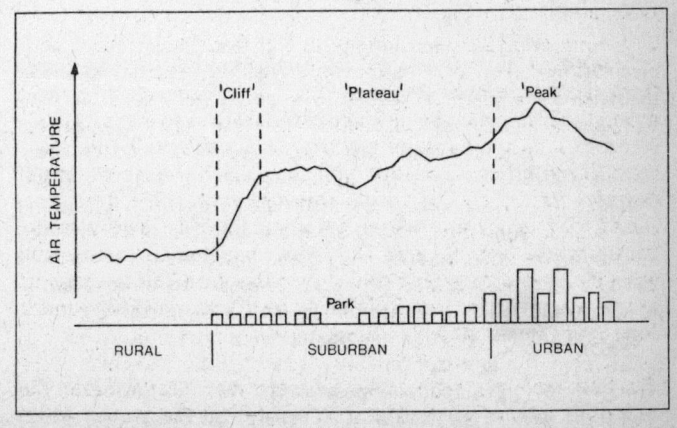

Figure 20. Generalized cross-section through an urban heat island

and large bodies of water and the rapid removal of surface run-off all contribute to decrease local evaporation. One of the most notable features of urban climates is that they are generally warmer than the surrounding countryside, producing a **heat island** effect (Fig. 20). There are three main factors responsible for this: the direct production of heat from fires, industry, and central heating systems; the heat-conserving properties of brick and stone in the city; and the blanketing effect of atmospheric pollution on outgoing radiation. Measurements in the London area and elsewhere have shown that the greatest contrasts between town and country occur in summer, especially at night after a fine sunny day. From this we must conclude that the strongest factor at work in creating a heat island is the storage of heat from day-time insolation in the brickwork.

Some city atmospheres are notoriously liable to **pollution**, and this has the effect of blanketing the radiation over the area, cutting down the sunlight and providing abundant condensation nucleii. On days with some wind most of this waste is dispersed, but under stable anticyclonic conditions radiation fog may combine with excessive pollution and become trapped under a temperature inversion, forming a **smog**, as used to occur in London. In Los Angeles, recent summer and autumn smogs have been caused largely by the concentration of pollution from car exhausts under a day-time temperature inversion.

Climatic change

The connection between long-term climatic change, the general circulation and solar radiation was considered in Chapter 1. The evidence for changes of this scale is largely geological, deriving from glacial and interglacial deposits, traces of the former distributions of plants and animals, and isotope records from deep ocean sediment cores. There is also ample evidence of a different kind that climate has fluctuated in the historical period on much shorter time-scales. Contemporary observations, records of floods, harvests, port closures and openings, and instrumental records in the last one hundred and fifty years, are used to reconstruct the general trends. The evidence indicates that for northern Europe, the period AD 400–1200 was on the whole dry and warm, with relatively few major storms. This was the time of the great Viking voyages to Greenland and possibly to America. After 1200, a period of weather variation and general decline set in, with a number of devastating floods recorded around 1300 and the abandonment of Viking colonies in Greenland and Iceland. The period 1550 to 1800 has been called the **Little Ice Age**. Then, glaciers reached their most advanced positions in the Alps and Norway since the end of the last major glaciation 10,000 years ago. It was also a time of general agrarian stress in the northern countries of Europe, and in England the Thames froze over frequently (Fig. 21).

The beginning of the period of instrumental records in the first part of the nineteenth century witnessed a gradual amelioration of climate. This warming trend appears to have begun about 1820,

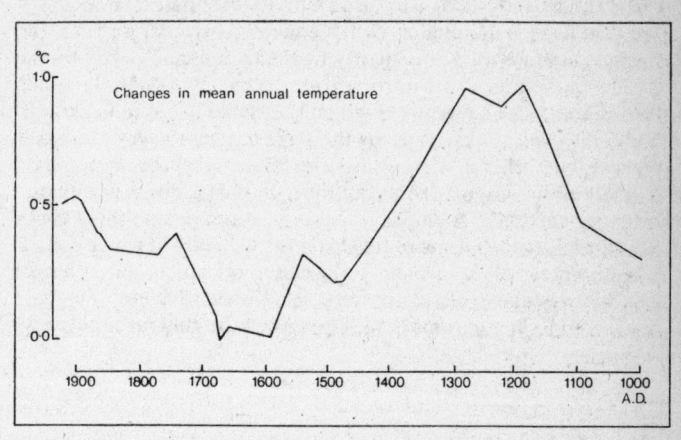

Figure 21. Temperature trends in central England since AD 1000

and continued up to the 1940s. The trend also seems to have been world wide, as expressed by a general rise in the temperatures of the world's oceans by 0·7°C. Since 1950, average temperatures in northern Europe appear to nave declined slightly.

There seems little doubt that the immediate cause of these recent climatic fluctuations is linked to the strength of the general circulation, especially the westerlies. The effect of an intensified circulation is to increase oceanic influence, especially in winter, thereby raising mean temperatures. H. H. Lamb has shown that the climatic amelioration in the 1820s was linked to an increase in the vigour of the westerlies in the North Atlantic, together with a northward shift in depression tracks. In other parts of the world, similar relationships between climate and circulation intensity have been observed. In the past 35 years, the atmospheric circulation has been weakening, with an increasing occurrence of low zonal index situations. This first became evident a little before 1940, but it was not until the 1950s and 1960s that an extension of polar ice in the Icelandic and northern European sectors became apparent.

Summary

Global climates can be classified according to effects or causes. Based on the pattern of the general circulation, seven major climatic zones can be recognized, plus mountain climates. The equatorial rain zone is dominated by the equatorial trough all year, the tropical summer rain zone partly by the trough and partly by the trade winds, and the subtropical dry zone by dry trade winds throughout. The subtropical winter rain zone has summer trades and winter westerlies, whereas the large temperate westerlies belt receives westerlies at all seasons. The influence of the westerlies is still felt in the subpolar zone, but the high polar zone is dominated by polar easterlies. Significant local variations within these zones are caused by the effects of relief and the presence of water bodies. The character of the ground surface also influences local climate and is particularly distinctive in cities. Recent changes in climate are linked to fluctuations in the strength of the general circulation.

Chapter 6
Rocks and Relief

The branch of geography which studies the Earth's relief features is known as **geomorphology**. This is concerned not only with the shape of landforms, but also with the agencies which create them. Land-forming processes may be grouped broadly into two types: internal or **endogenous** processes stemming from the tectonic forces beneath the Earth's surface; and external or **exogenous** processes related to surface weathering, water, wind, ice, and the sea. Nearly all the Earth's major relief features, such as mountain chains, ocean trenches, basins and plateaux, are tectonically formed, even though their detailed landforms may be the result of exogenous sculpturing. It is important that we know something of the structure of the Earth's crust and the forces at work within it, particularly in the context of the modern concept of plate tectonics. Another way in which geological considerations are important in landform studies is that different rocks vary considerably in their resistance to erosion, and this aspect will also be looked at in this chapter.

Layers of the Earth

From a study of earthquake waves, it is known that the Earth is made up of a series of concentric zones: the crust, mantle, outer core and inner core. The **crust** varies greatly in thickness: beneath the oceans it is as little as 5 km in places, but extends down to 70 km beneath mountain ranges. Although many kinds of rock are found in the crust, they fall into two main groups. The ocean basins are underlain mainly by basaltic rocks containing much iron and magnesium and having densities of between 2·8 and 3·0. In continental areas, granitic rocks predominate; these are rich in silicon and magnesium and are lighter in both colour and weight (densities of c. 2.7). The oceanic crust does not appear to extend beneath the continental crust, as formerly envisaged.

The base of the crust is marked by a surface called the **Moho**, named after the seismologist Mohorovicic who discovered it. Below the Moho lie the even denser rocks of the **mantle**. The upper part of the mantle is solid to depths of about 100 km and, together with the crust, forms a relatively rigid shell round the

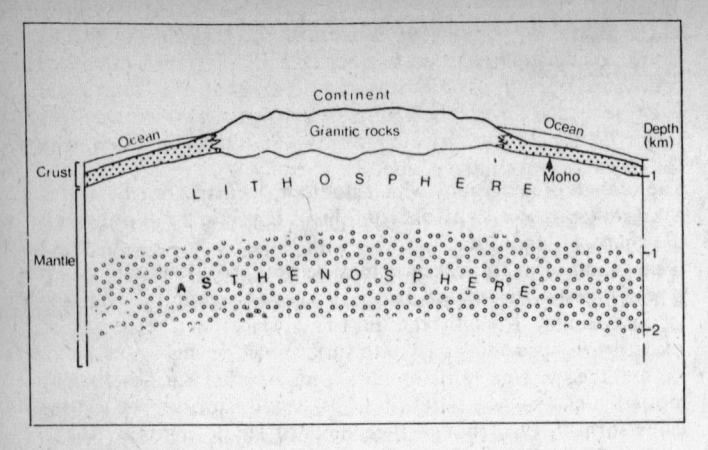

Figure 22. A section through the upper layers of the Earth

Earth called the **lithosphere**. Underneath this in the mantle there exists a partially-molten layer which is capable of slow flowage. This zone is known as the **asthenosphere** and reaches minimum strength at depths of around 200 km; below this, strength again increases. The recognition of these two zones (Fig. 22) is fundamental to the understanding of large-scale crustal movement.

Crustal movements

One of the major geological discoveries of this century is that parts of the crust are capable of slow horizontal movement and have caused the continents to change position in relation to each other over long periods of geological time. The idea of **continental drift** was originally put forward by A. Wegener in 1915, but for many years there was considerable opposition to his theories. However, since about 1965 new discoveries have confirmed his broad thesis and have led eventually to a body of theory which is known as **plate tectonics**. It is now known that the lithospheric shell round the Earth is broken into several sections or plates, each of which can move over the asthenosphere, carrying oceanic and continental crust alike. At the mid-oceanic ridges in the Pacific, Atlantic and Indian Oceans (Fig. 23), the plate margins are characterized by the creation of new crust from the underlying asthenosphere, and in a process called **sea-floor spreading** the plates migrate slowly away from these central ridges (Fig. 24a). Elsewhere, as around the edge of the Pacific Ocean, plates move past each other or collide. At many zones of collision one plate overrides another (Fig. 24b), the lower plate being reabsorbed into the mantle in a **subduction zone**. This makes up for the new crust coming out of the ocean ridges, thus maintaining total material balance over the globe.

Movements of the plates cause pressure and tensions to build up at the Earth's surface, in many cases leading to deformation of the land and the creation of major tectonic landforms. The general term **diastrophism** is sometimes applied to the bending, folding, warping and fracturing of the crust. On a broad scale, earth movements can be divided into two types.

Epeirogenic movements are those involving forces acting along a radius from the Earth's centre to the surface, and are characterized by large-scale uplift or submergence of parts of the crust. The movements involved are often so slow and widespread that no obvious fracturing or folding is produced in the rocks. One kind of epeirogenic movement involves the principle of **isostasy**. This term describes the state of balance that is thought to exist between the lighter areas of the crust and the denser rocks of the mantle. Each continent is underlain by a root zone of similar material projecting down into the asthenosphere (Fig. 22), rather as an iceberg floats in water. If, say, material is moved by erosion from a continental area and deposited on its margins, it will in-

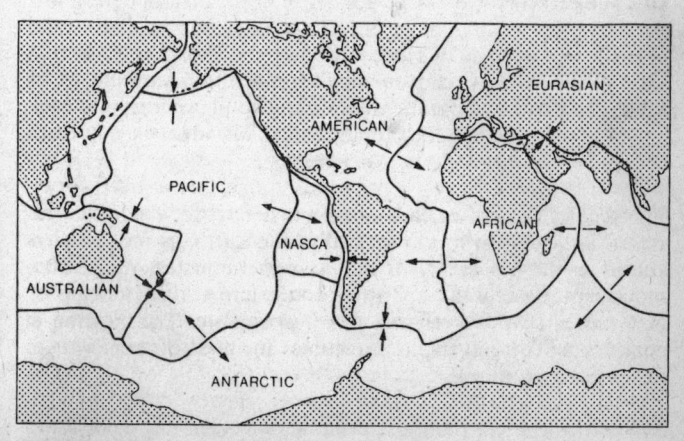

Figure 23. The major lithospheric plates

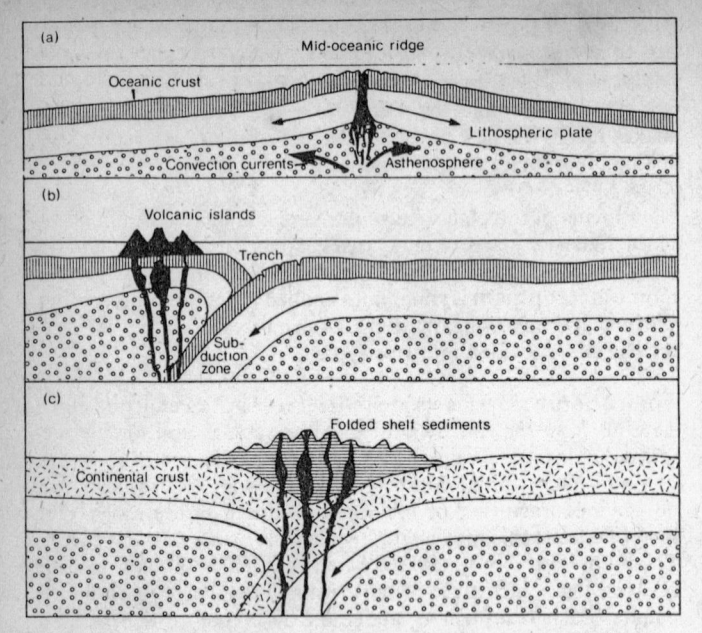

Figure 24. Types of plate margin (for explanation see text)

volve isostatic adjustment whereby there is a rise in the level of the area subject to erosion and subsidence in the area of deposition. Similarly, the addition of weight to a continental area, in the form of ice or a large body of water, will cause slow isostatic changes to take place. Much broad crustal warping today appears to be related to isostasy. Isostatic uplift is taking place in regions such as Scandinavia and Arctic Canada, which were depressed beneath ice caps during Pleistocene glaciations.

The second type of earth movements are those which are generated at a tangent to the surface of the Earth, as primarily involved in the movement of the lithospheric plates. Where such movements have been responsible for the formation of fold mountain ranges they are referred to as **orogenic**. The creation of complex fold structures, as sometimes involved in orogenesis, is called **tectogenesis**.

Earthquakes are the most prominent present-day evidence of tangential forces, and are the result of deformation in the lithosphere, which finally ruptures abruptly. Earthquakes are important to landform development because they can trigger off rapid erosion and deposition. These include large-scale landslides and mudflows, and some surges in glaciers. **Tsunamis** are seismic seawaves generated by earthquakes and can arrive at coasts with great force, causing considerable damage. They are most common in the Pacific Ocean.

Large-scale tectonic landforms

The major mountain chains of the world appear to have formed as the result of the movement of plates during the geological past and mark the closure of former oceans on the margins of which large thicknesses of sediment accumulated. The most notable present day chains are the Alpine-Himalayan system and the circum-Pacific system comprising the Andes, the Rockies, and the island chains of Japan and the western Pacific. All these mountains are comparatively 'young', having been created in the last 50 million years, and contain intensely crumpled and folded rocks. The transformation of the sediments into mountains seems to have been the result of both compressional forces associated with colliding plates (Fig. 24c), and also isostatic uplift. The intrusion from beneath of large bodies of igneous rocks, particularly granite, appears to be a common feature of mountain-building episodes. The introduction of these lighter rocks allows the whole orogenic belt to rise isostatically.

Many of the world's largest mountain ranges exist beneath the sea. The **mid-oceanic ridges** (Fig. 24a) form distinctive features rising out of the flat abyssal plains of the major oceans. All mid-oceanic ridges are composed of basaltic lavas and represent the formation of new crust. Other oceanic mountains are revealed as **island arcs**, as in the West Indies and the west and south-west Pacific. Associated with them are deep ocean **trenches**. Both arcs and trenches are the result of the type of plate collision shown in figure 24b, the trench reflecting the downward plunging of the lower plate into the mantle, and the island arcs being an expression of volcanic activity in the subduction zone.

Block mountains are usually composed of rocks much older than those found in young fold mountains. However, in many cases they themselves were once fold ranges, but have been worn down by erosion and altered by earth movements. They now form rigid blocks, often bounded by faults of considerable vertical displacement. An uplifted block is called a **horst**; a downthrust block, a **graben**. Horst-and-graben structure is well exemplified by the Vosges and Black Forest mountains (horsts) and the Rhine rift valley. The Basin-and-Range country of western North America is a large-scale tract of block mountains, consisting of a series of major subparallel faults and differentially uplifted and tilted blocks. **Rift-valleys** are of a similar nature, being elongated grabens bounded by parallel faults. One of the most extensive rifts is that in East Africa, where broad warping has lead to tensional stresses in the crust, causing it to fracture. As in East Africa, volcanoes are often associated with rift valleys, taking advantage of the crustal weaknesses set up by faulting.

Volcanoes form an important primary landform group, in this case being constructional in origin, a result of the outflow of magma (lava) at the surface rather than of crustal deformation. As a result of chemical differences in the magma which feeds different outlets, volcanic landforms are diverse, but two broad types may be recognized. Outpourings of fluid **basaltic lava** are not usually accompanied by violent eruptive activity, and individual lava flows are normally only a metre or two thick. Over a long period of time repeated flows build up domed or **shield volcanoes**, as exemplified by Mauna Loa and Mauna Kea on the island of Hawaii. Some continental areas are covered with widespread accumulations of basaltic lava, also made up of many thin flows, which have come from fissures instead of a single vent. The resulting landform is a plateau rather than a volcanic cone; the Columbia and Snake River Plateaux of the north-west United States are good examples of this. By contrast, in the second type, cooler and more viscous **andesitic lavas** build volcanoes which are characterized by explosive eruptions, resulting in cone-shaped **strato-volcanoes**. Extremely viscous rhyolite magmas result in either very violent eruptions or the creation of a lava plug which chokes the vent and remains as a resistant rock landform long after the flanks of the volcano have been worn away.

Most active volcanoes today are found in well-defined zones, mainly along plate margins. The most extensive of these is the circum-Pacific 'Ring of Fire', which is dominated by explosive andesitic volcanoes. Some chains of volcanic islands, for example the Hawaiian group, show an increasing age away from the most recent vent. This progression is the result of the gradual passage of a plate over a stationary 'hot-spot' in the underlying mantle.

Lithology and structure

External weathering and erosion processes gradually become the dominant factors in the development of the landscape as tectonic activity ceases or becomes very slow. The influence of geology remains important but passes to a more detailed level in which rock type (lithology) and structure may strongly influence local relief features. In all landscapes, the critical factor is not so much the absolute resistance of a rock as its resistance relative to the rocks around it. It is this which creates the pattern of high and low relief. For instance, in south-east England chalk is a relatively resistant rock in relation to adjacent strata, but in Northern Ireland it is soft compared to surrounding basalts.

Rocks are normally classified into three major groups according to their origin. **Igneous** rocks are those formed directly from magmas as described earlier in the chapter. These can be classed into extrusive (volcanic) and intrusive types, the latter cooling within the crust. **Sedimentary** rocks are composed of the broken-down products of older rocks, redeposited on land or under water by surface processes. Sedimentaries are subdivided into clastic rocks, formed by the mechanical aggregation of materials (as in shales or sandstones), and organic or chemical rocks, formed by the precipitation of soluble minerals (as in limestone). **Metamorphic** rocks are those which have undergone change because of great heat or pressure. This may occur to igneous, sedimentary, or even rocks that are already metamorphic. However, from the point of view of landforms it is the mineralogical composition of rocks that is more significant than their origin, especially in determining weathering characteristics. Table 1 lists in terms of their percentage occurrence the six most important rock-forming mineral groups found near the surface of the continental crust. These types constitute over 90 per cent of the total; most of the remaining groups, including the economic minerals, have only a limited effect on relief.

Structural features in rocks which are important to relief include folding, faulting and jointing. In a simple series of folds, **anticlines** (upfolds) may be distinguished from **synclines** (downfolds). Degrees of increasing asymmetry can be recognized in overturned and recumbent folds (Fig. 25a). In this example the relationship between the relief and folding is direct. Quite frequently however, synclines form high ground and the anticlines are deeply eroded, as occurs in the Weald; this is known as indirect or **inverted relief** (Fig. 25b). It would seem that during folding, fracturing of the apex of the anticlines creates a zone of weakness which is rapidly exploited by processes of erosion. In general, folded structures become most significant to landforms where several rock types are involved. Their relative erodibility will be most apparent when dips are at a high angle, and least so when dips are low.

MINERAL	WEATHERING CHARACTERISTICS	OCCURENCE
Feldspar group (39%)	Hard, but liable to chemical alteration (especially calcium types) to clay and sand.	Igneous and metamorphic rocks
Quartz (28%)	Tough and inert. Otherwise known as silica.	Main constituent of sandstones
Mica group (18%)	Flaky cleavage, easily weathered to microscopic clay minerals	Common in granite and metamorphics
Carbonates (9%)	Physically hard, but very prone to solution, especially calcite.	Mainly sediments
Iron (4%)	Includes earthy (limonite, hematite) and metallic forms. Stable.	Sediments and igneous rocks
Amphiboles, Pyroxenes, Olivine (2%)	Hard, dark coloured, but readily weathered chemically to clays. Major minerals in lower crust and in mantle.	Basic igneous rocks

Table 1. The six most important rock-forming minerals found in surface continental rocks

Faulting in rocks occurs on many scales, but in all cases its significant effect on landforms depends on contrasting rock types being brought together to create features of differential erosion. The main types of fault are depicted in figure 25c. Normal faulting may produce a **fault scarp**, a well-defined cliff-like feature. Where a softer rock was originally uplifted relative to a harder rock, in time the weaker rock may be more rapidly worn away and the resistant rock may come to form the higher relief on the fault-line scarp. Faults frequently occur in zones which may be characterized by crushed or shattered rock known as fault **breccia**, presenting a situation favourable to rapid erosion. The fjords of Norway largely coincide with such zones, indicating that fluvial and later glacial erosion were structurally controlled.

Jointing develops in rocks as they consolidate and crack under the stresses set up by cooling or by pressure changes. Some extrusive igneous rocks develop columnar joints on cooling, as in the case of basalt. Sedimentary rocks usually develop joints at right

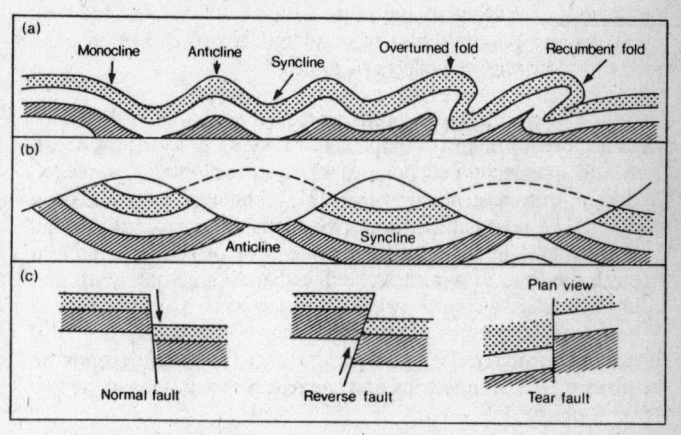

Figure 25. (a) types of fold; (b) inverted relief; (c) types of fault

angles to their bedding planes. It is significant to landform studies that joint frequency in many rocks apparently decreases with depth; that is, many joints are formed near the surface. It seems that these joints open up only when surface erosion relieves pressure on the rock. This process is known as **unloading**, and probably applies to most of the right-angled joints in sedimentary rocks. In rocks with no original structures, for example many granites, a special type of unloading named **sheeting** may occur, creating joints parallel to the existing ground surface and helping to perpetuate the original granite form.

The significance of joints in promoting erosion is therefore complicated since many of the joints themselves seem to depend on erosion. This relationship appears to be self-perpetuating in many cases, since there is a distinct tendency for joint-orientated landforms such as domes and cliffs to persist. This is an example of feedback in geomorphology, whereby the form (e.g. the cliff) controls the unloading, which in turn determines the form.

Distinctive rock-controlled landscapes

It is not possible to make broad generalizations about the effects of all specific rock types on relief, and distinctive rock dominated landscapes are relatively few. Rock types form different kinds of relief in various structural situations, and may react differently to weathering according to the climatic zone (Chap. 7). However, limestone and granite may be considered as two exceptions, and both illustrate well the effects of jointing.

Limestone relief largely results from two related facts. First, the rocks are predominantly composed of varying proportions of calcium and magnesium carbonate, which are soluble in rainwater. Second, limestone strata are permeable, allowing the transmission of water. The permeability is of two kinds: water passes through the pore spaces in the rock (the property of **porosity**), and also through the lines of weakness, such as bedding planes, joints and faults, which are widened by concentrated water solution. Nearly all limestone landscapes are thus characterized by a high degree of subsurface drainage. Detailed variation in the relief depends on the precise type of limestone and the relative variations in the two types of permeability.

Karst scenery may be found on hard massive limestones where bedding planes and joints are well developed. This type of landscape is dominated by large-scale solution features such as sinks, caverns and steep-sided gorges. Horizontally-bedded strata create limestone pavements with their own distinctive microrelief of widened vertical joint planes, as found on the limestones of the Pennines, where glaciation has exposed a step-like arrangement of relief. In contrast to the angular features of karst, rounded forms tend to develop on chalk, a porous and very pure carbonate limestone. Chalk has a much smaller-scale and more weakly developed jointing pattern than massive limestones and fewer underground solution features. Instead, solution at or near the surface is relatively high.

Granite is popularly considered to be a 'hard' rock, and therefore a distinctive relief-former. It originates in **batholiths**, large domed igneous intrusions which cool at depth, but which quite commonly become exposed. Where batholiths are found amongst hard crystalline rocks, as in many instances in the Highlands of Scotland, they have little obvious effect on the relief, but where they have been intruded into sedimentary rocks, as in south-west England, the effect is much more obvious.

The effects of jointing in granite can be most marked. The development of sheet jointing is common, maintaining domed forms where bare rock is exposed. Notable examples occur in the Yosemite National Park, California.

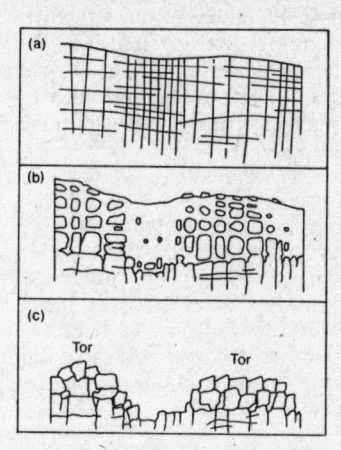

Figure 26. Stages in the joint-guided development of tors

In warm climatic zones, varying joint patterns may promote selective weathering. The origin of **tors**, small rocky hills which are a distinctive feature of many granite landscapes, may be related to this (Fig. 26). They are most probably the product of a period of deep chemical weathering, guided by the joint pattern, followed by the later removal of the weathering products after a change of base-level or climate. Tors are well-known features of Dartmoor and Bodmin Moor. Similar forms appear to develop on rocks other than granite wherever selective weathering takes place on joint planes and the products of weathering are removed downslope. In the Pennines, the gritstone tors and edges which are usually flanked downslope by blockfields are likely to have been formed in this way.

Some authorities regard granite relief as **zonal**, by which they mean that it varies fundamentally with climatic regime. Thus, in the humid tropics weathering produces a deep mantle of fine debris covering the solid rock; in sub-tropical areas with a wet and a dry season, granite domes may form by the massive exfoliation of material (as in the Sugar Loaf of Rio de Janeiro); and at the other extreme, in cold regions freeze-thaw action reduces granite to masses of angular debris. In classifying granite relief in this way we must bear in mind the possibilities of climatic change (Chap. 5) and the effects of local variations in the texture of granite.

Summary

The solid Earth is made up of a series of concentric rock zones of which the lithosphere and the asthenosphere are the two most significant to geomorphology. Major relief features such as fold mountain chains, ocean trenches, island arcs, and volcanic landforms can be related to the history of the movement of the Earth's lithospheric plates. On a smaller scale, lithology and structure, including folding, faulting and jointing, strongly influence the types and rates of surface denudation processes. For most rock types, mineral composition is a reliable guide to their resistance to erosion; particular lithologies such as granite and limestone sometimes form distinctive landscapes.

Chapter 7
Slopes

Although all landscapes, subaerial, subglacial or even submarine, are made up of slopes, in practice 'slope studies' in geomorphology are primarily concerned with **hillslopes**, that is, the slopes connecting interfluve crests with river channels in valley bottoms which dynamically integrate the subaerial landscape. Geomorphologists have spent much time arguing about slopes, for three main reasons. First, slope forms have often been simply estimated by eye, or drawn from contour maps, rather than having been precisely measured in the field, and this situation has inevitably led to various misconceptions. Second, slope processes are undoubtedly complex: it is sometimes difficult to unravel cause and effect: does the slope angle control the process, or the process control the slope form? Third, slopes have been at the centre of major theories of landscape evolution and this has led to doctrinaire attitudes about slope development. The best known of these schemes was the Davisian cycle of erosion, which is briefly reviewed at the end of the chapter.

Approaches to slope studies

Slopes reflect a wide range of adjustment between form and process, that is, some slopes are in close equilibrium with present-day processes, whereas others reflect past situations. An *historical* approach to slope study emphasizes the latter aspect; certainly the present-day slopes of much of Britain need to be seen in the context of recent phases of glaciation and periglaciation (Chap. 9). However the understanding of the mechanics of slope development will be fundamentally advanced only by adopting a *dynamic* approach which studies the slopes produced by contemporary processes. Formerly, there was a tendency to assume that modern processes working on slopes could be largely ignored, as they were either too slow or too catastrophic to measure. Recent improved techniques have rendered even the slowest movements measurable, and many slope studies have become field orientated and at least partly quantitative.

One useful dynamic approach is to regard slopes as **open systems**. This gives us a framework in which we can identify

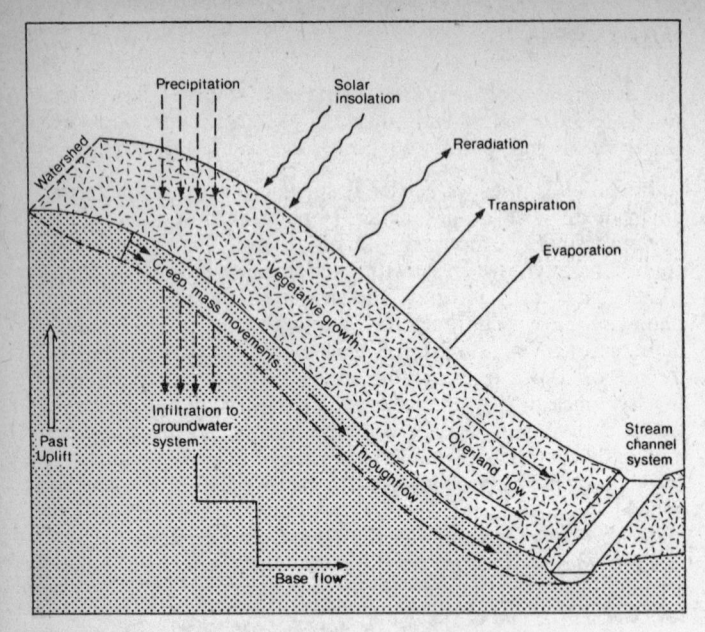

Figure 27. A hillslope regarded as an open system

forces at work and in which we can regard slopes as continually striving to approach a condition of equilibrium. In Figure 27 the watershed and the river mark the upper and lower boundaries of the system. Movements of energy and matter occur across these boundaries, causing adjustments to the slope form through the processes of erosion and deposition. The main inputs into the system include the potential energy and matter of the relief, precipitation and solar radiation. Some of this energy is lost back into the atmosphere by conduction, evaporation and outgoing radiation. The input of water and heat promotes weathering, and the material passes through the system by: infiltration, carrying with it particles of clay and silt (the process of eluviation); throughflow and overland flow, which may initiate gully erosion; and mass movements. The material is lost at its lower end into the adjacent stream channel; the activity in the stream in turn adjusts itself to the water and debris supplied to it by the slope. These slope processes form part of a continuum, but for convenience we can consider them as being of three types: weathering, mass movements, and the action of water.

Weathering

The first essential phase in the denudation of slopes is the weathering of rocks *in situ* by natural agents. Weathering prepares rock materials for transportation by other agents of erosion, and it is also an important prerequisite to the formation of soils (Chap. 12). Many weathering processes are understood only in outline and, although it is usual to refer to them individually, in reality rock disintegration at any one locality is likely to be the result of several processes acting in combination. Two general types of weathering are normally recognized: the physical or **mechanical weathering** of material into smaller particles, and **chemical weathering** in which some or all of the minerals in the rock suffer decay or alteration. Biotic influences, involving plants, animals and bacteria, frequently play a significant role in both types. Table 2 summarizes the main processes at work.

PHYSICAL WEATHERING

1. Thermal expansion — Daytime heating of rocks and night cooling weakens rock surfaces.
2. Ice crystal growth — Forces apart rock particles and fissures.
3. Salt crystal growth — Crystals grow, creating pressures in pore spaces and cracks.
4. Pressure-release — Erosion of surface rocks promotes development of joints (see page 67).
5. Biotic agencies — Root growth forces rocks apart. Animal burrowing weakens rocks.

CHEMICAL WEATHERING

1. Solution — Pure water dissolves rock salts
2. Carbonation — Rainwater contains CO_2 and acts as a weak carbonic acid, altering and dissolving limestones
3. Hydration — Some minerals expand on taking up water: a prerequisite to hydrolysis.
4. Hydrolysis — Hydrogen ions in water decompose feldspars leaving clay minerals.
5. Oxidation — Freshly exposed rocks with iron or manganese take up oxygen and alter to oxides (i.e. they 'rust').
6. Biotic agencies — Plants release humic acids. Carbonation enhanced by CO_2 from soil animals.

Table 2. A summary of the main types of weathering

These weathering processes are universal in the sense that they can potentially take place in nearly all environments, but the two main factors which ultimately determine the type and course of weathering are the rock type itself and the climate. In particular these control the availability of moisture in the weathering zone; water is vital to nearly all types of weathering. Broadly speaking, chemical weathering predominates in tropical or temperate humid climates, and physical weathering in cold or dry regions. We may note, however, that chemical weathering may be more important in deserts than one would perhaps imagine, since it has been shown that the thermal splitting of rocks is at its most effective in the presence of moisture.

Weathering itself is to a large extent dependent on the operation of other processes to transport away the products of weathering and re-expose fresh rock, otherwise weathering will necessarily slow down. If the waste is moved away slowly, a soil will develop. We can re-emphasize that weathering, soil formation, transport and erosion on hillslopes are closely interdependent and should be viewed as parts of a unified system.

Mass movements

In all mass movements, the downslope movement of material is a response to the application of shearing stresses caused by gravity and the weight of the material and soil water. These forces increase with increasing angle and height of slope. Resistance is provided to these stresses by the cohesive properties of the soil particles and their internal friction. This in turn is dependent on the pressure exerted by the soil water occupying the pore spaces of the soil. The addition of water to a slope not only increases the weight of slope materials but also introduces high **pore water pressures** which effectively reduce soil strength. Hence we may expect many landslides to occur after heavy rain. The role of water in mass movements is clearly very important. This can be used as one basis for classifying mass movements, namely as a continuum from rockfalls with hardly any water involved through to mudflows in which there may be as much water as rock debris.

Rock and debris falls are liable to occur wherever steep walls are maintained by erosion, for example on sea cliffs or glacial headwalls, or on artificially-created precipitous slopes in road or railway cuttings. The actual fall is set off by some trigger mechanism, such as frost bursting, chemical weathering, thermal changes or wind action. At the other extreme, in terms of speed, **creep** describes the very slow downhill movement of debris and soil. Leaning fence posts, the accumulation of earth on the upslope side of walls, the bending over of bedrock strata near the surface, all may indicate that creep is taking place. The cause of creep almost always lies in a combination of processes, including rainsplash impact, frost action and the activity of animals and plant roots. Ploughing can also cause the appreciable downslope movement of material. Solifluction is a special type of creep which takes place in periglacial regions (Chap. 9).

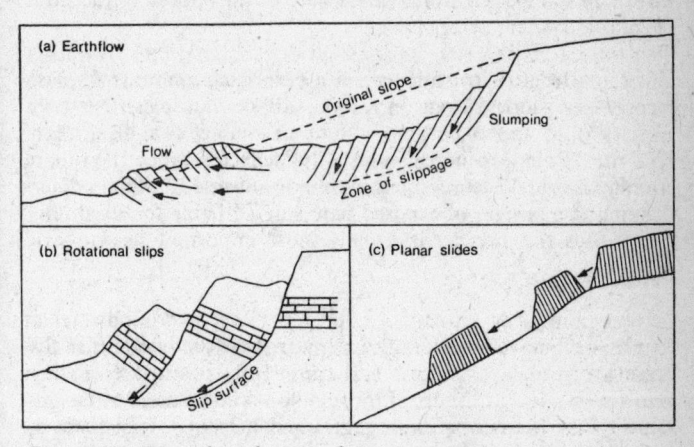

Figure 28. Examples of types of mass movement

Flows depend on there being sufficient water to saturate the soil mass comprehensively. In all flows the velocity is greatest at the surface, decreasing downwards, and these may be distinguished from slides, in which the velocity at the base is similar to that at the top. Mudflows and earthflows have bowl-shaped source areas leading to a chute through which the slope material rapidly passes before spreading out in the terminal zone. In **landslides**, there must be one or more shear surfaces on which movement takes place. Where the shear surface is approximately planar the strict meaning of the term slide is appropriate. However, another common type of landslide takes place on arcuate shear planes, and these are called **rotational slips** (Fig. 28). They are common in eastern Devon and at Folkestone Warren in Kent.

Most landslides move fairly rapidly; an impermeable stratum, perhaps of clay, often provides the zone in which shearing takes place.

Run-off on slopes

The direct action of water is one of the most common processes on hillslopes. The relationship between two fundamental factors determines whether there will be any surface run-off and what type of flow will take place: the *rate* of rainfall (not the total amount), and the infiltration capacity of the soil. An additional factor in some cases is that water may be introduced to the slope by groundwater springs.

First, **raindrop impact** causes a surprising amount of splash erosion on slopes. Even on a level surface, rainsplash has been observed to move particles 4 mm in diameter a distance of 200 mm. Raindrop impact is usually ineffective when the rate of rainfall is low. Vegetation has an important role to play in determining the amount of exposed bare surface liable to splash erosion; thus this process is usually most important in semi-arid regions.

Water infiltrating into the soil may either join groundwater at depth, or it may flow laterally as **throughflow**. Velocities in this case are usually fairly low and cause little subsurface erosion. However, concentrations of throughflow known as **piping** may lead to the heads of surface gullies and help to extend them by eroding subsurface material.

Overland flow occurs when the infiltration capacity of the soil is exceeded and the water flows down the slope in films, sheets or rills. We may distinguish this from channel flow (Chap. 8), in which the water occupies a distinct trough confined by banks. Initially, with heavier rain, **surface detention** will hold up some of the water in small puddles, but these will gradually fill up and overflow. As the water moves down the hillside, we can expect the volume of water to increase in proportion to the length of slope. Thus either the depth of the water or the flow velocity increases and erosion may be initiated. At the foot of the hill, the overland flow passes into a stream channel or lake.

Under stable natural conditions in a temperate humid climate, the rate of erosion by overland flow is slow enough to permit the soil cover to replenish itself, allowing a vegetation cover to be maintained. However, disturbance of this natural equilibrium by man, frequently through the removal of the vegetation cover, can lead to a state of accelerated erosion. Destruction of the vegetation cover greatly increases the likelihood of splash erosion and drastically reduces the resistance of the ground surface to erosion by overland flow. The results of such accelerated erosion are well known in the mid-west of the United States and in parts of the world where cultivation has been attempted under marginal conditions.

Controls on hillslope processes

On any slope a combination of weathering, mass movements and run-off is responsible for the hillslope form and its development. In turn, the interplay of these processes is conditioned by a wide variety of factors, including the bedrock and soil materials which comprise the slope; the prevailing climatic conditions; the vegetation cover, itself largely dependent on climate; the available relief; and 'downslope factors', that is, those operating at the foot of the slope, such as stream channel activity. The more important of these controls can be discussed briefly here.

Slope materials Some observations on the control exercised by specific rock structures on landforms were made in the preceding chapter. Geological factors have not only a direct influence on form in this way but also through their control of the type of weathered superficial deposits (the **regolith**). Resistant rocks normally produce slopes that are steeper than those on weak rock types. Geomorphologists S. A. Schumm and R. J. Chorley, working on scarps in the Colorado Plateau, concluded that the form of the slopes was related to four main geological variables. First, rock resistance, as controlled by the strength of the cementation of individual particles and by the porosity or infiltration capacity of the rock; second, the orientation and spacing of joints and bedding planes; third, the way in which the rock is dipping; and fourth, the thickness of any cap-rock at the top of the slope: once a cap-rock disappears, slopes will rapidly degrade.

Of these points, the infiltration capacity of bedrock and regolith appears to be one of the most significant factors. Highly permeable limestones or sandstones often have very steep slopes, whereas on impermeable rocks, such as clays, the high degree of surface run-off tends to produce gentler, concave slopes.

Climate and vegetation Since factors such as temperature and precipitation clearly influence the rates of weathering and run-off processes, then it would seem logical that climate is bound to influence slope form. But there has been much disagreement over this. On the one hand, some geomorphologists, such as Lester King, have forcibly argued that slopes develop similarly in nearly all climates, with micro-climate accounting only for minor aspects of slope form. On the other hand, many geomorphologists firmly believe that slope forms do vary with climatic zone. This view can be summarized in the following terms. Slopes in humid climates are smooth, relatively gentle, mantled with soil and vegetation, and consist of convex-concave profiles which decline with time. Slopes in arid climates are rough, relatively steep, barren of soil and vegetation, and consist mainly of straight slopes which retreat parallel to themselves to produce pediments (see Chap. 9).

Although these generalizations can be regarded as broadly correct, some qualifications are needed. For instance, it has been demonstrated that valley-side slopes in England are sometimes straight. At a detailed level, all types of hill form may be found in all kinds of climate; in other words, specific climates do not produce slope profiles unique only to that climate. Of course, some hillslope processes are more important in some environments than in others. For example, mass movement can only operate widely on low-angle slopes if both moisture and freeze-thaw action are prevalent. Only a periglacial climate fulfils both these criteria. This sort of observation lies at the basis of **climatic geomorphology**, which states that each climatic zone has its own complex of processes. However, this is not the same as saying that each zone has its own specific forms. The reason is that there are inevitably innumerable combinations of climatic, geologic and other factors which will produce the same forms in many different places. This similarity of form for different reasons is known in geomorphology as the **convergence of form**.

Available relief and the drainage basin The amount of available relief – the difference between the highest and lowest points in the landscape – and the degree of dissection both affect slope morphology. Slope angles tend to be greatest in areas of high relief and where dissection is rapid, whereas in stable, low relief areas, slopes are usually less steep and more concavo-convex in profile. The connection lies in the activity of the valley streams. On the one hand, the stream will tend to adjust its gradient so that it can just transport away the amount of debris the slope supplies to it. On the other, the slope form will adjust so that it supplies the load the stream will be able to carry. Hence an area with gentle river gradients, for example, will support low-angle slope forms. This mutual interaction of slopes and streams means that if there were to be some change in the stream channel gradient, perhaps because of tectonic activity or because of a variation in discharge consequent on climatic change, then this would materially alter the slope form. Rejuvenation of the stream will hence lead to increased erosion of the valley sides.

Slope development

In any hillslope system there will be an inevitable loss of material through time (unless renewed uplift occurs), and slopes will gradually retreat. However, the precise manner in which the slopes develop is a difficult problem to unravel, especially in respect of very long-term trends. Most geomorphologists today adopt a pragmatic approach to the question of slope evolution, relying on the evidence of empirical work rather than on the hypothetical schemes of, say Davis and Penck, that have been so controversial in the past. Several modern field studies of slopes have shown that the way in which a slope develops very much depends on whether or not the rate of erosion at the foot of the slope exceeds the rate of weathering higher up. When slopes are eroded as fast or faster than the regolith can accumulate, there is no net build-up of the lower part of the slope and the soil mantle remains thin. This is most likely to occur where slopes are steeper than 35° and where a stream is available to remove the slope debris. Under these circumstances the slope undergoes **parallel retreat** or backwears (Fig. 29). On the other hand, if the rate of weathering exceeds the rate of erosion, then deep soils and regolith develop and mass movements such as creep become dominant, reducing the angularity and gradient of the upper slopes. The lower parts of the slope become relatively protected from erosion as the debris mantle thickens. The dominant manner of development is one of **decline** (downwearing).

Most geomorphologists today accept that slopes may retreat by downwearing, backwearing, or a combination of the two, depending on the relationships described above in each hillslope system. At the beginning of the twentieth century, W. M. Davis put forward the idea of a **cycle of erosion** (Geographical Cycle) in which he

(a) Parallel retreat (backwearing)

(b) Slope decline (downwearing)

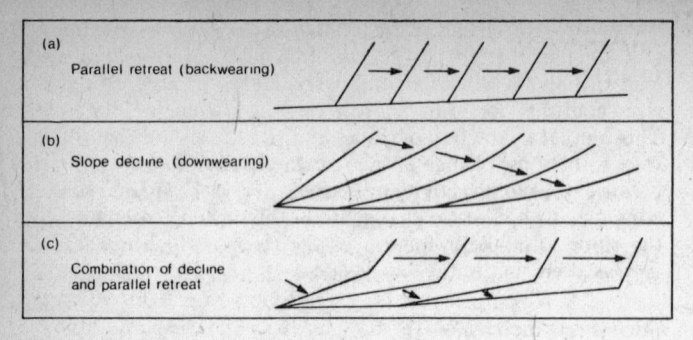

(c) Combination of decline and parallel retreat

Figure 29. Types of slope development

postulated that all slopes inevitably decline through time. He suggested that there was therefore a direct link between the gradient of a slope and its age: thus steep valley-side slopes were regarded as 'youthful', and progressively gentler slopes as 'mature' and 'old'. But we recognize now that geometry is little guide to the age of a slope, and that landscapes do not go through clearly defined stages to a predictable end-result, termed a **peneplain** by Davis. It is also very doubtful, given the changes of base-level and climate that have characterized much of the globe in the last few million years, whether the concept of an uninterrupted 'cycle' is a very realistic one. Certainly Davisian geomorphology, based on a model of very long-term landscape evolution, is not an acceptable framework for understanding how slopes actually do develop, whereas an open system model (e.g. Fig. 27) does serve to direct attention to the essential point, the relationship between process and form.

Summary

The most useful approach to the study of slopes is to view them as open systems in which the passage of mass and energy controls the form of the slope. This is achieved through the processes of weathering, mass movements and surface run-off. Their operation is related to inputs and outputs in the system provided by climate, bedrock materials, available relief and stream channel activity. The long-term development of a slope is not an inevitable sequence of gradient decline.

Chapter 8
Rivers

A stream or river is a body of water flowing in a defined channel as distinct from surface run-off on slopes. Both types of water movement, together with groundwater flow, are important components of the basin hydrological system described in Chapter 1. Channel flow can be recorded in the form of a **hydrograph**, which shows the variation of discharge with time. Figure 30 shows some of the typical features of river flow. It is usually possible to distinguish the level of base flow, resulting largely from ground water supply, from that of quickflow (flood flow), which produces sharp peaks in the hydrograph. The peak of discharge characteristically occurs sometime after the most intense rainfall has ceased. This time lapse is referred to as **basin lag**.

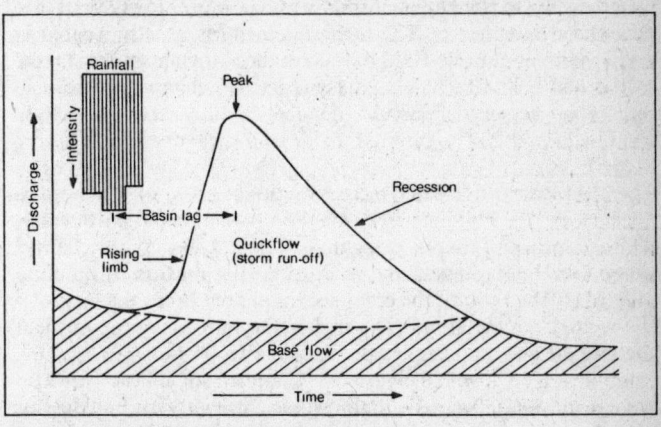

Figure 30. Components of a hydrograph

From such hydrographs a great deal of information can be gained about flood magnitude and frequency, data which is vital to the water engineer and the geomorphologist. The variation in hydrograph shape from river to river shows the dependence of the discharge on the geological and morphological characteristics of the catchment area. A hydrograph with a very sharp peak, for instance, results from high immediate surface run-off, with little absorption and storage of water in the basin.

Characteristics of channel flow

When water flows in a stream it is subject to two basic forces. Gravity exerts an impelling force and is opposed by the frictional resistance between the water and the bed of the channel. A stream's ability to work, that is, to erode and transport material, is related to these two forces. Potential energy is provided by the weight and elevation of the water. This is converted by gravity into downflow and hence into kinetic energy. However, something like 95% of this energy is lost because of the frictional forces, and the precise shape and nature of the channel bed can have a significant effect on this figure.

In all but the most sluggish streams, water flow is not steady and uniform but is affected by **turbulence**, which takes the form of chaotic movements and eddies. Turbulence is an important flow characteristic because it creates upward water motion which lifts and supports the finer sediments. The effect of friction ensures that water closest to the banks normally moves more slowly than that near the stream centre. The highest velocity is usually located in mid-stream about one-third of the distance down from the surface to the bed (Fig. 31), but in an asymmetrical channel the zone of maximum velocity shifts to the deeper side, and may cause significant erosion, as on the outside of a meander (Fig. 32).

The **discharge** (velocity x cross-sectional area) of a stream is affected by the characteristics of the channel itself, particularly width, depth, and channel roughness. The efficiency of the channel shape can be expressed by its **hydraulic radius**, a quantity defined as the ratio of the cross-sectional area (a) to the length of the wetted perimeter (p). The higher the ratio the more efficient the stream and the smaller the loss due to friction. Contrasting examples are shown in figure 31. Channel roughness can also have a marked effect. A rough channel, strewn with boulders or rock projections, creates considerable eddying and loss of energy, whereas a smooth channel minimizes the frictional loss. Channels in silt and clay tend to be deeper and narrower than those in sand and gravel, because the finer materials are cohesive and promote bank stability.

Discharge in a river normally increases downstream, and with this we find that channel width and depth both increase, but channel roughness decreases. The increase in velocity downstream occurs mainly because water flows more efficiently in large channels and

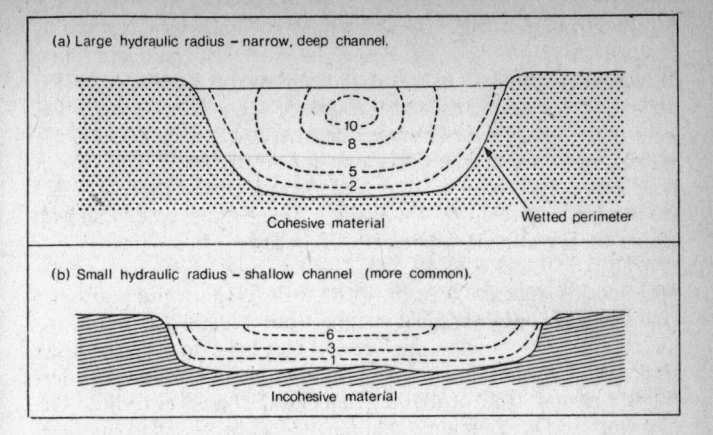

Figure 31. Typical velocity distributions (in cm/sec) in channels with different hydraulic radii

less energy is spent overcoming internal and external friction; hence the carrying capacity of the stream is increased and a lower gradient is required to transport the load. River gradients also tend to become less steep downstream as the load gradually abrades itself, particles becoming smaller in size and easier to transport. Only on the occasions when the river is at bankfull discharge does the velocity appear to be more or less constant downstream.

Channel patterns

Although geological features may determine the overall course of a stream or river, if we look at a detailed map we can observe a variety of channel patterns, including straight, crooked, meandering and braided. On natural courses, straight channels are rare, and most streams wander. Meandering and braiding are two of the most common channel habits and account for the formation of several specific features of erosion and deposition.

Meanders can be described by various geometric properties, some of which are illustrated in figure 32. Of these, wavelength is significant, since it is related to the square root of bankfull discharge. Wavelength is normally about ten times the channel width. This information may sometimes be useful in identifying **misfit streams**, those whose present discharges are too small for their meandering channel pattern. A meandering river is typically asymmetric in cross-section at bends, the deeps being known as **pools**, while the shallows between bends are called **riffles**. On a meander bend the surface water flows towards the outer bank, while the bottom water flows towards the inner bank, setting up helical flow, a corkscrew-like arrangement. This type of flow promotes local erosion and deposition in the meander: **point bars** develop on the inside of bends and eroded slip-off slopes on the outside where water flow is fastest.

Meandering appears to begin with the development of pools and riffles in more or less straight channels, but it is still not possible to define precisely the ultimate cause of this behaviour. We can say that straight channels are inherently unstable and that meandering is a natural state of affairs, given that the banks are adjustable. Contrary to Davisian ideas that meanders are limited to 'mature' or 'old' landscapes, streams of all sizes and at all altitudes can meander. Another false notion is that meanders are caused by obstacles: precisely the opposite is true; obstacles distort meanders and prevent their full development.

Braiding occurs when a stream has not the capacity to transport its load in a single channel, be it straight or meandering, and splits into several channels. Again, the precise causes are not fully understood, but it has been found that braiding occurs most readily where the river discharge is highly variable and the bank

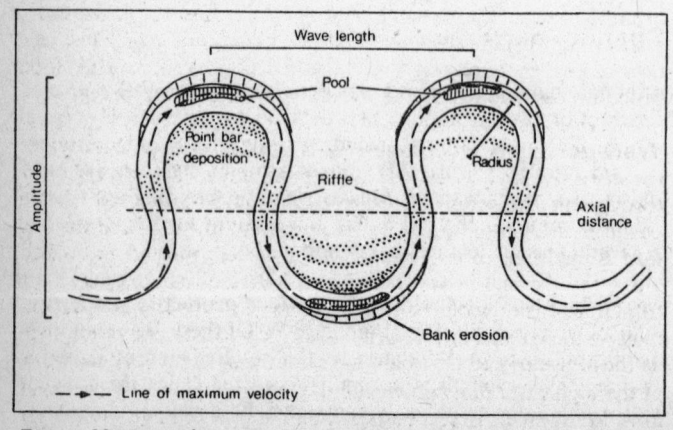

Figure 32. Meander geometry, erosion and deposition

sides are easily eroded, supplying an abundant bedload. Thus braiding is commonly found in semi-arid regions and on glacial outwash plains. One interesting contrast between braiding and meandering revealed by empirical studies is that for a given channel gradient, meanders will occur at a smaller discharge than braiding. This means that some rivers will change from a meandering to a braided habit with an increase in discharge.

Erosion, transport and deposition

Erosion takes place when the stream has an excess of energy, but excess energy does not always result in erosion; much depends on the resistance of the bed over which the water is flowing. Some erosion can be achieved by the force of the flowing water alone which exerts a dragging effect upon the bed, eroding poorly consolidated materials. This is termed **hydraulic action**. Erosion may also be achieved by solution (corrosion). But the principal method of erosion is by **corrasion**, the mechanical impact produced by the debris carried by the stream. This not only erodes the channel bed but also the load itself, grinding it into smooth and rounded shapes. Erosion by the stream allows the channel to extend in two ways. **Headward erosion** at the source of the stream results from undercutting, usually at the base of the soil layer or a vegetation mat. Percolation underground removes fine material and allows the development of subsurface pipes and tunnels which become exposed as open streams as they are undercut and cave in. **Channel widening** and deepening takes place primarily when the stream is in flood or flowing at bankfull discharge. Erosion of the channel sides causes the gradual migration of the channel and this, together with work of the slope processes, contributes to the overall widening of the valley.

Transport of the eroded material is accomplished in three ways: the *dissolved load* consists of soluble materials carried uniformly throughout the water; the *suspended load* is composed of fine particles held in the water by the turbulent motion; and the *bed load* is made up of larger materials bounced, pushed and rolled along the channel floor. The relative contributions of each to the total load varies widely with the nature of the river and is dependent on the volume and velocity of the flow. Semi-arid rivers such as the Missouri and Colorado have large suspended loads because of the high rates of sediment supplied to the channel by overland flow. Many rivers in southern England appear to have a relatively high percentage of dissolved load.

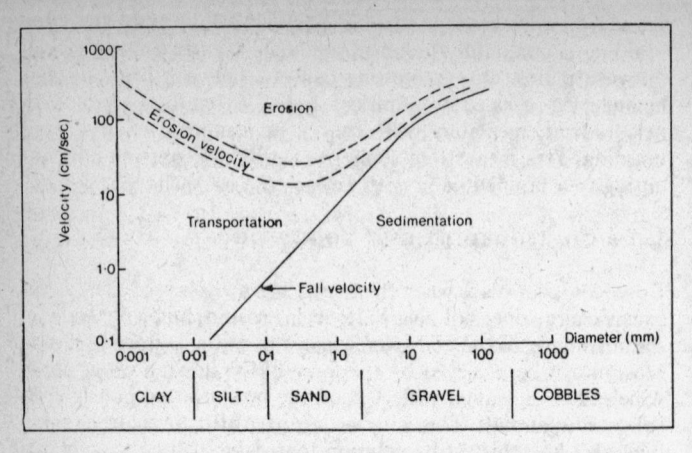

Figure 33. Erosion, transport and deposition related to velocity

The load carried by a stream increases with increased discharge and velocity. The term stream **capacity** denotes the largest amount of debris a stream can transport, and stream **competence** refers to the weight or size of the largest particles that can be moved. The lowest velocity at which grains of a given size can be picked up is said to be the **critical erosion velocity**. Figure 33 demonstrates some important relationships. An interesting point is that sand is more easily picked up than silt or clay; this is because the finer particles tend to be more cohesive. A wide zone rather than a single line is used in the graph to delimit erosion velocity, because its value varies with the depth and temperature of the water and with the density of the grain.

Deposition occurs when the river is no longer competent to transport its load. This usually occurs because of a reduction in the gradient of the stream channel, but may also result from an increase in the calibre of the load, perhaps brought in by a tributary into the main stream, or by conditions of accelerated erosion upstream. The largest calibre material will be deposited first, succeeded downstream by finer material, while the finest material may continue to be deposited even though the river energy has been reduced. This sequence of sedimentation is found in many of the depositional forms created by rivers.

The material deposited by rivers is known as **alluvium**. There is a wide range of alluvial landforms, of which the more important can be described here. A fundamental depositional feature of most river courses is the **flood plain**, built up partly by **channel deposits**, that is material laid down in and at the edges of the main channel, as in the point-bars of a meander, and partly by the horizontally-laid **overbank deposits** during flooding. In floods the coarsest debris is deposited as levees near the channel, and the finer silt and clay is spread over the rest of the flooded area, covering previously laid channel deposits. Natural flood plains often contain such features as ox-bow lakes and backswamps (Fig. 34a).

Alluvial terraces are formed when a river erodes flood-plain sediments previously deposited by itself. The river cuts into these deposits because of some environmental change affecting the channel gradient. In many cases the cause is a climatic one, but near river mouths, terraces may have been built and cut in response to sea-level changes. Terrace sediments and morphology are often used as evidence for interpreting the geomorphological history of a river valley, especially in relation to changes in the Quaternary period (Chap. 10). Some terraces may be benches cut in bedrock, but these are much rarer than alluvial terraces.

A depositional structure not directly related to flood-plains is the **alluvial fan**. Typically, these form where a stream carries a large load of coarse debris and emerges from a hilly area on to a plain. The stream gradient and velocity are drastically reduced, forcing the stream to rapidly aggrade, building a feature with a cone-shaped form. A similar rapid reduction in stream velocity occurs where a river flows into standing water, but in this situation a **delta** is constructed. The finest particles are carried furthest into the lake or sea, settling as *bottom-set beds*; coarser material is deposited as a series of steep-angled wedges (*fore-set beds*) which allow the delta to prograde into the water, and the coarsest channel deposits are dumped on the braided surface of the delta as *top-set beds* (Fig. 34b). Deltas with curving shorelines, such as that of the Nile, are known as arcuate deltas; the delta of the Mississippi is said to be of bird's foot type because of the long projecting fingers of its distributaries.

The long profile

In our earlier discussion in this chapter on water flow in channels, we noted that there was a tendency for channel gradients to become flatter downstream. The longitudinal profile of most

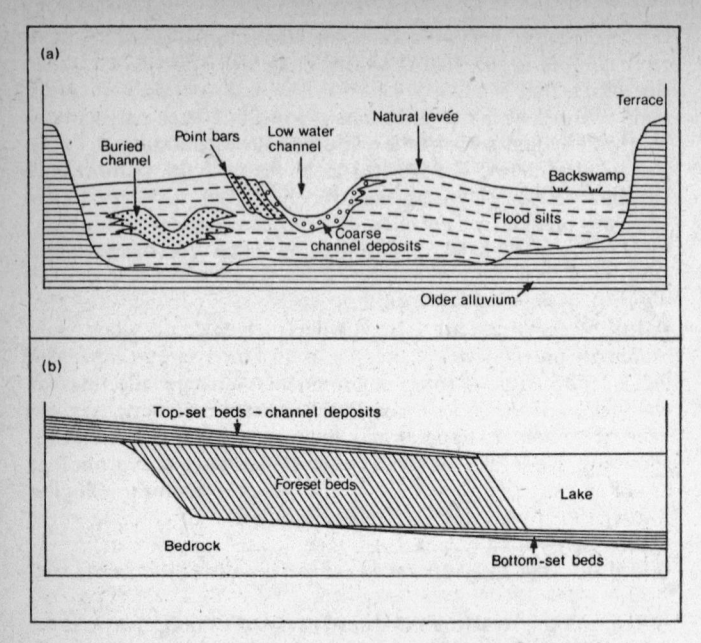

Figure 34. Sections through (a) a flood-plain; (b) a delta

rivers is therefore generally concave upwards. However, in detail the long profile or **thalweg** commonly shows many inflections called **knickpoints**. Many knickpoints have a structural or lithological origin; others may be the result of the steepening of the lower part of the profile by base-level changes. Quite frequently, however, knickpoints are simply the result of variations in the load and discharge characteristics of the river, as will occur at the junction with a tributary.

In time, irregularities such as rapids and waterfalls will be eroded away. Observations show that irregularities in alluvial channels disappear very rapidly. Rivers tend to obtain a condition of equilibrium with prevailing forces which is called **grade**. This term was first introduced by G. K. Gilbert, an American geologist. W. M. Davis regarded grade as a condition of balance between erosion and deposition, and linked the concept with the attainment of a smooth concave profile throughout the thalweg over a very long period of time (Chap. 1). But even streams with irregular profiles can be shown to attain a balance between erosion and deposition, and the best way to regard grade is as first defined by Gilbert: it is a condition of balance in which the slope, width, depth and other channel characteristics are adjusted to the prevailing volume of water and the load it is carrying. Minor fluctuations in erosion and deposition, say on a daily basis, tend to cancel each other out, such that over periods of time of several years a kind of oscillating balance or **dynamic equilibrium** is achieved in the river.

This state is self-regulatory; the river reacts to any change in the controlling factors by adjusting itself to absorb the change and establish a new equilibrium. For example, an increase in the volume of water supplied to a graded river would result in a change in channel characteristics whereby erosion would modify depth, width, and channel roughness to accommodate the new discharge. In summary then, the term 'graded' can be applied to rivers or parts of rivers which have reached a state of self-regulation and which maintain stable channel characteristics.

Drainage basin geometry

In order to understand more fully the relationships between the various components of river systems, and to facilitate comparisons between basins, geomorphologists in recent years have placed considerable emphasis on the quantitative investigation of the geometric properties of rivers and their basins. This type of analysis is called **fluvial morphometry**.

For any drainage basin, a hierarchy of stream orders can be applied. This is an instructive classroom map exercise. Although the idea was originally proposed by R. E. Horton, the amended systems of Shreve or Strahler (Fig. 35) are the ones generally used. Streams without tributaries at the head of river systems are designated first-order streams. Two first order streams join to make a third order stream, and so on. If a lower order unites with a higher order stream, the order of the latter remains unchanged. The basin order is named from the highest order stream in the basin: the example shown is a fourth-order basin.

The examination of a large number of systems has shown that if the number of streams is counted within each order, then that number decreases with increasing order in a regular manner, as demonstrated in figure 35. This is known as the law of stream numbers. A straight-line plot emerges if a semi-logarithmic graph is used (Fig. 35b). Similar straight-line plots can be obtained if

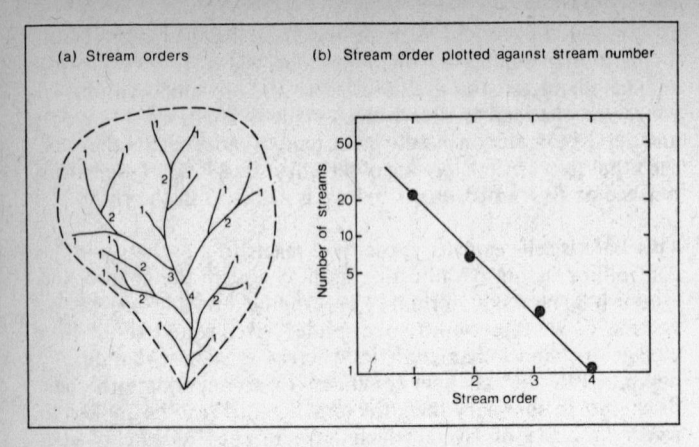

Figure 35. Drainage basin order and stream number

stream order is plotted against the total stream lengths per order (law of stream lengths) and against the total area drained by each order (law of basin areas). The **bifurcation ratio** is an expression relating the number of streams in a given order to the number in the next order. Most streams have bifurcation ratios of between 3 and 5. These various geometric properties show that in many river basins downstream changes are regular and determinable. The 'laws' described above are known collectively as the **laws of drainage composition**. Underlying them is a principle which in the biological sciences is known as **allometric growth**. This concept states that the relative growth of part of an animal is a constant fraction of the relative growth of the whole individual. The same can be said for the component parts of a river system.

Other useful indices that can be derived from the analysis of drainage basins include an index of **drainage density**, expressed as the total channel length divided by the total area of the basin. In the United States, wide ranges of density value occur: the lowest, 2 to 2·5 km per square kilometre, are found on resistant rocks in the Appalachians; values in excess of 200 are reported from badlands. **Stream frequency** is the number of channels per unit area: like drainage density, it is a measure of the texture of the drainage net and hence of the degree of dissection.

If the principles underlying the laws of drainage composition are accepted, then the application of these geometric techniques may give us some insight into the state of equilibrium between the components of the river system. At least they give us some objective ways of comparing drainage basin phenomena, and are to be much preferred to genetic terms such as 'consequent, subsequent and resequent' (W. M. Davis) which imply a speculative erosional history.

Summary

As part of the hydrological cycle, river energy is derived primarily from precipitation and gravity and lost by friction and work, namely erosion, transport and deposition. The efficiency of water flow is affected by channel characteristics such as shape and roughness. Natural channels are rarely straight, but commonly meander and braid. Erosion and deposition by rivers give rise to a range of alluvial landforms. A river or section of a river attains 'grade' when its channel characteristics become stable in relation to the prevailing discharge and its load. Geometric analysis of rivers and their basins serves to demonstrate the equilibrium relationships between the component parts of the river system.

Chapter 9
The Work of Ice

The profound effects of **glacier ice** on landforms is well known. Only about 10% of the world's land surface is currently occupied by glaciers and ice sheets, but their former expansion in the cold phases of the Quaternary left a marked legacy on much of northern Europe, North America, and similar mid-latitude regions. However, ice also occurs in guises other than glacial which are equally significant, even if the results are less spectacular. **Ground ice**, found within the soil and bedrock, characterizes about 20% of the present global land area, and is the basis of many **periglacial** processes and landforms. These too, were much more extensive during the Ice Age. The study of glacial and periglacial geomorphological processes is important not only because of present-day activity in cold regions, but also in the context of the understanding of landscapes in many parts of the British Isles and other countries once covered by glaciers and tundra.

Glaciers

Glaciers are part of the hydrological cycle (Chap. 1), and can be regarded as cascading open systems, moving energy and material downhill and accomplishing geomorphological 'work' on the way. The main mass input is snow. When this falls it has a density of only 0·1, but it undergoes settling and compaction, becoming **firn** (*névé*) at about 0·6, and eventually transforming into glacier ice, which has a density of 0·9. A glacier will only become established and grow if the annual accumulation of snow exceeds the annual melting or ablation. The relation between these two factors represents the **net budget** of the glacier, and like any budget, this can be positive, negative, or in balance. Over a period of years, the budget determines whether the glacier will grow or shrink and a study of the budget can be used to predict glacier behaviour. An *active* glacier is one that has sufficient annual accumulation of snow to keep it moving forward internally, even though the snout may be retreating because of a negative net budget. However, if accumulation ceases altogether, perhaps because of climatic change, then the glacier becomes *stagnant* and forward internal motion ceases. As described below, certain landforms can be related to active glaciers, others to stagnant ice.

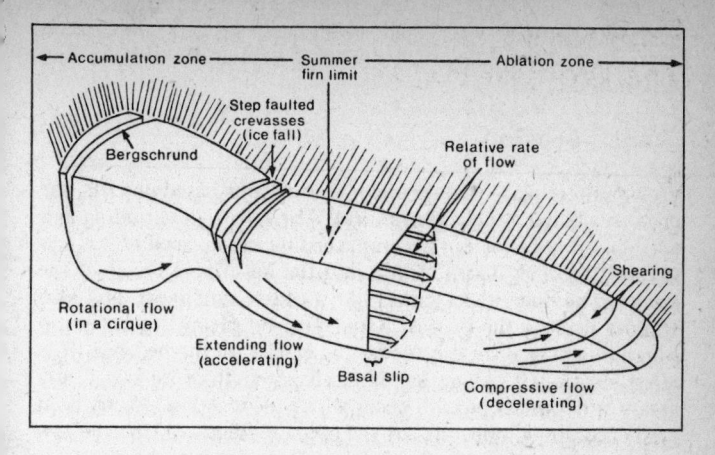

Figure 36. Section through a glacier, showing types of flow

In moving downhill under gravitational force, glaciers act partly as solids by sliding on their bases and by shearing internally, creating crevasses, and partly as plastic media, deforming under stress by reshaping and realigning their crystals. Bedrock exerts frictional drag on all moving glaciers and the maximum rate of flow is near the middle of the ice stream (Fig. 36). Most glaciers flow rather like a concertina: in some parts, **compressing** flow obtains, in which the shear planes thrust upwards. In other sections, **extending** flow takes place. Irregularities in the bedrock floor may initiate these patterns but, in turn, the flow patterns accentuate the bedrock morphology. In particular, compressing flow may favour erosion by moving material upwards away from the rock/ice interface.

Glaciers are not all equally cold. Of critical importance to glacial geomorphology is the temperature of the basal ice layers in relation to the theoretical pressure melt point (*pmp*), which of course varies according to the thickness of the glacier. We can recognize a distinction between **cold glaciers** whose basal layers are below *pmp* and are therefore frozen to bedrock, and **warm glaciers** whose basal layers are very close to *pmp* and are not frozen to their beds. Note that this division is not the same as that between polar and temperate glaciers, which is a geographical categorization, although many temperate (e.g., Alpine) glaciers are dominated by warm ice. Cold-based glaciers can only move by internal shearing and deformation, and will be unable to abrade their beds. On the other hand, warm-based glaciers can slide on bedrock, and have a much greater potential for erosion and deposition.

Glacial erosion

Erosion takes place mainly under active warm-based glaciers, the processes being largely mechanical. **Abrasion**, the grinding and crushing of rocks, is not accomplished by the ice itself as it is too soft, but by rock debris frozen into the lowermost layers of the glacier. The debris acts rather like a coarse sandpaper, and also abrades itself in the process. Quarrying or **plucking** occurs in response to the drag exerted by the glacier on the bedrock. It is not a simple tug-of-war, as the tensile strength of ice is not very great; rather, plucking will occur where the rock has already been weakened along joint-lines by the pressure forces and freeze-thaw action under the glacier.

The landforms of glacial erosion are extremely varied and it would be impossible to describe them all here. However, we can say that, in common, they are affected by four main groups of variables. First, by glacial variables such as ice thickness, velocity, and basal temperature; second, by bedrock variables, including lithology and joint type and spacing; third, by topographical variables such as valley gradient and relative relief; and fourth, by the variable of time, namely, the length of the glacial episode in which modification can take place. Another feature of note is the range of scales involved. The smallest-scale forms are striations and other scratches and cracks created by abrasion. Medium-scale forms include rock steps and **roches moutonnées** (Fig. 37); these are particularly instructive in that they demonstrate the relative roles of plucking and abrasion. Irregularities on the bedrock floor, perhaps the result of variable jointing, are subject to greater pressure on their upstream (stoss) sides than on their lee sides. Pressure melting allows sliding and abrasion to take place on the stoss side, whereas refreezing of the glacier to the bedrock in the reduced pressure zone of the lee side favours plucking. Since plucking tends to be more effective quantitatively than abrasion, in this way glacial erosion tends to accentuate pre-existing landforms (a positive feedback mechanism). Large-scale erosion landforms include U-shaped valleys, pyramidal peaks, and cirques, which are common features of glaciated mountain regions. Less spectacular, although as widespread, are glacially-scoured lowland landscapes, such as the Canadian Shield and the knock-and-

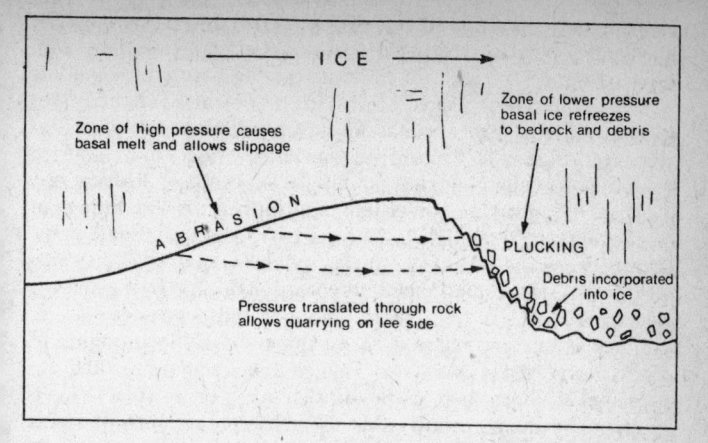

Figure 37. Erosion processes associated with a roche moutonnée

lochan topography created on the Lewisian gneiss of north-west Scotland.

Glacial deposition

The general term **glacial drift** is given to all debris deposited in a glacial environment, but we can recognize a difference between material directly deposited by ice which is known as glacial **till**, and **fluvioglacial** material deposited by glacial meltwater streams. Till is usually composed of a seemingly chaotic assemblage of partly rounded stones set in a finer mass or matrix of clay, silt or sand. There are several mechanisms of till deposition. At the base of the glacier, **lodgement till** may be formed as debris-rich layers of ice lodge against obstructions and become separated from faster-flowing and clearer ice above. **Ablation till** will be deposited when a stagnant glacier downmelts on the spot, allowing material in and on the ice to accumulate in heaps. Material reaching the surface of a glacier sometimes flows rather like a porridge, forming a **flow till**. With these several different possibilities for till deposition, a single glacier can build up quite complicated drift sequences. Landforms composed largely of till are called **moraines**. At the margins of a glacier, ridges and mounds may form an end-moraine complex (Fig. 38), although this may also include fluvioglacial material. The streamlined shape of **drumlins**, also composed of till, reflects their subglacial origin under moving warm-based ice.

Fluvioglacial drift is sorted and stratified into layers by the meltwater, but this stratification can often change rapidly over short distances because of the ever-varying nature of a melting glacier. Material deposited against ice is known as **ice-contact drift**, and this can account for several distinct landforms, as depicted in figure 38. **Eskers** are long narrow ridges of well-sorted material deposited in sub- or en-glacial tunnels; **kames** are isolated mounds which may represent former crevasse fillings or be the remains of small deltas; **kame terraces** accumulate in the area between the side of the glacier and the confining valley walls; **kettle-holes** are small enclosed depressions formed by the melting of buried blocks of ice. Areas of mounds and depressions of ice-contact origin are referred to as kame-and-kettle topography. **Proglacial drift** is carried beyond the ice margins, and the principal landform here is the outwash plain or **sandur**. This is built up by the constantly shifting meltwater streams, dumping the coarsest material at the proximal end near the glacier margin and the finer material at the distal end. Where proglacial material is deposited in a lake, a delta will form, similar to that in Figure 34

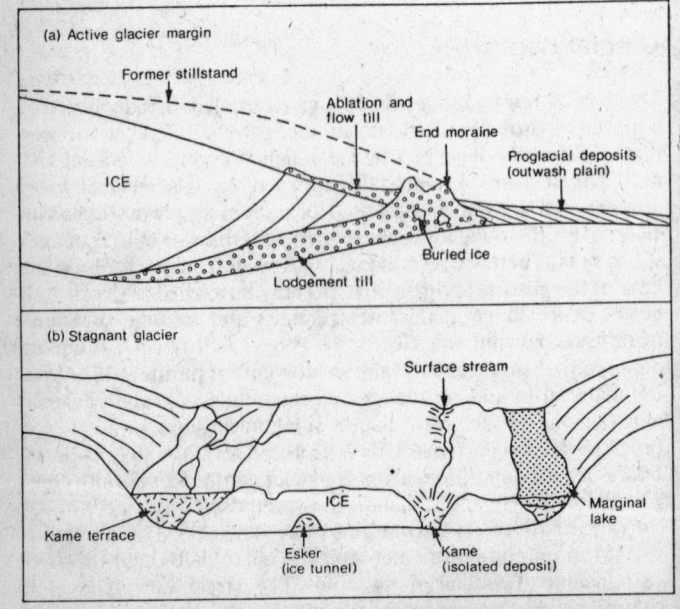

Figure 38. Some features of glacial and fluvioglacial deposition

except that the bottom-set beds will often be varved, each **varve** consisting of a coarse layer representing summer deposition and a finer layer resulting from the slow winter precipitation of the suspended material in the lake.

Other effects of glaciation

Glaciation has important effects on the landscape beyond the direct modifications caused by ice erosion and deposition. We may recall here the example of glacial isostasy (page 64). In northern Britain, slow recovery still continues from the effects of the weight of an ice sheet present some 15,000 years ago. The growth and retreat of ice sheets have also been responsible for large fluctuations in global sea-level; the effects are discussed in more detail in Chapter 11. On a local scale, advancing ice sheets have frequently disrupted pre-existing drainage lines, initiating new courses which in many cases have persisted after the ice has disappeared. In the English Midlands, much of the area now drained by the Warwickshire Avon was once part of the Trent catchment until Pleistocene ice sheets advanced into the region and blocked the northward-flowing pattern. Similarly, the Thames formerly flowed eastwards through the Vale of St. Albans and northern Essex, but was diverted to its present course by an ice sheet which reached as far as Finchley (Fig. 40).

The periglacial environment

Geomorphologically, periglacial regions are very active. Mechanical splitting of rocks by ice (**gelifraction**), frost heaving of the ground (**geliturbation**), solifluction and nivation are all important processes. In addition, each spring large quantities of water from melting snow and ice rapidly erode the debris scattered and moved down the slopes. The disturbed ground and scarcity of vegetation also allow wind action to play a significant role in some areas.

The formation of ground ice within the soil and upper bedrock layers is basic to several processes. As it forms, **ground ice** tends to segregate into needles, lenses or veins, causing considerable local disruption to the ground morphology. The freezing of water in the soil is also capable of disrupting the colloidal binding of soil particles so that, on melting, the soil layers are rendered incohesive and mobile. Sediments most susceptible to frost disturbance in these ways are in the silt size range.

In some parts of the periglacial zone, geomorphic activity is promoted by a large number of freeze-thaw cycles and high snow precipitation (Icelandic type of region). Other areas (Siberian type) are characterized by relatively light snow precipitation, few freeze-thaw cycles, but very low temperatures, resulting in the formation of **permafrost**, the name given to perenially frozen ground. Permafrost consists of a permanently frozen layer which may reach to depths of several hundred metres and an **active layer** nearest the ground surface which unfreezes in summer. This arrangement produces a number of unique effects, as explained below.

Patterned ground

The repeated passage of freeze-thaw cycles in the ground has the effect of differentially sorting the finer frost-susceptible materials away from the coarser soil particles. In plan view, this produces various types of **sorted patterned ground** (Fig. 39). On flat ground, individual stone circles or nets of sorted polygons may form, each with a coarse border and a fine centre. On steeper ground, the polygons elongate into garlands, and stone stripes form on gradients of 7° or more. Many of these features can be observed today near the summits of some of the higher mountains in Britain. Where the soil is more uniform and the sorting of material less obvious, the ground may be heaved into small mounds or hummocks (**thufurs**). This is one kind of **unsorted**

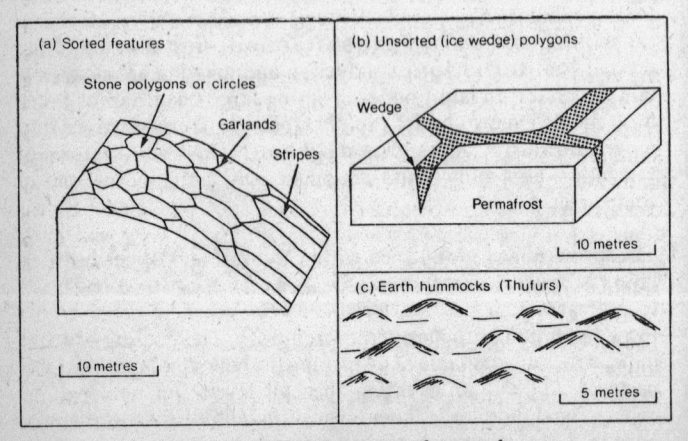

Figure 39. Types of periglacial patterned ground

patterned ground. Another common type of unsorted patterned ground is the **ice-wedge polygon**, found only in permafrost regions. Here, the intense cold causes the ground to contract and crack into polygonal networks. The initial crack becomes wider each year because in summer it is filled with moisture which freezes at depth and prevents the crack from closing. Fossil ice wedges may be preserved by an infilling of sand or other debris and can occasionally be seen in gravel pits in Britain.

Pingos are large ground ice mounds, anything from 5 m to 70 m in height, found in the high Arctic. They have an ice core supplied by water moving upwards through permafrost under hydrostatic pressure. An artesian situation would provide a suitable environment for this to occur. The upward growth of the mound eventually exposes the ice core to sub-aerial melting, and the feature disintegrates to a landform with a central depression surrounded by a rampart. Relict pingos have been identified at Walton Heath, Norfolk, and at Llangurig in central Wales.

Periglacial slope processes

One of the most ubiquitous processes in these regions is that of **solifluction** (gelifluction), and it is particularly significant where permafrost is present. The permanently frozen ground prevents the downward percolation of water in summer and this, combined with the incohesion caused by surface freezing and thawing, produces a highly mobile active layer. In addition, there is no deep-rooted vegetation to bind the soil, hence solifluction can occur in permafrost regions on very low-angle slopes and has the general effect of removing debris from interfluves and filling up valleys and hollows, giving a smooth appearance to the landscape. This type of solifluction appears to have been common in southern Britain during the Ice Age; the relict solifluction debris is known as **head**, or as **coombe rock** in chalk areas. Solifluction can also occur in non-permafrost periglacial regions under conditions of frequent freeze-thaw cycles, high precipitation and steep slopes. Here, the process typically results in the creation of solifluction lobes and terraces, which move slowly downhill.

The presence of snowbanks on hillsides can favour local solifluction by providing additional moisture to the ground; the moisture also increases the effectiveness of freeze-thaw action. In this way snow can have an erosive effect (nivation) and create slope depressions known as **nivation hollows**. Large hollows of this type may develop into true glacial cirques. At outcrops of hard rock the combination of frost-shattering and removal of the debris by solifluction produces angular free-faces and **tor-like forms** where joint structures intersect at right-angles. These tors are often very similar in appearance to tors produced by deep chemical weathering in warmer environments of the globe. Blockfields of angular debris may accumulate at the foot of many free faces and tors. Related features include **altiplanation terraces**, semi-horizontal structurally-controlled benches cut into hillsides by a combination of frost-shattering and solifluction.

The Ice Age in Britain

The last two million years of geological history is known as the Quaternary period. Throughout the globe this has been dominated by alternations of marked climatic change. In Britain and other temperate lands, the cold oscillations have been times of active periglacial and glacial activity. Although it is now recognized from ocean-core evidence that over twenty glaciations

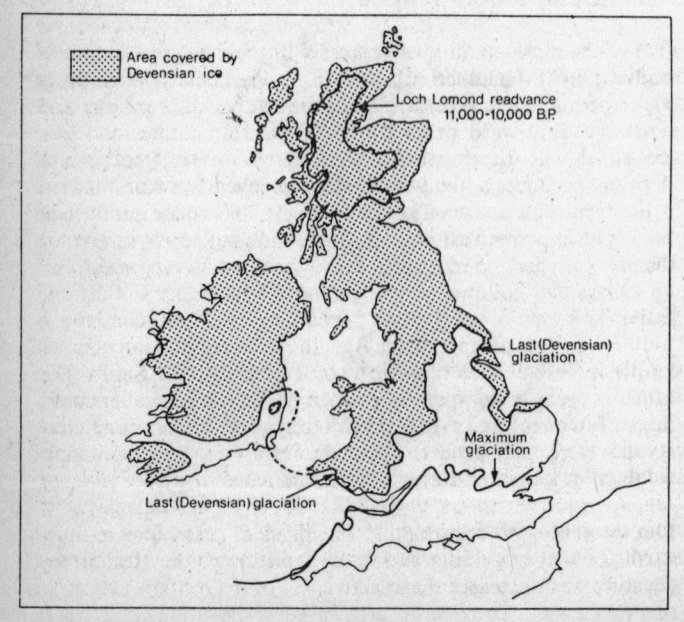

Figure 40. Glacial limits in the British Isles

have occurred in the Quaternary, it is thought that while earlier cold phases were dominated by periglacial conditions, only the last three glaciations led to ice sheets in the British Isles, known as the Anglian, Wolstonian, and Devensian (last) glaciations. In the **Anglian** stage, both British and Scandinavian ice sheets contributed to the widespread deposition of till over much of East Anglia. Ice at this time reached into the London Basin, forming the southernmost limit of glaciation in eastern England. Elsewhere in Britain there appears to be only scattered evidence of an Anglian glaciation. The results of the **Wolstonian** glaciation are best seen in the English Midlands, where a prominent end-moraine exists at Moreton-in-Marsh. A huge glacier covered much of the Irish Sea basin, reaching as far as the Isles of Scilly and the north coasts of Devon and Cornwall (Fig. 40), forming the maximum limit of glaciation in western Britain. Anglian and Wolstonian glacial drift together are sometimes known as the **older drift**, in contrast to the generally fresher morphology of the Devensian stage (newer drift).

The **Devensian** glacial stage lasted from about 110,000 to 10,000 years ago, but ice sheets did not advance substantially in Britain until after 25,000 years ago, much of the earlier time being of tundra rather than glacial conditions. The limit of Devensian ice is marked by large end-moraine complexes in the Vale of York and in southern Ireland. The retreat of the main ice sheet took place about 14,000 years ago, but this was followed by another regrowth of glaciers, known as the **Loch Lomond Readvance**. This led to the establishment of a small ice cap in Scotland and cirque glaciers in other mountain areas, the final appearance of ice in Britain.

Summary

Ice plays an important role in geomorphology, not just in the form of glaciers but also as ground ice in periglacial regions. Glacier budgets, motion and temperatures are aspects of glaciology that are fundamental to the understanding of glacial erosion and deposition. Fluvioglacial landforms are mainly the product of stagnant glaciers. In periglacial regions, some landforms result from the presence of permafrost, others from intense freeze-thaw activity. The British Isles has been strongly affected by former glacial and periglacial activity.

Chapter 10
Wind Action

Wind as a geomorphological agent is usually associated with arid regions, but two points need stressing in this respect. First, winds blow everywhere and have the potential to be an important sculpturing force wherever vegetation is sparse. This is particularly true in coastal environments with onshore winds, in thinly vegetated periglacial areas, and where dry areas are ploughed by man for crops. Second, large tracts of arid regions are not dominated by dunes, as is sometimes popularly imagined, and water-based processes contribute a great deal to desert landforms.

Wind moves sand by surface creep, by **saltation** – that is, in a series of hopping movements – and in suspension. The particles moved by these processes are remarkably uniform in size, between 0·1 and 0·5 mm. Particles smaller than this are often carried considerable distances to be deposited elsewhere (e.g., as loess). Particles larger than this, coarse sand and gravel, remain on the ground as lag deposits. The trajectories of grains undergoing saltation (Fig. 41) are very significant in building dunes and other similar features. Turbulent wind flow near the ground creates a variety of short, steeply sloping ascents, followed by a much more

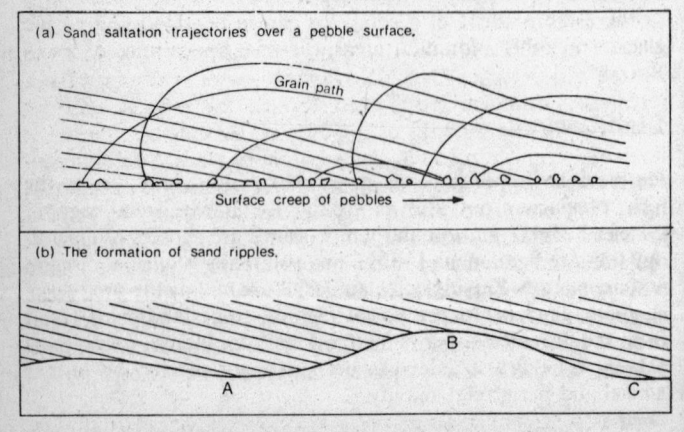

Figure 41. The effects of sand grains undergoing saltation

horizontal path before the grain hits the ground. The impact of the grain may cause other particles to move by creep.

The main depositional features created by wind include small-scale sand ripples and ridges and large-scale dunes. The formation of **ripples** is closely connected with saltation. Small irregular sand surfaces facing the wind (*AB* in Fig. 41) will receive more bombardment from saltation than will lee slopes (*BC*). Material creeps up to *B* faster than it can be removed, and creeps away from *A* and *C* faster than the supply down the sheltered lee slope. The crest at *B* thus grows and the hollows deepen at *A* and *C* until an optimum regular ripple amplitude is developed in equilibrium with the prevailing wind speed. This equilibrium is reached because the crest at *B* cannot grow indefinitely, as with increasing height it interferes with the wind flow and grains are blown off the crest into the hollow. **Sand ridges** are larger features than ripples and are composed of material too coarse to be lifted by the wind. The particles in this case are shaped into ridges by the impact of grains undergoing saltation which can move material up to six times their own size.

There are many shapes and sizes of **dune**, and particular complications occur where some vegetation is involved, as in many coastal dune systems (see page 106). In desert areas, however, two basic types can be recognized. **Barchan** dunes (Fig. 42) are crescentic in plan with their horns pointing downwind. Material is moved by the wind up the windward slope of a sand mound and accumulates near the top of the lee slope, which gradually becomes steeper. Eventually it shears, the material slipping to the bottom of the slope. The dune slowly migrates as this process is repeated. The horns are created because the process operates faster on the lower flanks of the mound; the rate of advance is inversely proportional to the height of the slip face. **Seif** (longitudinal) dunes are long and straight, often occurring in subparallel lines. They may have various origins; some seif dunes may form in the lee of obstacles such as hills, but others are not connected with obstacles and develop in multi-directional wind patterns where cross winds elongate barchan dunes (Fig. 42). In Australia, great longitudinal dunes have a sinuous pattern, rather like a braided river. It has been suggested that they are related to dried-up river courses, for this is where the sand supply will be concentrated.

Wind also has important erosive effects, of two distinct kinds. The wholesale removal of sand from an area is termed **deflation**.

Where this is localized, a deflation hollow may be created. The action of deflation over large desert areas leaves behind a gravel-strewn surface known as **hamada** in most of the Sahara. The other type of wind erosion is the process of **abrasion**; this is confined to the saltation zone, normally within a metre or so of the ground. Wind abrasion is responsible for the undercutting and

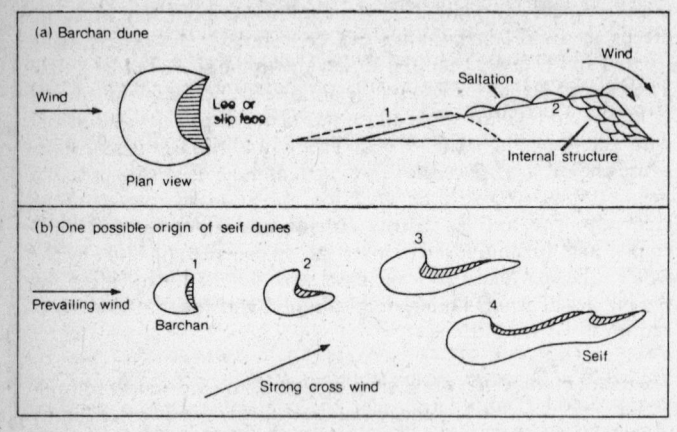

Figure 42. Barchan and seif dune types

fluting of rocks, polishing hard rock surfaces and shaping individual stones into faceted forms (ventifacts). Soft rock may sometimes be fashioned into **yardangs**, parallel U-shaped troughs separated by sharp ridges.

Wind and water in deserts

Although extensive sand 'seas' occur in most of the world's hot deserts, the occurrence of these and other smaller dune areas depends on suitable dune-building sand being available. In some cases this may occur within ancient basins of centripetal drainage; in other cases near outcrops of easily eroded sandstone rock. The depositional effects of wind in deserts thus tends to be regionalized and is certainly not universal. Large areas of desert are potentially subject to deflation, and some well-known large depressions, such as the Qattara in the Egyptian desert, seem to be the result of this process. However, many geomorphologists believe that both deflation and abrasion are only really effective in the presence of moisture, where chemical weathering disintegrates the ground surface, creating sand particles that can be easily picked up by the wind. In this sense, the principal role of wind in deserts seems to be to rework material locally. Many would argue that the role of water is much more important than is generally realized. It is significant not only as a weathering agent, but also in the form of run-off. Although this may occur on only a few days per year, hence the tendency to underplay its role, it can have dramatic effects. The interaction of long periods of drought between intermittent bouts of rainfall allow weathering and wind action to create large amounts of loose surface debris. **Flash floods**, which are caused by heavy convectional storms, flow as sheetfloods or as concentrated streams in wadis, picking up enormous loads which accomplish a great deal of erosion.

Thus, although dunes are significant landforms in deserts, over considerable areas a landscape of vast flat or low-angle surfaces is more typical, sharply broken by isolated hills, scarps or mountain fronts. This assemblage is essentially moisture controlled through the action of weathering, mass movement and run-off, and wind plays a relatively minor role. A typical desert landscape is illustrated in figure 43. An additional factor to bear in mind is that many desert landforms may be partially relict; that is, they are more related to former phases of wetter climate than they are to prevailing conditions. Many extensive wadi systems seem to be of this nature.

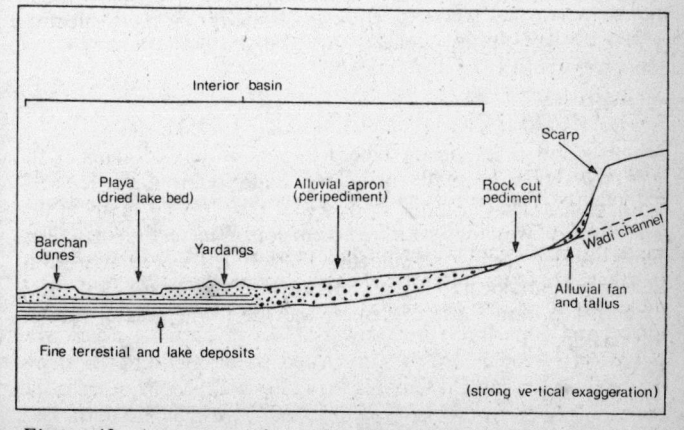

Figure 43. A composite desert landform assemblage

Wind in coastal areas

Active coastal dunes occur only where there are sandy beaches fed by an adequate supply of marine sand and where the wind is on-shore. The biggest coastal dunes are found on west-facing coasts in the temperate storm belts of the world. The main difference between desert dunes and coastal dunes lies in the presence of vegetation, mainly marram grass and sea-couch grass in Britain, which traps blowing sand, resulting in different basic dune forms. At the back of the beach, **foredunes** develop in the form of a ridge or ridges parallel to the line of the beach. A dried-out berm (see Chap. 11) may provide the initial foundations. Landwards of the foredunes there occurs a seemingly chaotic accumulation of **secondary** or **transgressive** dunes, originally derived from the erosion of the foredunes. However, certain recognizable forms can usually be found. These include **parabolic** dunes of crescentic ground form with their horns facing the wind. This is opposite to barchan form because vegetation impedes the downwind migration of the lower slopes of the dune. A hairpin dune is an exaggerated form of parabolic dune. **Blowouts** are quite common in coastal dunes, and develop particularly where the wind manages to breach through a hairpin dune, leaving a deflated central area flanked by walls of sand.

Coastal dunes are liable to be particularly mobile if the vegetation cover becomes thin or is removed. A common cause of this in Britain is excessive trampling in holiday areas. Artificial replanting with marram grass or trees is normally the most effective means of re-stabilizing the system.

Summary

Wind action is important wherever unconsolidated sand exists and vegetation is relatively sparse. Saltation is a particularly significant mode of sand transport and accounts for many of the landforms of wind deposition and erosion. Wind action in deserts tends to be locally significant, whereas elsewhere moisture-controlled landforms may be important. Dune forms in coastal areas differ from those of deserts because of the greater role of vegetation.

Chapter 11
Coastlines

A wide variety of landform environments exists on coasts, from the mud flats of protected inlets, where wave energy is very low, through sandy and pebbly beaches to hard-rock cliff coastlines where wave energy may be very high. This range of coastal types is shaped not only be wave erosion, transport and deposition, but also by tides and currents and by subaerial processes such as weathering and mass movements on cliffs. In turn, these processes are conditioned by several major factors, listed below.

The marine agencies, waves, tides and currents, are the result of oceanographic and climatic forces. The most fundamental of these are the Earth's atmospheric circulation features (Chap. 3), which control wind direction and force and hence the generation of waves and currents. Climate also affects the rate of weathering on cliffs and partly controls the biotic factor in coastal environments. Geological factors of structure and lithology influence the general trend of the coastline, its detailed configuration, cliff profiles and offshore gradients. Rock type also controls the local type of beach material. Biotic factors include vegetation, which plays an important role in both sand dune areas (Chap. 10) and in salt marshes. In addition many tropical coastlines are distinctive because of the presence of coral and other reef-building organisms. The factor of sea-level change is significant on nearly all coastlines, since there are many landforms which are not in equilibrium with present processes, but rather result from former periods of higher or lower sea-level. Finally, man must also be regarded as a significant factor in coastal geomorphology, since he modifies both physical and biological processes through coastal protection works, reclamation schemes, leisure activities and pollution.

Waves, tides and currents

Waves are by far the most important agents of shoreline modification. Apart from those very occasionally started by earthquakes (tsunamis), all other waves are produced by wind. The wind exerts a drag on the surface water particles and sets up small orbital motions in the water. There is some small lateral displacement of the water, but the wave itself moves much faster through

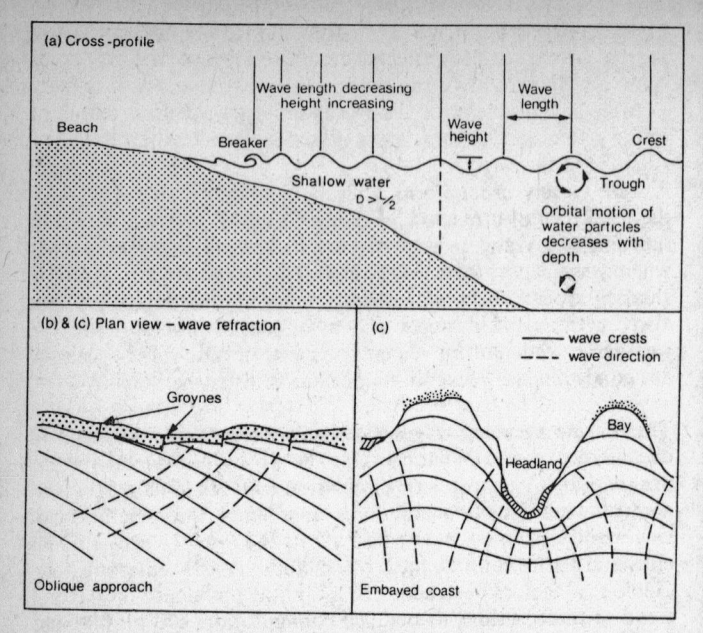

Figure 44. Changes in wave form in shallow water

the sea, growing as it travels. Three factors govern the size of the wave: the wind speed, the duration of the wind, and the distance or 'fetch' over which the wave travels. The largest waves will be produced by prolonged gale-force winds blowing over ocean surfaces.

When waves reach shallow water near a coast, their dimensions are substantially altered (Fig. 44). Principally, the wavelength (L) is shortened, but the wave height (h) increases: the **wave steepness** (h/L ratio) increases until the faster upper part of the wave topples over at the breakpoint line. In the breaker or **surf zone**, the wave force is translated up the beach in the form of a **swash**. This returns as **backwash** either in sheet flow (under-tow) or as a rip-current, a localized concentration of backwash. Wave steepness is a critical parameter determining the erosional or depositional character of waves: **constructive waves** (spilling breakers) have a low index of steepness; **destructive waves** (plunging breakers) have a relatively high h/L ratio. Waves are also subject to **refraction** as they approach the coast. Where oblique waves approach a straight shore, the frictional drag exerted by the sea floor tends to turn the waves so that they break more nearly parallel to the shore. On embayed coasts (Fig. 44c), headlands interfere with the waves first and set up a refraction pattern that concentrates wave attack on the headlands and reduces it in the bays.

The most important effect of **tides** on coasts is that their range controls the vertical range of wave action. A large tidal range (macrotidal environment) creates a broad shore zone; in a microtidal environment the wave energy is concentrated at a more constant level and large intertidal beaches or shore platforms will not exist. The configuration of the coast has a marked effect on tidal range, the highest tides in the world occurring in funnel-shaped embayments, such as the Bristol Channel. Onshore winds may also locally increase the height of a tide; where they combine with the effects of a depression, which allows an additional slight rise in the level of the ocean surface, a **storm surge** may result. One well-known catastrophic example occurred in the southern North Sea in 1953, causing widespread flooding, erosion and loss of life in the Netherlands and eastern England.

Several kinds of **currents** affect coasts, as the term describes any mass movement of water. Ocean currents (Chap. 1) are of considerable indirect importance to coastal geomorphology since they act as a major control on the supply of offshore heat energy, which in turn influences local winds and biotic activity in coastal areas. Tidal currents are created as the tide ebbs and flows and are usually powerful enough to move fine sediments in estuaries. Local winds may create currents in gulfs and estuaries and locally along the shore. Contrary to earlier beliefs, the longshore movement of beach material is no longer attributed to such currents, but to wave action; overall, currents are probably more important in shaping sea-floor topography than in modifying beaches.

Beaches

A beach is an accumulation of sediment on a shore, and is usually composed of either sand or shingle. On a global scale, sandy examples predominate; shingle beaches are more common in higher latitudes, where there is more coarse material, supplied by past and present glacial and periglacial action. A notable exception is southern England where much of the shingle is flint, derived from chalk cliffs. The constant movement of material both up and down and also along beaches means that beach sediments tend to become well rounded.

Beach **cross-profiles** vary partly because of the variations in particle size: shingle beaches are normally steeper than sandy beaches because they allow greater water percolation, reducing the combing-down action of the backwash. However, within the limits set by the size of material, the main controller of beach profiles is wave steepness. We can identify the relationships in a process-response model (Fig. 45). Steep (destructive) waves comb

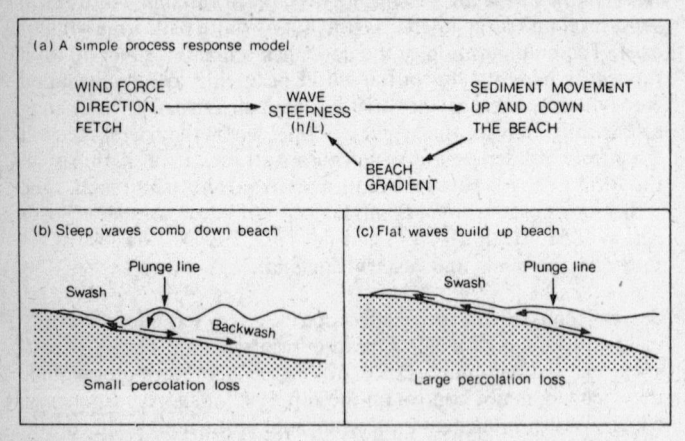

Figure 45. Process-form relationships in beach cross-profiles

down the beach by moving sediment seaward in their powerful backwash. However, the reduction in gradient allows the wave length to become longer, automatically reducing the wave steepness. Thus the process of combing down does not go on indefinitely but rather an equilibrium is reached between the beach gradient and the prevailing waves. Similarly, flat waves shift sediment landward, steepening the beach; in this case the increase in gradient will eventually shorten the wavelength, making the waves more destructive. Again a balance is achieved. These adjustments are a good illustration of the working of negative feedback between form (the beach) and process (wave action).

The small landforms typically found on beaches in Britain vary from season to season. In summer, when constructive waves predominate, a **berm** is built up at the limit of wave action. Sometimes several berms may be observed, related to a spring-neap tide sequence. In winter, storms produce much flatter profiles, especially on sandy beaches. However, on shingle beaches a **storm beach** may be flung up by the spray to create a backshore ridge. It remains there as a semi-permanent feature because the coarseness of the shingle allows the backwash to percolate down rather than wash away the surface. **Ripples** are common on the mid- to low-tide parts of sandy beaches, and are formed by bottom currents induced by wave movement when the tide is higher.

The general orientation of beaches is again a function of wave action. Material is moved along beaches by waves breaking obliquely on the shore. The sand or shingle is pushed up the beach

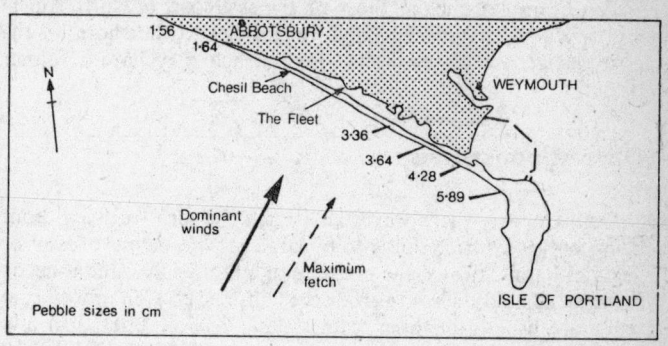

Figure 46. Chesil Beach, Dorset: orientation and pebble sizes

at an angle by the wave, but returns in the backwash down the steepest gradient; each particle therefore moves in a zigzag fashion. Over a long period of time, longshore movement of material means that beaches will tend to orientate themselves at right angles to the direction of approach of the dominant waves. Chesil Beach is one such **swash-aligned** feature. Here, there is a marked gradation of pebble size along the beach (Fig. 46); this is a reflection of conditions in which wave energy is greatest at the eastern end of the structure where the offshore profile is steep. The coarsest pebbles are found here: throughout the beach, the sediments have moved to a point where they are in equilibrium with the dominant wave energy. Where there is strong unimpeded longshore transport on a coast obliquely aligned to the dominant waves, **drift-aligned** features may be apparent, orientated parallel to the direction of maximum drift, and this is commonly the alignment found in many spits.

Spits are a very common form of coastal depositional structure and are usually sited at points where the shoreline undergoes a sharp change in direction. Longshore drifting extends the beach into open water. Many spits are recurved at their extremities, the recurves being produced by wave refraction round the head of the spit, or by wave approach from a different direction. Drift of material along a shore from opposing directions may result in the building of a **cuspate bar** or foreland, of which Dungeness in Kent is a classic example. **Offshore bars** can often be seen on gently shelving coastlines, and where such bars are long and continuous they form **barrier beaches**. They are usually swash-aligned features but may have originally been created by longshore drifting; in other words, they are extended spits. But the largest examples, such as those on the east coast of North America, appear to have been piled up parallel to the shore by the post-glacial rise of sea-level. Chesil Beach may have a similar origin.

Cliffed coastlines

Sea cliffs occur where waves can reach the local rocks without being prevented from doing so by large accumulations of sand or shingle. Paradoxically, the presence of a limited amount of beach material can aid the sea to erode the cliff. The erosion processes at work are usually of three main types. Physical **abrasion** and corrasion are important where beach material is available. The sea uses the material as tools of erosion in much the same way as a river. In the abrasion zone at the foot of the cliff both the bedrock and the material become smoothed and rounded. **Chemical erosion** may also take place: sea water is very effective in dissolving a number of rock-forming minerals and this type of erosion will be important not only in the swash zone but also higher up the cliff in the spray zone. **Hydraulic action**, the force of the waves themselves, produces tremendous instantaneous compressions of air in cracks and crevices, suddenly released as the wave recedes. This is a very effective erosion agent on well-jointed rock or on man-made structures with lines of weakness. In addition to these three marine processes, sub-aerial slope processes (Chap. 7) are very important on sea cliffs. Some of the largest landslides and rockfalls in Britain are triggered by active marine undercutting. In other, less exposed situations, the sea may act as an efficient agent of debris removal of the products of weathering and slope processes.

The precise form of any cliff is controlled by the lithology and structure of the rocks and the relative effectiveness of marine as opposed to sub-aerial processes. In addition, the past geomorphological history of the cliff may be relevant. Within the limits set by geology, the largest active cliffs occur where exposure to waves is greatest. Cliffs are nearly always most vertical around headlands rather than in bays. The highest cliffs in Europe occur in Portugal and on the west coast of Ireland, facing the biggest Atlantic swell waves. Where, through a combination of rock type and exposure, the rate of retreat is especially rapid, **hanging valleys** may be created, well exemplified by the Seven Sisters in Sussex.

Except where offshore water is very deep, many cliffs are fronted by a **wave cut platform**. In the British Isles, most are the result of marine abrasion and have a gentle concave-upward profile which ideally is an equilibrium gradient just steep enough to allow debris to be removed by wave action. The junction between platform and cliff is marked by a rounded **notch** which lies just below high-tide level. The seaward limit of the abrasion platform is determined by the maximum depth at which material can be moved by waves. This is about 10 m below low-tide level for the biggest waves. Processes other than abrasion may also create platforms. Concentrated chemical and biological action in the intertidal zone may create a rough platform which can be further trimmed by wave action. Another possibility is that rock disintegration may be caused in the spray zone by the constant alternate wetting and drying of rocks, again creating a bench. This process is called **water-layer weathering** and occurs on some subtropical coasts.

Low energy coasts

Within estuaries, behind spits and bars, and in deep embayments, protected conditions exist in which wave energy is usually very low and in which tidal range has an important geomorphological role to play. Here, finer sediments settle out forming mud flats, allowing salt-loving plants to colonize the area. In such environments three zones related to tidal activity may be recognized. The **sub-tidal zone** is made up of the permanently occupied creeks and channels; in plan view these channels often exhibit many of the features of a dendritic drainage system. The muddy flanks of the channels comprise the **intertidal slopes**, which are covered by every high tide. These slopes are normally bare of vegetation except near their upper parts. The **high-tide flat** is, as its name suggests, a level surface built up at the extreme limit of marine deposition, just above the mean high-water mark. These three units can be recognized in a wide variety of climatic environments, wherever the low-energy conditions are suitable. In temperate latitudes, the high-tide flat is colonized by **salt-marsh**; in tropical regions, by **mangrove swamps**. The plants take advantage of the conditions of sedimentation but, once established, the plants themselves aid deposition by trapping sediment and stabilizing the morphological features. Low-energy zones in general are very much dependent on protection, and if this is removed for any reason, such as by the erosion of a spit or bar, then the break-up of the adjacent marsh is usually very rapid.

Changes of sea-level

Although modern wave action and other processes adequately account for the detailed morphology of beaches and other mobile coastal areas, the general configuration of most coastlines is complicated by the effects of past changes of sea-level. These changes occur as a result of **eustatic** or global changes in the level of the sea, as has occurred with the successive growth and waning of ice sheets during the Pleistocene, or of **tectonic** changes in the level of the land. Tectonic changes may be: isostatic, that is, adjustment to load, as in glacial isostasy; epeirogenic, related to broad scale tilting; or orogenic, related to folding and flexuring. Glacial eu-

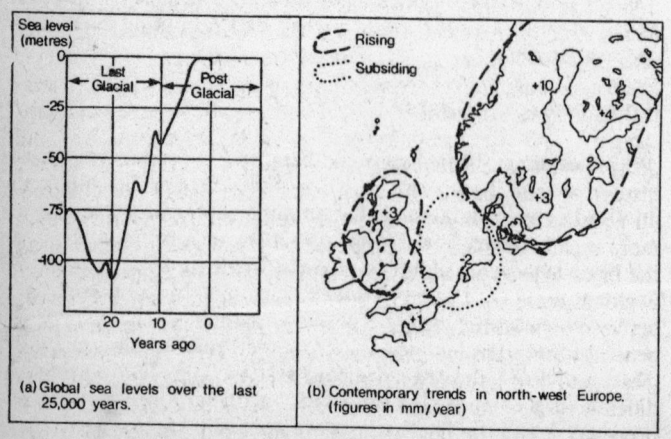

(a) Global sea levels over the last 25,000 years.

(b) Contemporary trends in north-west Europe. (figures in mm/year)

Figure 47. Trends of sea-level change

stasy and glacial isostasy account for most of the sea-level changes that have affected Britain in the recent past.

The level of the sea has been both higher and lower than now, and has left **emergent** (raised) and **submergent** (drowned) features, sometimes on the same stretch of coastline. Submerged effects include **rias** and **fjords**. **Raised beaches** and **platforms** and abandoned clifflines are among the main emergent features. In areas affected by isostatic recovery a complex series of raised beaches often exists, reflecting the interplay of isostatic and eustatic causes. In Scotland and around the Baltic, each raised beach becomes progressively lower away from the former centre of glaciation, reflecting the difference in subsequent uplift.

The generalized trend of global sea-level change over the past 25,000 years (Fig. 47a) shows that it has remained relatively steady for the past 5,000 years or so. However, small-scale fluctuations still continue: on the evidence of tide-gauge records, the level has been rising for the last fifty years at an average rate of 1·2 mm/yr. Some areas such as the Baltic (Fig. 47b) are still undergoing isostatic uplift at rates faster than this.

Coastal classification

Because of the large variety of coastal landforms many attempts have been made to categorize them, but in many cases it is as difficult to remember the classification as it is the individual landforms. One of the most commonly used classifications has been that of D. W. Johnson, who based his categories on sea-level change, recognizing: shorelines of submergence; emergence; neutral shorelines; and compound shorelines which have both submergent and emergent features. This classification has the disadvantage that it requires that we know something of the past history of the coastline. Strictly speaking, we would expect nearly all shorelines to be compound. A recent and potentially much more useful scheme is that proposed by J. L. Davies. Primarily on the basis of **wave energy environments**, he suggests that on a global scale it is possible to recognize significant differences between high-latitude coasts (frozen for part of the year, and with generally low wave energies); mid-latitude coasts (high wave energies); and low-latitude coasts (swell wave environments). The differences are emphasized by climatic conditions acting on processes above the tidal limit. This threefold division of latitudinal zones has been superimposed on a map of the major wave

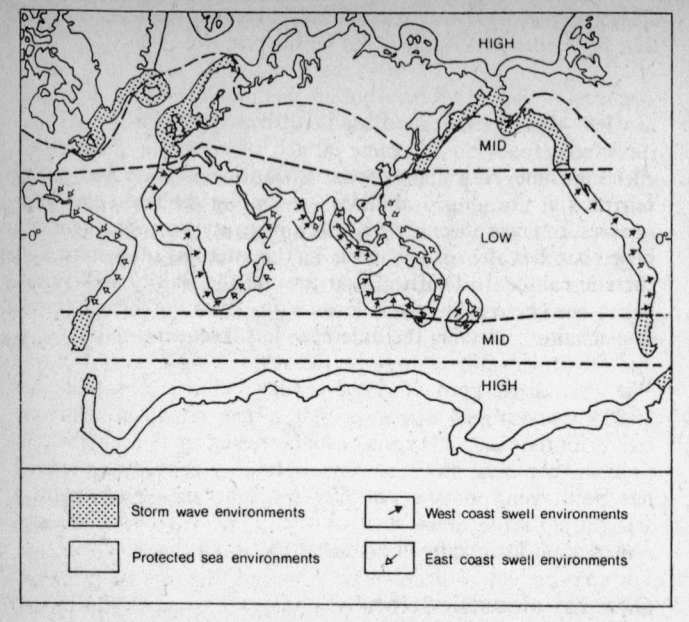

Figure 48. Global shore process zones, based on wave environments

environments (Fig. 48). The concept of differing wave energy environments can also be applied on a much more local scale, as has been illustrated by some of the landform examples in this chapter.

Summary

Of the wide range of factors affecting coastlines, waves are the single most important force creating change, wave steepness being the most significant parameter. Beach gradients are a function of both wave steepness and particle size, whereas their orientation is related to the direction of wave approach. Factors of geology become more important in cliffed coastlines, and tidal range and vegetation play a significant role in low energy coasts. Although all coasts have been affected by changes of sea-level, present processes offer a better basis for classifying them.

Chapter 12
Soils

Although there is no universally agreed definition, soils can be regarded as the uppermost weathered layer of the Earth's crust, consisting of decomposed and disintegrated bedrock which has been altered to the extent that it can support plant life. Soils are therefore an integral part of both ecosystems and geomorphological systems, and play a vital role in the link between vegetation and climate. The scientific study of soils is known as **pedology**, and the process of soil formation as pedogenesis.

Composition of soils

Soils contain solid, liquid and gaseous matter. The solid part is partly inorganic, made up of mineral particles derived from the weathered rock material, and partly organic, consisting of living and decayed plant and animal materials such as roots and worms. The end-product of this biological decay is **humus**, black amorphous organic matter. Soil is also permeated by gases and by soil water, a dilute but complex chemical solution derived from precipitation and groundwater. The soil atmosphere fills the pore spaces of the soil when these are not occupied by water. After heavy rain the pore spaces will be entirely filled with water, but the water moves out rapidly by gravitational movement until the coarser pores are empty and water is no longer being supplied to gullies and field drains. The soil is then said to be at **field capacity**. Further removal of water may occur by evapotranspiration, until the pore spaces are largely air-filled and the soil becomes parched.

The **texture** of a soil refers to the sizes of the solid particles composing the soil. These range from gravel to clay and will vary from soil to soil and from layer to layer within the soil. Standard soil textural classes can be defined according to the ratio of sand, silt and clay. A **loam** is an admixture of these three main particle sizes. Texture largely determines the water retention properties of a soil: in a sandy soil, pore spaces are large and water drains freely; in a clay soil, the pore spaces are too small for adequate drainage. The **structure** of a soil is a function of the way individual particles aggregate together into **peds** or lumps. These can

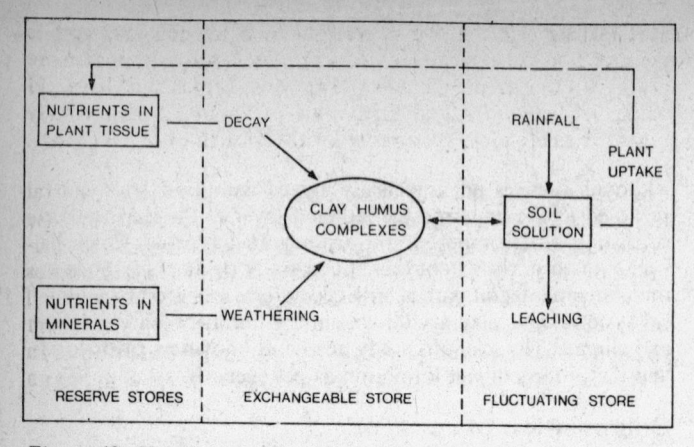

Figure 49. Nutrient exchange in a soil

be described as being blocky, platy, crumbly, or prismatic. Clay soils tend to have a prismatic structure whereas, at the other extreme, some sandy soils may lack aggregation altogether, in which case they have a **single grain** structure. Soils with a crumb structure are best for cultivation and are said to have a good tilth.

Within the clay fraction of the soil are **soil colloids**, tiny particles with unusual properties. The colloids may be organic, made up of very finely divided humus, or mineral (clay minerals). Together, the two types make up a **clay-humus complex**. The clay minerals have a profound effect on the chemical and physical characteristics of soils, since they largely control the mechanism of cation (base) exchange through which plant nutrients are made available. The negatively-charged clay minerals are able to attract and hold positively-charged bases such as calcium, potassium, magnesium and sodium occurring in the soil water. These bases may be taken up by plant roots in the process of **base exchange** as nutrients for growth (Fig. 49). Over a period of time this will make the soil more acid unless the bases are replaced by further weathering or by nutrient recycling from plant and animal decay. The removal of vegetation by man cuts off one source of replenishment, and the soil will become impoverished unless artificial fertilizer is used.

Soil **acidity** is a property related to the proportion of exchangeable hydrogen in the soil in relation to other elements and is measured on the logarithmic pH scale which ranges from extreme acidity (0) to extreme alkalinity (14). Most British soils have pH values of between 4 and 9; a value of about 6·5 is normally regarded as the most favourable for the growth of cereal crops.

The **colour** of a soil will be determined by its parent material (especially in recently formed soils), its humus content, and the processes of soil formation. In cool humid areas, most soils contain a relatively high amount of humus and are blackish or shades of brown. Reddish colours are associated with the presence of ferric compounds, whereas greyish or bluish colours reflect reduced iron compounds, indicating poor drainage conditions. In arid areas, little humus is usually present and soils are light brown or grey.

A vertical section through a soil is known as a **soil profile**. In each profile there are normally several layers or **horizons**, which can be distinguished on the basis of some of the characteristics

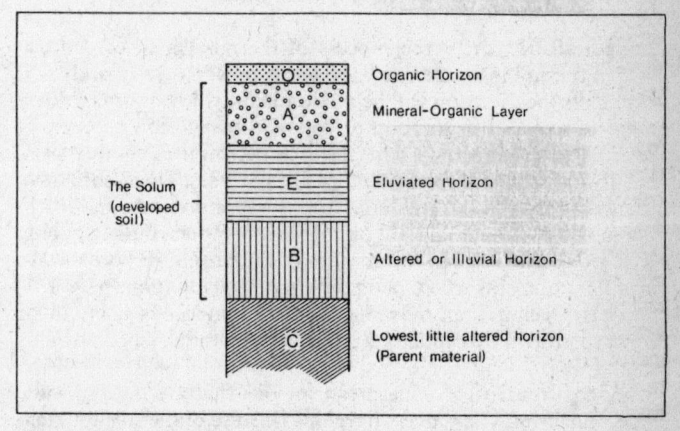

Figure 50. Soil profile and horizon nomenclature

outlined above. The horizons are labelled according to a system of capital letters and subscripts (Fig. 50). Horizons *A*, *E* and *B* represent the true mineral soil or **solum**; horizon *O* is entirely organic, and horizon *C* consists of weathered parent material. This particular notation system is that currently used by the Soil Survey of England and Wales.

Pedogenesis

Soils can be regarded as another example of open system phenomena. In the formation of soils there are gains and losses of material to the profile, movement of matter from one part of the profile to another, and chemical transformations within the soil. In theory, if all gains and losses were balanced the soil would remain unaltered, but not all changes are towards long-term equilibrium. Following rock weathering (considered in Chapter 7), the principal processes involved are organic changes, translocation, podzolization, gleying, and desilication.

1. **Organic changes** ensue as soon as plant material becomes established. Accumulation of organic matter takes place mainly at the ground surface as plant material decays and is degraded by the action of fungi, algae, small insects and worms. Over a long period of time the resulting humus will itself decompose in mineralization, which releases nitrogenous compounds into the soil. Degradation, humification and mineralization are not separate processes and always accompany each other.

2. **Translocation** is the process of the movement of material within the soil, principally by the agent of water. In humid environments the direction will be predominantly downwards. Movement of material in solution or colloidal suspension is generally referred to as **leaching**, whereas **eluviation** involves the physical downwashing of clay and other fine particles. The E horizon of the soil profile has lost material in this way. Eluviation and leaching may move material right out of the soil system, but commonly it is redeposited in the lower parts of the profile (B horizon). In arid environments where potential evapotranspiration (page 138) exceeds precipitation, movement of soil material is likely to be upward, drawn by capillary action towards the drying surface.

3. **Podzolization** is widespread in soils that are on the acidic side of neutral. The process develops because of the strong leaching action of certain organic compounds known as **chelating** agents, which are richest in heath plants and conifer needles and poorest in grass and deciduous trees growing in base-rich conditions. In the upper parts of the profile, the chelating agents remove many of the minerals, leaving behind an ash-grey sand horizon. The lower illuvial horizons become enriched with sesquioxides, particularly of iron, and in some cases the enrichment is concentrated in the form of a thin tough **iron-pan**.

4. **Gleying** occurs in very wet or waterlogged soils, where oxygen-deficient (**anaerobic**) conditions favour the proliferation of specialized bacteria which use up organic matter. In the process of **reduction**, they reduce ferric iron to a soluble ferrous state. This results in the creation of a gley horizon, a compact layer of sticky structureless clay, usually bluish-grey in colour. This horizon normally occurs within the zone of permanent groundwater saturation. Above this, where the soil periodically dries out, the process is not so uniform and gives the soil a mottled or blotchy look, typified by patchy red colours.

5. **Desilication** only takes place to any marked degree under the sustained warm conditions of the humid tropics. Here, silica is more mobile than iron and aluminium oxides and is progressively removed from the soil along with many of the bases. This process contrasts with podzolization in which the iron and aluminium oxides are the more mobile. Desilicified soils are appropriately enough known as **ferralsols** (Fe + Al). Such soils also often have a low organic content because of rapid decomposition by micro-organisms. Hard **lateritic** horizons may form where ground-water movements within the soil concentrate the iron and aluminium oxides into layers near the surface.

The controlling factors

The operation of these processes varies considerably from soil to soil, since they are controlled by local factors which are not constant from place to place. These controls can be summarized as: parent material, climate, the biotic factor, topography and time.

Immature soils will be very similar to their **parent material**, but in well-developed soil profiles only the *C* horizon will reflect the underlying bedrock. It is a popular misconception that the type of parent material alone determines the kind of soil present. The main lasting effects are through texture and fertility. For instance, soils developed on sandstones will be coarser than those developed on clays. Equally, calcareous rocks tend to give rise to fertile base-rich soils, whereas soils on non-calcareous rocks are liable to podzolization and acidity.

Climatic regime influences the rate and type of soil formation through temperature and precipitation levels. The rate of chemical and biological reactions in the soil is related to temperature, so that in cool climates bacterial action is relatively slow and a thick layer of decomposing vegetation covers the ground. In the tropics, although the leaf fall in forests is great, it is rapidly consumed by bacteria. Absolute precipitation figures need to be taken in conjunction with the amount of moisture lost through evapotranspiration, as this ratio controls such processes as the intensity of leaching.

The **biotic factor** includes the action of organisms ranging from microscopic bacteria to large mammals, but probably the most important link is that between vegetation and soils. Plants are an essential part of the nutrient cycling system (Fig. 49). Different types of vegetation require different proportions of basic nutrients: trees, especially conifers, use little calcium and magnesium, whereas grasses recycle abundant quantities of these. Thus certain major soil types (Fig. 51) are associated with specific vegetation zones, and a change of vegetation may cause a change of soil. In addition, plants are important to soils in intercepting direct rainfall and binding the soil with roots, thereby checking soil erosion.

Slope angle is probably the most significant of the **topographic factors** affecting soils. Soils on steep slopes are normally thinner than those on flat sites, since the susceptibility of soil to erosion increases with gradient. However, a hillside soil tends to be much better drained than those in valleys, where gleying may take place. Situation is also important in that a flat hilltop may be a material-exporting site, whereas an equally flat lowland site will receive downwashed material (see Fig. 27). The combined result of these topographic effects sometimes gives rise to a soil **catena**, a typical assemblage of soil types occurring on slopes in an area of similar relief.

Soils vary greatly in their rates of development, and **time** is a difficult factor to assess in soil formation. It is certainly not the case that all thin soils resembling their parent material are young, or that deep profiles indicate maturity beyond which there will be no further development. Some environmental factors will ensure that certain soils will always be thin, independent of the time factor. Renewed evolution takes place in soils when climate or other external factors change, causing the soils to adjust. When this happens, some of the characteristics of the old soil profile will remain in the new soil, producing a **polycyclic** soil profile. This is common in British soils.

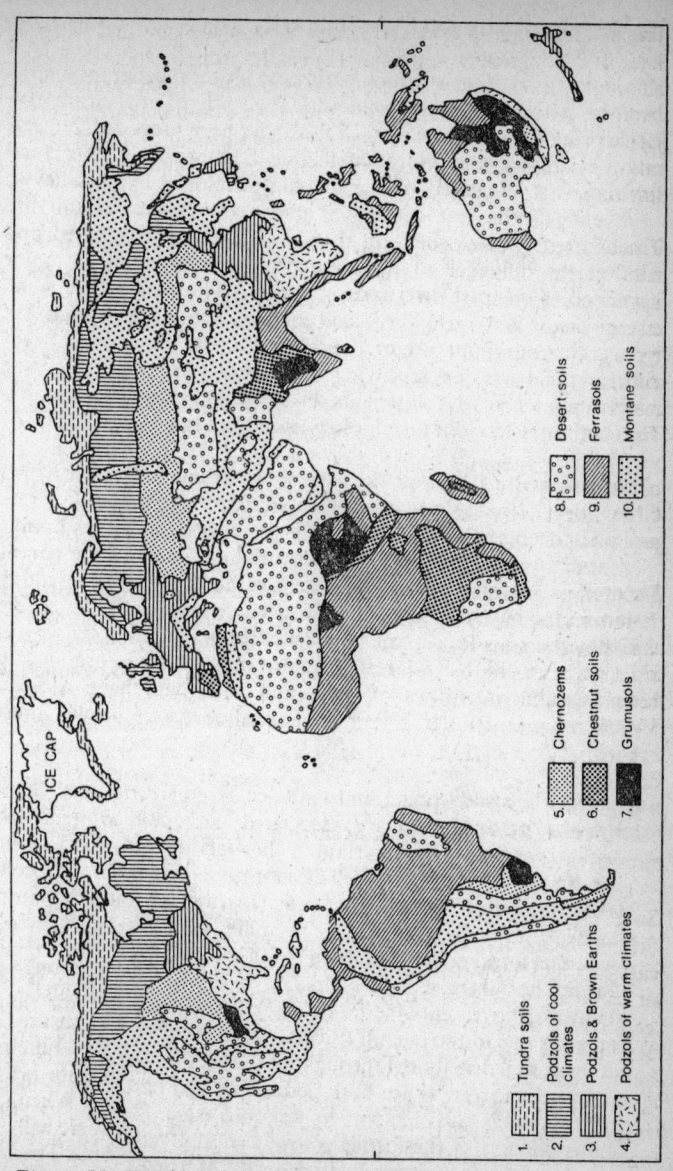

Figure 51. World soil map (zonal types)

Major soil types

As in the case of many other features in physical geography, soils can be classified according to either their origins or their observable properties. Many classifications have been proposed, but one of the simpler and more intelligible frameworks is the zonal system, first suggested by the Russian pedologist Dokuchaiev at the end of the last century. Three main classes of soil are recognized: **zonal** soils are those that are well developed and reflect the influence of climate and/or vegetation as the major controlling factors; **intrazonal** types are formed where some local factor overrides the zonal factors; and **azonal** soils are those that are immature or poorly developed. The zonal concept forms the basis for reviewing world soil types here (Fig. 51), although recent developments in soil analysis are taken into account and modern terminology is incorporated.

Tundra soils (1) reflect the extreme environments under which they form. Where slope conditions are fairly stable, the slow rate of plant decomposition results in the presence of much raw humus or peat. In areas of active frost disturbance, much of the parent material consists of shattered particles and soils are inevitably thin. In the most extreme conditions, where plant growth is barely viable, the soils lack humus almost entirely (ahumic). By way of contrast, in the birch-forested tundra margins there are usually considerable quantities of loess, and soils here have a thick dark organic *A* horizon and are known as Arctic brown forest soils.

Podzols are widespread and embrace several variations. **Cool climate podzols** (2) are associated with cold winters and adequate precipitation distributed throughout the year. Low in bases and fertility, they are well developed under coniferous forest. **Grey-brown podzols** (3) or brown earths, are found equatorwards of the main podzol zone in milder climates supporting a deciduous forest cover. Leaching is still evident in the profiles, but of a far less intense nature than in true podzols. There is no downward movement of sesquioxides, and their dispersed distribution gives rise to the overall brown colour of the soil. In addition, humus is well distributed throughout the profile. The **podzols of warm climates** (4) are both podzolized and partly desilicified: warm summers and mild winters promote bacterial action and the humus content of these soils is low. Red and yellow colours are typical, reflecting staining by hydroxides of iron.

Chernozems (5) and their variants are found in association with steppe or prairie vegetation. The light rainfall of these areas leads to incomplete leaching, with the result that chernozems are rich in calcium. The base-rich mineral matrix gives a deep dark colour to the upper metre or so of the soil, although the humus content of this layer is often no more than 10 per cent. An important factor in middle-latitude chernozem soil development is the presence of loess, widespread in the mid-west of North America and in Russia and northern China. **Chestnut soils** (6) are a more arid type of chernozem, but with an illuvial carbonate layer closer to the surface and with a lower organic content. **Grumusols** or tropical chernozems (7) are dark clayey soils of savanna or grass-covered areas which have a warm climate with wet and dry seasons. There are no eluvial or illuvial horizons, but the whole solum is rich in bases, especially calcium, hence its dark colour. These soils are characterized by a high degree of dry season cracking.

Sierozems or desert soils (8) can be regarded as extreme forms of chestnut soils in which the lime and gypsum come even closer to the surface because of upward capillary attraction. Not unexpectedly, organic matter is these soils is low, but when irrigated sierozems can be very fertile because of their high base status. **Ferralsols** or latosols (9) are typical of humid tropical areas and are typified by deep desilicification. The remaining sesquioxides of iron and aluminium account for the red, brown or occasionally yellow colour or these soils. Profiles are often very deep, but with poor horizon differentiation. These soils are low in fertility because of the lack of humus and bases.

Montane soils (10) are not a single type, but embrace a mosaic of many other categories, depending on local factors of climate, vegetation and drainage. They particularly include various types of azonal soil.

On the zonal scheme, **intrazonal** soils include: gleyed or hydromorphic soils, associated with marshes, swamps, and poorly drained upland; calcimorphous soils, developed on calcareous parent materials, and halomorphic or saline soils, developed in extreme conditions of upward alkaline movement in deserts. Immature or **azonal** soils may exist because of the characteristics of the parent material or the nature of the environment, or simply the lack of time for development. Active flood plains often provide an example of the latter case, since the alluvial soils are repeatedly buried under new sediments. Similarly, soils on steep slopes (lithosols) may be removed by erosion as fast as they are formed.

Soils in Britain

In generalized terms, soils in Britain broadly reflect the traditional division between highland and lowland parts of the country. Within the highland zone, most soils are acid and intensely leached and on the zonal scheme can be classified as various types of podzols. Another characteristic feature is a peaty surface horizon together with gleying of various intensity. The peat in places may reach a depth of several metres or be only a few centimetres thick. A typical **peaty gleyed podzol** has a peaty surface passing sharply into an eluvial horizon which has some mottling, and below this is an irregular but continuous iron-pan. In figure 52, three main highland soil types are depicted: (1) podzols, (2) peaty soils, including blanket peat soils and peaty gleyed podzols; and (3) acid brown soils, which are less intensely leached and are otherwise known as low base status brown earths.

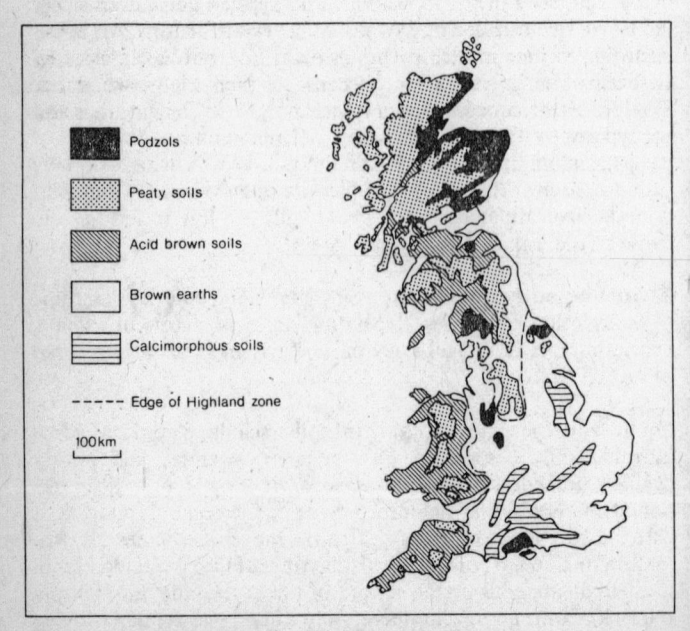

Figure 52. A generalized map of British soils

In lowland Britain, most soils can be regarded as **brown earths**; that is, they still show some tendency towards podzolization but horizon differentiation is less apparent. However, many detailed variations of soil type occur in southern Britain which are a result of changes in the parent material rather than in climate and vegetation. Organic soils occur in the Fenlands, Somerset Levels and parts of Lancashire; fertile, fine-grained alluvial soils are to be found in many broad river valleys; podzols occur on many southern heathlands, such as the New Forest, and calcimorphous soils occupy the large expanses of chalk and limestone bedrock (Fig. 52). Exposed chalk gives rise to a thin **rendzina** soil with pH values of between 7 and 8·5.

Summary

Soils are composed of both organic and mineral particles which determine the texture, structure and base status of the soil. These characteristics vary down the profile and allow various horizons to be distinguished. Pedogenic processes involve chemical changes as well as the movement of both water and minerals up and down the profile. The processes will vary from place to place according to the influence of a number of controlling factors. On the basis of the zonal system, major soil groups of the world are largely a reflection of vegetation and climate. In Britain, soils are predominantly variants of podzols and brown earths.

Chapter 13
Ecosystems

The study of plant and animal distributions, or **biogeography**, must rest on a clear understanding of the principles of **ecology**. This is concerned with the relationships between plants and animals and their environment. An **ecosystem** is a functioning unit of organisms together with their physical surroundings and, as with other natural systems, they are open systems characterized by energy flow. The concept of an ecosystem can be applied on a very flexible basis according to the scale of study, from a small pond to a major tropical rain forest.

Functional structure

There are four basic components to an ecosystem; these are illustrated in figure 53, using a lake as a model.

1. The **abiotic** part, or non-living environment. In the lake this is made up of the water and sediments and all the basic organic and inorganic compounds contained in them. Most will be in the sediments which act as a nutrient reserve for the ecosystem.

2. The producers or **autotrophs**, green plants capable of producing their own food by using the energy of sunlight to make carbohydrates from water and carbon dioxide. This process is called **photosynthesis**. In the lake, these can be large rooted or floating plants, or microscopic plants called phytoplankton which are very important for producing food in the system. In deep ponds or lakes they usually produce a much greater amount of food than the large plants.

3. Consumers or **heterotrophs**, animals which obtain their food by eating plants or other animals. In any ecosystem the heterotrophs can be divided into groups by their feeding habits: herbivores eat only plant material; detritovores feed on dead plant and animal material; carnivores eat other animals; and omnivores eat both plant and animal material. In a lake, the herbivores will consist of herbivorous fish and minute zooplankton which feed on the phytoplankton. The carnivores will include predacious insects and game fish.

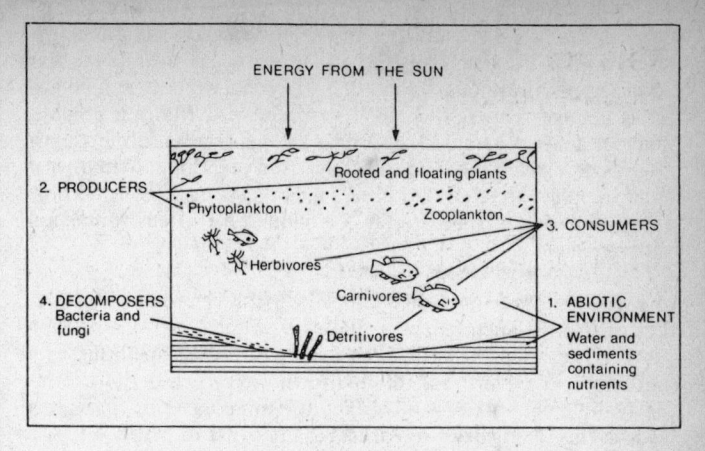

Figure 53. A freshwater ecosystem

4. **Decomposers**, such as bacteria and fungi which promote decay. They will be especially prolific in lakes at the sediment/water interface where dead plants and animals accumulate.

The organization of feeding in an ecosystem is known as its **trophic structure**. The sequence of consumer levels is known as a **food chain**. There are two basic sorts of food chains: grazing food chains in which the plants are eaten live by herbivores, and detrital food chains in which the plants are eaten as dead material by detritivores. Food chains can be linear, e.g. plants – herbivores – carnivores – detritivores, but are often more complicated, forming interconnected food webs. For instance, carnivores may eat other carnivores as well as several different herbivores. Organisms feeding at the same number of steps from the autotrophs on a food chain are said to be at the same trophic level, the green plants being at the first trophic level, the herbivores the second, and so on. This trophic classification is one of function, not population numbers, so that an omnivorous species could occupy more than one trophic level.

Species structure

The role an organism takes in an ecosystem is known as its **ecological niche**. Some animals are specialists in their feeding habits, whereas others are generalists, consuming a wide variety of food. Usually the specialists are more efficient at using their resources and therefore become abundant when their particular food supply is abundant; however, they are vulnerable if conditions change so that their food becomes rare. Many mammals, such as foxes, bears and squirrels, are generalists, occupying a broad ecological range and switching from one thing to another if food supplies are short. Although generalists may never become locally abundant, they are far less vulnerable to environmental change.

A species may occupy a different niche in different places, depending on factors such as the availability of food and competition from other animals. Man is an example of this, operating as a herbivore, carnivore and omnivore in various situations. Similarly, different species may occupy the same niche in equivalent ecosystems. Kangaroos in Australia and cattle in North America both function as grazing herbivores in ecosystems where the main autotrophs are grasses. Most ecosystems contain a great variety of ecological niches and so have a mixture of generalists and specialists.

The **species structure** of an ecosystem refers to the numbers of species present, and their relative abundance and diversity. Characteristically ecosystems contain a few relatively common species, the **dominants**, and a large number of rare species, the **incidentals**. However, the so-called dominants may not actually impose the greatest effect on the rest of the system and the incidentals may be extremely important ecologically. The species with high numbers will probably be specialists, exploiting prevailing conditions and so becoming abundant. In changing conditions they may not be so successful, and the rarer species may be able to exploit the new situation better and so increase in abundance. The incidentals thereby form a **reserve of adaptability** in the system which allows a continuation of energy flow and productivity if environmental conditions change.

Energy flow and productivity

Starting with the energy of sunlight fixed in photosynthesis by green plants, energy flows through ecosystems via the food chains and webs from one trophic level to the next. The flow can be imagined rather as water channelled through pipes whose width is proportional to the amount of flow (Fig. 54). Storage in the system (boxes) is expressed by the amount of living plant and animal material; this amount is known as the standing crop, usually expressed as the weight of living material (biomass) per unit area. Usually the amount of standing crop at each trophic level decreases with each step along the food chain, forming a **trophic pyramid**. There are two main reasons for this. First, there are large losses of heat energy between trophic levels as herbivores convert plant substances into animal substances. Second, there will be energy losses within each trophic level: respiration by all organisms involves the oxidation of carbohydrates which releases energy. The flow of energy will thus decrease at each level, enabling less standing crop to be supported.

The rate of production of organic matter in ecosystems is known as **productivity**; primary productivity occurs at the autotroph level, and secondary productivity at the heterotroph level. Productivity can be further divided into *gross* productivity, the total amount of organic matter produced at each level, and *net* productivity, the amount of organic matter left after some has been used in respiration. **Gross primary productivity** will depend on

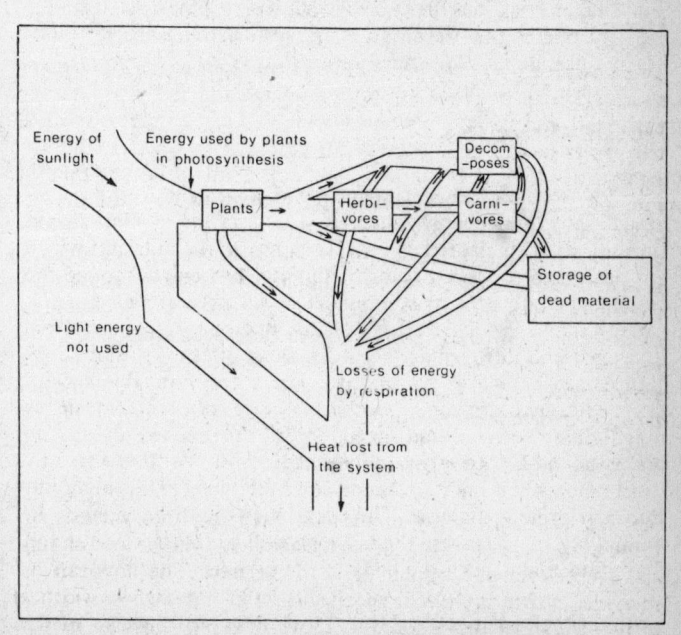

Figure 54. Ecosystem energy flow: an hydraulic analogy

the amount of light energy coming into the system and the efficiency of photosynthesis. Quantitative studies indicate that of the light energy impinging on the surface of vegetation, as little as 1% to 5% may be trapped and converted into food energy; yet despite these low figures, enough energy is trapped to maintain all life. Net primary productivity is determined by the relative rates of respiration (using up carbohydrates) and photo-synthesis (producing carbohydrates). **Secondary productivity** will depend on the conversion of plant to animal substances and, as we have seen, the efficiency of this process is low in terms of energy conversion. Most studies estimate it to be about 10% in natural ecosystems. The majority of animals have their greatest rates of net productivity when they are young; it is an ecological advantage to grow quickly in order to compete with other animals for survival.

The model of energy flow shown in figure 54 belies the fact that in nature, energy flow paths are rarely simple. Frequently there are feedback loops: one species may feed on the faeces of another so that energy in the faecal system does not go to the decomposers but is taken back into the system at a lower trophic level. It should be remembered that the model is simply an extreme abstraction of reality, despite its neat visual impression.

Nutrient cycling

The flow of energy in ecosystems is one way: light energy is converted into food energy which is stored in the system, passed through it, or dissipated as heat. In contrast, the nutrients which are needed to produce organic material are circulated round the system and are re-used several times. All natural elements are capable of being absorbed by plants, but only oxygen, carbon, hydrogen and nitrogen are needed in large quantities. These substances are known as **macronutrients** and form the basis of fats, carbohydrates and proteins. Other nutrients, such as magnesium, sulphur and phosphorus, are needed in minute amounts and are known as micronutrients or **trace elements**. Both macro- and micro-nutrients are taken into plants and built into new organic material. The plants may die or be eaten by an animal but in either case the nutrients will be returned to the soil and atmosphere when the body of the organism decomposes.

Nutrient cycles can be represented by a model in which each cycle has a **reservoir pool**, a large, slow-moving non-biological component, and an **exchange pool**, a smaller, more active portion where the nutrient is exchanged between the biotic and abiotic parts of the ecosystem. There are two basic types of cycle: **gaseous** ones, in which the reservoir pool is the atmosphere, and **sedimentary** ones, in which the reservoir pool is the Earth's crust. Generally the gaseous cycles are more complete than the sedimentary ones. Under natural conditions, both types of cycle are assumed to be stable, but the sedimentary types are more susceptible to disruption, particularly by human interference.

A general indication of some of the terrestial nutrient cycles is given in figure 55. The **nitrogen cycle** is a good example of the gaseous type, and is one of the most complete of the nutrient cycles. The reservoir pool is the atmosphere and the exchange pool embraces organisms and the soil. Nitrates in the soil are absorbed by plants and pass through food chains. Ultimately they are released as ammonia when organic material decomposes; the ammonia is changed back to nitrates by the action of bacteria. If the nitrates are not re-absorbed by plants they are lost from the exchange pool in two ways; either they are broken down by denitrifying bacteria and the nitrogen contained within them is released to the atmosphere (N_2), or they are leached from the soil into sediments. Atmospheric nitrogen in the reservoir pool cannot be used directly by plants but has to be 'fixed' into nitrates, and this is done mainly by organisms, mostly bacteria, algae and fungi, which operate either independently in the soil or in association with a plant, particularly those of the legume family, such as clover.

The **carbon cycle** is more complicated, involving both important marine and terrestial parts, and gaseous and sedimentary components. The cycle begins with the fixation of atmospheric carbon dioxide by photosynthesis; this forms carbohydrates, with the simultaneous release of free oxygen into the atmosphere. Some of the carbohydrate is directly consumed to supply the plants with energy and the carbon dioxide so generated is released back to the atmosphere either through the plant's leaves or through its roots. Part of the carbon fixed by plants is consumed by animals, which also respire and release carbon dioxide. Plants and animals die and are ultimately decomposed by micro-organisms in the soil. Some of this carbonaceous matter may enter into the sedimentary carbon cycle, which is dominated by a large **fossil fuel** reservoir, but the rate of modern addition to this is very slow. Moreover, there are considerable losses because of fossil fuel mining, par-

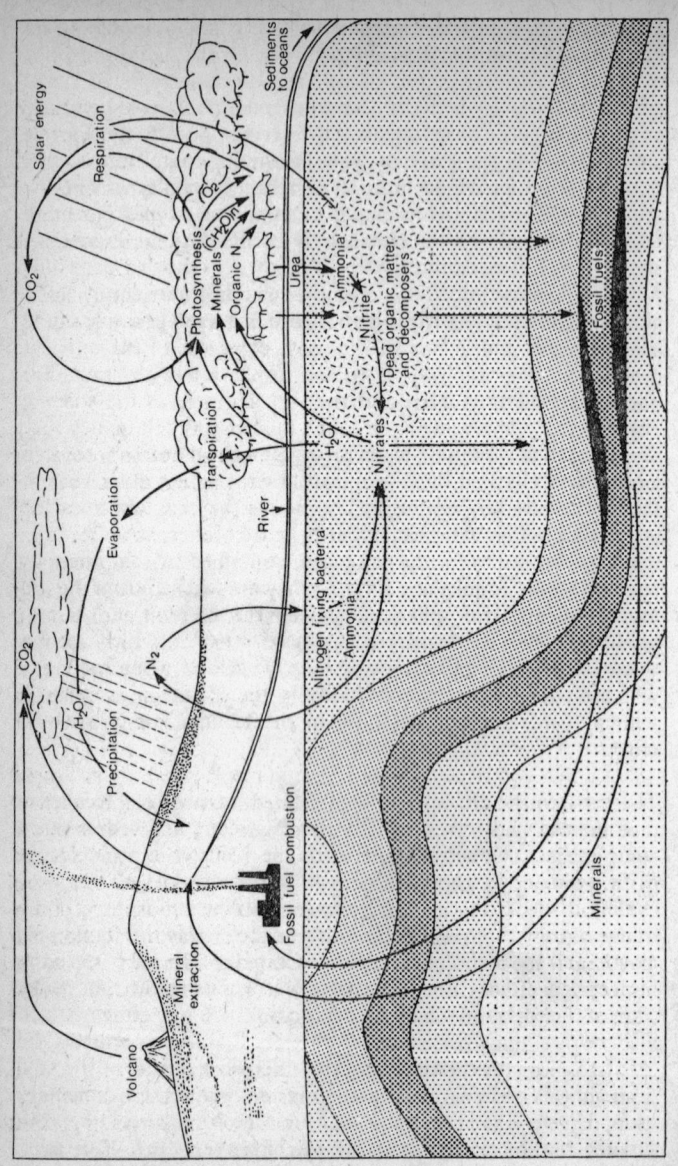

Figure 55. Major terrestial nutrient cycles

ticularly of coal and oil. Combustion of this material adds to the carbon dioxide in the atmosphere.

Broadly similar pathways to that of carbon are followed by many of the other major elements; each are present in a variety of forms, undergoing a number of inorganic and biological reactions which convert them from one form to another. Elements which have gaseous forms, such as nitrogen, carbon, and sulphur, are constantly recycled, whereas elements in sedimentary cycles, released only by rock weathering, are recycled on very much greater time spans and may potentially come to be in short supply. This applies especially to **phosphorus**, which is used as a nutrient by all organisms.

Environmental controls

The plants and animals forming the biotic part of an ecosystem are those which can tolerate the prevailing environmental conditions. The principal environmental factors which have some effect on the life and development of organisms are: climate, including light, temperature, water availability and wind; topography, especially slope angle, orientation and altitude; and edaphic (soil) factors such as pH and fertility. In addition there are **biotic controls**, such as competition between species, which are discussed later. In practice, these factors are closely interrelated and it is not always easy to isolate the influence of individual forces. In theory, every species has a minimum and maximum range for each environmental factor and a range of **tolerance** between these limits which includes an optimum condition. Narrow ranges of tolerance can be indicated by the prefix **steno-** (e.g. stenothermal indicates narrow range of tolerance to temperature), whereas wide ranges are indicated by **eury-** (e.g. eury-thermal). Species with wide tolerance ranges for all factors should be the most widely distributed. Any factor which approaches or exceeds the range of tolerance may be a limiting factor on the distribution of a particular species. The following summary considers the more universal factors. Other specific regulators such as fire and pollution are assessed in Chapters 14 and 15.

Light is not only the vital source of energy for ecosystems but can also act as a control of functions such as reproduction and migration. Excess light can be a limiting factor by damaging plant tissues and decreasing productivity. Three aspects of light are of great interest, its wavelength or quality, its intensity and its duration. The *quality* of light becomes significant with altitude since on high mountains invisible ultra-violet light becomes intense. This retards plant growth by deactivating the hormones which cause the stems to elongate, and flattened rosette plants are typical of such habitats. Light *intensity* is an extremely important controlling factor everywhere, since it governs the rate of photosynthesis. As photosynthesis only occurs in the light, carbohydrates respired at night must be replaced before there is any gain in growth. The point at which photosynthesis balances the energy used in respiration is known as the **compensation point**, and plants vary in the light intensity required to achieve their compensation points. Species which grow best in high light intensities are known as **heliophytes**, and these have high rates of respiration and photosynthesis and hence high compensation points. Shade-loving plants are called **sciophytes**. There is considerable global variation of light intensity: low latitudes receive more intense light than high latitudes, and tropical ecosystems have a higher energy input and productivity than arctic ecosystems (Chap. 14). Light intensity also varies *within* plant communities: tall plants will shade those beneath them, creating a range of ecological niches of varying light intensity. This frequently leads to layering in vegetation communities, typically in a sequence of trees, shrubs, tall herbs and ground plants.

The response of organisms to variation in day length is called **photoperiodism** and this affects many aspects of behaviour in plants and animals. Flowering in many species of plants is initiated by a certain number of hours of darkness; day-light duration stimulates reproduction and migration in many birds; and similarly, metamorphosis and hibernation in insects is influenced by the length of day. This imposes broad latitudinal controls on the life-habits of species.

Temperature has both direct effects on organisms and indirect effects in modifying factors such as relative humidity and water availability. Generally, aquatic plants and animals have narrower temperature tolerance ranges than those on land which have to cope with far more temperature variations. For terrestial ecosystems, there are broad latitudinal patterns: tropical plants often do not tolerate temperatures below 15°C; many temperate plants are intolerant of temperatures of less than −2°C; whereas evergreen coniferous forests may withstand intense freezing. In high temperatures, plants are cooled by transpiration through the leaves, but wilting or death may result if the water supply is not adequate. Under low temperatures, plant growth may be inhibited not only by the lack of photosynthesis but also by a **physiological drought**. This occurs when water in the soil cannot be absorbed by the plants either because it is frozen or because the temperature is too low for its uptake. Plants may survive cold winter conditions in several ways: by overwintering as seed (annual plants); by existing in a state of dormancy, as in the case of bulbs; by adopting a deciduous habit, typical of many temperate trees; or by increasing the density of the cell sap, reducing its freezing-point, as in evergreen conifers.

In terms of temperature tolerance, **warm-blooded animals** have a distinct advantage over cold-blooded ones since they can remain active despite the temperature of their surroundings. They have various mechanisms which allow them to increase their temperature range, such as possessing thick layers of insulating fur or fat, shivering to keep warm, and sweating to loose heat. **Cold-blooded animals** have much more limited mechanisms and will only be active when environmental temperatures are suitable.

Water availability is essential for all organisms. In the case of animals, it usually only acts as a limiting factor when it is in short supply. There is great variation in the amount of water needed, but usually cold-blooded animals require less than warm-blooded ones, which use it for heat regulation. In plants, water provides tissue support and is essential for photosynthesis. If there is insufficient water, plant cells lose their rigidity and wilt; the stomata on the leaves close, helping to prevent further transpiration, and the plant may survive in this condition for a long time providing the temperature is not too high. Plants can be divided into broad groups depending on their water requirements. **Xerophytes** are plants which can survive in arid areas, by either evading or enduring drought. Desert plants which complete their life cycles very quickly after rain and survive as seeds are **ephemerals** or drought-evaders. Drought-endurers include water-storing succulents such as cacti and deep-rooted acacias. **Halophytes** are plants tolerating saline conditions, and have many features in common with xerophytes. **Hydrophytes** are adapted to living submerged in water. Between these rather extreme types are the **mesophytes**, a broad unspecialized group embracing the majority of temperate plants.

Some of the important interchanges between plants and water

are illustrated in Figure 56. In general, water availability to plants depends on the effectiveness of precipitation; this is largely a matter of the balance between evaporation and precipitation, although the type of vegetation also affects the amount of water reaching the soil. **Potential evapotranspiration** is a useful measure of the effectiveness of the water factor: it is the amount of moisture which would be evaporated from the soil and transpired from vegetation in a unit area if there was sufficient water for this to take place to its maximum extent. Thus, drought can be thought of as a condition arising when the amount of water required for potential evapotranspiration exceeds that available from the soil.

Topography can influence ecosystem development in three major ways: first, through the direct effects of altitude on temperature (Chap. 5); second, through its related effect on relative humidity (Chap. 2); and third, through local variations in slope orientation and angle. The strong contrasts in insolation on south-facing and north-facing slopes leads to equally significant contrasts in species structure and productivity on the sides of valleys.

Edaphic characteristics have been described in Chapter 12. Soil and the rest of the ecosystem are one functional unit. Particular attributes of soil, such as texture, pH, soil climate and organic content operate in a closely interrelated fashion to exert control

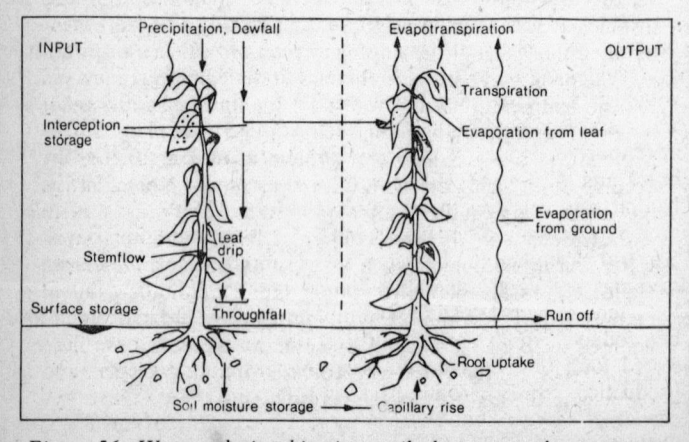

Figure 56. Water relationships in a soil-plant-atmosphere system

on rates of decomposition, nutrient cycling, and plant distribution and productivity. The relationship between plants and soil acidity is particularly noteworthy. Although many plants have a wide range of tolerance to pH for survival, they tend to have a much narrower range in which they can achieve maximum growth. One very important influence on soil acidity is the calcium content. The presence of calcium ions in the soil solution inhibits the uptake of other ions such as boron, magnesium and phosphate. Because of this, some plants cannot live on calcareous soil and these are called **calcifuges**, whereas **calcicoles** are plants restricted to calcareous soils. This broad distinction is reflected in the distribution of many plants in Britain.

Biotic factors

Biotic factors in ecosystems are the interactions that occur between living things. Some species are beneficial or even essential for the existence of others, whereas some may be detrimental. **Competition** arises if the resources of a habitat are insufficient to meet the demands of all the plants and animals living there. Generally, competition is most intense between individuals of the same species, or between different species that have the same ecological niche, especially in the early stages of the life cycle.

One of the main forms of competition between plants is for light. The dominant plants will be those that grow tallest and modify the light conditions for the rest of the community. They will shade plants growing beneath them and exclude any species which require high light intensities. The struggle for light above the ground will also influence root development and the competition for water and nutrients in the soil. **Reproduction** in plants is also an important aspect of competition. **Asexual** reproduction by bulbs and rhizomes is a safe way of maintaining a place in the habitat, and can lead to an aggressive spread of a species in an area by excluding other plants from the same community layer. **Sexual** reproduction by seeds is far more precarious because seedlings are very vulnerable. Large seeds, containing a lot of food, tend to be heavy so they cannot be dispersed far and few can be produced. At the other extreme, very small seeds have little stored food but they can be much more widely dispersed and production can be prolific. Individually, small seeds have less chance of survival, but because there are so many of them it is likely that some will find suitable habitats. The most successful species will be the ones that have vigorous, tolerant seedlings that are widely dispersed.

In animals, the **population** of any species oscillates between an upper limit which is determined by the energy flow through the ecosystem and by a lower limit which will be the minimum number necessary to continue the species. There are two basic controls on population. **Density-independent** controls include all the environmental factors previously outlined, especially the climatic ones. **Density-dependent** controls operate in relation to the numbers present. Of these, **predation** is probably the most frequent control on animal numbers. It usually involves a complex food chain, but if a predator's preferred food becomes scarce it will switch to an alternative and the food species will have a chance to recover its numbers. In this way predation rarely causes extinction, which is more likely to be related to external forces. **Territorial animals** frequently exhibit density-dependent control mechanisms. Since they require definite territories for hunting and breeding, weak individuals will be unable to establish territories if there is competition for space. They will be excluded from reproduction and hence **natural selection** favours the stronger animals.

Man is by far the most important biotic factor and has caused fundamental modifications to ecosystems by fire, hunting and agriculture. With industrialization and the intensification of farming methods, large areas of natural habitat have been obliterated or polluted. Further consideration of this theme is given in Chapter 15.

Succession and climax

The final factor influencing ecosystem development to be considered here is that of **time**. The nutrient cycling and energy flow in an ecosystem will depend not only on the species present but also on the degree of development. The species in a community at any specific place and time will be those that can tolerate the prevailing conditions, but since organisms modify their environment by influencing soil formation and microclimates, the physical conditions in any location will not be constant. In turn, the species structure will evolve. Typically, there will be a sequence of different assemblages of species, each known as a **seral stage** or **sere**. Change of community structure through time in this way is called **succession**. If it takes place on a bare area which has not been vegetated before, such as a delta or volcanic ash cone, it is called primary succession; changes occurring in an area already colonized represents secondary succession.

Some ecologists regard succession as an orderly and predictable process of change in species structure which will lead to a stable, self-perpetuating community, called a climax. This is usually a type of forest, representing the greatest possible development of an ecosystem for any climatic zone, and is hence a **climatic climax**. Examples would include tropical rain forest and boreal (coniferous) forest. However, although there are recognizable trends in succession, there is also a large random factor which renders prediction in succession difficult. In particular, climates are constantly oscillating and ecosystems are in a constant state of adjustment to new environmental conditions. By the time ecological adjustments have come into effect the climate may have changed again. As in the case of landforms, many ecologists think that ecosystems should be viewed not as an expression of the theoretical climax they have reached, but as an expression of all the environmental factors, such as climate, topography and soil, which influence them.

Summary

Ecosystems consist of abiotic and biotic components. The organisms within them have a trophic or functional structure and a population structure. Energy flow in ecosystems governs productivity at different trophic levels. Ecosystems are also characterized by nutrient cycles which can be of gaseous or sedimentary types. The functioning of ecosystems is controlled by a wide variety of environmental factors, of which climatic ones are among the most important. There are also biological regulators within each system. Successional changes take place with time, but communities are unlikely to reach a state of perpetual equilibrium.

Chapter 14
Major Natural Habitats

There are a number of large areas in the world within which ecosystem structure and functioning are broadly similar. A basic distinction can obviously be made between the **marine** ecosystem and **terrestial** ecosystem types. The structure of the marine ecosystem is very similar for all oceans and it can be considered as one unit, but in the case of terrestial ecosystems a threefold division must be made. **Forest** ecosystems have a complicated layered structure in which the dominant plants are tall and create a variety of ecological niches beneath them. **Grassland** ecosystems have a simpler and more uniform structure. In cold or warm **biological deserts**, vegetation is low-growing and the plants and animals have to tolerate extreme conditions. An instructive comparison can be made between the primary productivity of these ecosystems, as indicated by average daily rates of biomass produced (Fig. 57).

Forest ecosystems

Forest is the vegetation type most likely to result from the process of succession in land areas, unless conditions of climate, soil or biotic factors arrest development at an earlier seral stage. Trees become the dominant plants of the community because they grow taller and live longer than anything else, although they do have considerable problems in regenerating their own kind, as the germination and growth of tree seedlings is precarious. Once the forest is established, however, it forms a complex ecosystem with a large standing crop. Much of this is made up of wood which is non-productive but represents energy stored in the system; the productive part, the leaves, forms an extensive surface area for photosynthesis. Food webs tend to be complex, the detrital food chains being responsible for the majority of energy flow. The presence of a large standing crop means that many nutrients are locked up within organic material, and forest ecosystems immobilize nutrients for longer periods than other types.

Trees, whether evergreen or deciduous, vary greatly in their ecological tolerances, and occupy many different climatic zones. Many differing classifications of forests in relation to climate have

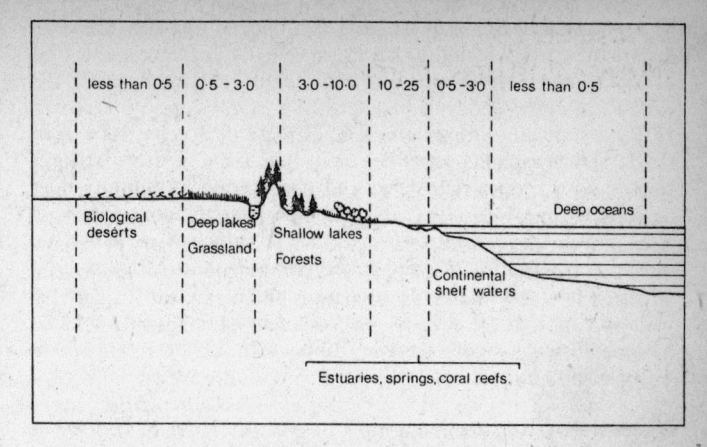

Figure 57. Primary productivity in major ecosystems ($g/m^2/day$)

been devised, but the most significant ecological contrasts lie between tropical rain forests, temperate deciduous forests and boreal forests.

Tropical rain forests occupy low-altitude areas near the equator (Fig. 58) and show great similarity of structure and function. They are all broad-leaved evergreen forests of high primary productivity, diverse fauna and a great deal of animal biomass. In these conditions there is intense competition for survival, leading to specialization. All green plants strive to reach the light, so they either become very tall, adopt a climbing habit, or live as **epiphytes**, plants living on other plants but not deriving food from them. Beneath the tree canopy there is usually a well-developed layering of understorey vegetation. Many of the heterotrophs, particularly snakes and mammals, are adapted to live in the trees because this is where the bulk of the food exists. Providing the rain forest is undisturbed it is the most diverse and productive type of forest ecosystem, but very few nutrients are stored in the soil, and if the canopy is depleted the system rapidly becomes disturbed and the soils infertile.

Temperate deciduous forests have been severely modified by human activity, but were very extensive in the past and are the natural vegetation type of much of Europe, eastern North America and eastern Asia. Species composition is poorer than tropical forests: there are only twelve dominant species in Europe, mainly different sorts of oak, beech, and ash. North America has sixty dominant species, including several species of chestnut, maple and hemlock. In most forests, sufficient light reaches beneath the canopy to allow understorey vegetation to develop, but this will vary dramatically with the tree species present. Beech casts a dark shade and few plants grow below it, but oak and ash cast light shade and a species-rich shrub and herbaceous community may develop. Primary productivity in temperate deciduous forests is less than in tropical rain forests but still sufficient to allow the development of diversity and to support long and complex food chains. There is a large bulk return of nutrients from the trees to the soil with the leaf fall each autumn. Characteristically the leaf litter is nutrient-rich and decays with the action of bacteria to form a **mull humus**.

Boreal forests are made up of a vast expanse of coniferous evergreens and occupy a belt extending across North America and Asia on the southern margins of the tundra zone. The conditions of life are harsh because of the adverse climate. The growing season is only of three or four months' duration and even during

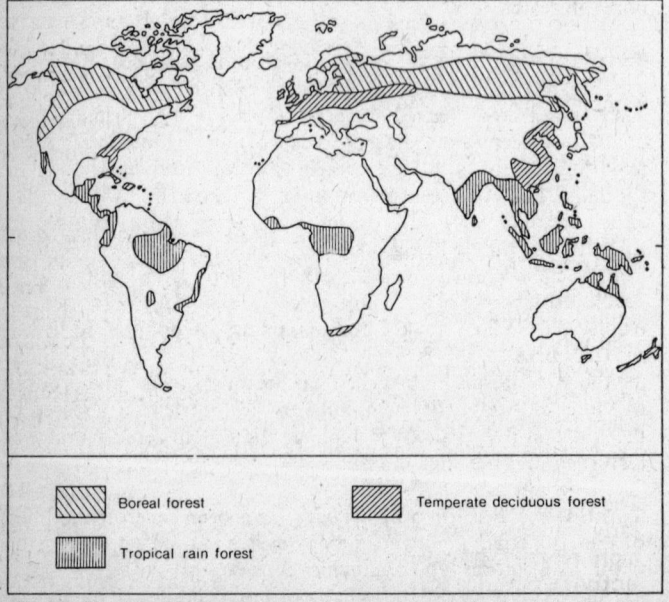

Figure 58. World distribution of forest ecosystems

this time the energy input from solar radiation is small because of the high latitude. Despite the climate, coniferous trees form a dense canopy which intercepts a great amount of light and precipitation, so that there is little opportunity for undergrowth to develop. The trees themselves show little variety across the whole formation, with species of pine, spruce and fir being dominant in most places. Being evergreen, they are able to make full use of the growing season, but nevertheless primary productivity is low. This means that only a limited amount of energy is available for use at secondary levels and typically there is a very small amount of animal biomass as well as a lack of diversity. For instance, carnivores, such as the wolf and lynx, and large omnivores, such as the black and grizzly bears, are scarce. The nutrient cycles tend to be slow and impoverished: few nutrients are demanded by the evergreen plants and few are returned to the soil in the leaf litter. Most decomposition is fungal because bacterial activity is slow in these conditions, and the resulting humus is of the **mor** (acidic) type.

Grassland ecosystems

The grass family has a world-wide distribution, exhibiting a remarkable range of tolerance to habitat factors. Grasses can be annual, biennial or perennial in habit, but all have a similar life form and are **herbaceous** (non-woody) with the exception of bamboo. They all grow from their base and consequently can tolerate grazing or burning better than most plants. They also have extensive root systems, and once a sward has formed it is very difficult for other species to invade it.

Grassland ecosystems have a much smaller biomass than forest ecosystems; the annual primary productivity is only about one eighth or ninth of an adjacent forest area and there are more limited nutrient reservoirs in grassland. Turnover of nutrients is relatively rapid. Since much of the plant food occurs in the soil, a large soil fauna, notably made up of decomposers, is a characteristic feature. Surface animals are frequently large: herbivores adapt their behaviour to the relatively open and unprotected habitat by congregating in herds and being fleet of foot.

The ecological status of grasslands has given rise to much debate: early workers thought that grasslands were too dry for trees, but more recently increased study has shown that **fire** and **human activity** have for long been an important element in the maintainence of these open habitats. The most extensive 'natural'

grasslands occur in sub-humid continental areas of low relief and
two main types can be distinguished: temperate grasslands, in
which woody growth is absent or negligible, and tropical grassland or savanna, in which scattered trees are much more common.

Temperate grasslands include the prairies of North America,
the steppes of Asia, the pampas of South America and the veldt of
South Africa (Fig. 59). Precipitation in these areas ranges from
250 to 1000 mm per annum and the grasslands extend over a wide
range of soil conditions, including chernozems and chestnut soils.
The geographical isolation of these grasslands from each other
has led to some species differentiation, but most other features are
similar, as typified by the prairies. Here, there is a transition westwards from high-grass prairie in Michigan and Illinois to short-
grass prairie on the high plains. This change is partly related to
climate but also to **grazing pressure**, since longer grasses reap-
pear in the west if grazing is eliminated. There is a notable lack of
ecotone or transitional zone between the edge of the eastern
prairies and adjacent forests. Grazing and fire, not climate, seem

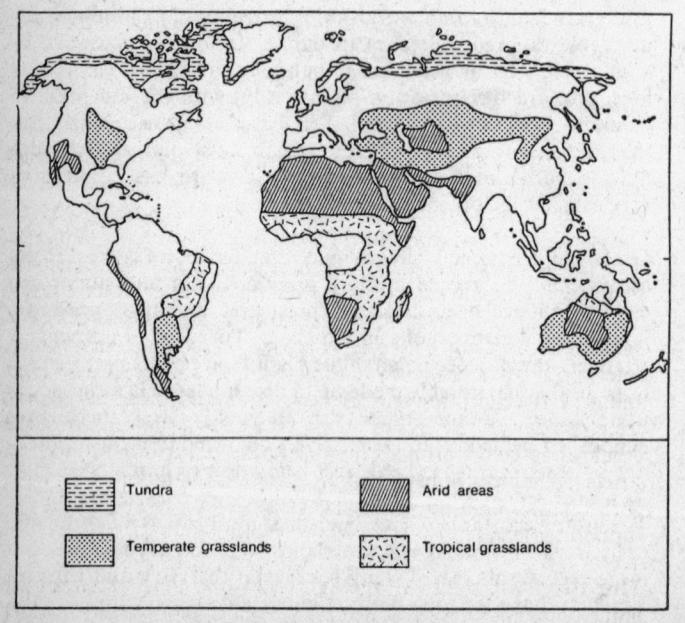

Figure 59. Grasslands and biological deserts

to have been the two most important factors in bringing about this situation: large herds of bison once roamed the prairies and Plains Indians frequently used fire as a means of herding bison. It would seem that the prairies and other similar grasslands may originally have been of climatic origin, but they have been extended and maintained by other factors.

Savannas are ecologically dominated by sedges and grasses but added variety is afforded by wooded plants. All areas experience marked seasonal drought and many of the plants, both grasses and woody species, exhibit xerophytic features. The ferralsolic soils frequently include near-surface lateritic crusts in which nutrients are markedly lacking, and it has been suggested that edaphic factors, as much as climate, favour the xerophytic tendencies of savanna plants. Savanna/forest boundaries show only a poor correlation with precipitation amounts, and again this strongly suggests that factors of soil, fire and grazing are important in maintaining the character of these tropical grasslands. Many of the trees appear to be fire-resistant. The great variety of herbivores and carnivores in these areas suggests that the ecosystem is of considerable antiquity and has extended into areas where climatic conditions are in theory suitable for trees.

Biological deserts

There are extensive regions of the world where biomass and organic productivity are very low, resulting either from a lack of water (as in hot deserts) or from extreme cold (as in tundra). Despite the obvious differences between these two types of region, they have a number of ecological characteristics in common. Plants and animals show less species variety than other ecosystems but a much greater degree of specialization, imposed by the harsh environment. There is a mosaic of small communities, determined by micro-relief and micro-climate. There are no trees and, with the exception of giant cacti, both tundra and hot deserts are characterized by plants of low growth in which much of the organism is below ground. Inevitably the lack of plant food restricts the number of heterotrophs that can be supported. Finally, both types of area are particularly susceptible to ecological disruption by man.

The tundra includes all types of vegetation found between the limits of boreal forest and the polar ice caps. Plants have to adapt both to sub-zero temperatures and to the shortness of the growing season. The low growth form of tundra plants enables them to take advantage of slightly higher temperatures near the ground and avoids extreme wind exposure. Photosynthesis in most tundra plants starts immediately soil temperatures rise above 0°C. Reproduction may take place vegetatively, or in other plants by seed production which may need two or three seasons to be completed: flowers, often vivid, are formed in one season and maturation occurs in the next. Not surprisingly, annuals are rare. Broad transitions in tundra vegetation are related to the poleward increase in the severity of environmental conditions. Where undisturbed, the southern parts of the tundra in the northern hemisphere are characterized by stands of dwarf willow, birch and alder. Further north, these give way to heaths of cowberry or crowberry and peaty swards. Under the harshest conditions only mosses and lichens survive.

Animals in the tundra are limited in number and variety by the lack of food, the intense cold, and the impossibility of finding underground shelter where permafrost exists. Warm-blooded animals must either possess extremely good insulation or they must migrate. Cold-blooded animals, of which the insects are by far the most numerous, can survive in larval form throughout the winter. The total biomass is relatively small and undergoes marked seasonal fluctuations in volume, especially in species such as the lemming or Arctic fox. Some authorities regard this as a manifestation of **inherent instability** in the tundra ecosystem. Because the types of prey at any particular trophic level area so few, any variation in numbers has major repercussions on the next level. This instability may be a reflection of the short time in which the system has been able to develop: the tundra in its present position can only date from the recession of ice sheets after the last glaciation.

Hot deserts are typified from a biological point of view by a lack of water availability rather than a complete absence of water. With one or two notable exceptions (e.g. the creosote bush), there are in fact very few desert plants capable of withstanding extreme dessication or very high temperatures. Up to 60% of the flora is made up of annual or emphemeral species which complete their life cycles within a few weeks of any rain, their seeds remaining quiescent throughout dry periods. **Succulents**, such as cacti, combat the water problem with water storage organs and low surface area/volume ratios. In addition to physical drought, a **physiological drought** is created in deserts by saline ground conditions, and plants need to have halophytic as well as xerophytic characteristics. Desert vegetation is more discontinuous than tundra, but on the other hand it is more diverse in composition and form. Flora of different deserts have tended to evolve in isolation from each other, whereas the tundra is more continuous. Related to varying degrees of aridity, desert vegetation includes low scrub formations, cacti communities, intermittent swards of perennial grasses and ephemeral herbaceous vegetation. In a few areas of extreme aridity or mobility (e.g., on dunes), vegetation may be excluded entirely.

Protection against water loss and high levels of body heat pose similar problems for animals as for plants. Nocturnal activity and summer dormancy are common features. In smaller animals the burrowing habit is widely developed, since the deeper soil layers remain humid and have a more temperate climate than the free air. Morphological protection may be given by such features as an impermeable body covering and a light colouring. The sparseness and marked seasonal fluctuations of biomass at the autotroph level is reflected in animal populations: synchronization of breeding cycles with periods favourable to vegetation growth causes an explosion of life within a few days of the onset of rain. A detrimental side effect of this synchronization occurs where man irrigates deserts and provides an abundant source of food without predators: spectacular locust plagues are one result of this. Desert ecosystems are as precariously balanced as those of the tundra.

Marine ecosystems

In many ways the marine environment is more favourable to life than land areas: it is more equable, oxygen and carbon dioxide are readily available, and many of the nutrient minerals found in the Earth's crust are dissolved in the sea in varying amounts. The main environmental gradients are related to temperature, salinity and light intensity. Both vertical and horizontal ocean currents play a major role in equalizing variations in chemical and physical composition. The most **saline** conditions occur where temperatures, and hence evaporation, are highest; the lowest values occur near melting ice or river mouths. Many marine organisms have very narrow tolerance ranges to particular salinity concentrations, which may therefore localize them to particular depths or areas. The availability of light exercises as much control on photosynthesis in the sea as it does on land. In addition to horizontal variations caused by latitude, light energy and photosynthesis falls

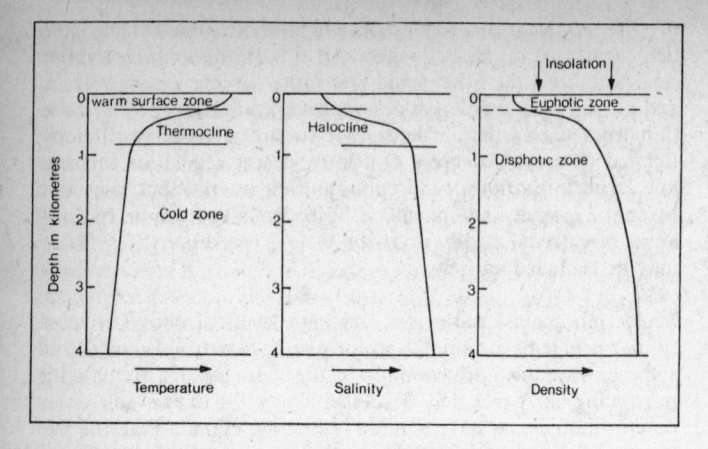

Figure 60. Environmental gradients in marine ecosystems

off with depth. The depth of the compensation point (page 136) varies considerably: it may be as little as 10 m in inshore waters and as much as 100 m in open seas. This latter figure roughly separates the **euphotic** zone (enough light for photosynthesis) from the **disphotic** zone (dim light insufficient for photosynthesis).

Marine plants are confined to the euphotic zone. They are dominated by algae: the most obvious visible types are seaweeds, but 99% of marine vegetation is phytoplankton (microscopic floating algae) and these are responsible for nearly all the primary productivity in the marine ecosystem. Nutrients absorbed by phytoplankton sink to deeper layers of the sea when the plants, or the animals that feed on them, die. Nutrient return is dependent on upwelling sea-water; thus, maximum primary production occurs with upwelling cold currents or on continental shelves where mixing is promoted by waves. Near-shore areas receive additional nutrients from rivers, and coastal and estuarine areas are among the most fertile parts of the marine ecosystem. Productivity may also vary with season: in higher latitudes, maximum productivity takes place in spring and autumn. In summer a **thermocline** develops, a sharp temperature inversion between warm surface waters and colder waters lower down which prevents upwelling. In tropical waters a thermocline is a more permanent feature, and this may inhibit nutrient return to such an extent that certain doldrum areas are virtual biological deserts.

Marine fauna is very diverse, and food chains long and complex, but because of the tiny size of the phytoplankton large herbivores feeding directly on the land plants do not exist. Instead, the bulk of the grazers are zooplankton. These in turn are one of the main sources of fish food – the shrimp-like **krill** zooplankton provide the main diet of Antarctic whalebone whales. Zooplankton are not directly dependent on the light and can exist at all depths, probably deriving food from detrital material. Zooplankton is eaten directly by surface water (**pelagic**) fish and by marine invertebrates, such as molluscs and worms, which in turn are eaten by bottom-dwelling (**demersal**) carnivores such as cod, haddock and plaice. Food chains become complicated at this level as certain fish and invertebrates prey on each other. At the top of the food chain, the fish themselves are eaten by sea-birds, seals and man.

Summary

Major terrestial ecosystems can be distinguished on the basis of structure. Forest ecosystems are layered, have a large standing crop, and are among the most productive of habitats. Differences in life form distinguish tropical rain, temperate deciduous and boreal types. Grassland ecosystems include temperate and tropical types, but both associations result from a combination of climatic, edaphic, human and fire-regulating factors. Biological deserts, where productivity and biomass is low, include the tundra and warm arid areas. Both these ecosystems are delicately balanced and susceptible to disruption. The marine ecosystem is globally more complex than terrestial systems and is dominated at the autotroph level by phytoplankton; these are grazed by zooplankton which in turn support complex carnivorous food webs.

Chapter 15
Environment and Man

Man's relationship with his natural environment is a complex one. Although he is subject to certain natural controls and events, he also acts as the dominant force in many of the Earth's physical and biological systems. In some parts of the world, man has so transformed the environment that few elements of its original nature are detectable. Even extreme habitats, such as the tundra or hot deserts, have not escaped untouched, since they are often the most sensitive to the slightest interference. Many apparently natural systems are in fact **control systems** in which man acts either consciously or inadvertently as a regulator. At best, except perhaps for large-scale weather phenomena and tectonic activity, natural systems are mostly **modified systems**. Although man's primary object in altering the natural environment has been part of an attempt to improve his own lot, in many cases these modifications have created major long-term problems and in others they have been catastrophic.

Atmospheric modifications

Human impact on the atmosphere may be divided into four categories: (1) the introduction of solids and gases not normally found in the atmosphere, i.e., pollutants; (2) changes in the proportions of the natural component gases; (3) alterations to the Earth's surface in such a way as to affect the atmosphere; and (4) planned weather modifications.

1. **Pollutants** in the atmosphere include particulate matter – solid and liquid particles – and gaseous substances such as sulphur dioxide, oxides of nitrogen, carbon monoxide and hydrocarbon compounds. Their main sources are cities, industrial sites and mining and quarrying activities. Natural sources of foreign matter in the atmosphere include forest fires and volcanic explosions. Atmospheric pollutants are conducted upwards from the emission sources by rising air currents as part of the normal convective processes. Larger particles settle under gravity and return to the ground as **fallout**. Smaller suspended particles are brought to the earth by precipitation as **washout**. While in the atmosphere, the primary pollutants may undergo a number of chemical reac-

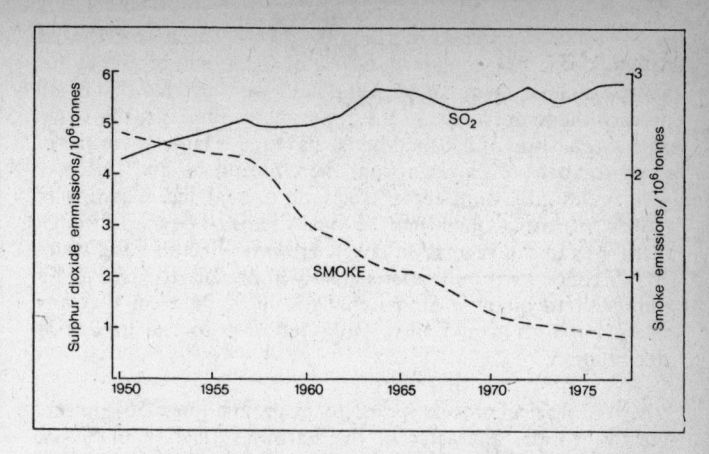

Figure 61. Recent trends in smoke and SO₂ emissions in Britain

tions, generating **secondary pollutants**. For example, sulphur dioxide (SO_2) combines with oxygen and suspended water droplets to produce dilute sulphuric acid. **Photochemical** reactions are brought about by the action of sunlight: ozone (O_3), which can have a severe effect on plant tissues, is produced in this way from nitrogen oxides and organic compounds.

In Britain, recent trends in **smoke** emission (containing much particulate matter) show a welcome decline; this is largely the result of a major swing away from the use of coal for both domestic and industrial use. The Clean Air Act of 1956 introduced strict smoke control measures which accelerated the decline (Fig. 61). However, SO_2 levels show a steady increase and this can be attributed to the greater number of power stations brought into use since 1950. The harmful effects of air pollution are well known. Many pollutants are irritants to the eyes and dangerous to the lungs. Lead and other toxic metals are a particular cause of concern. In addition, pollution causes great damage to materials: limestone structures suffer considerably in many cities unless treated with preservatives.

2. Of the main **natural gases** in the atmosphere, those most critical from an environmental point of view are carbon dioxide, oxygen and water vapour. Although nitrogen comprises four-fifths of the atmosphere, it has an inert chemical nature in this form. Since the Industrial Revolution, **carbon dioxide** levels

appear to have increased by about 10%, largely because of the use of fossil fuels. The long-term effects of this trend, especially for climatic change, are not clear, but it has been suggested that it will increase the temperature of the atmosphere. Similarly, the large-scale combustion of hydrocarbon fuels requires large quantities of **oxygen** to be withdrawn from the atmosphere, and this may have undesirable long-term effects on animal life. Changes in **water vapour** content may be locally induced by man through alterations to the vegetation cover. However, in this case, water vapour content naturally varies greatly from place to place and it is difficult to quantify global changes. It would seem that any excess build-up would be rapidly returned to the oceans as precipitation.

3. Meteorological processes close to the ground (page 56) are very sensitive to the character of the Earth's surface, and can be strongly affected by deforestation, agriculture and urbanization. The effect of cities on local humidity, wind and temperature values was reviewed in Chapter 5. Another noteworthy example is the effect on heat and evaporation budgets when a desert region is placed under irrigation. There is a marked drop in surface albedo and much of the incoming insolation energy is used up in evaporating the water. Thus day-time temperatures are markedly lower than in the surrounding desert. A very common man-induced local modification to climate is the lessening of wind-speeds caused by hedges, walls and shelter belts. If these are too effective in stilling the air, frost pockets may develop on cold nights immediately to leeward of the barrier.

4. Conscious attempts to modify weather systems have been mainly centred around the principle of **cloud seeding**. The artificial supply to clouds of hygroscopic nuclei such as dry-ice particles or silver iodide smoke to accelerate the Bergeron rain-making mechanism (Chap. 2) has been applied with only limited success in Britain and America. As a technique for increasing precipitation, it works best where unstable masses of moisture-laden air are already present. It will not produce rain out of dry air. Seeding has also been tried in an effort to reduce the severity of hurricanes, relying on the theory that it causes the rapid condensation of super-cooled liquid particles and drains off reserves of latent heat in the system. Again, success has been limited. In general, many atmospheric processes operate on such a large scale and with such large energy inputs that, as yet, man has had little direct impact on them.

Landsurface modifications

Where man excavates or piles up material, he can be regarded as a direct agent of geomorphological change. Such man-created landforms include road and rail cuttings and embankments, land reclaimed from the sea, and coal tips and other waste heaps from mining and quarrying. Many of these features are inherently unstable, allowing various forms of mass-movement to develop. When saturated with heavy rain, spoil tips are frequently liable to gullying and flowage, supplying sediment which clogs adjacent stream channels. Extensive engineering works may be required to stabilize over-steepened slopes. **Land scarification** is a term sometimes applied to describe man-made disturbances created by the extraction of mineral resources. Strip-mining is one of the more devastating examples of landform alteration of this kind. **Subsidence** landforms such as flooded depressions or flashes may result from underground mining, as in some of the salt and coal mining areas of Britain.

Indirect man-induced modifications to landforms occur where natural landform processes are caused to accelerate or diminish as a by-product of human activity. These indirect effects are far more widespread than direct effects. Many of the most significant are connected with man's interference with natural vegetation cover, in particular with the clearing of forest for agriculture. A stable vegetation cover acts as an effective regulator of natural erosion, protecting the ground from direct raindrop impact, absorbing some of the run-off and making the slope more cohesive. With the removal of vegetation the surface loses its plant litter, causing a loss of soil structure, cohesion and porosity. Overgrazing of grasslands has similar consequences. The end-result is **accelerated erosion**, often typified by multiple shoestring rills and gullies. In addition, wind deflation may be promoted on the friable soil surface. The **Dust Bowl** of the Great Plains of North America in the 1930s is the classic example of this type of land catastrophe, but very similar effects can be observed today in many overgrazed semi-arid areas, particularly in Africa and the Indian sub-continent.

Alterations to the infiltration capacity and run-off on slopes have two profound effects on adjacent rivers: they increase both the discharge and sediment supply. There seems little doubt that many of the floods that occur on rivers in mid-latitude areas would not take place if the vegetation were in its natural state. At times of flood, discharge levels become higher and achieve their maximum more quickly (Fig. 62). Similar effects occur with **urbanization**: the ground surface is rendered impervious by paths, roads and buildings, and precipitation is channelled directly and rapidly to rivers through drains and sewers. Construction works, as well as mining and quarrying, increase the sediment load. When land is taken into cultivation, sediment levels in rivers increase by a factor of about two or three. Such increases may considerably effect the long-term viability of dams and canals and, in severe cases, large amounts of sediment supply may cause valley aggradation.

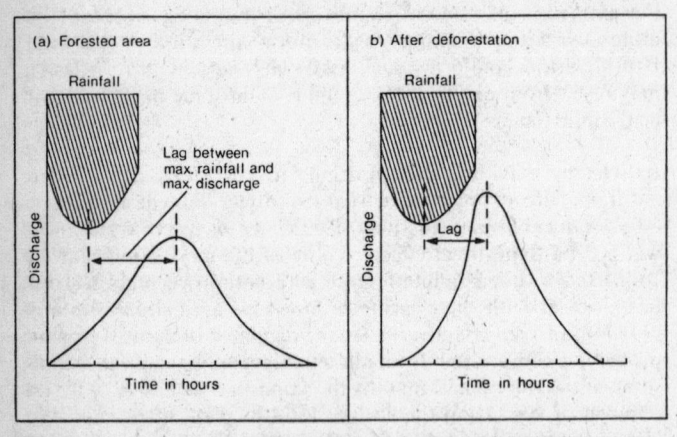

Figure 62. The effects of forest removal on a hydrograph

In **coastal areas**, although man has relatively little impact on the forces that govern waves, tides and currents, erosion and deposition can be materially affected by the building of groynes and breakwaters, and also by the removal of beach material for ballast or construction. Experience has shown that these structures cause long-term problems. By interfering with the natural sediment transport system, a groyne may starve a down-drift beach of material. This will lead to a narrowing and steepening of the beach and an increase in direct wave attack on the backshore or the cliff behind. Similarly, steeply sloping or vertical seawalls may reflect storm waves which then contribute further to the height of the next incoming crest-line, increasing its erosive power. It would seem that many coastal structures have been built without a full understanding of shoreline processes.

Ecosystem modification

Primitive man managed to live within ecosystems without altering their main characteristics, but with the beginnings of agriculture far-reaching effects were introduced. The **simplification** of ecosystems is the most widespread general effect that has come about (Fig. 63). Man's prime concern is to direct energy and material cycling in ecosystems towards himself so that he can easily crop them. Species other than the ones he wants to crop are regarded as **weeds** or **pests**: hence reduction in species diversity, often to a single species population, is a notable characteristic of man's impact on the living environment. Food webs are consequently made much simpler in the process. In arable farming, man removes all other consumer organizations and crops the primary producers. In pastoral farming, he retains a single herbivore species, namely sheep or cattle, and himself occupies the position of sole carnivore.

Ecosystem simplification of this type can result in severe side effects. A single-species population offers great opportunity for the spread of disease, pests and parasites, whereas the potential for survival is much greater in natural multi-species ecosystems. The more the species diversity, the better the chance that there will be a balanced inter-relationship between organisms. Man-created **monocultures** are thus ecologically unstable and can only be sustained at the price of high inputs of energy (machinery, weeding) and matter (fertilizers). Without these, soil infertility quickly sets in. Intensively managed monocultures can be very high yielding, but only at the expense in the long-run of non-renewable resources, namely fossil fuels and minerals.

Major nutrient reservoirs are inevitably destroyed as part of the ecosystem simplification process, notably the natural vegetation and the soil systems. The clay-humus complex is replenished to some extent if fertilizers are used as a substitute, but not all the elements used in fertilizers are retained. Some of the **nitrates** are rapidly leached into rivers and lakes, where the increased nitrogen input permits accelerated growth of plants, algae and other phytoplankton. This chemically-induced increase in productivity is called **eutrophication**. In extreme form it is ultimately harmful, since the plants and animals grow, die and decompose at such a

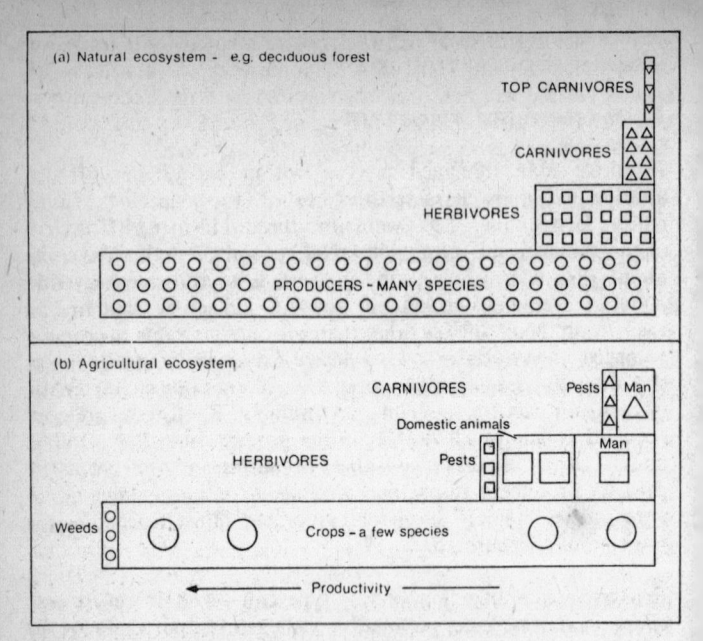

Figure 63. Natural and agricultural ecosystem structure compared

rate that oxygen levels fall and aquatic life becomes impossible. Similar problems of eutrophication arise with the **phosphates** contained in detergents and sewage effluent.

The effect of man's impact on **individual species** in ecosystems takes two major forms. First, many species have become extinct or drastically reduced in numbers: this comes about in some cases by hunting and conscious elimination, but in most others by the fragmentation of habitats. Second, species have been accidently or purposefully introduced as **aliens** into other ecosystems. Some animals and plants have flourished in this way at the expense of native species. Rhododendrons and grey squirrels are two examples in Britain. Other species have taken advantage of new artificial ecosystems created by man, particularly in cities. Pigeons, rats and cockroaches fall into this latter category.

With the increasing impact of man, severe signs of **imbalance** or declining efficiency are being observed in many ecosystems. This is shown for example by: the progressive devastation of formerly good fertile agricultural or grazing land through over-intensive use, particularly in Third World countries; the reduction of species variety and numbers when secondary forest replaces primary forest; a general loss of biological productivity in grassland ecosystems; and an increasing amount of pollution.

Environmental management

Many of the problems outlined above are not insoluble. The term 'environmental management' implies a clear understanding both of the nature of the interactions between the various systems in the natural environment, and that man's use of the landscape should be directed within an integrated context. Drainage basin or **watershed management** is one example of this. It emphasizes that drainage basins are a natural unit for the operation of many physical and biological systems, including human activity. As an example of a specific applied case, an integrated approach is essential when dealing with **flooding**, since its origin and control will embrace climatic, geomorphological, hydrological and biotic factors. The feedback relationships between slopes and rivers, emphasized in Chapters 7 and 8, provide the fundamental theoretical base. There are two common approaches to flood alleviation. Flood *control* attempts to control the flood in the river channel by building large dams, retaining embankments or diversions. These measures can obviously be costly, and have their own consequences on river velocity and patterns of erosion and deposition, but the works can be sited where they are most needed, usually close to populated areas. Flood *prevention* aims to stop the flood forming in the first place by careful integrated management of the whole catchment, particularly by reafforesting slopes where possible or by building small dams on first-order tributaries.

As applied to biogeography and ecology, environmental management embraces **nature conservation**. This is concerned with the preservation and protection of wildlife and natural habitats from modification or depletion by man. To this end, nature reserves of various sorts have been set up in many parts of the world. However, they have not always been successful. For instance, in East African game-parks, animals such as elephant, hippo, and buffalo, whose populations had formerly been kept in check by hunting by natives, increased in numbers to such an extent that widespread devastation of their natural habitat resulted. The general lessons for environmental management are twofold: first, that ecosystems cannot simply be preserved, but are dynamic in character; and, second, that man is an important habitat factor in many cases: the ecological niche occupied by him cannot suddenly be left vacant. Ecosystem management also includes the concept of maintaining sustained yield from organic resources. This idea is implicit in **forestry** practice, as well as in **soil conservation**, the aim of which is to sustain agricultural fertility. Many authorities would regard this as by far the most important aspect of ecosystem maintenance and feel that, in the face of growing pressure on food resources, the protection of wildlife for non-productive reasons is a luxury we can ill afford.

The principles of organic resource management also apply to environmental **resources** in general. Some of the resources, such as solar energy, are virtually **inexhaustible**. Similarly, the total amounts of air, water and rock are so great that there will always be enough. Other resources can be regarded as **exhaustible but renewable** with reasonable management. This applies to fresh or usable water, fresh air, vegetation and animal life. Because the reproductive capacity of most organisms is relatively high, there will always be recovery in most ecosystems if man-induced damage is not too severe. A third category of resources must be regarded as **irreplaceable** if lost. This applies to soils, certain minerals and fossil fuels, and to rare species of plants and animals. Developed soils can take thousands of years to form, yet be destroyed in a matter of weeks by unchecked soil erosion. The fossil fuels are combusted and dispersed in an even shorter time-span.

Summary

Major parts of the natural environment have been affected by man. In the atmosphere, particulate and gaseous pollution has had significant effects on regional climate, and micro-climatic modifications are important near the ground. Widespread changes have taken place in rates of erosion and deposition on slopes and in rivers through interference with the natural vegetation cover. Many ecosystems have been drastically altered by simplification, which has involved the elimination or control of all species in direct competition with man and the depletion of nutrient reservoirs. Environmental management attempts to redress some of these problems by adopting an integrated approach to resource conservation.

Chapter 16
Population Patterns

Population geography or the geography of population – the terms may be regarded as synonymous – is concerned with the study of demographic patterns and processes in an environmental context. The emphasis, as in other fields of geographical enquiry, is on the spatial variations in population patterns and processes. It is in this essential respect that population geography may be distinguished from **demography** which is the science of population *per se* and which is little concerned with the influence of environment on demographic processes, and even less with the impact of man on his environment. Given such a definition of population geography, it becomes clear that the description, analysis and explanation of patterns of population density and distribution constitute the foundation of this branch of human geography. The strength of this foundation in turn depends on the quality, accuracy and reliability of the population statistics available for any given country or region.

Population data sources

It has been remarked that 'the demographer is devoted to numbers and depends heavily upon statistical methods, whereas the population geographer relates numbers to area and relies upon maps'. This statement reflects the geographer's interest in the spatial aspects of population, but it should not be taken to mean that geographical study of population is non-quantitative. Demographic statistics provide the key to precision in the description, classification, comparison and analysis of population patterns. At national level two main sources of data are available to the geographer: census reports and various registers of population. The former have been described as 'the counting of heads' and the latter as 'the recording of demographic events'.

A **census** has been defined as 'the total process of collecting, compiling, evaluating, analysing and publishing demographic, economic and social data pertaining at a specific time to all persons in a country or a well-defined part of a country' (UNO). In the UK the first census was held in 1801, and, with the exception of 1941, a census has been conducted on a regular decennial basis since that date. The census of 1981 will be the eighteenth full census to be held in the UK. Over the years the UK census schedule has become longer and more complicated as more and more categories of questions have been added, although some questions have been short-lived and appeared on only one or two occasions. The latest schedule asks questions about housing arrangements and amenities, household composition, as well as the age, birthplace, previous residence, education, occupation, workplace and many other facts about individual household members. All of this is needed to provide the essential data base for demographic analysis and future planning. The British census indicates where members of the population were actually residing on the day of the enumeration (usually a Sunday in April). This is known as the *de facto* approach, in contrast with the *de jure* approach which is used in the USA, for example, and which records individuals according to their normal place of residence.

Registers of population are statistical records of demographic events such as births, deaths, marriages and divorces. In the UK, for example, the local registrar must be notified of all births, deaths and marriages within a prescribed time. This registration is a compulsory legal requirement. The registrar in turn sends his local statistics to the General Register Office, and the resultant aggregate statistics appear in the quarterly and annual publications of the Registrar-General. Population experts suggest that in those countries which have adopted this type of registration of vital events, the data contained in registers of population are more accurate and reliable than those of census reports, although the categories of information which they provide are, of course, much more restricted.

It should be realized that both population registers and census reports are subject to a certain degree of error and inaccuracy. Generally speaking, good quality, reliable statistics exist for the developed nations of the world, but demographic data for the developing nations need to be interpreted with caution. A significant number of births and deaths escape registration, and the accuracy of census returns is reduced by omissions, misstatements, double-entries and various other errors. Probably the most difficult problem faced by the population geographer is that of making comparisons between different countries. Despite the efforts of the UNO to standardize census procedures, the various nations of the world include different categories of questions in their census schedules, classify their results in different ways and conduct their censuses in different years and at varying intervals, with the result that international comparisons are made extremely difficult, if not impossible. Furthermore, many countries held their first census only relatively recently so that historical comparisons are impossible. It has been estimated that even at the present time more than one-quarter of the world's population escapes regular enumeration.

Population density and distribution

The term **population density** is an expression of the ratio between total population numbers and the area occupied by that population. Crude population density, for example, is a measure of the average number of individuals per unit area. For instance, the UK has an average population density of 230 persons per km^2. Such a figure is of limited value, for there are, of course, wide variations on either side of that mean figure. As a measure, crude population density is most useful when used in studies of small areal units such as parishes, census enumeration districts or city wards. It can, however, be modified in various ways to improve its value. For example, densities can be calculated for inhabited areas or cultivated areas only, rather than for total area. This may give an improved and more realistic value. Population density is usually shown cartographically by means of **choropleth maps** which use a series of shadings to show density values.

The term **population distribution** refers to the spacing of the individuals of a population within a given area. In the analysis of population patterns it is often necessary to determine whether the population is concentrated around a central city or clustered in a particular district, or whether it tends towards a uniformly even distribution or is merely randomly scattered over the area in question. Geographers have developed various statistical techniques or borrowed techniques from other disciplines in order to clarify, measure, describe and compare population distributions. For example, a measure known as **mean distance between nearest neighbour**, originally devised for the analysis of plant distributions, is now widely used in the study of population patterns. This provides an index value for any distribution on a scale ranging from the hypothetical extremes of total concentration to perfectly even distribution (Chap. 28). The mapping of population distributions is usually done by means of **dot distribution maps** or by the use of proportional circles or spheres, or by a combination of these techniques.

A useful graphical device for studying changes in population distributions through time is known as a **Lorenz curve**. This can be used when both the areas and population totals of sub-units within a given territory are known, for example, the sizes and population totals of states, counties or other sub-divisions within a national territory. These units are arranged in descending order according to their population totals, and cumulative percentages of population are plotted against cumulative percentages of area. The resultant curve is known as a Lorenz curve. Changes in the form of the curve through time show whether a population distribution is becoming more concentrated or more dispersed or remaining relatively static. For example, Figure 64 indicates that between 1960 and 1978 the population of the USA became more dispersed.

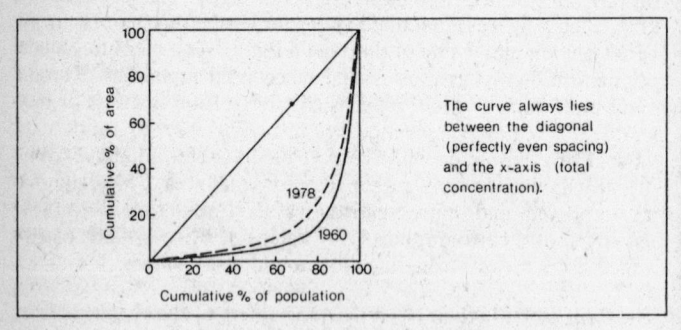

The curve always lies between the diagonal (perfectly even spacing) and the x-axis (total concentration).

Figure 64. Lorenz curves for US population 1960 and 1978

Influences on population distributions

Patterns of population distribution in almost every part of the world are influenced to some degree by environmental conditions, but various historical, economic and social factors must also be taken into account in seeking an explanation. From a superficial examination of the distribution of world population it is tempting to conclude that physical influences alone, such as climate and terrain, exert a dominant and controlling influence on population numbers and their distribution (Fig. 65). However, this type of interpretation in which patterns of settlement and economic activity are held to be determined by environmental factors alone does not stand up to close examination. It is a view known as **geographical determinism** which found favour with many geographers during the early years of this century. For example,

Ellsworth Huntington and others even went so far as to describe climate as 'the mainspring of civilization, the impulse for migrations and the determinant of the energy and character of nations'. It is now realized that man is capable of modifying and controlling his environment to a considerable degree and is not a passive and powerless creature totally constrained and dominated by his surroundings. His environment offers various possibilities and opportunities which may or may not be fully exploited. According to this viewpoint, which is referred to as **geographical possibilism**, man is the dominant element in the man/environment relationship.

Thus, in the context of population analysis, reference should be made to both physical and human factors. **Physical influences** on patterns of population distribution include latitude, altitude, relief, seasonal variations in temperature and precipitation, availability of water supply, soil quality and the geographical distribution of mineral resources. Numerous studies have demonstrated the importance of one or more of these factors in different parts of the world. **Human influences** include the type of economy practised in any area, the degree of urbanization and industrialization, the level of technological development, the role of government in the fields of economic and physical planning, and especially the age and duration of settlement in a given area. The importance of these individual factors has been demonstrated in numerous specific areas. Clearly, the distribution of population in any given area is the product of many influences, some physical and some human. In such a multi-factor situation it is difficult to ascribe a particular degree of importance to any single factor or even set of factors. The problem of analysis is made even more difficult because patterns of population distribution are constantly changing in response to changes in birth rates, death rates and migration trends (Chap. 18). It follows from this that the influences on population patterns have no stable values through time. Factors which were important a century ago may now be relatively insignificant, and new influences come into play in response to economic developments, technological changes and planning decisions. It has been remarked that 'the general human cover is thickening over the globe ... but it is thickening particularly in certain areas and becoming thinner in others ... The population map for the beginning of the 19th century bears no resemblance to the present one, and the latter probably looks very different from the one which future generations will see after the year 2000. However, through all the changing circumstances one can always see the three great and fundamental influences; natural conditions, economic conditions, and the events of history.' (J. Beaujeu-Garnier).

World distribution of population

Total world population in 1977 was estimated at 4,123 million. This population occupied a land area of 135,830,000 km^2 to give an average world population density of 30·4 persons per km^2. Such a figure has, of course, limited value, for one of the most

	Population (Millions)	% of world total
Africa	424	10·3
North America	242	5·9
South & Central America	342	8·3
Asia (excluding USSR)	2,355	57·1
Europe (excluding USSR)	478	11·6
Oceania	22	0·5
USSR	260	6·3
Total	4,123	100·0

Table 3. Distribution of world population by continents, 1977

striking features of the world's population is its uneven distribution. Within Western Europe alone, for example, national densities vary from 12 persons per km^2 in Norway to 339 per km^2 in the Netherlands. Elsewhere the variations are even greater; for example, the vast, virtually empty lands of Australia (2 persons per km^2) may be contrasted with the tiny, overcrowded territory of Hong Kong (4,320 persons per km^2). Taking a broad view of the world pattern, two main features are evident. First, the northern hemisphere with about 90% of the world total is much more heavily populated than the southern hemisphere, even after making allowances for its greater land area; secondly, the so-called Old World (defined here as Europe and Asia) with about 75% of the world's population, supports much greater numbers than the New World (the Americas, Africa and Australia). These facts are reflected in the distribution of world population by continents (Table 3).

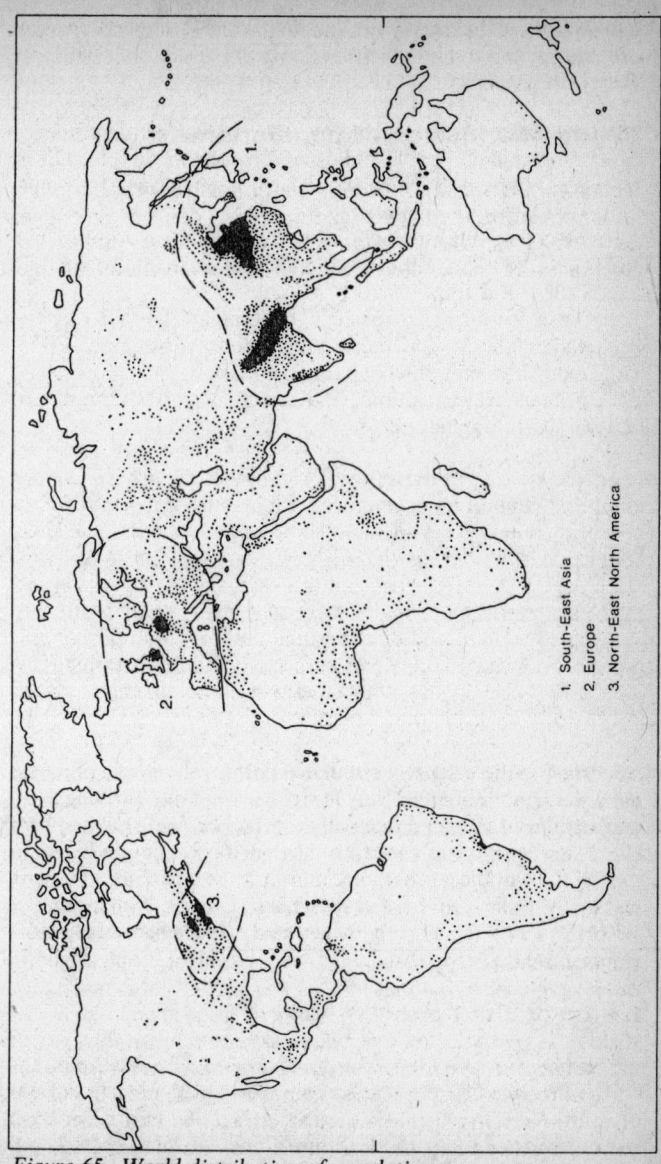

Figure 65. World distribution of population

Examination of figure 65 reveals three major regions of outstandingly high population density. These regions, referred to as the **primary concentrations** of population, are listed below.

1. **South-East Asia** (including the Indian sub-continent). About 2,000 million people, almost 50% of the world total, live in this region. India and China alone have populations of 625 million and 865 million respectively.
2. **Europe** (including the USSR west of the Ural Mountains). This region contains almost 700 million people, approximately 15% of the world total.
3. **North-East North America.** (The region bounded by the Great Lakes, the St. Lawrence Valley and Washington, D.C.). With about 150 million inhabitants, this is by far the smallest of the primary concentrations, and accounts for less than 4% of the total world population.

Secondary concentrations of population are smaller in extent and contain fewer numbers, but are also important within the world context. They include the western seaboard of the USA, the lowlands bordering the Plate Estuary in South America, South Africa, the Mediterranean coastlands of North Africa, and south-east Australia. Finally **tertiary concentrations** are even more localized and often assume the form of linear concentrations or localized clusters; respective examples include the lower Nile Valley of Egypt and the high mountain basin centred on Mexico City in Central America.

In contrast to these densely populated parts of the world, there are vast areas containing relatively few people and often having average densities of less than one person per km^2. These include high latitude areas (the lands north of latitude 60°N contain less than 0·5% of the world's population), mid-latitude and tropical deserts such as the Sahara and Great Australian Deserts, high mountain and plateau areas such as the Andes and Himalayas and equatorial forest areas such as Amazonia and the Zaïre Basin (Fig. 65).

Ecumene and nonecumene

The term **ecumene** (derived from an ancient Greek word meaning the inhabited part of the known world at that early time) is sometimes used to refer to the settled lands of the Earth. The term **nonecumene** refers to the uninhabited or very sparsely inhabited regions of the Earth. It is impossible to draw a precise division between the two, for clearly the permanently settled lands merge gradually into the uninhabited areas. Nevertheless, it has been estimated that approximately 60% of the world's land surface may be classified as ecumene and about 40% as nonecumene. The line, or more realistically the zone, between ecumene and nonecumene may be regarded as the limit or **frontier of settlement**. Throughout history the ecumene has been progressively expanded. Explorers and settlers from Europe entered sparsely populated or empty lands and extended the frontiers of settlement into equatorial forests, arid regions and sub-arctic environments. At the present time this type of process is unusual. There are some exceptions – the Israeli colonization of the Negev Desert, the Brazilian development of Amazonia and the Soviet building of new towns in Siberia – but more typically frontiers of settlement are static or even show signs of retreat. However, if the world's population continues to grow at its present rate (Chap. 17) and if the pressures on land and resources continue to increase, it seems likely that in future years greater efforts will be made to develop areas which at present remain only sparsely populated.

Summary

The geographical study of population relies heavily upon two main data sources, census reports and national registers of population. Using these statistical sources a preliminary stage in population analysis is concerned with establishing patterns of population density and distribution which are influenced by both physical and human factors. The world's population is very unevenly distributed and striking contrasts exist between the main concentrations of population and the sparsely inhabited regions. These contrasts underlie the division of the Earth's lands into areas of ecumene and nonecumene.

Chapter 17
World Population Growth

In 1960 the total world population was almost 3,000 million. By 1970 this figure had risen to 3,610 million and had reached 4,123 million in 1977. From these figures it can be seen that since 1970 the world's population has increased on average by more than 73 million each year. The significance of this figure should be carefully considered. Each year the world's population increases by an amount far in excess of the total population of the UK. Each month the world increase is greater than the population of Scotland, and every single day of the year a population larger than that of Newcastle or Portsmouth is added to the world total.

The contemporary rate of increase becomes even more alarming when compared with earlier figures. The first 1,000 million of population was reached by about 1820, the second by about 1930, the third in 1960 and the fourth in 1975. In other words, after requiring hundreds of thousands of years to reach the first 1,000 million, the second was added in a little over a century, the third in just thirty years and the fourth in a mere fifteen years. As a United Nations Population Bulletin of 1951 pointed out, 'It took 200,000 years for the world's human population to reach 2,500 million; it will now take a mere thirty years to add another 2,000 million.' That forecast of 1951 has proved to be remarkably accurate. Currently the UN demographers are forecasting a world population of between 6,000 and 7,000 million by the end of the century. Given that at least half the world's population is at present underfed and living in conditions of grave poverty, there can be little doubt that this uncontrolled increase in numbers is one of the most serious and urgent problems facing mankind during the closing decades of the twentieth century.

In the context of world history this rapidly accelerating rate of growth of the human population is a relatively recent feature. Due to the almost total lack of census statistics prior to 1800, we cannot be absolutely certain of earlier numbers and growth rates. However, it does appear that the beginning of the present accelerating growth rate occurred during the mid-17th century (Fig. 66). Experts have suggested a total world population of approximately 500 million for the year 1650. For example, A. M. Carr-Saunders and W. F. Willcox give figures of 545 million and 470 million respectively. The same authorities also suggest a total of about 1,000 million for the year 1820. Growth rates appear to have doubled between 1650 and 1850, doubled again between 1850 and 1920, and yet again between 1920 and 1970.

This accelerating growth rate was not caused by any significant increase in birth rates, but rather by a progressive reduction in mortality rates. As a recent UN bulletin on *Population and Food Supply* pointed out, '... in a world which since the beginning of history has sustained terrible visitations of plague, cholera, smallpox and diphtheria, there has not been a major pandemic since 1919 when influenza is believed to have caused 25 million deaths around the world. In other words, world and national population growth has shifted from a wave-like pattern of gains and losses to a steady upward trend. In consequence of these changes, a fertility rate which only a few generations ago was essential to mere survival now results in a rapid multiplication of numbers, by reason of ever better control of mortality.'

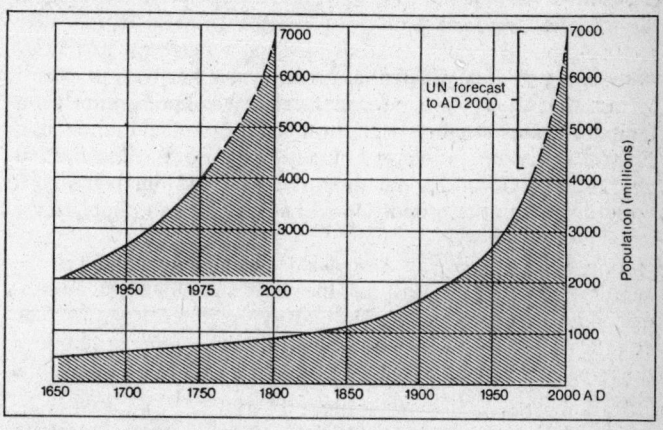

Figure 66. World population growth since 1650

Having established the overall amount and rate of recent world population growth, some other points require examination. Where is the growth taking place? Do certain continents or regions account for the bulk of the increase or is the rapid growth of numbers a worldwide phenomenon? During the 18th and 19th centuries total world growth was very largely accounted for by

Europe and Asia. During the 19th century there was also massive emigration from Europe to the New World, so that part of the growth in the Americas, Africa and Australia can also be indirectly attributed to Europe During the present century national growth rates in Europe have slowed down to very low levels, so much so that some European countries have even been characterized by a slight decrease in numbers in recent years; for example, during the 1970s Scotland had an average annual decrease of population of 0.5% per year. On the other hand, Asian growth rates show few signs of slackening, and Asia is now the largest contributor to the world's total growth of numbers. Pakistan, Bangladesh and India had average annual growth rates of 3.2%, 2.4% and 2.2% respectively during the 1970s. Annual increase rates of over 3.0% are also evident among the Arab nations of the Middle East. Tropical Latin America too is characterized by very high growth rates, over 3.0% per year in the case of Mexico, Ecuador and Peru, although these high growth rates are being applied to much smaller base populations than those of South-East Asia. It is worth noting at this point that an annual growth rate of 3.0%, if maintained, will cause a population to double in approximately 25 years.

One effect of these differential growth rates has been to cause a progressive shifting in the world distribution of population. Comparison of recent figures with those for 1920 reveals a number of interesting points (Table 4). Since 1920, Europeans as a percentage of the total world population have declined from over 18% to less than 12%; the proportion of Latin American population is

	Annual increase (percent)		% of total world population	
	1920–30	1970–77	1920	1977
Africa	1.1	2.7	7.9	10.3
North America	1.5	0.9	6.5	5.9
South & Central America	1.9	2.8	5.0	8.3
Asia (excluding USSR)	1.1	2.2	53.3	57.1
Europe (excluding USSR)	0.8	0.6	18.1	11.6
Oceania	1.8	2.0	0.5	0.5
USSR	1.1	1.0	8.7	6.3
World	1.1	1.9	100.0	100.0

Table 4. *Population growth by continents 1920–1977*

now greater than that of North America, and the Asian population now accounts for a massive 57% of the world total.

The demographic transition model

Many attempts have been made to formulate models or theories of population evolution. Despite a number of valid criticisms, probably the most useful model of this type is still the so-called **demographic transition model** which suggests that any population will pass through a series of stages as it develops from a primitive, pre-industrial, agrarian type of economy to a complex, modern, urban-industrial type of economy and society. The various stages are based on the pattern of population changes which took place in Europe from about 1700 through to the present day. The European experience is used as the foundation of the model simply because Europe is almost the only part of the world for which reasonably reliable demographic statistics are available for the pre-twentieth century period. During the period from 1700 onwards Europe also experienced the changes in economy and society – industrialization and urbanization – which the model assumes are at present taking place or will take place in the underdeveloped nations of the world. On the basis of changes in birth rates and death rates, the demographic transition model identifies four stages through which it is assumed any population will pass.

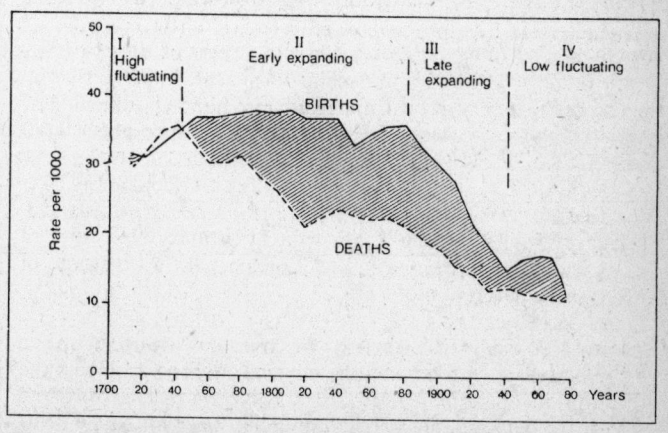

Figure 67. The four stages of demographic transition as illustrated by birth and death rates for England & Wales 1700–1980

Stage 1. High fluctuating or primitive demographic regime This stage of development is characterized by very high birth rates and death rates (over 30‰). Both are subject to short-term fluctuations so that the growth of population is slow and intermittent. In Britain this situation lasted until the mid-18th century. At the present time every country in the world has moved out of this situation, although some in Central Africa and South-East Asia have done so only recently.

Stage 2. Early expanding or youthful demographic regime During this stage the birth rate remains high and may actually increase, but the death rate shows a progressive decline from its former high level. Stage 2 lasted in Britain from about 1750 through to about 1880, a period of some 130 years. Currently almost every nation in the developing world finds itself in this situation of an enormous excess of births over deaths. Examples include Nigeria with crude birth and death rates of 52·2‰ and 25·5‰ respectively, and Bangladesh with a birth rate of 49·5‰ and a death rate of 28·1‰. Furthermore, most developing nations have entered a phase of declining death rate only recently (Fig. 68). Given that Stage 2 of the demographic transition lasted well over one hundred years in Britain, are we to expect that the developing nations will continue to be characterized by explosive growth rates until late in the twenty-first century?

Stage 3. Late expanding demographic regime This stage is characterized by a progressive reduction in birth rate from its very high level (40‰ or more) down to a level of 10‰ to 20‰. Death rate also continues to decline during this stage, so that by the end of Stage 3 both birth and death rate stand at quite modest levels. These trends were evident in Britain between about 1880 and 1940. Countries which at present exhibit these characteristics include those of Mediterranean Europe, the USSR and many New World countries such as the USA, Australia and New Zealand. Specific examples include Spain with birth and death rates of 18·2‰ and 8·0‰ respectively, and Canada with a birth rate of 15·5‰ and a death rate of 7·3‰.

Stage 4. Low fluctuating or mature demographic regime A very small number of countries, all European with the exception of Japan, may be regarded as having entered this final stage of the demographic transition model. They all have low or moderate birth and death rates with very little difference between the two, so that the natural increase of population is slight. In

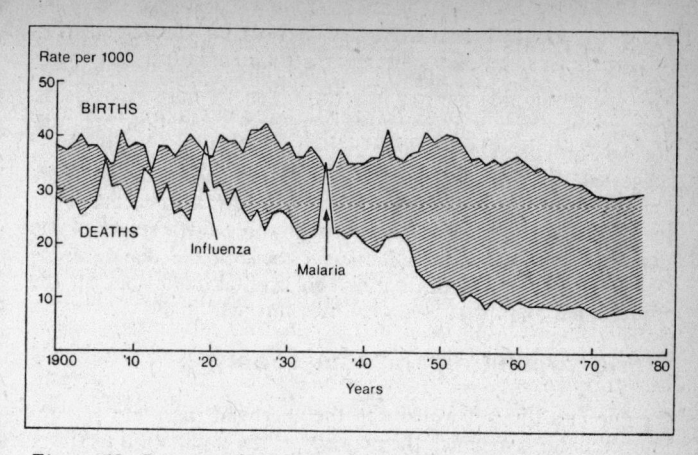

Figure 68. Demographic change in Sri Lanka 1900–77

some instances periods of slight increase may alternate with periods of actual decline. Examples include the UK with identical birth and death rates of 11·7‰ in 1977, and Sweden with a birth rate of 11·6‰ and a death rate of 10·7‰ in the same year.

The pattern of demographic change shown in figure 68 is typical of many developing nations. In the case of Sri Lanka an important factor accounting for the decline in death rate has been a long and vigorous campaign to eradicate malaria, following a severe epidemic in the mid-1930s. Other general improvements in medical services, health care, diet, housing and hygiene have also played their part. As a result the death rate of the island (8‰) has been reduced to a 'western' level, and is in fact significantly lower than that of the UK. On the other hand, Sri Lanka's birth rate (30‰) is almost three times as high as that of the UK. As a result its population is increasing by more than 1·6% each year. On the evidence of figure 68 in Sri Lanka may be said to have entered Stage 2 of the demographic transition model in about 1920. The critical question is whether or not it will take the same length of time to pass through Stage 2 as did the UK. Is the demographic transition model, based on the European experience, applicable to developing nations such as Sri Lanka?

Many experts have suggested that the demographic transition model is not applicable to the present-day developing nations. They have pointed out that contemporary growth rates in the

Third World are higher than those of 18th and 19th century Europe and are being applied to much larger base populations. Also the developing nations lack the outlets for massive overseas emigration which did so much to relieve population pressure during Europe's stage of most vigorous growth. It has also been suggested that foreign aid and investment and education programmes may cause a reduction in the length of time taken for the developing nations to pass through the growth stages of the model. Nevertheless, despite these criticisms, the demographic transition model provides a useful conceptual framework for the study of national population changes through time.

World population and food supply

We live in a divided world. On the one hand there are the developed nations in which the majority of the population enjoys a level of material presperity which the world has never before experienced. On the other hand there are the developing nations whose people have little or no share in that prosperity – a world of affluence and a world of want. The distinction between the 'haves' and the 'have nots' may be quantified in various ways. In purely monetary terms, 20% of the world's population living in the eighteen richest nations enjoys 70% of the world's total income, while 50% of the world's population living in the fifteen poorest nations shares less than 10% of the world's total income. In terms of the availability of food supply, it has been variously estimated that between 50% and 65% of the world's population suffers from lack of food. Between 2,000 million and 2,600 million people do not get enough to eat.

To form a picture of human food requirements it is useful to refer to the number of calories needed to satisfy the body's energy requirements – about 2,400 calories per day for an average active adult. It should be pointed out that expert nutritionists disagree on the exact calorific requirement, some placing the figure as low as 2,000 calories per day and others as high as 2,800 calories per day. Additionally, specific elements such as proteins, mineral salts and vitamins are also necessary for the maintenance and improvement of muscle and bone structures and for the efficient functioning of the body. In other words, calorific intake provides only a very general measure, for not only are the number of calories important, but also their quality, nutritional content and the balance between different components such as carbohydrates, proteins and fats. Protein is an especially important dietary element, each person needing at least 70 grammes per day, of which 20 grammes should be animal protein. In this respect the population of India consumes on average a mere 5·9 grammes of animal protein per day, compared with a per capita figure of 53·4 grammes per day in the UK. Reference to figure 69, which shows the per capita calorific intake of the various nations of the world, reveals that most countries in Africa, South-East Asia and tropical Latin America provide an average of less than 2,400 calories per day for their inhabitants.

In these countries a large proportion of the population suffers from undernourishment or malnutrition. **Undernourishment** is used to describe a diet which is inadequate in quantity, whereas the term **malnutrition** refers to a diet which is defective in quality. Both result in a reduction of body energy and a withdrawal from physical and intellectual effort, and cause a variety of **deficiency diseases** such as kwashiorkor, anaemia, marasmus, beri-beri, trachoma and goitre, as well as lowering resistance to other diseases and infections such as tuberculosis, malaria and bilharzia.

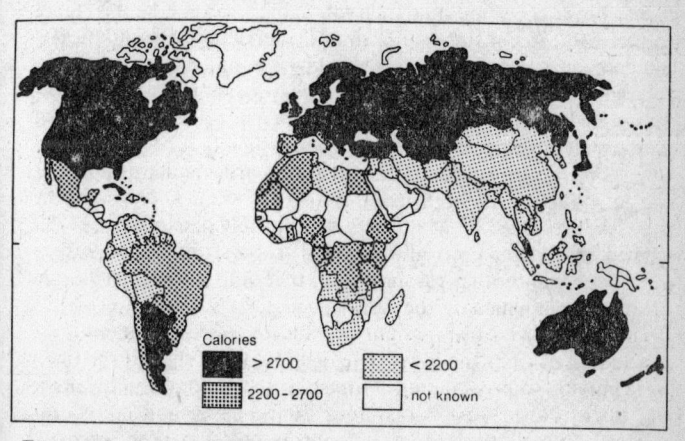

Figure 69. Per capita calorie intake per day 1977

Not only are there chronic shortages of food in the world today, but there are also clear indications that the situation is becoming worse year by year. Frequent outbreaks of famine over wide regions - in Biafra, Bangladesh, Ethiopia and Chad in recent years -

give an indication of a worsening situation, while statistical evidence tells a similar story. Between 1967 and 1977 rates of population increase were higher than rates of increase in food production in thirty-six of the developing nations of the world. In most parts of the Third World, food production is increasing on average by less than 2·0% per year, while annual rates of population increase are generally higher than 2·0% and in some cases as high as 3·5%. Consequently in most developing nations the per capita supply of food is actually decreasing year by year.

One of the earliest writers to discuss the relationship between population growth and food supply was **Thomas Malthus** (1766–1834). In his *Essay on the Principle of Population*, published in 1798, Malthus argued that the growth of population is a function of the growth of food supply. If the supply of food is increased, then population will also grow. In other words, any attempt to improve living standards will be self-defeating because population will simply grow until a subsistence level is reached again. Malthus suggested that population tends to increase in a geometric ratio (1, 2, 4, 8, 16, 32 ...) doubling every 25 years, while food production tends to increase in an arithmetic ratio (1, 2, 3, 4, 5, 6 ...) over the same time interval. The key phrase here is 'tends to increase'. According to Malthus, the tendency of population to increase in a geometric ratio would be counteracted by checks such as war, famine and disease, so that the actual growth would be somewhat less than that derived from a geometric progression. Conversely, the increase in food production might be greater than that resulting from the application of an arithmetic ratio due to the introduction of improved farming techniques. Nevertheless, the view presented by Malthus is a completely pessimistic one. He argued that population always tends to outstrip any increase in food supply and other resources and that only when it reaches the absolute limit which can be sustained on available resources will it become stabilized by 'famine, vice and misery'. Throughout the nineteenth century the ideas developed by Malthus had relatively little impact. Improvements in transport technology and the opening up of New World grasslands for ranching and cultivation allowed Europe to feed its growing population with imported grain and meat. The crisis predicted by Malthus seemed very remote. However, in recent years many writers have attempted to apply the principles developed by Malthus to the contemporary world 'population explosion'. According to this **Neo-Malthusian** view, the widening gap between the present run-away population growth and the feeble growth of food supply is clear evidence that the gloomy predictions of Malthus were essentially correct.

On the other hand it is often pointed out that there are many ways in which the world output of food could be greatly increased. Possibilities exist for extending agriculture far beyond the 11% of the Earth's land surface which is at present cultivated. The development of new strains of seeds requiring a shorter time to mature and ripen might allow an extension of agriculture into areas which are at present unsuitable for production; irrigation schemes could permit further extensions of farming into arid and semi-arid areas; new farmland might be reclaimed from the sea, as has been done in the Netherlands; swamps might be drained, heathlands made productive and forests cleared. The elimination of pests and diseases might permit large-scale ranching on the savanna grasslands of the tropics. Then there are ways in which existing farmland could be made more productive by the development of higher-yielding, disease-resistant strains of seeds. The considerable success of Dr Norman Borlaug and other agronomists in initiating the so-called **Green Revolution** in the 1960s pointed the way in this direction. Greater use could be made of fertilizers and pesticides, and increased mechanization would improve farming efficiency. More productive breeds of livestock could also be developed by selective breeding. These various possibilities for increasing food supply would all require a high level of capital investment by national governments, as well as programmes of education to combat the deep-rooted traditions and resistance to change of most peasant farming communities. The potential wealth of the world's marine resources is usually mentioned in the context of this discussion. It is generally agreed that by systematic and controlled fishing, the seas and oceans could provide far more than the 2% of world protein supply at present obtained by haphazard methods which are destructive of fish stocks. Elimination of loss and waste of food caused by inadequate transport and storage facilities would also improve supplies. For example, 20% of the grain imported into India is lost to rats and decay. Finally, the possibilities also exist for producing protein synthetically from unicellular organisms such as bacteria, algae and yeasts. These can be grown in a culture-solution to produce a substance known as SCP (single cell protein) which could be a useful dietary supplement.

The fact that these possibilities do exist for increasing food production suggests that it may be wrong to adopt a Malthusian attitude of total pessimism towards the world food problem. The apocalypse is probably not just around the corner. Nevertheless, there is cause for genuine concern just as long as such a large proportion of the world's population is living at near-starvation level. Massive investment and international co-operation is needed on an unprecedented scale. Unfortunately, experience suggests that it may be a very long time before that is achieved.

Optimum population, overpopulation and underpopulation

Many writers, including Malthus, have discussed the question of what is the ideal or optimum population for any country. **Optimum population** may be defined as 'the size of population which allows the highest standard of living under present economic and technological conditions'. It has no absolute value. Criteria other than material welfare may also be used in defining 'optimum'. **Overpopulation** exists where there is 'an excess of population over utilized or developed resources'. It may result from a growth of population or a decline in resources, and is often characterized by low incomes, poor living standards, high unemployment, strong out-migration and high population density. Population density alone can never be used as an indicator of overpopulation. It must always be related to resource development. **Underpopulation** is relatively rare at the present time. It is defined as 'a population which is too small to fully utilize its resources, or a situation in which resources could support a larger population without any reduction in living standards'. The enormous territory of Canada with a population of only 23 million could be regarded as underpopulated.

Summary

Since about 1650 the world's population has been increasing at an accelerating rate. Current increase is about 1·9% per year which produces an annual increment of over 70 million. The demographic transition model is widely used in the study of national population growth, but there is no certainty that the developing nations will duplicate the earlier pattern of European growth. Increases in food production are not keeping pace with population growth and this is the cause of widespread hunger and starvation which constitutes one of the most serious problems facing the world today.

Chapter 18
Population Dynamics

In the previous two chapters reference was made to the dynamic nature of patterns of population density and distribution. The changes taking place in any area are the product of three factors which are referred to as the **components of population change** or the **basic demographic processes**. The three factors in question are: first, the number of births occurring in an area over a given period of time; second, the number of deaths occurring during the same time span; and third, the number of persons moving in and out of the area. In other words, population changes are the result of three processes: fertility, mortality and migration. Thus, considering population change over a given time span, the population at any point in time is equal to the total at an earlier point in time, plus the births, minus the deaths, plus immigration, and minus emigration. The latter processes may be combined into a single positive or negative value known as **net migration balance**. Changes in numbers over time may therefore be reduced to the following basic demographic equation:

$$P_2 = P_1 + B - D \pm M$$

The equation may be illustrated by reference to population change in the UK between 1971 and 1977. In 1971 the total UK population was 55,610,000. During the period 1971–77 there were 4,486,200 births, 4,009,200 deaths, and a negative net migration balance of 234,300 persons. By using these values in the equation it can be calculated that the 1977 total for the UK was 55,852,700. The difference between the first two components of the equation (births and deaths) constitutes what is termed **natural increase or decrease**. In this chapter the three components of population change will be examined in turn.

Fertility: Trends and determinants

Before discussing the spatial variations in fertility and their main determinants, it is necessary to consider how these variations can be measured and in what forms they can be expressed. The most commonly used of the various measures is **crude birth rate**, although it is unsatisfactory in one important respect. Crude birth rate is simply the ratio between the number of live births (usually in one year) and total population (usually a mid-year estimate for the year in question). Thus, the crude birth rate for the UK in 1977 was:

$$\frac{657{,}200 \text{ (total births 1977)}}{55{,}852{,}700 \text{ (total population 1977)}} \times 1{,}000 = 11 \cdot 8‰$$

Crude birth rate has the advantage of being easy to calculate, but it does not take into account the effect of age structure on birth rates. Consider two towns such as Worthing with a very high proportion of elderly retired people, and Stevenage, a new town with a high proportion of young married couples and relatively few old people. Any meaningful comparison of the fertility of the two towns would have to take into account their differing age structure. Crude birth rate fails to do this. To overcome this problem a more complex index known as **standardized birth rate** can be employed. This involves calculating what the birth rate for an area would have been if its age composition had been the same as that of the country as a whole. Having adjusted crude birth rate in that way, it is then possible to make valid comparisons of standardized rates for different towns and regions. Another useful measure is known as **gross reproduction rate**. This is defined as the average number of female babies born per 1,000 women during their reproductive period. This measure can be further refined into **net reproduction rate** to allow for the fact that not all female babies survive to reproductive age, nor do all those that survive actually have children themselves. During the period

	Crude birth rate	Crude death rate	Natural increase
Africa	46	20	26
North America	17	9	8
South & Central America	37	9	28
Asia (excluding USSR)	34	13	21
Europe (excluding USSR)	16	10	6
Oceania	23	10	13
USSR	18	8	10
World	31	13	18

Table 5. Birth rates, death rates and natural increase rates (per 1,000 population) by continents 1965–77

1961–71, gross and net reproduction rates for the UK were 1,300 and 1,260 respectively. It has been argued that a net reproduction rate of 1,000 (or 1·000 as it is often expressed) means that just enough female babies are born to maintain any population at its existing level.

World variations in fertility In 1977 crude birth rates for the various nations of the world ranged from 8·2‰ (Monaco) to 52·2‰ (Niger) with an average world value of 31‰. Countries with very high birth rates (often in excess of 40‰) are found in tropical Latin America, Central Africa and parts of South-East Asia and the Middle East. In contrast, countries with low birth rates (under 20‰) are found in Europe, North America and Oceania together with USSR and Japan. Table 5 includes variations in birth rates by continents.

It has been said that 'no other single characteristic distinguishes developed areas from developing areas as clearly as does birth rate'. Most of the developed nations have been characterized by a progressive reduction in birth rates since the late nineteenth century. As seen in figure 70, the reduction has not been a steady one, nor has the rate and timing of the reduction been the same in all nations. Contrary to the general trend, a period of higher birth rate occurred in many Western countries during the years after World War II. Nevertheless, the overall trend has been clearly downwards. Some reductions in birth rate have also occurred in the developing nations, but the gap between developed and developing nations still remains very wide. India, for example, reduced its birth rate from 47‰ to 36‰ between 1920 and 1977, but its present level is still over three times that of the UK.

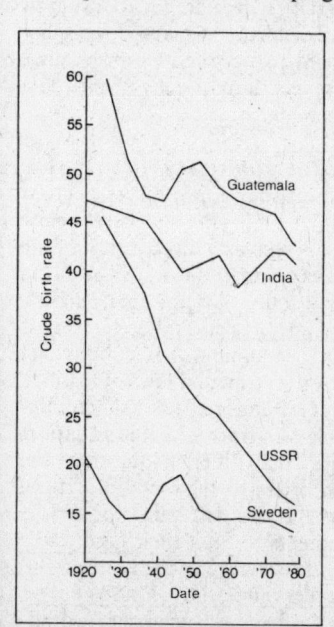

Figure 70. Decline of birth rate in selected countries 1920–77

Influences on birth rates Many writers discussing the influences on fertility make a basic distinction between 'natural' and 'controlled' birth rates. The term **natural birth rate** is used to refer to the situation in many developing countries with crude birth rates in excess of 40‰. In these countries, techniques of birth control are not widely practised, and it is often argued that birth rates are determined essentially by social customs and taboos (such as attaching great importance to producing a male heir) and religious beliefs and traditions, as well as diet and the general state of health of the population. For example, the demographer, Josué de Castro, in his book *The Geography of Hunger* demonstrated that a high level of fertility is characteristic of the poorest peoples and those most seriously undernourished. The consistently high birth rate for all Muslim countries – for example, Algeria and Saudi Arabia with crude birth rates of 48·7‰ and 49·5‰ respectively – indicates the influence of religious prescription on fertility. Some would even add various environmental factors, such as climate, to these influences on so-called natural birth rates. A number of studies have drawn attention to seasonal variations in the number of births in many developing nations (the same phenomenon used to be true of Europe too), and have suggested that human sexual activity may show some response to seasonal changes of climate.

The term **controlled birth rate** or **voluntary birth rate** is used to describe the situation in most developed nations. These countries have birth rates of less than 20‰ – in many cases below 10‰ – and the low level of fertility is seen as a direct result of the widespread use of various techniques of birth control. 'In addition to the primeval factors in the birth rate – natural environment, biological make-up and traditional customs and taboos – there is another fundamental one, which is the human will. It is this which permits individuals to escape from the elemental laws of instinct, and families to adjust the number of children to their circumstances or their desires.' (J. Beaujeu-Garnier.) In this situation, any analysis of birth rates requires that different questions are asked from those which are appropriate to the study of natural birth rates. In particular it is necessary to determine the factors which influence the decision of parents to limit their family to a particular size. A great deal of work has been carried out on this question by sociologists, demographers and others. Family limitation has been shown to be related to income, social class, educational attainments of parents, race, religion, cycles of national prosperity and depression, and a host of other factors. Clearly, in a situation such as this, in which so many variables are operating, it is difficult to ascribe a particular level of importance to any one specific factor. J. Clarke hinted at the complexity of these interrelated factors when he wrote that 'the fertility of any community is affected by a wide range of direct and indirect influences, which act as differentials. For example, there tend to be substantial differences between the fertility of urban and rural populations, negroes and whites, Catholics and Protestants, miners and office workers, rich and poor. Such differences determine regional patterns of fertility which are of special interest to geographers'.

The problem of forecasting birth rates and of understanding the factors influencing parental decisions about family size can be illustrated by reference to recent birth rate trends in the UK. Contrary to almost all the official forecasts, the UK birth rate fell steeply between 1964 and 1977. Every year from 1965 onwards the Government Actuary calculated figures for the future population of Britain on the assumption that birth rate would quickly recover towards the peak year of 1964. Every year except one, the actual birth rate showed a further fall. After rising for the previous ten years, a long decline in birth rate started in 1964 and eventually fell below replacement level in 1973. As a result, the population of Britain actually decreased in 1974, the first time that had happened in peacetime since the early 18th century. The reasons for the decline are still not clear. The introduction of the contraceptive pill in 1963 and the legalization of abortion in 1968

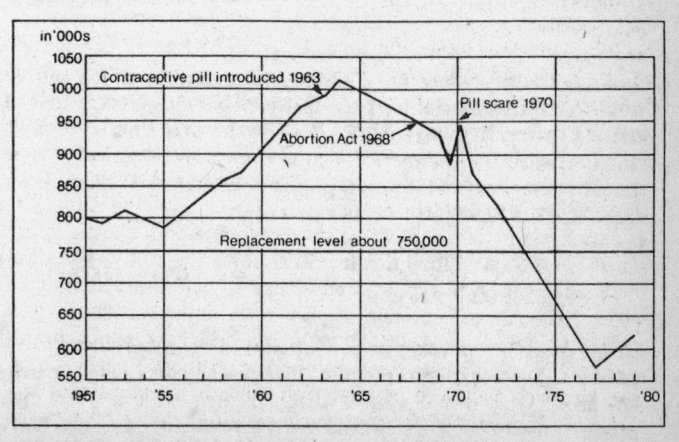

Figure 71. Numbers of live births in the UK 1951–79

were clearly important factors. It is interesting to note that a scare about the safety of 'the pill' in 1970 was followed by a short-lived 'baby boom' in 1971. But contraception and abortion are only the means to an end. It is still not apparent why people are making use of those facilities to have 25% fewer children than they did in the early 1960s. The explanation of the Office of Population Censuses and Surveys is that families are only postponing having children. They will eventually catch up, it is argued, and over their complete child-bearing cycle will have families very nearly as large as before. Since the production of a family can be spread over twenty years or more, it can take a long time to discover what the completed family size is going to be. A slight upward turn in birth rate since 1978 gives some support to that hypothesis.

Patterns of mortality

Mortality, the second of the components of population change, differs from fertility in that it tends to be more stable and predictable and less prone to short-term fluctuations. With very few exceptions – the recent UK situation described above is one of them – death rate in almost every part of the world is lower than birth rate. However, that is not to underestimate its importance in determining patterns of population change. It is the decline in mortality, rather than any increase in fertility, which has been largely responsible for the population explosion of the present century.

As with fertility, there are a number of measures which can be used to express mortality. The most widely used index is that of **crude mortality rate** or **crude death rate**. This is simply a ratio between the number of deaths over a given period of time (usually one year) and the total population. A worked example for the UK in 1977 is given below:

$$\frac{655,300 \text{ (total deaths 1977)}}{55,852,700 \text{ (total population 1977)}} \times 1,000 = 11.7‰$$

Crude mortality rate can be converted to a **standardized mortality rate** to take into account the age structure of any particular area. One would expect that an area with a very high proportion of old people would have a relatively high mortality rate. A standardized mortality rate simply makes an allowance for that fact. Another useful measure is **average expectation of life at birth**. By its very nature this is a standardized measure and is unaffected by variations in age structure. Mortality may also be expressed by means of **age-specific and sex-specific death rates**. Figure 72 shows a set of values of this type for the UK in 1977. Notice that more deaths occur in early childhood than in later childhood, adolescence and early adult life. Age-specific rates start to rise significantly from about age 40 to give a J-shaped curve for the whole life span. The deaths of very young children are often considered separately from other deaths by means of an **infant mortality rate**. Infant mortality is usually defined as the number of deaths of infants under the age of one year, expressed per 1,000 live births. It has been described by Lewis Mumford as 'perhaps the most sensitive barometer of the fitness of the social environment for human life'. In Britain, for example, infant mortality is more than twice as high in the mining and old industrial towns of South Wales and northern England than it is in the middle-class dormitory towns of south-east England.

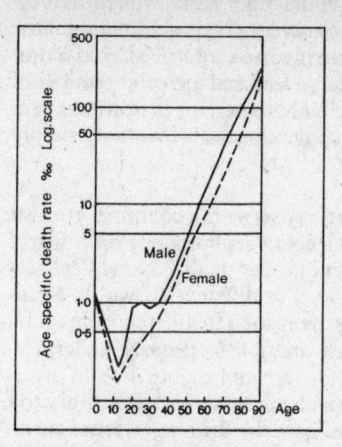

Figure 72. Age-specific death rates by sex, UK 1977

World variations in mortality In 1977 crude mortality rates ranged from 3·8‰ in Brunei to 28·1‰ in Bangladesh, with an overall world value of 13‰. Table 5 shows mortality values by continents calculated for the period 1965–77. Countries with mortality rates significantly above the world average are found chiefly in West and Central Africa, the Middle East and South-East Asia. In these regions of high death rate a large proportion of the total deaths are those of infants and very young children. In many Central African countries infant mortality accounts for up to one-third of the total deaths in any one year. Mortality rates below the world average are experienced in North America, Europe, Oceania, parts of South America, USSR and Japan. During the present century death rates have been reduced in every part of the world as a result of improved medical services and campaigns against infectious diseases. Infant mortality has been reduced and the average expectation of life has risen worldwide, so that it can be said with some justification that 'there is now much greater equality in the face of death'. On the other hand, while the average length of life has been increased everywhere, it does not follow that the quality of life has necessarily been improved. Reduction of death rate means more mouths to feed and a greater number of elderly people to be supported. Unless reductions in death rate are matched by increases in resource development then they simply create a new set of problems.

Regional variations of death rate within countries are also of interest. The same basic influences which operate on a world scale, such as standards of nutrition, the quality of medical services, hygiene and housing, also act as differentials within countries. In many cases these factors are related to differences in social class. That is to say, the poorest and most seriously underprivileged sections of any population are obliged to live in overcrowded substandard housing and are unable to afford a good balanced diet or proper medical care. In Britain, regional variations in mortality show a close correlation with variations in the distribution of different social classes. For similar reasons the black population of the USA has a much higher death rate at all ages than the white population. Regional variations in mortality can also be related to occupation structure. In Britain, communities based on mining and deep sea fishing, both occupations with a high level of accident risk and health hazards, have above-average mortality rates. In a more general way, significant differences can also be noted between urban and rural areas. Despite a better provision of medical services, urban areas with their overcrowded housing and often poor working conditions, high traffic densities and atmospheric pollution, have higher death rates than country areas.

Causes of death may be divided into two main categories; namely, **exogenetic** or environmental causes of death and **endogenetic** or degenerative causes. Exogenetic causes are the result of environmental conditions and include various infections, pulmonary and digestive diseases associated with contaminated food and water supply and inadequate housing and hygiene. Typical examples include malaria, typhoid, dysentery and influenza. Endogenetic causes are the result of the failure or gradual exhaustion of body functions. Examples include senility, heart disease and cancer.

A striking feature of countries with low death rates is that they show a predominance of endogenetic causes of death, whereas those with high death rates are dominated by exogenetic causes. The demographic transition described in the previous chapter is therefore accompanied by changes in the main killing diseases. In the primitive type of demographic regime where there is little control over disease, environmental causes hold sway but are progressively eliminated until, in the low fluctuating type of demographic regime, heart disease and cancer are left as the main killers. Such is the situation in Britain today. Just over a century ago about 30% of the deaths in Britain were caused by infectious diseases such as typhoid, scarlet fever and tuberculosis. Today less than 0·5% of deaths result from infectious diseases. On the other hand, deaths from heart disease, cerebrovascular disease and cancer have risen steadily to the point where together they now account for almost 75% of all the deaths in Britain.

Migration

Migration, the third component of population change, is usually defined as 'a movement of population involving a permanent change of residence of substantial duration'. Such a definition clearly excludes seasonal or short-term movements such as transhumance, tourism and commuting, as well as nomadism, but is ambiguous in respect of certain other types of movement. What is to be regarded as a 'substantial duration' of time? If a person leaves the UK on business for a year should he or she be recorded as an emigrant, or should a five year absence be regarded as the qualifying time? For reasons such as this, migration statistics should always be treated with caution. Different countries define migration in different ways and use varying methods for the collection of their migration statistics. The problem is made more difficult by the enormous variety of types of migratory movement. J. Clarke has noted that 'we read of seasonal, temporary, periodic and permanent migrations, of spontaneous, forced, impelled, free and planned migrations, as well as internal, external, interregional, international, continental and intercontinental migrations.... Moreover, many migrations which are similar in cause are different in character, and *vice versa*'. In the face of this complexity there is a tendency to refer simply to **international migration** which involves the crossing of national boundaries, and **internal migration** which refers to movements of population within national units. International migration causes a change in absolute numbers in both the sending and receiving countries, while internal migration produces a change in the distribution of population but has no effect on total numbers.

The causes of both types of migration are similar. Studies of the motivation for migratory movements are usually organized in terms of so-called **'push-pull' factors**. The 'push' factors are the adverse conditions in the sending area which stimulate individuals and families to make a change of residence. These include a wide variety of factors such as low wages, housing shortages, poor employment prospects, inadequate social amenities, and even adverse climatic and other environmental conditions. The 'pull' factors are the attractions (real or imagined) of the destination area. These include higher wages, improved housing and employment prospects, and the physical attraction of a particular environment. This concept of 'push-pull' factors provides a useful framework for the study of various types of internal migration such as rural depopulation, urbanization and retirement migration, but is less satisfactory when applied to international migration. Internal migration is a relatively free, spontaneous process, but international migration flows are distorted by a variety of legal and political barriers such as entry restrictions, quotas and the like.

Models and theories of migration Many attempts have been made by geographers and others to formulate general models and theories to explain patterns of migration. As early as the 1880s, E. G. Ravenstein presented papers on *The Laws of Migration* to the Royal Society in London. Ravenstein's main proposition was that migration occurs in a series of stages. As he put it, 'the great body of migrants only proceed a short distance and consequently there takes place a universal shifting or displacement of the population which produces currents of migration setting in the direction of the main centres of commerce and industry which absorb the migrants'. He also noted that 'the inhabitants of a country immediately surrounding a town of rapid growth flock into it; the gaps thus left by the rural population are filled by the migrants from more remote districts, until the attractive force of a rapidly growing city makes its influence felt, step by step, in the most remote corner of the kingdom. Migrants enumerated in a certain centre of absorption consequently grow less with the distance proportionately to the size of the population that furnishes them'. This basic principle proposed by Ravenstein is now referred to as **chain or stage migration**.

Also implicit in Ravenstein's writing is the idea that the volume of migration between any two centres of population is related to the distance separating them. This same concept has been expressed more precisely by G. K. Zipf in his **Inverse Distance Law** which states that 'the volume of migration is inversely proportional to the distance travelled by migrants'. This may be expressed by the following formula

$$N_{ij} \propto \frac{1}{D_{ij}}$$

in which N_{ij} is the number of migrants moving from town i to town j and D_{ij} is the distance between the two towns.

Other researchers have examined not only the effect of distance on migration, but have also taken into account the influence of 'opportunities' in the fields of housing and employment. For example, the **Theory of Intervening Opportunity** developed by S. Stouffer suggests that 'the number of persons going a given distance is directly proportional to the number of opportunities at that distance and inversely proportional to the number of intervening opportunities'. Again, this may be expressed mathematically as

$$N_{ij} \propto \frac{O_j}{O_{ij}}$$

in which N_{ij} is the number of migrants moving between towns i and j, O_j the number of opportunities at j, and O_{ij} the number of opportunities between i and j.

Another interesting and rewarding approach to migration flows involves the use of what is termed a **gravity model**. Gravity models used in social sciences are so called because of their analogy with Newton's law of universal gravitation which states that 'any two bodies attract each other with a force that is proportional to the product of their masses and inversely proportional to the square of the distance between them'. In migration studies, the amount of interaction or movement between two cities may be estimated by substituting population size for 'mass' and by expressing distance in various forms such as geographic distance, time or cost. In its simplest form the gravity model may be expressed by the following formula:

$$N_{ij} \propto \frac{P_i \times P_j}{D{ij}^2}$$

N_{ij} represents the number of migrants between towns i and j, P_i and P_j are the populations of the two towns, and D_{ij} is the distance between the towns. The formula tells us that as the size of one or both of the towns increases so does the volume of migration between them. It also indicates that the greater the distance between two centres the smaller the amount of interaction between them. In other words, distance has a frictional effect on movement. Geographers in fact use the term **friction of distance** to refer to this latter effect.

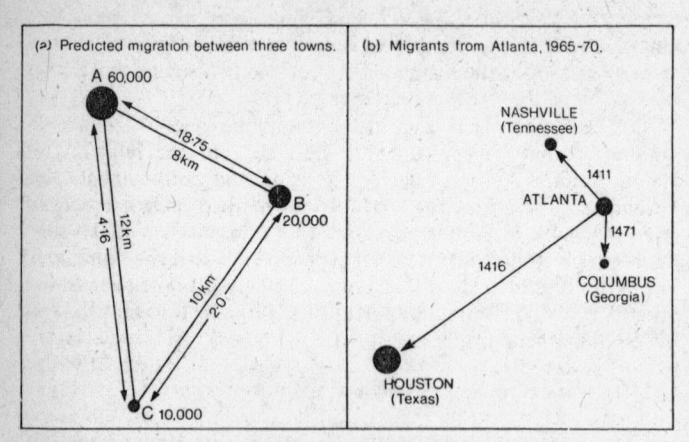

Figure 73. Aspects of the gravity model

Figure 73a shows the location, sizes and distances apart of three hypothetical towns, together with the estimated volume of migration between them according to the gravity model formula. For example, the predicted movement between A and B is arrived at by multiplying the populations of the two towns and dividing the result by the square of the distance between them.

$$N_{AB} \propto \frac{P_A \times P_B}{D_{AB^2}} = \frac{60 \times 20}{8^2} = 18 \cdot 75 \text{ units}$$

Figure 73b shows how the gravity model helps us to understand the actual amount of movement between four cities in the USA over a five year period. The number of migrants from Atlanta to Houston, Nashville and Columbus (Georgia) is almost equal. Houston is the largest of the three destinations but lies furthest from Atlanta; Nashville is smaller than Houston but closer to Atlanta, while Columbus is the smallest destination city but is also the closest to Atlanta. The attraction of each destination appears to be related to a combination of distance and size according to the prediction of the gravity model.

In recent years there has been something of a reaction against the abstract, impersonal, mathematical approach to migration typified by the gravity model. More attention is being given to the fact that any migration flow is the product of innumerable individual and family decisions about when and where to migrate. Increasingly, therefore, geographers are seeking to understand why people decide to migrate, how they perceive alternative destinations and how they make decisions relating to these things. This is referred to as the **behavioural approach**.

Summary

Population changes are the product of the three components of population change: fertility, mortality and migration. Values for fertility vary widely between developed and developing nations, but everywhere are affected by a wide range of socio-economic factors. Mortality rates show less variation, but are affected by nutritional standards, housing and medical services. Lowering of death rate is accompanied by a change from exogenetic to endogenetic causes of death. Migration, which is divided into internal and international migration for study purposes, has long attracted the attention of geographers who have formulated a number of models and theories of migration to aid analysis.

Chapter 19
Population Composition

The terms **population composition** or **population structure** are used to describe those characteristics of any population which can be measured, however inadequately. In reality the terms refer to those aspects of population for which census data are available. Geographical studies of population composition normally make reference to the age structure, sex composition, occupation structure and ethnic composition of particular populations, although elements such as language, religion, family and household composition and marital status are sometimes also examined. However, it is more usual for these latter aspects of population to be studied by sociologists rather than by geographers. In the study of population composition the field of geography clearly overlaps with a number of other social sciences.

A distinction is often drawn between the **physical** or **innate characteristics** of any population, such as age, sex and race, and the **social** or **acquired characteristics** such as occupation, language and marital status. In this chapter just three aspects of population composition will be examined; namely, age structure, sex ratio and occupation structure. It is hoped that reference to these three characteristics will serve to illustrate the geographical approach to population structure, which, as always, places emphasis on the spatial variations of these elements.

Age structure

The term age structure refers to the numbers of males and females of different ages within a given population. The age structure of any population is a product of the processes of population change (described in the previous chapter) as they have operated during the lifetime of the oldest member of that population. In a sense age structure is a record of the demographic history and to some extent the socio-economic history of an area over a period of about a century. Age structure is a factor of very considerable economic, social and even political importance, since it has a direct influence on, for example, patterns of purchasing and consumption, on the size and characteristics of the labour force in any area, as well as the type and range of social and welfare facilities required to serve the needs of a given population. It is not surprising, therefore, that a number of well-established techniques are available for the analysis of age structure.

Since the average age of a very large population provides only a very limited indication of its age characteristics, it is normal to use a system of **age groups** for the analysis of age structure. Three age groups, which are defined in various ways by different authorities, are normally used for this purpose.

1. **Infants and adolescents** (0–14 or 0–19 years) This group is largely non-productive and is essentially supported by the second group.
2. **Adults** (15–59, 15–64, 20–59 or 20–64 years) This group is the most active economically, and basically supports the other two groups. It is also the most mobile of the three age groups. It is sometimes divided into two sub-groups; young adults and older adults, with a division at age 35.
3. **The aged** (60 and over or 65 and over) This age group is largely non-productive and for the most part is supported by the adult population. A striking characteristic of this group is the fact that it contains a predominance of females.

By examining the percentages of population in each of the three age groups, a clearer picture of age structure emerges than might be obtained by simply calculating a mean age for any population. In fact, on this basis three distinct types of age structure can be identified; namely, a **West European type** with about 30% children and about 15% aged population, a **United States type** with about 40% children and about 10% aged, and a **Brazilian type** with 45 to 55% children and only about 5% aged population. Most developing nations with their very high birth rates and relatively high mortality rates fall into this latter category. It should be noted that the proportion of adult population is lowest in the Brazilian type of age structure; in some cases up to 60% of the population consists of economically non-active children and aged people who have to be supported by the remaining 40% of the population. This is, of course, a very heavy burden and makes economic progress difficult.

Age structure can also be studied by means of a graphical device known as a **population pyramid**. A population pyramid consists of a vertical scale divided into either single years or five-year age groups. On either side of this vertical scale a series of horizontal bars are drawn. The bars on the left represent the percentage of males in each age group, and those on the right represent the percentage of females in each age group. With a little practice it is possible to derive a great deal of information from the shape of any population pyramid. Long-term changes in birth rate and death rate show up very clearly, as well as lesser influences on age structure such as the persistent in- or out-migration of a particular age group or sex, large-scale wars, and even major epidemics. Although no two national population pyramids are ever exactly the same, it is nevertheless possible to identify four basic types. These are shown in figure 74.

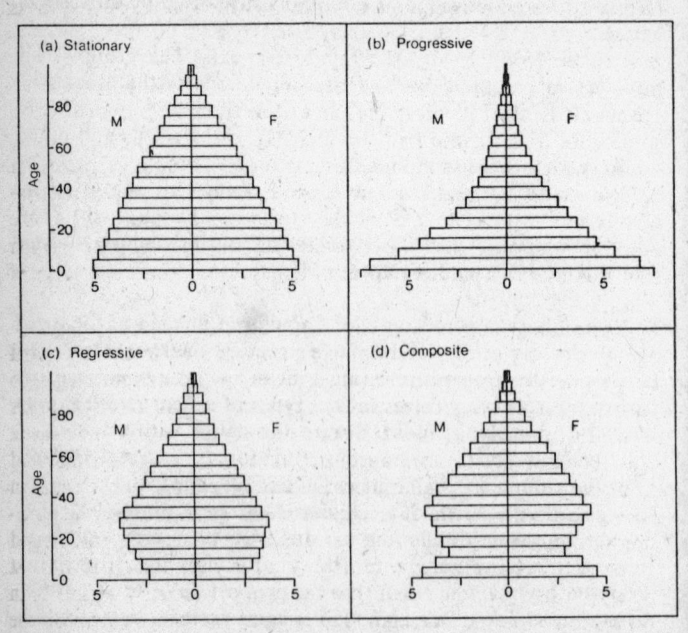

Figure 74. (a) Stationary, (b) progressive, (c) regressive and (d) composite forms of population pyramid

A **stationary population** is one with stable mortality and fertility rates over a long period of time. Such a situation produces a regular and evenly tapering pyramid as shown in figure 74a. A **progressive population** is characterized by a high and increasing birth rate combined with a high level of mortality. The resultant pyramid, shown in figure 74b, is broad-based and sharply tapering. A consistent decline in birth rate over a long period of time and a relatively low mortality rate are the main characteristics of a **regressive population**. The associated pyramid, shown in figure 74c, with its narrow base, is sometimes described as 'bell-shaped'. As well as these three basic forms of pyramid there are numerous **composite** or **intermediate types** which display a combination of two or more of the other forms. An example is shown in figure 74d. This latter type of pyramid is the result of one or more changes in fertility or mortality trends during the last hundred years or so. For example, a long period of declining birth rate followed by a period of increasing birth rate will produce a pyramid which is regressive in its upper part and progressive at its base.

Sex composition

Although the numbers of the two sexes are not widely different in most areas, there are, nevertheless, localized examples of imbalance. The **sex ratio** of any area is normally expressed as the number of males per 100 or 1,000 females or *vice versa*, although the numbers of each sex may also be expressed as a percentage of the total population.

It is a feature of the human population that male births exceed female births. For example, in the UK in 1977 there were 106 males born for every 100 females. The same imbalance of the sexes is found in every set of birth statistics which may be examined. The reasons for this are not clear. Some writers have suggested that the cause may be biological, while others are of the opinion that the cause is social. It is suggested, for example, that the widespread completion of families on the achievement of a male child could produce an imbalance. But what is clear is that in almost every part of the world male mortality is consistently higher than female mortality at all ages. Differential mortality rates for the two sexes are particularly evident in the case of infant mortality. What this means is that the excess of males at birth is gradually eliminated, so that from the age of about 30 years upwards there is a progressively larger excess of females in the population. There are a few exceptions to this generalization, notably in those countries where women suffer a deprived and subordinate role in society or are subject to unusually high levels of maternal mortality. The fact that women have a considerably longer expectation of life than males in almost every country of the world confirms the validity of the general statement. However, this 'normal' sequence of a male excess at birth being gradually transformed into a female excess by differential mortality rates is complicated by the process of migration, which is sex-selective.

Migration and sex ratios As early as the 1880s, E. G. Ravenstein pointed out in his *Laws of Migration* that 'females are more migratory than males over short distances'. Ravenstein's assertion was based on his observations of the sex-selectivity of internal migration in Britain during the second half of the 19th century when large numbers of young women migrated to the towns and cities to work in domestic service or light industry. This same type of sex-selectivity noted almost one hundred years ago still applies today. As a result there is a predominance of females in London and south-east England and other highly urbanized regions, while in regions with a predominantly rural population, such as Lincolnshire and East Anglia, the sex ratio shows an excess of males. Among the urban centres of the UK, those which show the highest proportion of males are military towns, mining towns and centres of heavy industry.

In the developing nations the situation is the reverse of that found in Britain and Western Europe. In many parts of Africa and Asia, for examples, males searching for employment form the bulk of the migrants to the cities, while most females remain in the villages where they are often responsible for tending crops and livestock in the absence of male members of the family or community. Certain of the black townships around Johannesburg in South Africa have as few as 17 females per 100 males in the 15 to 45 age-group. Indian towns too are characterized by a similar imbalance of the sexes. Calcutta, for example, has 175 males for every 100 females.

In the past, international migration was also dominated by young single males. As a result the populations of Australia and the USA at the turn of the century had 110 and 106 males respectively for every 100 females. At the same time many source areas of migrants, such as parts of Italy and Scandinavia, were depleted of their young adult males. A more recent example is provided by the movement of West Indians to Britain during the 1950s and early 1960s. The majority of these early West Indian migrants to Britain were males, although in many cases wives and dependents followed later, after the male head of the family had established a place of work and residence. In recent years international migration has tended to become more balanced between the two sexes, although the former pattern still persists in the case of migration to 'pioneer' regions or regions of physical hardship. The sex ratio of Alaska with 135 males per 100 females provides a well-known example of this latter situation.

Occupation structure

The proportion of any population which is economically active – that is to say, employed in remunerative occupations – varies quite considerably from country to country. The size of any national workforce depends very largely upon the age structure of the population, but is also influenced by a wide variety of social and economic factors. Published statistics indicate that employed population as a percentage of total population varies from 24% in the Ivory Coast to 55% in the USSR. The proportion of 'active' population is generally higher in the economically developed nations than in the developing nations, with typical values of about 50% and 30% respectively. Closer examination of such figures shows that the main cause of these differences lies in the size of the female workforce. Whereas the proportion of 'active' males varies within only relatively narrow limits, the proportion of females in paid occupations shows enormous variations. For example, in Pakistan less than 4% of the female population is economically active. This is clearly a reflection of Muslim beliefs and the social customs and traditions of that country. At the other end of the scale, more than 50% of the female population of the Soviet Union and Romania are in paid occupations, a situation made possible by the liberation of many women from domestic work by the provision of crêches, nurseries and other social services.

Significant variations in the relative size and sex composition of the working population also exist within countries. The most striking contrasts are those between urban and rural areas. Most types of urban employment provide the security of pension schemes for the elderly, so that the length of working life is usually shorter in towns than in the country where similar benefits are less common. For example, many farm-workers are in employment for virtually the whole of their lives. Towns also provide more varied and rewarding employment opportunities for women. This is the main reason for the type of migration mentioned earlier in which large numbers of women of working age migrate from village to town.

Occupations are of an almost infinite variety, and numerous systems of classification have been proposed. For example, the ILO (International Labour Organization) distinguishes nine groups of occupations. These are: (1) Agriculture, forestry, hunting and fishing; (2) mining and quarrying; (3) manufacturing; (4) building and construction; (5) electricity, gas, water and sanitary services; (6) commerce, insurance and banking; (7) transportation, warehousing and communications; (8) other services, and (9) occupations not classifiable elsewhere. National census reports classify occupational statistics in a variety of other ways, so that at national level there is a very low level of comparability of published statistics. French statistics, for example, are classified very largely on the basis of their social and professional characteristics, and cannot be compared directly with their British counterparts. In the face of such difficulties a solution which is often adopted is to simply group occupations into three or four very large, basic categories.

1. **Primary activities** (Agriculture, forestry, fishing and extractive industries).
2. **Secondary activities** (Manufacturing including building and construction work).
3. **Tertiary activities** (Transport, communications, wholesaling, retailing and other service trades and professions).
4. **Quaternary activities** (Research and higher education).

The latter category, quaternary activities, is a relatively new addition to this basic system of occupational classification. Its use has emanated from the USA where the quaternary sector forms a small but rapidly growing section of the workforce.

Ignoring the quaternary group of activities which only form a significant employment category in a few countries, it can be noted that the proportions of workers in the other three groups vary according to the stage of economic development of any country. In developing countries 80% or more of the workforce is employed in the primary sector (chiefly agriculture), with a mere 5% in secondary activities and about 15% in tertiary activities (chiefly petty trading and domestic service). An example is given in Table 6 opposite.

The processes of rural depopulation, urbanization and industrialization produce striking changes in employment structure. In the economically advanced nations a mere 5% of the workforce re-

Example	Primary sector	Secondary sector	Tertiary sector	Economic stage
Sudan	86·4	5·2	8·4	Developing
Ghana	59·6	16·5	23·9	Intermediate
Australia	11·6	44·8	43·6	Developed
USA	4·9	28·6	66·5	Highly developed

Table 6. Distribution of workforce by industrial sectors, 1976

mains in agriculture and other primary activities, while approximately 50% is employed in manufacturing and a further 45% in service trades. A final stage of development involves the transfer of more and more workers into the service sector at the expense of the other two categories. In the USA 66% of the workforce is now employed in the tertiary sector, and far more workers are employed in support services than actually produce material goods.

Summary

The qualities of any population can be referred to collectively as the composition or structure of any population. Physical characteristics, such as age structure, are essentially the product of the processes of demographic change which have operated in any area in recent decades; social characteristics, such as occupation structure, are determined by recent economic and social changes. Studies of population composition often make reference to age structure, sex ratio, marital status, family and household structure, language, religion and many other elements, although only three characteristics have been selected for study in this chapter.

Chapter 20
The Geography of Economic Activity

Economic geography is concerned with the study of man's economic activity over the surface of the Earth, and there are three basic inter-related questions to be answered. What type of economic activity is taking place? Where is it taking place, not only in absolute terms, but also in relation to all other types of economic activity? Why is it taking place where it is?

This study of **form, pattern and process** is fundamental to all aspects of geography. In geomorphology, for example, features typical of glaciated landscapes are fjords. Their form, measured by their cross and longitudinal profiles, has to be established as has their distribution normally on the western sides of the continents between latitudes 55° and 70° N and S. These can then be explained by the processes which have formed them, namely the erosive powers of ice-borne rocks in glaciers. Similarly, in the geography of settlement, the form of major industrial towns, as measured by the size and nature of their CBDs' (see p. 295), industrial zones and suburbs has to be established, as has the pattern of their distribution in the economically advanced countries in the middle latitudes. These can then be explained by the processes which have formed them, namely the processes of industrialization and urbanization.

There are, therefore, two basic problems to be solved in economic geography, as there are in all aspects of geography, the problem of description and the problem of explanation.

The problem of description

Two major aspects of the geography of economic activity have to be described: the **forms** of economic activity and their **patterns** over the surface of the earth.

As described in the previous chapter, the **forms** of economic activity can be subdivided into four major groups. Fishing, forestry, agriculture and mining are **primary** activities concerned with the production of raw materials for foodstuffs and industrial use. These materials are then processed, fabricated or manufactured in the **secondary** group which covers manufacturing industry. The exchange and distribution of these products of primary and secondary activities through systems of transport and wholesale and retail distribution networks forms a major part of the **tertiary** group of activities which is concerned also with the provision of personal services through the service trades and professions. With the increasing complexity of economic activity a further subdivision is now used, and **quaternary** activities can be recognized which are concerned with research and development, education and communications. Of course, all these activities are interlinked, but as noted on page 201, the relative proportions in any one country vary with the level of economic development that has been achieved.

The forms of economic activity can be studied either **regionally**, to produce an industrial geography of Germany or an agricultural geography of Denmark, or they can be studied **systematically**, to produce a geography of dairying or of the steel industry. In both cases a fundamental task will be to identify **patterns of economic activity** within which two basic components need to be considered. First, it is necessary to identify and describe the **distribution** of economic activity. This involves not only general distributions but also specific locations. When, for example, the oil refining industry in Britain is examined, it is necessary to explain not only why almost all of the refineries have coastal locations, but also why Fawley was built on the western side of Southampton Water and not on the eastern side. Similarly, the description of distributions also involves the measurement of quantity, because it will be important to know not only where the refineries have been built but also their size and number. This creates problems because there are many ways of measuring size, such as physical output, area occupied, numbers employed and so on, and different measures can give very different results.

The second component of pattern is concerned with **relationships**, because a specific economic activity does not operate in total isolation but is part of a much greater interconnected whole, and the nature and the pattern of these connections need to be analysed. These connections are of a number of types, the simplest constituting basic lines of communication such as roads or railways. Rather more complex are the functional linkages that operate in particular industries, such as those between sheep farming, textiles and the clothing industry, or between iron-ore mining, steelmaking and motor-car assembly. Such activities also include many lateral linkages. At the most complex level, the whole range of economic activity can be analysed as a **system**. A system can be defined as 'a set of objects, together with the relationships between the objects and between their attributes', and the study of human activity within a systems framework can give coherence to what are often apparently unrelated activities. The over-all functioning of economic and social systems is not the main focus of the geographer, who is much more concerned with their geographical aspects. These aspects involve the study of, first, the **spatial system** of human activity as man interacts with man over the surface of the earth through his economic and social activities, and secondly, the **ecological system** as man interacts with the physical environment to exploit its wealth. The task of the geographer is to identify the various elements in the system, understand how they work, discover how they are related to each other and then study their interaction as a functioning whole. This **systems analysis** approach could ideally provide a framework for the whole range of human activity but the size and complexity of reality necessitates the subdivision of the global system into its more manageable components (see also page 9).

It is also important to identify different **types of spatial pattern**, and, to facilitate this, attempts have been made to study human geometry, or the distribution of man in geographical space. The three basic characteristics of geometrical space – point, line and area – have been applied to geographical space in the form of locations, interactions and regions. In the analysis of geographical space, the **location** of settlements, factories or farms can be seen as point patterns, and these can be described as being regular, random or clustered. If locations can be seen as points, then the connections between them can be viewed as lines along which **interactions** take place. These interactions involve flows of people, goods, services and information and the system of interchange can be studied as a vast functioning network made up of points and lines which can be subdivided into a number of smaller networks. Finally, the ways in which areas of the earth's surface are organized and subdivided need study to identify the distinctive divisions of space which are known as **regions**. There have been many attempts to recognize sensible divisions of geographical space, but the aim has always been the same, to identify areas which have a central unity and which are different from surrounding areas. Early attempts produced **formal** or homogeneous regions based on the uniformity given by a particular characteristic such as physical condition or agricultural activity.

However, regions can be more profitably seen as systems or **functional units** and the idea of the city region has gained wide acceptance. A city region is the area around a city which is served by the city for shopping facilities, jobs and services, and which in turn supplies the city with food, water, labour and so on (Chap. 30). Unfortunately it is not possible to divide space without overlapping between regions, and regions are probably best seen as ideals or models rather than an objective reality; nevertheless, the idea of regions can be very useful. **Programming regions** are a third type and are used to designate areas for specific purposes. The Tennessee Valley Authority was one of the first programming regions and was intended to co-ordinate the efforts of seven states in improving economic and physical conditions in the valley of the Tennessee after 1933. Economic planning regions are now a common feature of government activity in many countries and are used in promoting and aiding regional policy (page 250).

The problem of explanation

However, description is only the first step and increased attention is being given to identifying and analysing the reasons for particular forms and patterns of human activity. The study of spatial processes is an essential element in the **explanation** of the geography of economic activity.

The process of economic activity involves man in using the Earth to supply his needs and wants. This interaction between man and the physical environment produces **resources** which may be defined as anything man needs or wants in order to live. Since wants vary from time to time, from place to place and from society to society, and since many resources are not in unlimited supply, resources must be regarded as a relative rather than an absolute concept (page 160). Economically resources can be classified into **renewable resources** which include biological resources such as plants and animals, and sources of energy such as HEP, tides or wind; and **non-renewable resources** which include the fossil fuels and minerals, the increasing use of which raises questions about their potential exhaustion. The use of a resource involves a **resource process** in which the resource is extracted, used and returned as waste to the environment. Concern is also being expressed about the effect of environmental pollution at each stage in the process (page 152).

Despite the concern about resource exhaustion and the problem of pollution the **demand** for resources is increasing rapidly and is dependent on two basic factors. First, the nature of the demand depends on the type of society. Industrial societies have demands that are different from agricultural societies, and even within industrial societies demand will differ according to differences in economic, social and political attitudes and historical tradition. All societies are bound by custom and taboo but their importance varies enormously between societies. Second, the volume of demand depends on the size of the population measured both absolutely and in terms of the standard of living. Thus, other things being equal, two people will consume twice as many resources as one, but a person in an advanced industrial economy may consume forty times as many resources in his lifetime as some one in a developing country.

Unfortunately, the **supply** of resources is rising less rapidly than demand. Resources are created by the interaction of man and the physical environment and the supply is affected by four basic factors, the first of which is the physical availability of a commodity that man wants. Water may be needed in the Sahara but it simply is not available. Second, technology represents man's ability to utilize commodities and thus turn them into resources. Nuclear fusion could produce unlimited energy but it is currently beyond our capabilities. Third, the economic costs of extraction or transport may be too high to utilize a mineral, but if the price rises above the cost then it becomes an active resource. Fourth, resources are affected by political factors. For example, Rhodesian chrome was unavailable in the UK throughout the 1970s. As a result, both supply and demand are constantly changing and this makes projections about the adequacy of the earth's resources very difficult.

Since the Earth's surface is not uniform, nor man's distribution over it, nor his pattern of production and consumption, an elaborate **system of exchange** has been developed to balance supply and demand, and a very complex economic organization has developed to facilitate and regulate it, involving the whole spectrum of transport and trade.

The process by which resources are allocated is extremely complex and is affected by a whole range of economic, social, political and physical factors. Because of the scale and complexity of economic activity it is necessary to simplify reality in order to understand and explain the underlying structure of its forms, patterns and processes. This simplification involves the identification of the fundamental elements and principles having general application and which need to be separated from those which only apply in particular circumstances. Since economic activity is not a random process it should be possible to identify regularities in the geography of economic activity and to relate them to the processes that have created them. The search is for general laws which can be used to develop a body of **theory** which will enable us to explain the complexity of reality.

The methods of explanation which were initially used to explain locations, distributions and interactions in more general terms were empirical and **inductive**. Attempts to explain the location of industry, for example, involved the examination of a large number of factories, and the specific reasons for their locations were drawn into general conclusions. More recently the trend has been much more theoretical and **deductive**, whereby assumptions have been made about the location of industry involving probable reasons why industry is located where it is. These assumptions have then been tested against real world locations. If they adequately explain reality then the assumptions are valid, if not they must be reformulated. This approach involves a great deal of hypothesis testing and has been one of the major causes of the application of quantitative methods in geography during the past twenty-five years.

The search for general explanations of the geography of economic activity have produced two major types of theory. **Normative theory** has largely been borrowed from economics and involves the establishment of theoretical spatial patterns which should result from processes operating under ideal circumstances. This gives us a model of what the world would be like if it were a perfect place inhabited by perfect men. Such theories are discussed in Chapters 25 and 28 and include the theories of Von Thünen, Weber, Lösch and Christaller. They involve the establishment of theoretical 'norms' against which the real world can be measured so that we can identify the underlying patterns of human activity and the processes which have produced them. However, normative theories have been criticized because they are unreal, and more recently **behavioural theory** has been developed to explain real world deviations from the theoretical norms. In this, an attempt is made to understand locations by examining the decisions which have produced them and the factors which affected the decisions. This involves the study of the decision-making process and much work has been borrowed from psychology to examine how reality is perceived by man and how this then affects his environmental behaviour. Man is more likely to be satisfied with what he sees as a good location than with an endless search for the optimum location of normative theory. One of the main objectives of behavioural theory is to determine the extent to which man can be considered a **satisficer** rather than an **optimizer** in his economic activities.

Summary

Our task here is to describe and explain the locations, distributions and interactions of economic activity not only to enable us to understand the complexity of the world at present, but also to enable future planning to be more sensible and efficient. The world economic system has become one complex, interrelated, functioning whole, and primary, secondary, tertiary and quaternary activities are all part of the same system of production. They are discussed separately in the following chapters but their essential unity should not be forgotten.

Chapter 21
Transport and the Adjustment of Space

Transport plays a central role in economic and social activity and is a major factor affecting the development of land use and settlement patterns. This chapter discusses the reasons why transport links develop, how distance operates to constrain movement, how different modes of transport compare in terms of their abilities to overcome distance economically, and the characteristics of movement patterns and transport systems.

Why transport links develop

People and agricultural and industrial resources are distributed over the earth's surface in an uneven and discontinuous pattern, and to bring people together and to move resources from areas of supply to convenient places where they can be processed and sold to meet demand requires considerable movement. This movement of people, goods, services and information results in the development of extensive and complex transport networks. These develop under the influence of a wide variety of economic, social, political

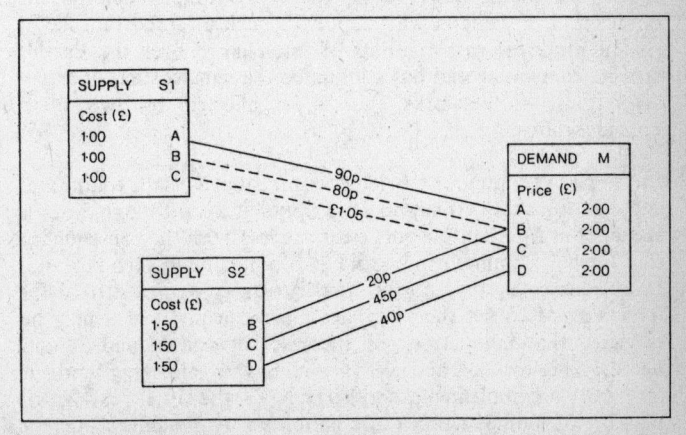

Figure 75. Complementarity, intervening opportunity and transferability (after Ullman)

209

and strategic factors to overcome the effects of physical separation and to bind society and the world economy together. Figure 75 illustrates a simple model developed by E. L. Ullman to explain the conditions which affect the development of transport links. Ullman identified three basic factors affecting interaction between areas: complementarity, which operates to encourage movement between areas, and intervening opportunity and transferability, which operate to constrain or redirect it.

If there is a demand for a commodity in one area and it can be supplied by another area, then the two areas can be said to be complementary, and this **complementarity** is the basis for interaction between them. In figure 75 there is a demand for four commodities in area M. Areas S_1 and M are complementary in the three commodities A, B and C and Areas S_2 and M are complementary in B, C and D. However, the simple existence of complementarity does not necessarily result in movement because the movement of commodities must be profitable for both supplier and customer. In the case of the commodity A, the cost at source is £1·00 per unit to which must be added 90p per unit transport costs, but since the price the customer is prepared to pay at M is £2·00 per unit, then the supplier can make a profit of 10p per unit. A similar complementarity exists between S_2 and M in respect of commodity D and it may be expected that A will be transported from S_1 to M and D will be transported from S_2 to M, assuming that M has the resources to pay the price. Complementarity, the connection of demand with supply, is such an important factor that it produces vast amounts of interchange over the Earth's surface every year and has stimulated the construction of extensive transport networks, but it is affected by two other considerations.

In the case of commodity B, let us assume that S_1 is the traditional supplier, but that new supplies are found at S_2. Although the cost is higher at S_2, the transport costs are less, with the consequence that the new supplies can be sold at 10p per unit less than the old. In this case, S_2 presents an **intervening opportunity** for buyers at M to get their supplies more cheaply, and it may be expected that interaction will increase between M and S_2 and decrease between M and S_1. In a constantly changing world it follows that complementarity also changes, and the appearance of new opportunities makes trade patterns very dynamic. Different sources of supply may be used because old ones become too expensive, new sources may be discovered, and new or substitute products may become available. For example, supplies of cheaper tin from Malaya replaced Cornish tin in England, the discovery of iron ore in Australia was of major benefit to the Japanese steel industry, and the development of synthetic fibres reduced demand for animal and vegetable fibres in Western Europe and the USA.

In the case of commodity C, although there are supplies at S_1, the cost of transport is so high, because of the greater distance or the inefficiency of the transport system, that C would cost £2·05 per unit at M and therefore could not be sold below the market price of £2·00. As a result, C is not transferable from S_1 and this **transferability** is a necessary requirement for interaction. If there were no other supplies and demand remained high at M, then the price would have to rise, but since alternative supplies are available at S_2, demand will be met from there. This transferability is a fundamental factor of location (Chap. 24) and if the cost of transfering a commodity is high, then it will either attract industry or lead to a search for new supplies or substitutes. On the other hand, commodities which are easy to transfer or are universally available have little locational power. At the heart of the question of transferability lies the role of distance, a fundamental factor affecting the location and distribution of human activity.

The importance and role of distance

Movement takes place when demand in one area is met by supply in another, but problems arise when supply and demand are located in different places because **distance** discourages movement. This discouragement has two causes. First, and most important, reducing distance involves a cost which can be measured directly in terms of cash payments such as fares or freight charges, or indirectly in terms of time, effort and inconvenience. As a general rule, movement decreases as costs increase. Secondly, distance affects levels of information. As a general rule, much more is known of near places than far places, and movement is more likely between known places. The resulting decrease in movement as distance increases has been expressed as the principle of **distance decay**. Attempts to measure the relationship between distance and the volume of movement have shown that it is difficult to be precise about the way in which contacts decrease with distance except that the general pattern is for contacts to fall off sharply over short distances and then decline more slowly over longer distances, as can be seen in figure 76. It has been suggested that, as in Newton's Law of Universal Gravitation, interaction between

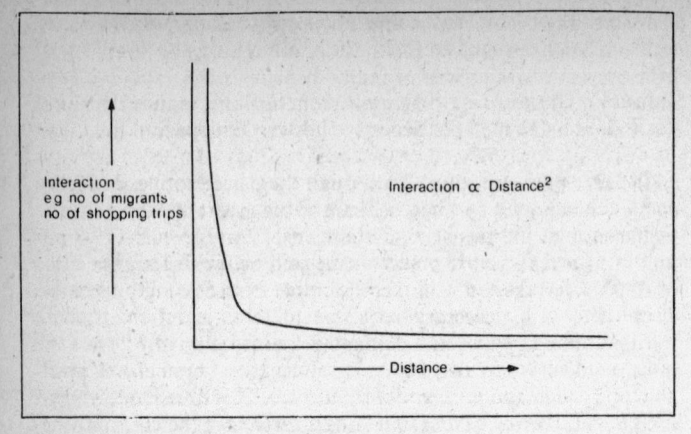

Figure 76. The form of the distance decay curve

two places will decline inversely as the square of the distance, but the application of physical laws to human activity cannot give as precise results, if only because of the difficulty of defining the term distance (page 190).

This may seem a simple problem, because distance can be defined as the extent of space between two points, but although distance in Newton's Law is an **absolute** measure, it is more variable when applied to the measurement of human activity. Human activity must take place within an absolute space that is measured in absolute distances, but even the simple question 'what is the distance between London and Manchester?' is difficult to answer in absolute terms. The distance by rail is 293 km, by road it is 302 km, and by air it is 245 km plus the 42 km journey to and from the airports. Therefore, even in absolute terms, Manchester is a number of distances from London, but any decision to travel or to send goods to Manchester would not be made on the basis of absolute distance but on the basis of the time, cost and convenience of the journey, and each of these can be considered a form of distance. Air journeys involve high *cost* distances but low *time* distances, coach journeys involve low *cost* distances but high *time* distances, and rail journeys reduce the *convenience* distance because of the large number of services offered. In addition, costs and journey times are constantly changing and the **cost**, **time** and **convenience distances** between Manchester and London have been radically altered during the past 200 years. This has come about as transport forms have improved and changed to make the journey easier.

Distance is therefore a **relative** rather than an absolute measure and it follows that if distance is relative, then space is relative, since space is measured in distances. The study of human activity in relative space has been one of the most interesting developments in geography in recent years, and transport is of fundamental importance in this study. The role of transport is to bring sources of supply and demand by reducing relative distance, and the history of transport is the development of increasingly successful methods of bringing places closer together in relative space. Transport is a **space-adjusting technique** and new forms of transport, new methods of propulsion and new methods of construction have brought London, for example, within three and a half hours of New York in time-space. In the movement of information and ideas, radio, television and the telephone have virtually annihilated distance.

Improvements in transport technology operate to bring places closer in two ways. First, they reduce distance, and second, they remove obstacles to movement. The **reduction of distance** can come about gradually as improvements in a form of transport are developed, and, over a period of 38 years, improvements to steamboats on the Mississippi reduced the journey time from New Orleans to Louisville by over twenty days (Fig. 77).

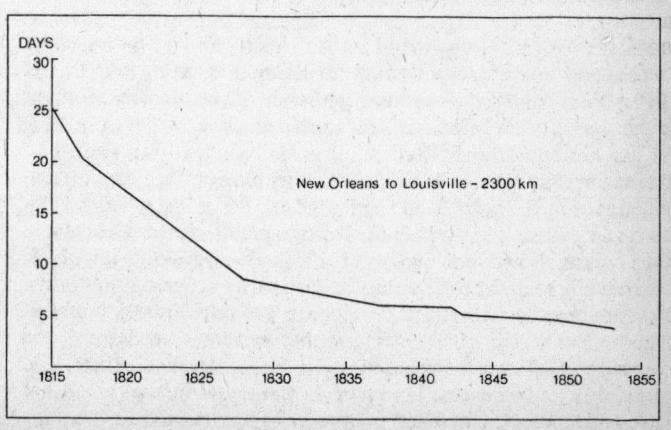

Figure 77. The reduction of steamboat journey times, 1815–53

The way in which places came together in relative space can be measured using the formula developed by D. Janelle in his theory of **time-space convergence**:

$$\frac{TT_1 - TT_2}{Y_2 - Y_1} = \text{Rate at which places converge.}$$

in which TT_1 and TT_2 are travel times in different years, and Y_1 and Y_2 are the years in question. In 1825 it took 603 hours to travel the 2300 km between New Orleans and Louisville, while 38 years later it took only 106 hours. Using the formula:

$$\frac{603 - 106}{38} = 13 \cdot 1 \text{ hours}$$

it can be seen that between 1825 and 1863, New Orleans was approaching Louisville at a rate of 13·1 hours a year. Since the steamboats travelled faster downstream, it must be remembered that Louisville was travelling even faster towards New Orleans! Reductions in distance can be even more dramatic when a revolutionary form of transport is introduced: the opening of the Liverpool and Manchester Railway in 1830 cut the journey time for passengers from over three hours by stagecoach to one hour and twenty-six minutes by rail. Since goods could take ten days by canal, the effect on freight traffic was even greater. More recently, transport improvements have reduced distance even further, and aircraft and motor vehicles have radically transformed space.

Obstacles to movement have also been removed by transport technology – the opening of the Erie Canal between Buffalo and New York in 1830 overcame the Appalachian barrier. Freight rates between Buffalo and New York immediately fell from $100 to $5 per ton and the transit time was reduced from twenty to eight days. By the same principle, the opening of the Suez Canal in 1869 removed Africa from the path of trade between Britain and the East, although it was temporarily replaced during the closure of the canal between 1967 and 1975. The development of the steamship reduced the size of the oceans by reducing the time it took to cross them, and the development of refrigeration removed the barrier to the transport of perishables across the Tropics and made a vital economic connection between the northern and southern hemispheres. However, it is the aeroplane which has been most effective in removing obstacles to movement by making it possible to move in a clear and continuous space.

Perceived distance and economic distance

Because distance can be measured in a number of ways it is a relative rather than an absolute feature which both varies between different modes of transport and changes over time. There are two types of relative distance which fundamentally affect human behaviour, perceived distance and economic distance.

Perceived distance is the distance we carry inside our heads, and the general principle that decision-makers base their decisions on the environment as they see it rather than on the way that it objectively exists is now well established. It is also well established that people vary considerably in their ability to judge distances and that different groups see the same distance in different ways. A young man may think nothing of his walk to the bus stop, but for the aged and the infirm it may be a major journey. Decisions to travel are made on the basis of how far we think places are and how attractive the destination is seen to be. It appears that people underestimate distance to places that they consider to be attractive and overestimate distances to places considered unattractive. In other words, people behave in a relative or subjective space which modifies objective reality. This is very important because it helps to explain why people do not always behave in the ways assumed in normative theory (Chaps. 20 and 25) and why distance decay is only a principle and not a law. Shoppers do not always go to the nearest store, but to the one considered most attractive at the time. However, although perceived distance is an important factor affecting personal movement, in the study of the large scale movement of goods and materials across the world, economic distance is the fundamental factor.

Economic distance is the measure of how far goods and materials can be profitably transported and is composed principally of cost distance, although time and convenience distance must also be considered. It is clear from figure 75 that the movement of goods will take place if there is a demand in one area which can be met from another, so long as the cost in the area of demand is lower than the market price. The maximum economic distance that any goods can be carried is the point at which the cost of the goods plus the cost of transport becomes greater than their market value, and this varies considerably with the type of goods involved. The transport costs needed to move cement are very high in relation to its value and therefore the economic distance that a tonne of cement can be carried is very much lower than that of a tonne of cameras. Economic distance is very much a relative measure because, first, it is being constantly changed as transport technology improves, and second, it varies with the mode of transport being used.

Transport modes

The ability of any mode of transport to reduce economic distance will depend on the type of goods to be moved, the absolute distance of the journey and the type of terrain to be covered. Decisions about which transport mode will be developed and used are not based solely on an ability to move goods but on an ability to move them profitably in the face of competition from other carriers and in compliance with government policies.

However, the costs involved in the actual movement of goods play a central role in determining which form of transport will be used, and three types can be identified. First, there are the **line-haul costs** which are made up of the costs incurred in physical movement such as fuel and labour costs. Secondly, there are the **overhead costs** which are made up of the capital and maintenance costs of terminals and equipment plus the administrative costs. Thirdly, there are the **transfer costs** which are made up of indirect costs such as the insurance cover for the cargo. The relative importance of these costs, especially between line-haul and overhead costs, varies between the different forms of transport, as might be expected from techniques developed to reduce distance in the very different media of land, sea and air.

As a result of this relative balance, some forms of transport are more effective over particular distances than others. This can be seen in figure 78, in which the overhead costs of road, rail, ocean and air transport are shown at T_1, T_2, T_3, and T_4. The terminal costs of ocean transport are very high because of the need for expensive port facilities, but the line-haul costs are very low because ships are efficient movers and costs can be spread over large cargoes. The terminal costs of road transport are very low because goods can be unloaded in the street, but line-haul costs are very high because of the cost of fuel and the fact that relatively small cargoes are carried. Rail transport occupies an intermediate position. Road transport is therefore cheapest over short distances (A–B), rail over medium distances (B–C) and ocean transport over long distances (beyond C). However, although this is generally true, reality is a little more complex, as can be seen from a

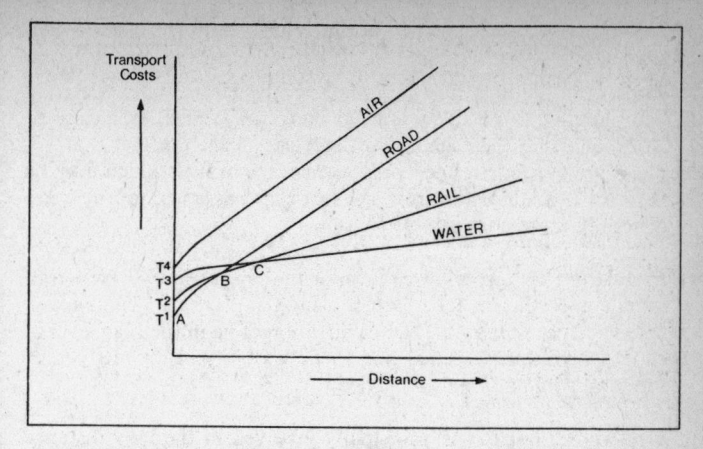

Figure 78. The cost structure of different modes of transport

study of the balance between advantage and disadvantage offered by the different transport modes. Air transport, despite having high overhead and line-haul costs, is still a prime mover of passengers.

The **railways** revolutionized land transport after 1830 and still play an important role today. The advantages offered by rail transport arise from the fact that movement takes place along a set, controllable route, and this results in a speedy and reliable service for passengers to convenient terminals in the centres of towns. Heavy loads can be carried efficiently over considerable distances because line-haul costs do not rise significantly with distance. The disadvantages offered by railways arise from the heavy overhead costs in establishing and maintaining a service; the inflexibility of a system operating on a fixed route where steep gradients and sharp curves have to be avoided; the difficulties of carrying awkward loads, and the relatively slow speeds of passenger services over long distances compared with aircraft.

A second revolution in land transport has come about this century as **roads** have increased in importance for the movement of goods and passengers. The advantages of road transport lie in its flexibility, the ability to carry a range of cargoes over many different routes; in its low overhead costs, not only because terminal costs are low, but because the user does not pay directly for the use of roads; in the presence of good road networks in the developed countries and the ability of vehicles to use bad roads in the Third World. The disadvantages offered by road transport come from the high line-haul costs involved, since only relatively light loads can be carried; from congested roads, especially in cities, affecting the reliability of services; from the fact that vehicles are dependent upon only one source of fuel, which may be variably available; and from the fact that passenger journeys are generally more comfortable by rail.

Pipelines are a specialized form of land transport and are direct, speedy and efficient for a limited range of products being moved between specific points. The disadvantages lie in the high level of capital investment needed and the inflexibility of the medium in terms of route and goods carried.

Ocean transport is principally involved in the long distance movement of bulk cargoes. The advantages offered by ocean transport arise from its very low line-haul costs, because ships move in an already available, interconnected and relatively frictionless medium where large cargoes can be moved over great distances. The disadvantages offered arise from the high capital costs involved in the building and maintenance of ports; the capital costs of ships; the relatively slow speeds attained by ships; the need for trans-shipment at **break-of-bulk points**, although this is being reduced by containerization; and environmental hazards such as storms and fog. Inland waterways are characterized by roughly the same range of advantage and disadvantage, although overhead costs in the maintenance of canals are higher, while environmental hazards are reduced.

Air transport is by far the most effective way of reducing time distance, and this is its principal advantage. In the free and limitless medium of the air, a regular and reliable service has revolutionized long distance passenger transport. The cost of air transport is a major disadvantage and is aggravated by the need for specialized terminals and close control, and as a result, only low-bulk high-value goods are carried.

Freight rates and government policies

The actual cost involved in moving goods over the Earth's surface is not the sole determinant of the price that the customer has to pay, because the price will also include the carrier's profit and may be affected by external factors such as government policy.

Freight rates are made up of costs and profits and will therefore vary considerably depending upon the type of goods to be carried, the volume and frequency of movement, the form of transport used, the distance and type of terrain to be covered, and the level of competition from other carriers and other forms of transport. The complexity is further intensified by the fact that special rates often apply. In the passenger field, for example, British Rail offer the passenger a choice of first or second class rates, and special **concessionary rates** for day and weekend periods. In the freight field, since costs do not always rise proportionately with distance (Fig. 76), freight rates may reflect this **long-haul advantage** and journeys of 2000 km may not be much more expensive than journeys of 1000 km. In addition, **back-haul rates** may be offered on goods travelling from place B to place A to avoid containers returning empty if there are large flows of goods from A to B.

Government policy also affects the provision and pricing of transport facilities for a range of economic, social, political and strategic reasons. The **provision** of an adequate transport system is vital, since transport forms a fundamental component of the economic infrastructure and plays a major role in economic and social interaction. There is also an important strategic need to make all parts of a national territory accessible, especially those adjacent to hostile neighbours. Since the provision of a transport network is so expensive and the returns are indirect or delayed, government must play a central role in its development. In the West in general, for example, governments provide the road network and private enterprise organizes the flows; because of the operating difficulties, such an arrangement is not possible for the railways, and there are various arrangements ranging from total state control to heavy subsidies; most national shipping fleets are subsidized to a greater or lesser extent, and most countries have a national airline. In other economic and social systems, state control is total. The **pricing** of transport facilities is also of central concern to government. Monopolist overpricing must be avoided and in areas which, for social or political reasons, need to be provided with transport services, subsidies must be applied from profits earned elsewhere in the system or from general taxation. In this way, the economic cost of providing a service may be less important than the social benefits, and the measurement of economic distance becomes very complex.

Transport systems

Although there are many different modes of transport, they rarely exist independently but compete with or complement each other. Road, rail and air services compete for custom between London and Manchester, but there would be nothing unusual in a passenger taking a rail journey to Heathrow, a flight to Ringway, and a bus journey into Manchester. This linking of services produces a composite transport system within a country which is then linked by international services into the world transport system.

This system is made up of a complex **network** involving a vast number of **links**, along which pass **flows** of people, goods, services and information. Because of changes in supply and demand, and changes in technology, transport systems are constantly changing, and decisions to establish, terminate or amend links within the system are made by the interaction of two closely related groups. First, the transport users, who provide demand for services and determine the nature and volume of the flows. Secondly, the transport agencies who supply the services and who must determine which demands to supply. The resulting networks can best be examined if attention is paid first, to the individual links, and second, to the network as a whole.

Individual links or routes are established for various reasons, but primarily to serve economic and social demands in the best possible way. However, the definition of the **best route** is not always easy to determine. In figure 79, it is assumed that within a national boundary there are no physical barriers between the six towns A, B, C, D, E and F, and the best route between towns A and B might seem to be the most direct route because the building and operating costs would be minimized. But if C and D were also sizeable towns, then the revenues from the increased traffic would outweigh the additional costs of building the route $ACDB$, and this would therefore be the most economic route. In reality, the most direct or economic routes are not necessarily the ones established or maintained, because other factors must also be taken into consideration. If E were a town in a region with strong separatist tendencies and F were a town with a military garrison protecting the other five towns from attack from the north-east, then the best political and strategic route between A and B would be $AECDFB$.

When individual routes are linked together, then the transport

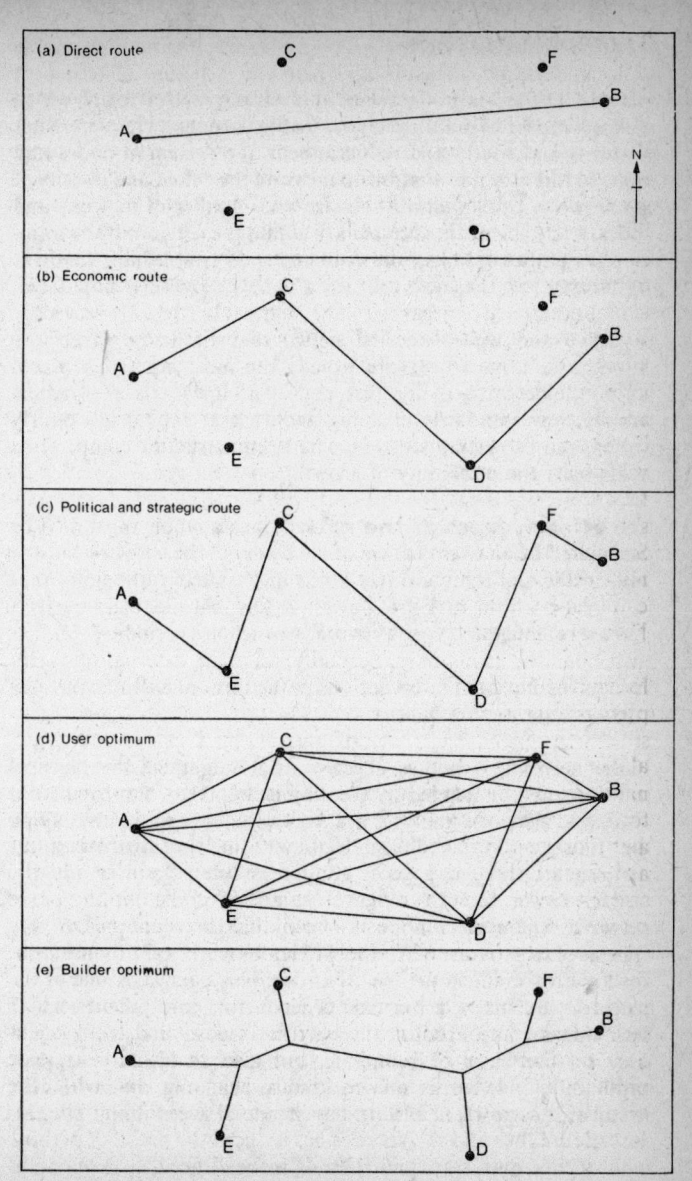

Figure 79. Best routes between six towns

network created can be studied by **network analysis** to enable us to understand, measure and plan the structure of transport systems. At the heart of network analysis is **graph theory** which makes a model of reality and ignores the particular characteristics of towns and routes and reduces them to a system of nodes and links. In this way it is possible to measure the extent and density of the network by examining the size and number of its links and nodes, and to measure accessibility within the network by examining the number of links from each node and establishing the **connectivity** of the network as a whole. Densely populated, economically active areas with few physical barriers are served by extensive and well-connected networks with many alternative routes, and large towns are usually the most accessible places within the network. In contrast, areas with low levels of economic activity, low standards of living and lack of capital are poorly served, and this lack of one of the basic infrastructure components holds back the possibility of growth.

The **effectiveness of the network** as a whole must also be considered by an examination of the ability of the network to cope with traffic and there are two kinds of obstacle to the flows that take place within it. First, there are physical obstacles such as narrow or congested roads, or roads which are periodically full at rush hours or at holidays. Secondly, there are external obstacles such as institutional interventions in the form of customs or tariff barriers, and import quotas.

If the network is not as effective as it might be, the physical problems can be tackled by creating new links or improving old ones, and network analysis is a very valuable tool in identifying the most profitable links. However, in the **planning of networks**, there is a basic conflict between the user and the builder, as can be seen in figure 79d and 79e. The optimum user network, where every node is directly linked to another, is very expensive to provide, while the builder network seeks to minimize costs with the shortest path structure. This conflict is one of the reasons why many governments have transport policies which seek to take into account the balance of costs and benefits not only on the basis of economic, but also social and strategic profitability. Networks are constantly changing, and while the motorway network in Britain has increased accessibility, the closure of rural bus and rail services has reduced the mobility of those who do not own cars, and there is a social need in many areas which must be subsidized. The social impact of transport is wider than the question of subsidies, however. There is increasing concern about noise and atmospheric pollution, especially from lead, but on the other hand, over 6,000 deaths and 80,000 serious injuries from road accidents each year in the UK appear to be an acceptable price to pay for economic and social mobility.

Summary

Transport is a vital part of economic and social activity and it plays a central role in the activities described in the following chapters. Transport is designed to equalize supply and demand by bringing places closer together economically, and many different transport modes have been developed to overcome the friction of distance, under the influence of a wide range of economic, social, political and strategic factors. A vast network of interchange has developed along which there are massive flows of people, goods, services and information.

Chapter 22
The Geography of Agriculture

Agriculture is the most fundamental of man's economic activities since it is concerned with the production of food and, although hunting and fishing have the same purpose, agricultural land-use dominates large areas of the world. Agriculture is the source of livelihood for over half the world's population who produce not only food but vital industrial raw materials such as animal and vegetable fibres, while crop-based alcohol may become an important source of energy in the future. Agricultural produce is also a major component of world trade.

Factors affecting the demand for agricultural products

The demand for agricultural products is dependent on a variety of factors which determine its volume and composition, and which operate in a complex, interrelated manner.

Population size is clearly the dominant factor affecting volume of demand and the exponential increase in the world's population has placed increasing strains on the supply of food and raw materials. However, size is not the sole determinant of the volume of demand since more affluent consumers have a greater buying power than poor ones. On the other hand, it is well established that agricultural demand does not increase proportionately with increases in income, at least not for food, but the **standard of living** of a country clearly affects the composition of demand: affluence encourages the consumption of more varied and expensive non-staple products. The composition of demand is also affected by the prevailing **attitudes and preferences** obtaining in society. Most societies have dietary preferences, be it for fish and chips or chapatis, and the influence of taboo is also important, not only for religious groups such as Muslims who ban the consumption of pork, but also for social groups such as the British who consume very little horsemeat and abhor the prospect of eating dogs.

Agricultural demand is not only for food. The **level of economic development** in a country will also affect its need for industrial raw materials. Because of the simplicity of its technology, the manufacture of textiles is one of the most easily adopted activities in the process of industrialization and stimulates an early demand, although as levels of technological achievement rise, the demand for natural products may be replaced by demand for synthetics such as nylon or rubber substitutes. **Physical conditions** also affect the nature of demand since woollen clothing will be less attractive in the Tropics than in Scandinavia.

Demand is also affected by the ability of any society to pay the costs involved in producing a supply, and potential demand will only become effective if these costs can be met. The tragedy of widespread hunger shows clearly how limited **effective demand** can be. Rapid population increases mean an ever increasing demand for food and clothing, but unless the supply can be increased the problem of poverty will be aggravated.

Factors affecting the supply of agricultural products

In deciding which crop to produce in order to meet this demand, the farmer, rancher or plantation manager is faced with the opportunity to produce and sell, but there are many constraints, both physical and human, which limit his opportunities. How the farmer perceives and evaluates the balance between opportunity and constraint depends upon his attitudes and abilities and these form the basis of his decision-making and consequent economic behaviour. However, although he is much more likely to be a satisficer than an optimizer, the farmer still needs his costs to be smaller than his income if he is to make a living. This depends upon his successfully balancing the various factors which affect his ability to supply his products and upon finding a market. It involves not only deciding which crops can be profitably grown, but also which of the profitable crops to choose.

The physical environment is a vital factor affecting the supply of agricultural products because in order to flourish, plants need warmth, moisture and mineral nutrients, and animals need food, water and shelter. As a result, the physical environment can impose absolute constraints upon production and even within areas where agricultural activity is possible, environmental factors affect the volume and costs of production.

Climate is the principal component in this environment and fundamentally affects the form and pattern of activity. All plants need warmth and the **temperature** must be over 6°C before growth can take place. Temperatures above this level must then be maintained through almost all of the plants' growth cycle and the growing season is generally limited to the period when the necessary warmth is available. A more precise measure of the temperature requirements is given by the calculation of **accumulated temperatures**, and maize, for example, ripens when the sum of daily maximum temperatures, counting only those days of 13·5°C or over, has reached 2,500°C. Plants also need **light** and many crops need sunshine to ripen. Available light varies with latitude and to some extent compensates for lower temperatures. Spring barley, for example, needs only 89 days to ripen in Lapland, but needs 107 days in southern Sweden. Finally, plants need **water** because it is used to carry food to the plant via the root system and although different plants have widely differing water requirements, a shortage or excess of water may lead to the complete destruction of a crop.

It is clear that climate prescribes the limits within which crops can grow, and cocoa, for example, will not grow in regions with annual temperatures below 18°C and less than 1,000 mm of rainfall. However, even within such climatic limits there can be periodic climatic disturbances which, if they affect the farmer adversely, may be considered **climatic hazards**. The frost hazard is a particular problem in middle latitudes and killing frosts in spring and autumn can cause serious damage. Wide variations in precipitation amounts can cause drought or flood hazards, while hail can effectively destroy crops over small areas. Excess snowfall is a major problem for animal farmers in winter and can cause additional damage in spring flooding. Crop damage can also be caused by abnormal winds, whether they be cold like the *mistral* or hot and dry like the *sirocco*. Strong winds are also constraining by increasing evapotranspiration in areas of low rainfall and by flattening crops. In this respect, major storms can create havoc, and 95% of the Dominican banana crop was destroyed by Hurricane David in 1979. It must always be remembered that changes in the weather, outside human control, introduce a major element of uncertainty into agriculture, not only when it is taking place on the margins of production, but even where conditions seem ideal.

Soil type and quality is a second major factor affecting agriculture since it provides the support for plant growth and also the essential minerals and trace elements which constitute plant food.

The suitability of a soil for farming depends upon its composition, texture and depth, and this in turn is the product of the type of parent material, past and present climates, relief and vegetation cover, the actions of soil organisms and past and present human use. At present, estimates of the areas of land with soils suitable for agriculture vary from 50% in Europe to 25% in Asia and 20% in North America. North America in particular illustrates the fundamental point that the soil is an exhaustible resource since in the USA alone, 5% of land suitable for agriculture or forestry has been completely ruined, 15% has lost three-quarters of its topsoil and 41% is subject to moderate erosion. Bad farming practice can initiate major environmental changes and reduce and even destroy the productive capacity of the soil.

Relief is a third physical factor and exerts an influence in three main ways. First, **altitude** affects climate and thus the type of crop which can be grown. In Western Europe the temperature falls 1°C for every 200 m of altitude and this puts the limit on barley growth, for example, at 800 m in central Switzerland. On the other hand, altitude ameliorates the high temperatures of low latitude countries and enables cattle to be reared in the Kenya Highlands and coffee to be grown in Brazil. Secondly, **aspect** is important agriculturally since a south-facing slope, in the northern hemisphere, protected from cold or strong winds, presents a favourable environment. This is particularly important in mountainous areas such as the Alps where north-facing slopes are generally shady and uninhabited and are known as **ubac** slopes in contrast to the sunny, south facing **adret** slopes where settlement and agricultural activity is concentrated. Thirdly, **gradient** affects the stability of the soil when the natural cover is removed and is a major contributing factor in soil erosion since the erosive power of run-off is increased. It also affects the use of machinery; for example the extensive level surfaces of the Prairies are ideal for large machines.

Biological processes also affect production, especially those related to the life cycles of plants and animals. The productivity of pastoral farming is clearly related to the breeding habits of animals. Pigs have a gestation period of 112 days and produce average litters of seven piglets, for example, while cattle have a gestation period of 280 days and normally produce only one calf. Reproduction is also a function of **season**, and this is more clearly a limiting factor in arable farming where constraints on production are imposed by periods of plant growth and rest. The rhythm of the seasons is much more pronounced in middle latitudes than in the Tropics where double and even triple cropping is a possibility. These rhythms not only affect the sedentary farmer but also affect the pastoral nomad as he follows his herds from summer to winter pasture.

The economic and social environment encompasses the second group of factors affecting the supply of agricultural products and it can be argued that over large parts of the Earth's surface they play a more important role than physical factors in determining the forms and patterns of production.

Technology represents man's abilities to reduce the constraints of nature and to create new opportunities for the utilization of the Earth. Because of this, the concept of the **ecumene,** that is the inhabited Earth, is a dynamic concept as man extends and intensifies his occupancy. As a result, production is growing not only by the occupation of larger areas, but also by gaining greater yields from the same area. Moreover, as technology advances, the physical environment is constantly being reassessed and land previously unused is brought into production. Technology is applied to agriculture in six main ways. First, it is used to modify the physical environment. Irrigation is used to overcome problems caused by low rainfall, land reclamation techniques such as draining and marling are used to improve soils, terraces are built to overcome the problems caused by steep gradients and methods such as cloud seeding are used to modify the weather. Second, it is used to modify plants and animals by selective breeding in order to produce, for example, drought tolerant wheat or sheep that regularly produce twin lambs. Third, it is used to maintain and increase the fertility of the soil by the use of crop rotation and natural and artificial fertilizers. Fourth, it is used to protect growing plants and animals from pests and diseases by the development of medicines, insecticides, herbicides and fungicides. Fifth, it is used to increase human efficiency and productivity by the application of machinery. Finally, it is used to develop special farming techniques, ranging from shifting agriculture in the Tropics where there is no other available method of maintaining soil fertility to factory farming in the West.

Social factors also play an important role through the operation of social attitudes and institutions. **Social attitudes** are important because a flexible, open society is more able to cope with the innovation and change which characterizes the modern world than traditional, closed societies. When rigid societies are put under stress, for example by environmental hazards, the consequences can be catastrophic. Social attitudes can be considered to be positive or negative, either favouring progress or opposing it, and are produced by levels of education, family structures, custom and tradition, and religion and taboo. They show themselves in varieties of agricultural practice and production. In some societies social attitudes allow and encourage innovation and the flexibility of Western societies has been a major factor in their economic progress, but in others the dead hand of custom has produced poverty and injustice. The most important **social institutions** affecting agriculture are land tenure and associated inheritance practices. **Land tenure** is important because it affects the size of holdings, the amount of investment and the type of farming practiced. Among primitive groups **communal ownership** is the common form of landholding, but in more economically advanced societies three main forms of tenure are found. First, **owner-occupation** (or freehold ownership) is the most common form in advanced countries. This gives the advantages of personal involvement and incentive and if inheritance customs involve holdings passing to the eldest son on the death of the owner (primogeniture), then there is the added advantage of continuity. On the other hand, if custom results in holdings being split between a number of heirs (gavelkind), then this results in fragmentation of holdings to a level where they are eventually uneconomically small. Second, **tenant farming** is practiced in two main forms. A cash tenancy involves a fixed cash rent being paid to the landowner and at its best the tenancy gives the opportunity to a man without capital to run his own farm. With security of tenure and a long and liberal lease, he has every incentive to manage the land carefully to his and the landlord's advantage. However, a short tenancy encourages the farmer to simply mine the land for short-term gain, and this is a particular danger in the second form of tenancy known as share-cropping. In this the landowner makes all the capital investment and the farmer provides the labour of himself and his family. The rent is paid in the form of a share of the crop and may be a fixed amount or a proportion of the crop, but the only incentive it provides is to produce as big a crop as possible with little regard for damaging consequences for the soil. Third, **state ownership** of land and the means of production characterizes most of the Communist world and the farm worker becomes a salaried employee of the state. In this situation incentive is low and in the USSR, for example, production of many commodities does not reach planned targets, with the consequent need for imports from the USA and Canada, where, under a different ideology, the problems are those of over-production.

Within the overall limits placed by the physical environment, **economic factors** play the major role in affecting the nature, volume, intensity and extent of agricultural activity. The farmer needs to make a profit to survive and this profit will depend on the price received being greater than the costs of production, transport and marketing in the face of competition from other producers in a fluctuating market. The costs of production depend upon the size and variety of the necessary inputs and the way in which agriculture is organized. The basic input in farming is the land, the value of which is based upon soil quality, climate, proximity to market and the past history of cultivation. Unless the land is held freehold and is free from mortgage, then the **rent** may be an important cost and in many Third World countries accumulated rents put peasant farmers in perpetual debt. The availability and cost of **labour** is a second factor and in peasant societies contributes the principal input where labour is cheap and plentiful and land and capital are scarce. In advanced countries, where wages are high and there are alternative forms of employment, the labour factor plays a different role. Here the availability of labour, especially in the face of seasonal demand, and labour productivity are the key elements. As a result, larger **capital** inputs are being substituted for labour inputs as machinery is employed and farms become efficient units of production with specialized buildings and fertilizers and feedstuffs bought in from outside. In the Third World the shortage of capital is a major concern, producing problems in the supply of inputs such as machinery and fertilizers and perpetuating forms of high interest credit which increase indebtedness to moneylenders. The availability of capital has been a major factor facilitating the trend in many Western countries to change agriculture to agribusiness, with large scale, capital intensive farming in efficient and profitable units. Many farms in the Third World, and even in Europe, are organized in small and fragmented units and this tends to hinder modernization. In Europe, for example, many farms are too small to support the farmer who must take a job elsewhere and work the farm in the evenings and at weekends on a **part-time** basis. On the other hand, many European countries are following active policies of **consolidating** small and fragmented holdings. One other way of overcoming the problem of small farm size is to organize a number of farms on a **cooperative** basis to enable the bulk buying of necessary inputs and to share expensive machinery. In countries such as Denmark and the Netherlands this has been encouraged and financed by the state.

Cooperatives can also play an important role in the **marketing** of produce and successful arrangements have been made, for example, for Dutch cheese and many French wines. Some farmers produce for specific buyers such as companies which freeze or can food, or for supermarket chains, and although contract prices may be lower than open market prices, a great deal of uncertainty is removed as the farmer is protected from price fluctuations. However, the existence of a commercial infrastructure to ensure that perishable agricultural produce is stored and distributed by an efficient network of wholesalers and retailers is necessary for most farmers and fundamentally affects his profitability. **Transport** is the second major component of the commercial infrastructure and involves the collection of inputs such as fertilizers and feedstuffs and the distribution of outputs such as food and raw materials. Distance, as expressed in transport costs, has always affected which crops can be profitably grown, and perishable or bulky crops such as milk or sugar beet tend to be produced near to a market. More expensive crops such as fruit or flowers can be grown at a greater distance, but transport costs cannot be greater than the difference between market prices and the costs of production or there will be no profit. Changes in transport technology have played a major role in affecting the patterns of agriculture by opening up new areas such as the Prairies and by making it possible for agricultural produce to reach markets many thousands of kilometres distant.

Of course, it must be remembered that the farmer does not operate in an economic vacuum and agricultural activity is fundamentally affected by the nature and level of **competition** from other crops, producers and land-uses. First, the farmer has to decide which crop to grow from a number of possible competitors, and the ability of the farmer to choose successfully is dependent upon his personal attitudes, abilities and resources. His decisions are affected by his desire to use the land effectively and to reduce risks in the face of economic and environmental uncertainty. Second, the farmer has to compete with other farmers from elsewhere whose production conditions may be quite different and the necessity to take into account market factors which are outside the farmer's control adds a further element of uncertainty. Third, the farmer may be under competition from other land uses, especially if he is farming on the urban fringe. As the value of the land increases, as it has in many parts of the USA, it becomes more heavily taxed and consequently adds to the farmer's costs. Underlying the whole issue of competition is the principle of **comparative advantage**: for a crop to be grown successfully in an area it must have a comparative advantage, usually in terms of a better profit, over competing crops. As a result, it may be better to grow an indifferent crop of barley than an excellent crop of potatoes. Similarly, the area in which the crop is grown must have a comparative advantage over areas where the crop could also be grown.

Finally, in the real world it is clear that profits are not completely dependent on the costs of production being smaller than the market price because governments may pay agricultural subsidies to cover deficits. **Government interest** in agriculture exists for a variety of economic, social and political reasons and operates in three main ways. First, through general government policy concerning matters such as taxation, food prices and wage levels. Second, by direct intervention in agriculture, the state can plan and control almost all aspects of agricultural activity as it does in Communist countries, but even in the West, government activity is increasing. This activity is concerned with general infrastructure improvements such as rural electrification schemes and the provision of agricultural research and education facilities; with encouraging mechanization and improvements such as land reclamation through the use of loans and grants; with direct attempts to control production by the imposition of production or acreage quotas; and with guaranteed prices and other forms of subsidy. Third, through controlling foreign trade by the imposition of tariffs to protect home producers against foreign competition or the relaxation of tariffs and the granting of export credits to encourage exports.

Farms as systems and farming systems

The various factors identified above affect demand for and supply of agricultural products, but they operate in complex interrelation rather than isolation. This complexity can be simplified in models of reality and a very useful model is the **system**, in which the parts are seen to be interconnected and flows of energy, materials and information take place within a functioning whole. Geographical systems are termed open systems because they do not operate in isolation and a single agricultural production unit such as a

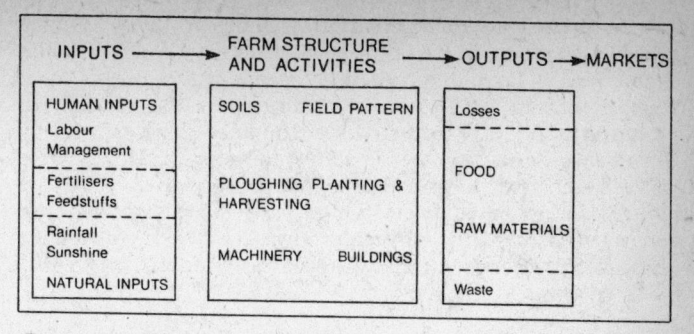

```
INPUTS ──────→  FARM STRUCTURE  ──→ OUTPUTS ──→ MARKETS
                AND ACTIVITIES

HUMAN INPUTS       SOILS    FIELD PATTERN      Losses
Labour                                         ─ ─ ─ ─ ─
Management
─ ─ ─ ─ ─ ─        PLOUGHING PLANTING &       FOOD
Fertilisers        HARVESTING
Feedstuffs                                    ─ ─ ─ ─ ─
─ ─ ─ ─ ─ ─                                    RAW MATERIALS
Rainfall
Sunshine           MACHINERY   BUILDINGS      ─ ─ ─ ─ ─
NATURAL INPUTS                                 Waste
```

Figure 80. A farm as an open system

farm, ranch or plantation can be studied as an open system (Fig. 80). Inputs are fed into the system which then works as an integrated unit to produce outputs which are taken from the unit within further systems of transport and marketing.

Individual farms operate as part of the much larger system of agriculture, but their interaction in particular combinations produces many subsystems over the Earth's surface which constitute **agricultural regions** within which distinctive forms of activity can be recognized. Unfortunately, it is not easy to classify agricultural activity but there are five basic criteria which should be taken into account, namely: economic aim, economic organization, type of product, intensity of input and type of physical environment. The first basic division in agriculture is between **subsistence farming**, as practiced by peasant farmers in Third World countries where crops and animals are produced for consumption by the producer, and **commercial farming**, where crops and animals are produced for sale. Second, commercial farming itself may be divided into **peasant farming**, as practiced in parts of Europe, **capitalist farming**, as practiced in Western economies in general, and **collective farming**, as practiced in the Communist bloc. The third division is that between **arable farming**, which is concerned with growing crops, and **pastoral farming**, which is concerned with animal management. However, a great many farms are **mixed farms** in which crops are grown both for sale and as feed for animals, and there is an enormous variety of possible crop and livestock combinations. Fourth, farming may be organized along **intensive** lines in which small areas receive large inputs of labour and capital, or along **extensive** lines in which these inputs are spread

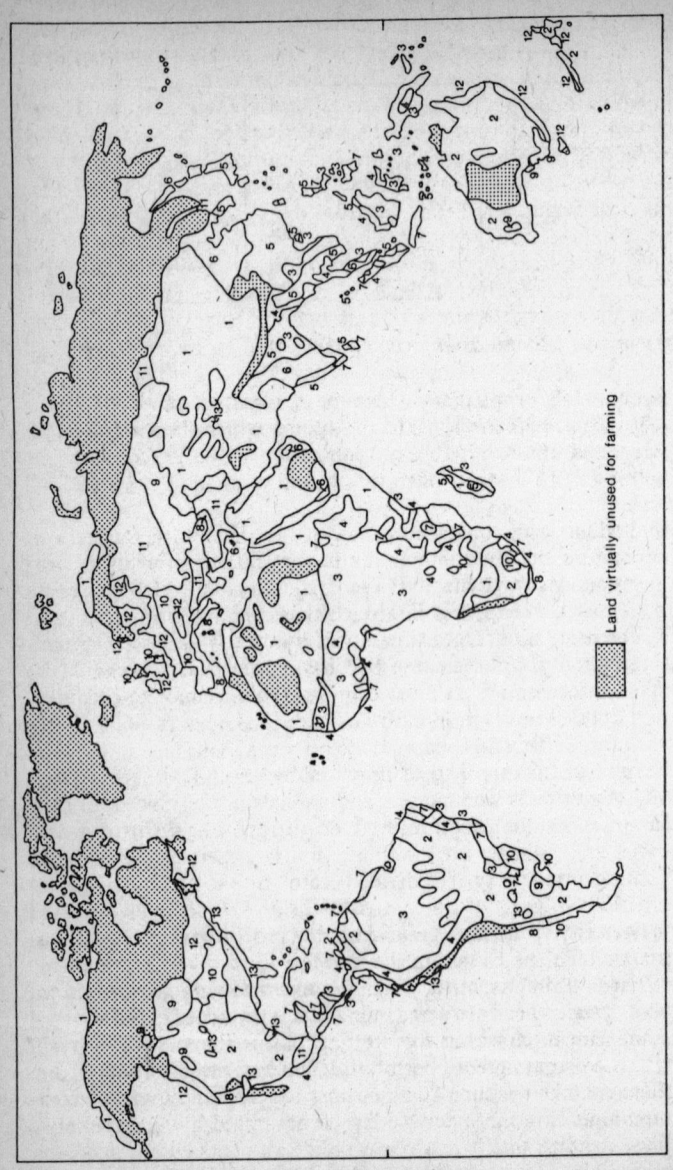

Figure 81: Principal types of world agriculture

over greater areas, with corresponding differences in output. Finally, there is a division between **tropical** and **temperate farming** based on types of crop grown and farming methods and organization appropriate to the different environments. These classifications are not mutually exclusive and, as a result, it is difficult to identify precisely world agricultural regions. However, the processes in which the various physical, economic, social and political factors interact do produce distinctive patterns over the Earth's surface, and one of the most satisfactory attempts to group these patterns into regions was made by D. Whittlesey in 1936. The regions are shown in figure 81, and are based on five criteria: namely, crop and livestock combinations, intensity of land use, processing and marketing of farm produce, degree of mechanization and types and associations of buildings and other structures associated with agriculture. There are thirteen main types of agricultural region, excluding land virtually unused for farming, and these are numbered on the map as:

1. Nomadic herding
2. Livestock ranching
3. Shifting cultivation
4. Rudimental sedentary tillage
5. Intensive subsistence tillage, rice dominant
6. Intensive subsistence tillage, without paddy rice
7. Commercial plantation crop tillage
8. Mediterranean agriculture
9. Commercial grain farming
10. Commercial livestock and crop farming
11. Subsistence crop and livestock farming
12. Commercial dairy farming
13. Specialized horticulture

Summary

Agriculture is a fundamental part of man's economic activity. This activity takes place within the margins imposed by nature, and although technology has managed to modify these margins to some extent, there are still large areas where conditions are too harsh. However, within the margins of possible cultivation, the nature, volume, intensity and extent of activity is produced by decisions taken within a socio-economic environment in which the margins are more flexible but just as critical.

Chapter 23
Physical Resources: Minerals and Energy Sources

The mining of physical resources such as minerals and energy sources is a second fundamental economic activity since these resources provide the basic materials of industry and provide the fuel and power for their collection, processing and distribution as finished products. In addition, large amounts of energy are required in the production of food. The use of these materials has increased enormously during the past 200 years as power has been applied to agricultural and industrial processes, and the industrialized countries are characterized by the large-scale exploitation and consumption of physical resources obtained on a world-wide basis. This chapter examines first, the factors which affect the supply of resources, and although they are identified separately, it must be remembered that in reality, the physical, technological, economic and political factors operate in very complex association. Second, the problems of resource supply and management in an age of high demand are examined.

Physical factors

Two groups of physical factors affect the supply of minerals and energy sources.

The first group is concerned with the **nature of a deposit**, including both its quality and its quantity. The **quality** of a deposit is a primary concern, because although many minerals are very common in the Earth's crust, a mineral only becomes an **ore** when it is found in sufficient concentration to warrant its commercial exploitation. This concentration varies from mineral to mineral, and although an ore containing 6% copper is considered very rich, an ore containing 20% iron is very poor. In the same way, the quality of an oil deposit varies with its chemical and physical composition, and deposits such as Orinoco heavy oil from Venezuela are not acceptable in US refineries at present for technical reasons, despite their proximity and the problems of guaranteeing supplies from the Middle East. The **quantity** of a material in a deposit is also important and large-scale deposits are much more attractive to exploit because the initial capital investment in mining or drilling is normally very heavy and a large-scale deposit of medium quality may be developed before a small deposit of high quality.

The second group is concerned with the **accessibility** of a deposit which fundamentally affects the cost of exploitation. This accessibility is affected by five conditions. The first concerns the **mode of occurrence**: minerals found in sedimentary rocks or alluvium are generally easier to mine than those in igneous rocks, because igneous rocks are generally harder. Also, the veins or lodes in igneous rocks containing minerals such as gold, silver, or tin are often very thin or difficult to follow. Faulting in coalfields such as South Lancashire can create similar problems of following the seam in sedimentary deposits, but materials such as coal and iron in sedimentary deposits can be very thick, level and easy to work. Second, the **depth** at which the deposits are found is important: materials found close to the surface can be worked by opencast methods and coal, iron ore, brick-clay and gravel are easily worked in the UK in this way. On the other hand, deep deposits involve considerable costs simply to reach them, and there are then costs and physical dangers in their extraction. Third, the **length of time** a deposit has been worked is likely to affect the ease of access. In general the most easily worked material is worked first and further exploitation not only requires increased investment but other costs, such as the time it takes a miner to reach the working face, also increase. Fourth, **environmental conditions** affect accessibility, and serious problems arise in the exploitation of materials in harsh environments. Additional costs have to be borne in the mining of iron in the Arctic conditions of Swedish Lapland or oil production on the north slope of Alaska, while the offshore oil industry, especially in the extreme conditions of the North Sea, is clearly at a disadvantage in relation to onshore wells. Finally, the **location** of deposits in relation to centres of demand is important and although the USSR, for example, has considerable reserves of oil, they will have to be sought in future in isolated and difficult areas such as the Barents Sea or the East Siberian Arctic Shelf.

Technological factors

The exploitation of physical resources is affected by technological factors in two ways. First, the specific technologies of mining, ore-dressing and transport play a fundamental role. Second, mining takes place within a general technological environment which affects both supply and demand.

Mining technology is basically concerned with the problem of extracting materials from the Earth's crust, and considerable progress has been made in developing techniques and machinery to strip surface deposits and to mine or drill for those occurring much deeper. A copper mine at Bingham Canyon in Utah covers 7·21 km^2 and is 775 m deep, gold is mined in South Africa at a depth of 3,840 m, and oil wells have been drilled down to 7,600 m. There are still problems, however, and at present, for example, about 70% of oil in commercial wells is left *in situ* because it is too difficult and costly to get it out. New methods of injecting gas, steam or chemicals are being tried to improve the recovery factor to 40 or 45%, but they obviously considerably increase the cost.

Beneficiation technology has also been developed in an attempt to make materials more moveable when they have been extracted. In the case of non-ferrous metal ores, concentrations are usually low and **ore-dressing**, in which the ore is crushed and separated from the surrounding waste or **gangue**, is necessary. In the case of an iron ore (taconite) found in Minnesota, similar techniques are necessary since the metallic content is only 20–30%, and in order to make the ore marketable it has to be crushed and the iron concentrated into pellets with a 63% metallic iron content.

Transport technology is also of central importance in ensuring a supply of materials to centres of demand. Historically, the railways played a vital role in opening areas such as the interior of North America to economic development, and the development of new forms of transport such as pipelines has continued. The improvement of old forms has also taken place and better ship technology has meant that very large bulk carriers have revolutionized the geography of iron ore. It is now possible, for example, to carry ore considerable distances from Brazil or western Australia to Japan, while the world supply of petroleum is dependent on the carrying capacity of supertankers of up to 500,000 dwt in size.

In the economy at large, **technological change** has had a fundamental effect on the exploitation of physical resources by creating new demands and enabling the use of known but unusable deposits. The development of the large-scale use of electricity has created the modern copper industry and increasing demand has stimulated the mining of uranium for nuclear power stations. The spread of the internal combustion engine created entirely new demands for petroleum and has revolutionized the geography of energy supply. Change has also taken place within specific industries, and the development of the Gilchrist-Thomas process in 1876 allowed the use of phosphoric iron ores such as those in Lorraine and Swedish Lapland which were useless until then.

Economic factors

A variety of economic factors are central to the exploitation of physical resources but they can be considered under five main headings: the size and nature of demand, world commodity prices, the cost of exploitation, the cost of transport from supply to demand, and pricing policies.

As discussed on page 205, the physical elements of the Earth's crust cannot in themselves be considered as resources, they only become resources when there is a **demand**. As a result, bauxite mining only began when the aluminium industry developed, and uranium mining only began in the nuclear age. Resources are anything that man finds necessary or useful and the size and nature of demand is dependent on two interrelated sets of considerations. The first set involves the needs and desires of a society, which are expressed in its economic and social aims and objectives, and the second set involves its values and skills. On the one hand, for example, the Amazon Basin can be considered a complete habitat, and many aboriginal peoples live contained lives within it. On the other hand, many Brazilians, brought up in the Western tradition with complicated aims and objectives, see it as a wilderness to be cleared and its resources, defined in the western sense, developed. Of course, there is a wide range of opinion about whether development should take place, and what type of development it should be but, in the past 200 years, the Western sense, developed. Of course, there is a wide range of opinion about whether development should take place, and what type of development it should be, but in the past 200 years, the creased and a new range of resources has been created as aspirations have risen and high standards of living have been achieved.

The level of demand is a major factor affecting **world prices** for commodities and prices play a fundamental role in determining which deposits are worked, especially those which are marginally profitable. In the case of Cornish tin deposits, for example, the rise in prices resulting from world shortages of tin in the late 1960s made it profitable to reopen mines which were unprofitable when prices were low, but in the late 1970s prices had again fallen below costs and some mines were taken out of production. On the other hand, the continuing rise in oil prices has taken the North Sea fields out of the marginal category and even small and expensive deposits can now be profitably developed.

The exploitation of physical resources is greatly affected by the cost and two major costs must be considered. The first concerns the **capital costs** involved in opening and running an extractive operation. Very heavy investments are usually necessary simply to get at deposits of commercial minerals in the stripping of overburden, the sinking of mine shafts or the drilling of wells, especially in difficult environmental conditions. Complex and expensive machinery is then needed to work the deposits. Initial investments in a new mine may be up to $300 million and in the oil industry there is considerable risk that wells may be dry. In a two year programme of offshore exploration begun in 1978 and costing $175 million, the Venezuelan government, for example, sank sixteen wells in the first year, of which only three were successful, and this was just part of a $3,000 million exploration programme planned for the period 1976–86. The second concerns **labour costs**, because wages and salaries contribute a major part of the running costs of a mine. In the developed countries there is usually a supply of skilled men available, but much mining takes place in sparsely inhabited and poorly developed locations and much labour has to be brought in from outside at a high cost. In inhospitable environments such as Alaska or the Sahara, high support costs are involved as new settlements have to be built in order to accommodate the workforce.

Transport costs are a major factor affecting whether or not a deposit can be worked and historically the difficulty of moving physical resources resulted in industry being located near to material deposits. Raw materials are usually heavy, bulky and difficult to handle and as a result they are expensive to transport. Moreover, they are of low value per unit and cannot bear heavy transport costs. In consequence, their location, in terms of the distance to be carried, the nature of the terrain to be covered, and the availability of transport facilities is of critical importance. Iron ore with easy access to deep water is transported all over the world, but inland supplies of low grade ores in highland areas are virtually immoveable without concentration. Nevertheless, if the cost of transporting a material is less than the difference between the costs of extraction and the market price, then it can be moved, and the world transport network is largely concerned with massive flows of bulk cargoes.

Pricing policies are also important in affecting demand. In the UK, for example, demand for gas has remained high because until recently governments have kept prices low, and a similar situation obtains in the USA in respect of petrol. There are economic reasons for such decisions, but there are also political considerations involved, and the two are often difficult to separate.

Political factors

Because the supply of materials and energy sources is uneven and widely distributed, and demand is concentrated in relatively few areas, there is always a potential difficulty because the world is not organized as a single political unit. In recent years political factors have played an increasing role in the availability of supply, especially in the international transfer of energy supplies. Moreover, this situation is likely to become more acute as demand for certain materials exceeds supply.

Even **within a country**, political considerations must be taken into account. On the one hand there are often objections to mining activity on environmental grounds, as illustrated by the opposition to coal mining in the Vale of Belvoir and to uranium mining in Orkney. On the other hand, there is also pressure to keep open uneconomic tin mines in Cornwall or coal mines in South Wales because of the political and social consequences which may result from closure and high unemployment.

Nevertheless, the main problem lies **between countries** and because the prosperity of the industrialized countries depends upon plentiful supplies of cheap materials obtained on a worldwide basis, the control of supplies is of vital importance. Although international companies extract and transport these materials, governments in producing countries are playing an increasing role in the regulation of supplies. This is clearly seen in the production of oil where supplies are regulated by increases in prices, the establishment of production limits, and even the complete severance of supplies in extreme cases. This is partly based on the legitimate claim that prices are too low, but it is also a reflection of political attitudes.

The response of the consumer countries in the face of uncertain or difficult supply has been to look for **alternative supplies**, from either alternative locations or substitute sources. The political instability of the Middle East was a major factor encouraging the development of oil supplies from the North Sea, despite the high costs, and by 1979 the UK was producing 1·7 million barrels per day (compared with 11·7 million b/d from the USSR, the world's largest producer), giving a notional 85% of UK needs. In electricity production, nuclear energy is being widely developed, especially in France, and many other energy sources are being investigated, from 'green petrol' produced from plant alcohol, to new forms of wind power. However, the whole question of the relationship between supply and demand is becoming of critical importance and the problem of resource management is now a major concern.

Resource management

Since the supply of known resources is finite, and demand is increasing because of population growth and increases in living standards, it would appear obvious that the supply of resources will run out very soon and disastrous consequences will result. However, this **Malthusian view** of the relationship between supply and demand is not universally accepted. If resources are relative rather than absolute features (page 205), created by the interaction of man and the physical environment and changing in importance from time to time and from place to place according to the level of human skill and ingenuity, then this **technological view** suggests that as resources run out, new ones will be created. In reality, the relationship between supply and demand is probably neither as pessimistic nor as optimistic as this and the sensible management of known resources is essential. There is a need to survey the Earth to learn the size of potential supplies and then manage them carefully so that small reserves are used with care until alternative supplies are available and large reserves are not squandered carelessly. The problem of ensuring resource supplies in the future has two aspects. First, there is a need to maintain or increase supply, and second, there is a need to steady or reduce demand.

The **increase in the supply of resources** can be achieved in a number of ways. First, technology can create a demand for resources such as uranium or bauxite, and make more efficient use of known ones. In the future, greater use of constant energy from the sun may be possible, instead of relying on the accumulated energy of fossil fuels. Second, the reduction of waste can dramatically reduce the need to exploit new supplies. Waste can be a direct loss when valuable metals such as steel or tin are simply dumped instead of being recycled, or a double loss when pollution is allowed to contaminate other resources such as land and water. The problem of pollution is so serious that releasing hydrocarbon wastes into the atmosphere might be a much greater threat to human life than the problem of resource exhaustion.

The **reduction of demand** is likely to be a much more difficult problem. Many governments, and even more religious groups, do not accept the need for population control, and those that do find it very difficult to implement their policies. On the other hand, there is some evidence that the rate of population growth may be slowing, but total growth continues and shortages of resources may be inevitable. Demand could also be reduced by cuts in living standards in the rich countries of the world, but politically this would be very difficult to implement.

Summary

The supply of physical resources such as minerals and energy sources is affected by a complex association of physical, technological, economic and political factors. In an age of high demand the problem of supply becomes critical, and supply and demand must be brought together into closer balance. However, there are enormous practical and political problems to be overcome.

Chapter 24
The Location of Manufacturing Industry

Manufacturing industry comprises the secondary group of economic activity identified in Chapter 20 and is concerned with the processing of raw and semi-finished materials, and with the fabrication and assembly of materials into semi-finished and finished products. Modern manufacturing industry is characterized by complex methods and structures, large workforces, the specialization of labour and the widespread use of machinery and inanimate power. The vast resultant output has enabled the industrialized countries to develop distinct and favoured economies with high standards of living. However, large scale manufacturing industry is not evenly distributed over the Earth's surface, and the present pattern of industrial activity has been produced by the complex interaction of a large number of factors.

Factors affecting the location of industry

Industry is located where it is as the result of millions of decisions made by people with less than perfect knowledge and ability in the face of a wide range of factors which operate to encourage or constrain the possibility of a successful location. Although these factors are isolated here in order that they may be examined, it must be remembered that they operate in a very complex interrelated manner and that their relative importance varies from place to place and from time to time. Although there is, in theory, such a place as an optimum location, in reality a successful location is one in which the favourable influences outweigh the unfavourable ones to give a manufacturer a comparative advantage over his competitors.

The factors affecting the costs of production can best be identified if a factory is examined as a system as in figure 82, with inputs of land, raw materials, semi-finished products and components, energy, water, labour and capital into manufacturing processes which lead to the output of products, by-products and waste materials. However, it must be remembered that many inputs may come from other factories and much of the output may supply further factories to produce a linked or integrated industrial system. As a result, there are other factors to be taken into account when considering location apart from the straightforward costs of production, including the size and nature of the market, geographical inertia, environmental factors, the geography of the firm and government intervention.

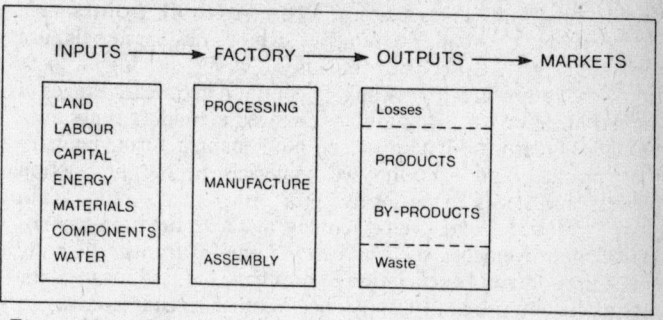

Figure 82. A factory as an open system

The first factor affecting the location of industry is concerned with the assembly of inputs and the distribution of output, and these **transport costs** play a major and central role. As discussed in Chapter 21, the world is characterized by variety, and raw materials, processing plants and consumers are rarely located in the same place. Men and resources are distributed in an uneven and discontinuous pattern over the Earth's surface. To bring supply and demand together, many transport forms have been developed over the years, but the assembly and distribution of materials and products against the friction of distance produces costs which the manufacturer has to pay. These costs are made up of the direct costs of transport plus the indirect costs of elements such as insurance cover, damage in transit and clerical costs. The manufacturer has to reduce his costs as much as he can to make or increase his profits, and a location close to supplies of materials and to markets involving few transport costs would be ideal. Unfortunately, this is rarely practical and the location decision must include consideration of the costs of assembly and distribution.

All industries use **materials**, either raw or semi-finished, or even complete parts that merely form part of a further assembly, and a location near to a supply of materials is desirable if a great deal of bulk or weight is lost in the manufacturing process. There is little point in transporting waste materials in large amounts. As a result, the smelting of copper in Zambia, for example, takes place close to the mines because metallic copper may constitute only 1% of the ore, and the refining of sugar beet close to the producing farms in East Anglia takes place for similar reasons. Often, when bulky materials such as grain or petroleum have to be transported, processing takes place at **break-of-bulk points** such as ports in consuming countries where raw materials are processed into a variety of products. However, although a location close to raw materials was very common in the early stages of industrialization, the situation has changed in modern times for a number of reasons. First, more and more manufacturing industry uses finished and semi-finished materials in the production process and needs to be located near other plants rather than close to mines. Second, even where raw materials are used, technological improvements such as better forms of transport or the concentration and beneficiation of ores have reduced the need for manufacturing proximity in the face of other considerations.

All industries must sell their products, and a location near a **market** is desirable, if the finished product increases in weight, bulk or fragility in the manufacturing process, in order to reduce the costs of transport. A market location is needed for products in this category such as cars or beer. However, it is not only low transport costs which make a market location attractive. Perishable goods such as bread or newspapers need a market location as do industries such as clothing manufacture where there is the need for close customer/manufacturer contact. A market location can also be attractive for industries assembling materials from a wide range of origins, while for those industries such as iron and steelmaking where economies of scale are vital to ensure competiveness, a large market is essential. Indeed, it can be argued that the market is the most important single factor affecting the location of industry, although the following factors must also be taken into account.

Given a location where materials can be assembled and products distributed without incurring prohibitive transport costs, the manufacturer must find a convenient **site**. Many industries have few site requirements but others such as iron and steelmaking need large sites with good loadbearing qualities in locations where materials can be easily assembled. Services such as a good supply of **water** are also vital in many industries. In the iron and steel industry, vast quantities are required since it takes about 200,000 litres to make a tonne of steel, while many other industries need water of a specific quality. Food processing is an industry which needs large amounts of pure water while even more stringent requirements must be met in industries such as that producing photographic paper. In an age of increasing concern about environmental pollution, a site with facilities to cope with the problems of **waste disposal** cheaply and easily is also likely to be attractive.

Industry is also dependent upon supplies of **energy**, although requirements differ from industry to industry in terms of volume and whether the demand is for fuel, as in the process of iron smelting, or for power to run machinery, as in the manufacture of textiles. Historically, the supply of energy has been a major factor affecting location and there is still a close correlation between the distribution of industry and the world's coalfields. It is still vital in industries such as aluminium smelting where power costs form a high proportion of production costs, but the role of energy as a locational factor has lessened. Improvements in fuel economy have meant that the volume of fuel needed in the iron and steel industry has been reduced, while easily transported energy sources such as electricity, natural gas and oil have meant that supplies are very widely available in industrialized countries and have only a weak locational role.

The **cost and availability of labour** is a much more important factor affecting location in many industries. In some industries, such as oil refining, the size of the labour input is so small in relation to the other factors of production that it plays a very minor role in location. In labour intensive industries such as clothing and textiles, labour costs are much more crucial. The cost of labour can only be measured against its productivity, and wage rates form only one element. Other elements include turnover rates, the degree of absenteeism and labour relations, and a high-wage, highly productive workforce can constitute a low cost input to an industry. The cost and availability of labour vary geographically and therefore have a locational effect. Areas with poor labour reputations such as Merseyside or Glasgow find it much more difficult to attract industry. The availability of labour involves not just quantity but also quality, and a skilled and adaptable labour force has a considerable attractive power for technologically advanced industries. A very specialized form of labour is **management**, and any area must be able to produce or attract managers in order to provide a successful location. The shortage of management skills is an important problem in many Third World countries.

The **mobility of labour** is also important, in terms of both its ability to change jobs or to move to new areas. A completely mobile labour force would have no locational effect but, in fact, labour is a relatively immobile factor of production. In many countries, new skills are not easily learned because of poor educational facilities, and changes in employment structures may be delayed by trade union resistance in others. Labour is also relatively immobile geographically, for social reasons such as family ties, or for practical reasons such as the shortage of housing at the right price. On the other hand, many young professional or skilled workers are highly mobile and can choose where they wish to work, at home or overseas.

The role of capital in location is best seen if the roles of money capital and physical capital are considered separately. Historically, the role of **money capital** was important because it was often only locally available, but with the development of national banking systems its locational role within developed countries has diminished considerably. On the other hand, many Third World countries are considered to be high risk areas and the availability of money capital is much more of a problem. In these areas, economic aid from developed countries is likely to be the only realistic source.

Physical capital is much less mobile and is one of the principal factors creating **geographical inertia**, or the tendency for industry to remain in an area despite the fact that the initial reasons for its location no longer apply. Thus, a factory or plant may remain in operation long after the local supplies of raw materials on which it was based have become exhausted, if importing supplies is cheaper than relocating. Some physical capital is mobile between uses, and washing machines can be made in plants built for making armaments but, on the other hand, there is not much one can do with redundant blast furnaces and capital immobility discourages change.

Inertia is also encouraged by the development in an area of **secondary advantages** which may offset the loss of initial advantages. These consist of, first, the presence of an economic infrastructure including many of the factors already discussed, such as good transport, water supplies and energy services.

Second, the presence of existing social capital such as housing and technical education facilities. Third, the presence of other industries which can easily supply materials or use the factory's products, or the presence of specialist service industries. As a result, **agglomerations** of industry develop in which there is a complex system of **linkages**. To these agglomerations other industries are attracted, and specialized industrial regions are developed which have considerable staying power, despite constantly changing conditions of supply and demand.

As factors such as materials and power supplies loose their traditional locational power, many modern industries are experiencing increasing freedom of location, and these **footloose industries** are subject to other influences. Areas which are attractive as places to live and work are becoming more and more important as industrial locations. In the USA, France, Germany and the UK, for example, there is a distinct trend for industry to move from less to more attractive areas, especially from north to south. **Environmental factors** such as climate have traditionally affected industries such as aircraft manufacture because of the need for good flying weather and the costs of heating large hangars, but the role of climate as a factor affecting the quality of life is a more recent locational factor. The **quality of life** is increasing in importance and the fast growing industrial areas in the USA are now found in the 'sunbelt', stretching from California to Florida. Moreover, as the centres of large cities become less attractive places to live and work, industry is being dispersed to suburban or small town locations.

Increasingly, location decisions are being made by groups of managers within corporate organizations rather than by individual entrepreneurs, and these decisions are made with reference to the **geography of the firm** as much as to the world at large. As a result, although profitable locations will be sought for new plants, this profitability will be considered in relation to the profitability of the firm as a whole, and smaller margins may be acceptable. Also, many corporate decisions are made by multi-national companies whose location decisions place much emphasis on factors such as political alignment or stability.

Finally, it must be remembered that while manufacturers locate where they think they will achieve the best returns, their choice is not entirely free, because **governments** are increasingly concerned to restrict or encourage industrial development in certain places for a range of economic, social, political or strategic reasons. In the planned economies of the Communist world, the location of industry is closely controlled, but national government influence is increasing even in the free-enterprise economies. There are a number of reasons for this. First, economic and social reasons are important because it is the duty of any government to ensure that a country's resources are being used to the best advantage and that there are no great inequalities in the distribution of wealth. Unfortunately, conflicts often occur because governments may encourage inertia where social costs are politically significant, while the manufacturer, with narrower social responsibilities, may wish to relocate in order to gain an economic advantage for his firm. Second, political reasons are also important since unemployment may lead to political instability, and most governments in Western Europe have regional planning policies to avoid serious imbalances. Finally, strategic reasons are also important where there is the need to maintain a capacity to produce materials of war or to locate industry in areas safe from attack. Within countries such as the USA, **local government** authorities are seeking to attract industrial development by offering physical or financial inducements to manufacturers in the form of cheap factories and tax concessions.

In the UK, for example, governments have attempted to encourage industrialists to locate in particular areas since 1934, in an attempt to reduce regional differences in unemployment and per capita incomes. Since that time, a variety of methods have been used to influence location decisions but they can be classified broadly into two types: first, attempts have been made to attract industry to areas selected by government by offering a range of incentives to industrialists such as grants, loans and tax concessions, help in training manpower, and infrastructure investment. Second, attempts have been made to control growth in more prosperous areas by requiring industrialists to obtain an Industrial Development Certificate (IDC) before they can undertake any development over a certain size. This mixture of persuasion and compulsion has been applied in varying degrees over the country as a whole, but the areas eligible for assistance have been increasing, and by early 1979, areas covering over 40% of the employed population were categorized as Special Development, Development or Intermediate Areas (Fig. 83a). However, the Conservative government elected in June 1979 decided to operate a more selective **regional industrial policy** by gradually reducing the assisted areas to cover only 25% of the employed population by

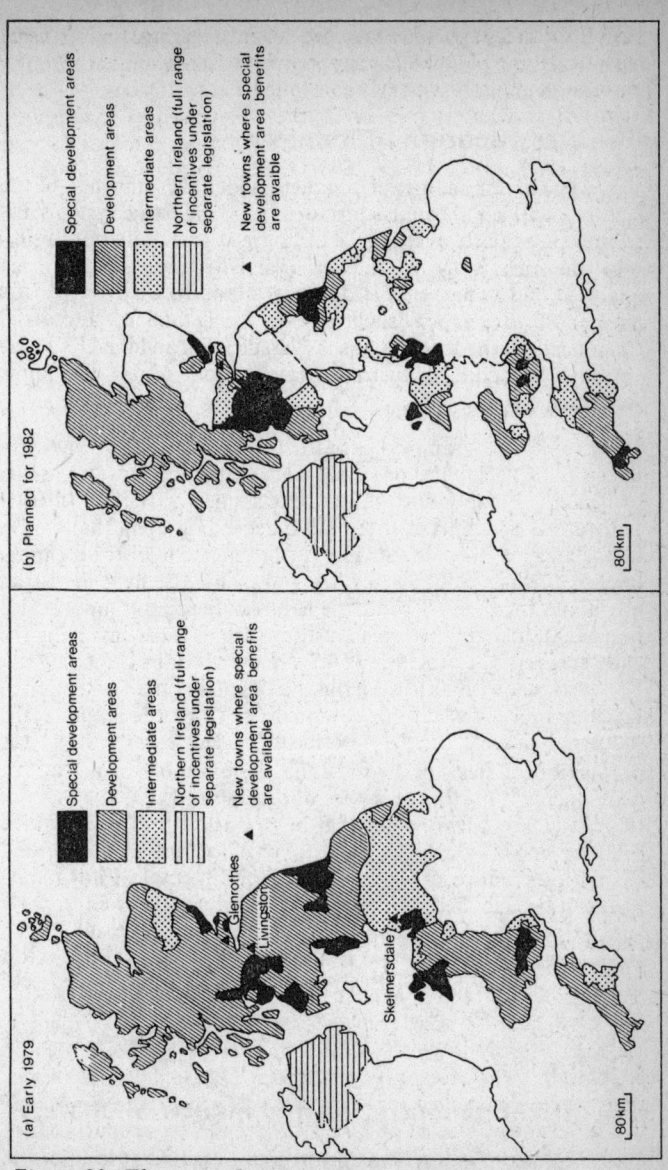

Figure 83. The assisted areas

1982 (Fig. 83b), by reducing the level of regional investment incentives, and by reducing the control on development through the partial abolition of IDC's.

The classification of industry

The demand for industrial products under the influence of the factors identified above has produced large industrial systems distributed irregularly over the Earth's surface. In an attempt to simplify the vast range of industrial activity, industry has been analysed, and a number of **industrial classification systems** have been developed such as the US Standard Industrial Classification, the British Census Classification and the UN International Standard Industrial Classification of all Economic Activities.

However, for geographical purposes it is useful to classify industry in terms of its inputs, processes and output, its location, or its ownership. First, industry can be classified as either **labour intensive** or **capital intensive**, depending upon the relative importance of either input. The petrochemical industry is capital intensive, while clothing, textiles and many assembly industries are labour intensive. Second, the nature of the labour input is also important, and **unskilled** industries such as those involving the early stages of the processing of raw materials or brickmaking can be contrasted with **skilled** industries involving the production of machine tools or electronic components. Third, the nature of the industrial process can be described as being **heavy**, as in the production of steel, or **light**, as in the assembly of motor car components. Fourth, the nature of the output forms the basis of the distinction between **capital** or **producer** industries which produce goods which are used to produce further goods, and **consumer** industries which produce for direct sale. Fifth, industries can be classified on the basis of their location as either **raw material based** or **market orientated**, or, depending upon the relative pull of the major factors of production, as either **tied** or **footloose**. Finally, industry can be classified on the basis of ownership as being either **private**, which may entail individual or corporate ownership, or **state** industry (nationalized industry in the UK).

Industrial concentration and industrial change

The tendency of industry to agglomerate at favoured locations in response to the factors discussed above has produced concentrations of industry over the Earth's surface (Fig. 84). The major belts are found in the north-eastern USA and California, Western Europe, Japan, the Ukraine, Volga, Urals and Western Siberia regions of the USSR, with smaller but significant concentrations in northern India, China, around the River Plate, South Africa and Australia among others. It can be seen that there are large parts of the Earth's surface with very little industry, especially in the Tropics and high latitudes, and that most manufacturing takes place in the middle latitudes, especially on coalfield areas in Europe and areas of European settlement. At a national scale also, industrial activity is characterized by concentration, and industrial regions such as the Midlands of England, the Ruhr in Germany and the north-eastern USA have developed in the advanced economies.

Because of the importance of the factors encouraging inertia, regions such as these remain as major industrial centres, but industry is characterized by constant **change**, and change in the relative importance of locational factors operates to produce changes in the location and distribution of industry. For example, in the USA, new industrial areas such as the Baton Rouge-New Orleans petrochemical corridor have been created while areas such as central New England and parts of Appalachia have fallen into decline. This is also apparent on a global scale and the rise of new industrial concentrations in Japan, Hong Kong and Korea has taken place as traditional industrial areas such as central Scotland and the Franco-Belgian coalfield have fallen into decline. These locational changes are being brought about for a number of reasons, including changes in the supply of materials, in the development of new industrial processes, changes in demand, and the changing balance of comparative advantage.

Changes in the supply of materials result from the operation of a number of factors. First, the traditional supply of a raw material may become exhausted, and the declining quality of the Lake Superior iron ores, for example, has made the location of iron and steelmaking on the east coast of the USA very attractive. Second, the discovery of new sources of iron ore in Brazil and Mauritania has reinforced this attraction since the ore can be brought easily to a coastal refinery. Third, new sources of supply may become available from known but unused supplies if the price of the commodity rises to a level which makes it economic to be worked. This happened with Cornish tin in the early 1970s, and the continuing rise in the price of oil is making the exploitation of

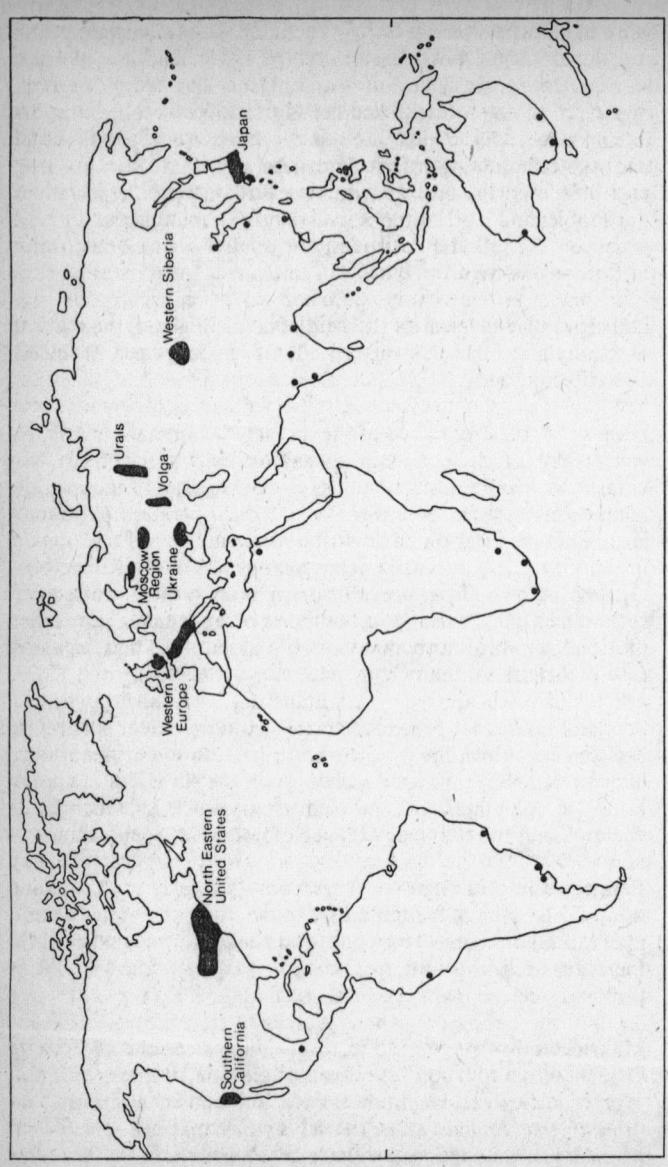

Figure 84. Major industrial concentrations

many small fields in the North Sea a viable economic proposition. Fourth, new materials may be created by technology, and the development of synthetic fibres and plastics has had a considerable effect on many textile and metal producers. Fifth, transport developments may change the relative positions of supplies and products within the world economy, and the development of very large bulk carriers, for example, has made possible the transport of iron ore on a world scale. Finally, political change can disrupt supplies, as the Western economies in general found to their cost during the revolution in Iran.

Changes in demand also affect location, and world population growth and the rise in living standards in developed countries have led to a considerable increase in the volume of demand and the establishment of new factories. There have also been changes in the nature of demand as products have become more sophisticated, requiring fewer basic raw materials and more finished parts in their construction: the proportion of steel used in the manufacture of motor cars, for example, has decreased as plastics have increased in importance. With the increasing sophistication of many products and the corresponding decrease in the locational power of traditional factors such as the costs of raw materials and transport, many industries have moved to more attractive locations, and the suburbanization of industry has been a major feature of developed countries since about 1950.

On the other hand, not all changes necessarily produce changes in location, and **changes in industrial processes**, especially in the development of innovations such as the basic oxygen technique and computer-controlled processes in steelmaking to create a high-technology industry will tend to reinforce many industries within the developed world. However, locations may change within countries as large manufacturing units become necessary to achieve economies of scale, and since it is uneconomic to think in terms of iron and steel plant with capacities of less than one million tonnes per annum, further concentration is likely.

In a constantly changing world, the initial advantages enjoyed by an area or an industry are constantly being reconsidered, and changes in the relative importance of location factors mean that an area may lose its **comparative advantage**. If sufficient secondary advantages have been developed and the area has become diversified, then the process of inertia may keep it viable.

In older industrial areas such as interior New England, southern Belgium or northern England, characterized by specialization and dependence on declining industries such as textiles or coal mining, lengthy periods of adjustment may be necessary.

Summary

Industry is located in an uneven pattern of concentration over the Earth's surface, but this is not a random pattern. It has been produced as a result of decisions taken in response to various factors which affect the location of industry. These factors are concerned with the assembly, processing and distribution of materials and products, geographical inertia, environmental circumstances, the geography of the firm and government intervention. Because many of these factors are constantly changing, industrial location is very dynamic, although relocation is restricted by the forces of inertia.

Chapter 25
Theories of Economic Location

As discussed on page 207, attempts have been made to explain the location of economic activity by the development of normative and behavioural theories which are also useful in the prediction of suitable locations for future development. Behind the search for theory is an assumption that there is some order in the location of economic activity and that location is not just a random process. This can be demonstrated, for example, by the fact that industry as a whole tends to be agglomerated in particular areas, and that plants in particular industries have similar locations. This patterning is to be expected given the fact that location decisions are taken within an ordered framework of opportunities and constraints offered by the operation of the many physical, economic, social and political factors discussed in previous chapters. The task is to simplify reality by identifying the most significant of these factors, establishing their relative importance, and explaining how they operate in order to develop an explanatory and predictive body of theory. Such theories of agricultural location are largely concerned with explaining patterns of land use, while theories of industrial location are more concerned with explaining specific locations. On the whole, normative theories are being modified by the development of behavioural theories, but it is possible to give only a brief outline here.

Theories of agricultural location

One of the earliest attempts to explain agricultural land-use patterns was made in 1826 by **J. H. von Thünen**, who simplified reality into an isolated, flat, featureless plain, (an isotropic surface), inhabited by maximizing farmers whose production costs are everywhere the same, served by a dense network of uniform roads, and dominated by a single city which acts as the sole market. In this situation, bulky products or those difficult to transport are grown near to the market, and lighter or easily transported products are grown further away, because transport costs, which increase in direct proportion to distance, account for variations in the cost of products at the market. Figure 85 shows how a farmer's returns at the market (M) decrease as distance, expressed as his transport costs, increases. *Crop 1* is a crop such as potatoes

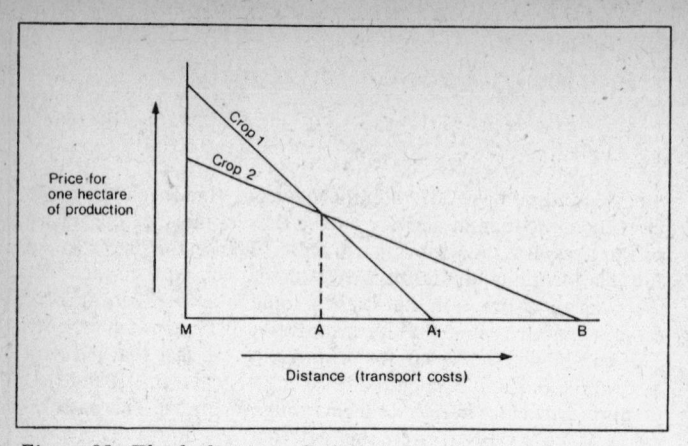

Figure 85. The declining profitability of two crops as distance from the market increases

which yields a large bulk per hectare and is expensive to transport, and *Crop 2* is a crop such as wheat which is less bulky per acre and is therefore cheaper to transport. As a result, the return from potatoes drops away from the market much more sharply than the return from wheat, and potatoes are more profitable than wheat only within MA. Beyond A_1 they cannot be grown profitably at all. In this situation, a farmer who wishes to maximize his profits will grow only potatoes within MA and only wheat within AB, and if A and B are rotated around M, then the pattern of optimum land use is a number of concentric zones around the market, as shown in figure 86a, and Map (a) in figure 87. Von Thünen realized, of course, that reality is not nearly as simple as this, and in figure 86b, he modified the pattern by the inclusion of two variables, a navigable river and a second market centre. Many others could have been selected such as variations in soil quality, transport method or demand.

However, although von Thünen's theory is both an important early approach to the problem of land use, and still valid in many of its underlying assumptions, especially concerning the role of transport, the use of normative models has been questioned, because real farmers are not **economic men**, possessed of perfect knowledge and ability and driven by a desire to maximize their profits. In recent years, attempts have been made to explain land-use patterns by understanding how man perceives reality and how

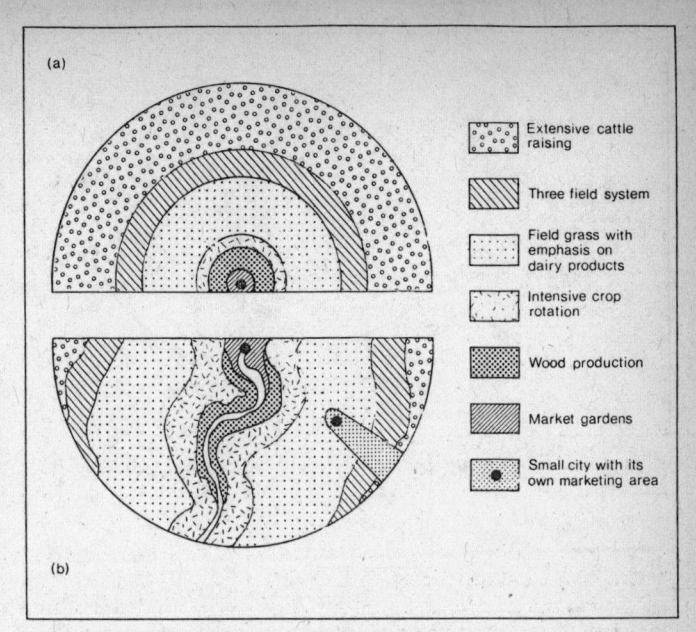

Figure 86. (a) concentric zonation of land use in von Thünen's isolated state (b) land use modified by two variables

he then, in a state of less than perfect knowledge and ability, behaves economically. To aid this understanding, the idea of a **behavioural matrix** has been proposed by A. Pred which enables the farmer's decisions to be analyzed in terms of the quantity and quality of information available to him, and his ability to use it. In figure 87 it assumed that the land-use pattern in Map (a) has been produced by optimizing farmers as shown in figure 85, and the location decisions of two of these economic men are plotted on the behavioural matrix. However, in reality most **decisions are sub-optimal** and a real-world land-use pattern would be more like that shown in Map (b), with farmers accepting less than maximum profits and with zones of transition rather than the rigid boundaries of Map (a). The decisions of a number of farmers growing *Crop 1* have been plotted on the matrix and a number of possible explanations of their decisions are offered. *Farmer 1* has used good information wisely and is similar to the economic men of normative theory. *Farmer 2* is ignorant and stupid, but lucky, and he appears to have made a good decision

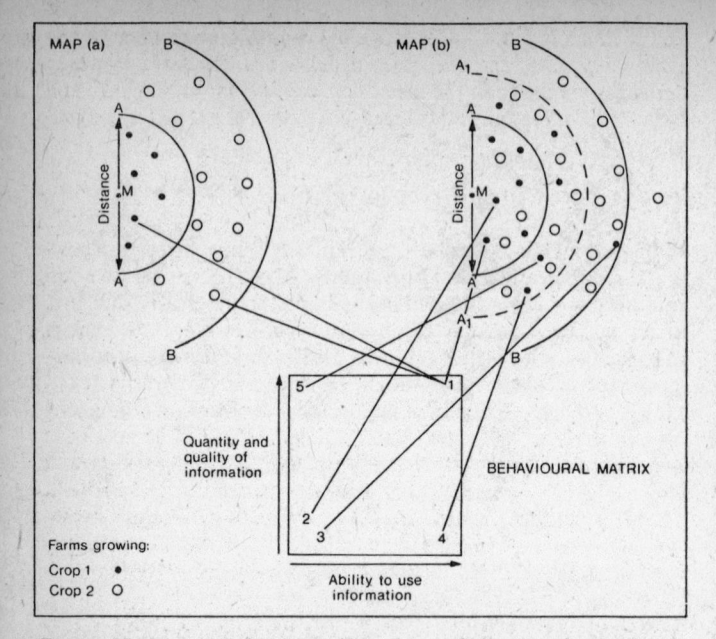

Figure 87. Location decisions plotted on a behavioural matrix

purely by chance. *Farmer 3* has similar characteristics but has not been blessed by good fortune and must soon be out of business. *Farmer 4* is able but lacks information and should really get together with *Farmer 5* so that they could make a sound decision between them. Unfortunately, it is difficult to quantify the behavioural matrix because information and ability are not easy to measure, but it is an interesting approach to the study of how sub-optimal decisions are made.

Another approach to the study of agricultural decision-making in order to understand land-use patterns is through the use of **game theory**. In an agricultural context, a game is set whereby the farmer plays the environment. The environment can hold wet year, dry year or average year 'cards', and the farmer's 'cards' are his crops or techniques which are suitable for wet, dry or average years. The possible ways in which the game may be played are then analyzed: whether, for example, the farmer gambles all on his judgement that the year will be wet and grows only crops which will give him high yields if he is right, or whether he plays it safe and plants a less profitable range of crops to take account of any eventuality. This analysis gives insights into the ways in which decisions are made in the face of environmental uncertainty and helps explain not only static land-use patterns, but also the dynamic ones.

Theories of industrial location

Industrial location decisions are similarly taken within a framework of opportunities and constraints although the operative factors affecting industrial activity (Chap. 24) are clearly different, and it has been possible to develop a body of theory to explain industrial location. Until recently most of these have been normative theories which have sought to establish **optimum locations** and have assumed that location decisions are taken by economic men. It has also been assumed that the best locations are those which give the **maximum profits**, and are therefore those with the **least costs** and the **maximum revenues**. However, maximum profit theories have been difficult to formulate in practice and most attention has been given to establishing separate least-cost and maximum revenue theories.

Least-cost theories assume that the best location is that where processing and transport costs are least, and the most important attempt to develop a least-cost theory was made by A. Weber in 1909. In order to understand how costs affect location, Weber assumed that there was a uniform demand for a product at all locations producing a uniform price, and therefore decisions about location would be based on variations in costs. Weber considered that transport costs were the key factor, and to find the least transport cost point he used a **locational triangle** (Fig. 88). Reality is simplified to one demand point (D) and two sources of materials (M_1 and M_2), and the least-cost location (L) is the point where the total transport costs, calculated by multiplying the weight of material or product by the distance carried, are least. In effect, each corner of the triangle exerts a 'pull' on L and in figure 88a, four tonnes of raw material have to be moved to produce one tonne of product. As a result, weight-losing industries such as iron smelting are raw-material-orientated, 'pulled' to M_1 and M_2. In figure 88b, one tonne of M_1 and one tonne of M_2 are needed to produce two tonnes of product and, as a result, weight-gaining industries such as baking are market orientated. It follows that only localized materials will have any locational effects, but it must be remembered that industrial costs consist of

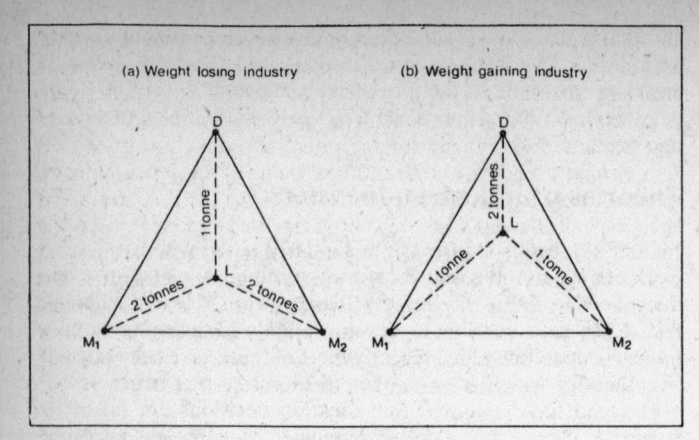

Figure 88. Weber's locational triangle

more than just transport costs, and the least-cost location is also determined by variations in labour costs, the benefits of agglomeration, and so on. However, even when the least-cost location is found it may not be the one that gives the best profits because demand varies as much as cost.

Maximum revenue theories attempt to examine variations in demand and assume that the best location is that which gives

P	Production point
OP	Price at production point
AQN	Demand curve
PQ	Quantity sold at P
A	No demand because price is too high

Demand curve rotated around production point to give cone AQP

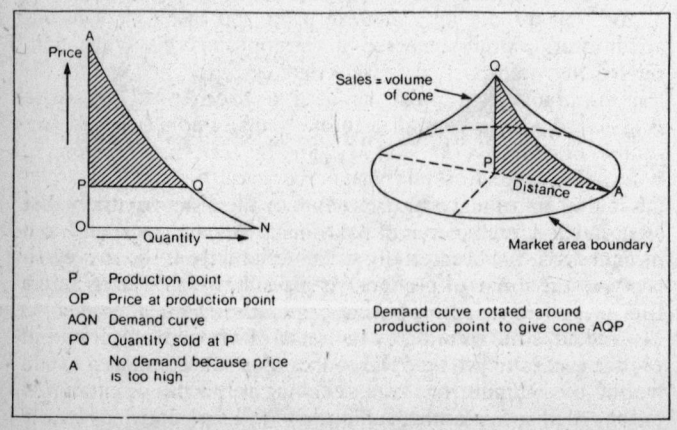

Figure 89. The theoretical shape of the market area (Lösch)

the maximum sales. Such a theory was developed in 1940 by A. Lösch (Fig. 89) which seeks to explain the size and shape of **market areas** around a production point. Reality is again simplified to a flat, featureless plain where costs are held constant and uniform and demand for a product varies with its price. P is the production point, and as can be seen from the demand curve, demand decreases as the price increases. If the increase in price is the result of increases in transport costs away from P, then the market area will be circular, as can be seen when the demand curve is rotated around P. The size of the market area is the volume of the cone AQP. Assuming that other producers locate on the plain to satisfy demand outside the market area of P, there will eventually be a hexagonal pattern of market areas (Fig. 90), as the circles become packed together.

1. Firms operate with circular market areas.
2. Competition increases to serve all the potential market.
3. To avoid overlap of circles and to serve all areas, market areas become hexagonal.
4. Final pattern of market areas.

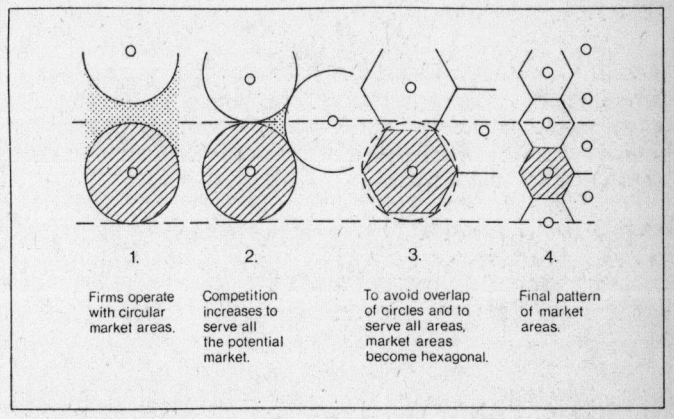

Figure 90. Circular market areas become hexagonal (Lösch)

Of course, in reality, both costs and demand vary spatially, but attempts to develop maximum profit theories integrating the two theories have not been totally successful and there is still no generally accepted normative theory of location. However, as in the field of agriculture, more recent approaches have attempted to explain industrial location by the use of behavioural theories and assume that establishing optimal locations is less important than finding the margins, or areas, within which some profit can be made and then explaining sub-optimal location decisions within these margins. It is assumed that the decision maker is not an

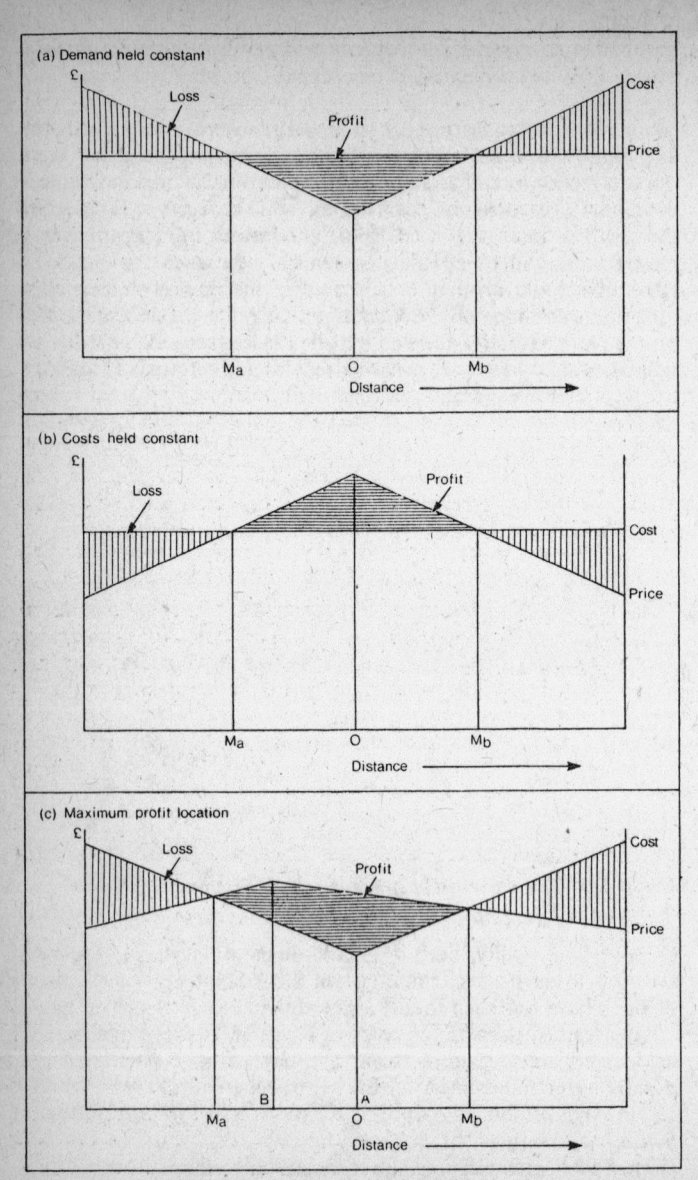

Figure 91. The spatial margins to profitability

economic man seeking to optimize his profits, but is a satisficer (page 208), making good, if not the best, profits.

The **spatial margins to profitability** were demonstrated by D. M. Smith in 1966 in a simple model which assumes that costs and revenues vary from place to place and that profitable locations are those in areas where revenues exceed costs. To identify such areas, Smith first holds demand constant and allows costs to vary, and in figure 91a it is assumed that costs per unit of production are less than revenues at O, but increase with distance from O, producing a V-shaped space-cost curve. At M_a and M_b, the cost curve cuts the revenue curve and beyond M_a and M_b no profits are possible. M_a and M_b are therefore the spatial margins to profitability and O is the least-cost location giving maximum profits. In figure 91b, costs are held constant and demand is allowed to vary. It is assumed that the price is greater than costs at O, allowing a profit to be made, but that demand declines with distance from O, producing a $\wedge$-shaped space-revenue curve. In this case, M_a and M_b are the spatial margins to profitability and O is the maximum revenue location giving maximum profits. In figure 91c, both costs and demand vary from place to place. Costs rise from location A and revenues fall from location B giving the spatial margins M_a and M_b. If the space-cost and space-revenue curves are steep because, for example, transport costs are high, then profitable production can only take place within a

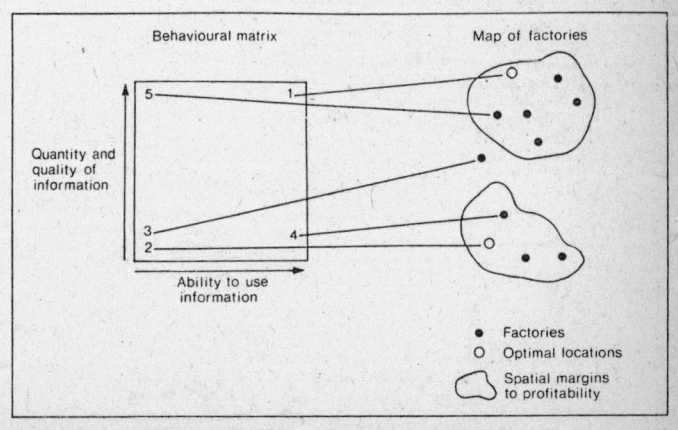

Figure 92. Industrial location decisions plotted on a behavioural matrix

small area, while shallow curves allow a widespread distribution of production.

In the example given, there is only one maximum-profit location and every other producer has to do with a sub-optimal location. Moreover, in reality it is very difficult to find the optimal location, and producers locate in a variety of sub-optimal locations giving different levels of profit – which is one reason why some companies are more successful than others. To explain these sub-optimal locations, the behavioural matrix can be used, and in figure 92, a map of some factories has been drawn with the spatial margins to profitability included, and the manufacturers' location decisions can be explained in the same way as in figure 87.

Summary

In an attempt to explain and predict the location of economic activity in a complex world, a number of theories have been developed which simplify reality in order to understand its fundamental characteristics. Early theories were attempts to construct an idealized reality inhabited by economic men in order to show optimal locations in optimal conditions. This normative approach has been modified in recent years by the development of behavioural models attempting to explain real-world location decisions made by real men with less than perfect knowledge and ability.

Chapter 26
The Geography of Economic Development

The type and intensity of economic activity varies from place to place over the Earth's surface in response to differences in the distribution of human and physical resources. The interaction of physical environments, cultural values, economic and political systems has resulted in widely differing levels of economic development, and the scale and distribution of this inequality, as measured by per capita incomes, is shown in Figure 94. This chapter briefly examines the theories which have been developed to explain these inequalities and then examines some of the problems facing those countries with low levels of economic development.

Models of economic development

The process of economic development is very complex because of the human and physical diversity of the world, and many attempts have been made to simplify it within an explanatory theory. The best known was published by W. Rostow between 1955 and 1960, and shows development taking place within a set of **stages of growth** (Fig. 93). *Stage 1* envisages a traditional society with

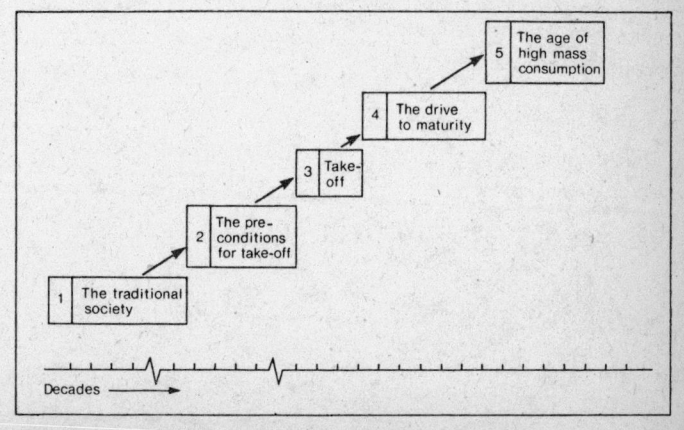

Figure 93. Rostow's stages of economic development

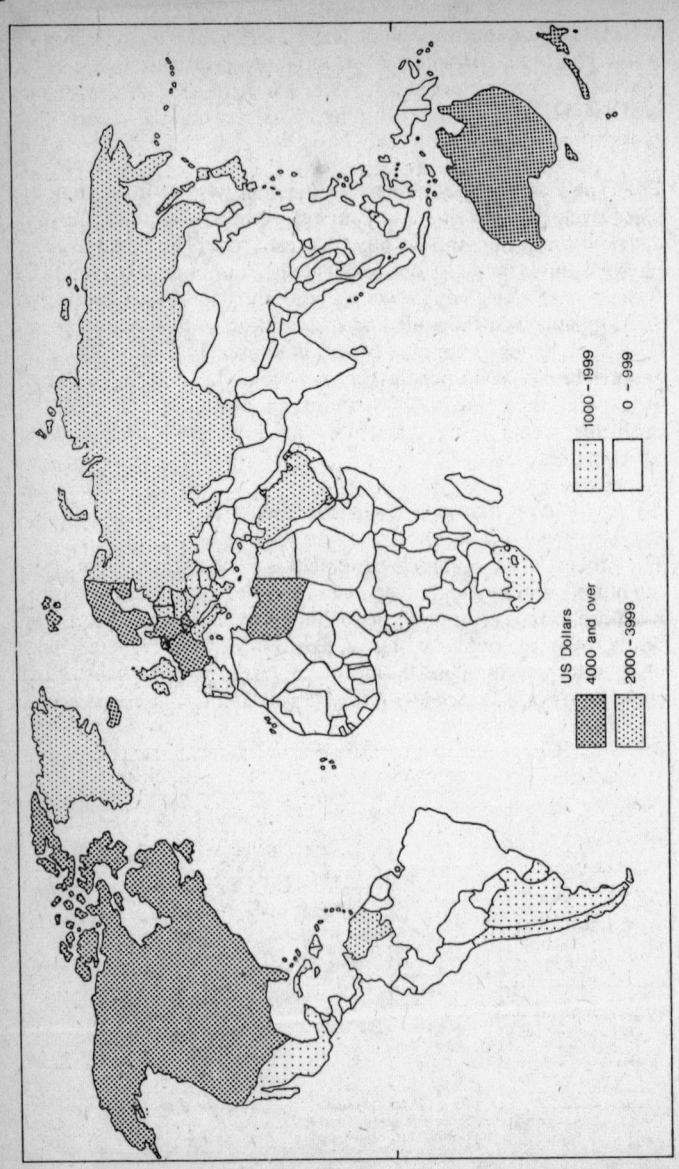

Figure 94. Per capita income 1974

limited science and technology and a hierarchical social structure which is then subjected to change as production begins to increase, infrastructure investments are made, and entrepreneurs are able to take up opportunities. This second stage establishes the preconditions which lead into the crucial third stage, when economy and society are transformed in such a way that self-sustaining growth takes place as leading manufacturing sectors are established and the economy 'takes off'. Further growth then takes place and is transmitted to all parts of the economy in *Stage 4*, and an age of mass consumption is eventually established in *Stage 5*. Criticisms have been made of the model, especially of its failure to establish a linking mechanism between the stages, but it is widely used. It also pays little attention to explaining spatial variations in development, although its emphasis on leading sectors may imply leading regions.

However, this gap is filled by G. Myrdal's theory of **cumulative causation**, published in 1956, which argues that economic development clearly does produce regional differences. Initially, development takes place in a region because of the advantages it can offer, and as it moves ahead of other regions, a process of cumulative causation takes place in which one development leads to another (Fig. 95), and secondary advantages are established. Once this growth has started, regional differences become even greater as labour, capital and commodities are attracted to the growth region, and this **backwash effect** on remaining regions

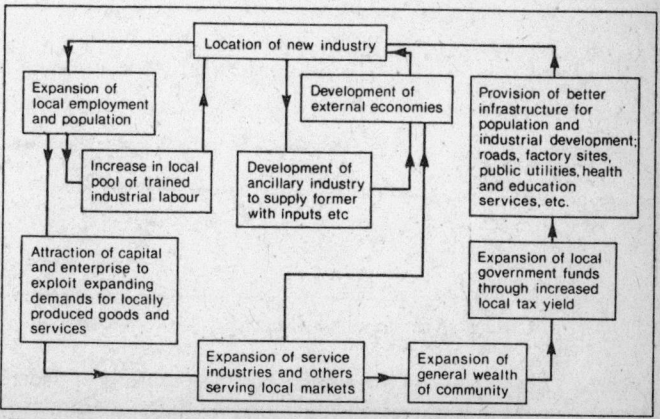

Figure 95. Myrdal's process of cumulative causation

is made even more acute as these regions receive goods from the growth region which flood their markets and prevent the development of local industries. On the other hand, it is expected that differences will eventually begin to diminish through a **spread effect** as general economic growth encourages the development of secondary centres of growth in regions where the backwash effect is not too great.

Nevertheless, the backwash effect seems to be much greater than the spread effect both within and between countries, and the world is characterized by great regional inequalities. Many countries are still in Rostow's first stage and the problem of underdevelopment is a major concern.

The problem of underdevelopment

The term underdevelopment is essentially a euphemism for poverty, and this poverty is extensive, deep-rooted and complex. Part of this complexity can be seen in figure 96 which illustrates the view of H. W. Singer that the problem of underdevelopment is made up of 'vicious circles within vicious circles and of interlocking vicious circles'.

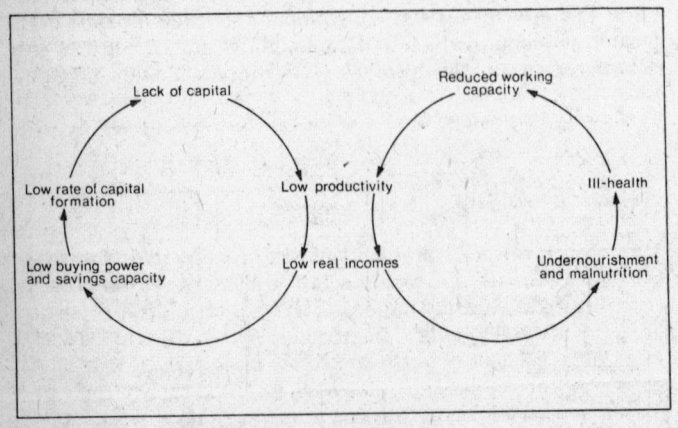

Figure 96. Circles of poverty and ill-health

Just two of these circles are shown, but the problems of underdevelopment can be examined under three headings: environmental and resource problems, social problems, and economic problems. These vary in their intensity and relative importance from country to country.

Environmental and resource problems

The world's poorer countries are generally located south of latitude 35°N and this north-south split in prosperity has some of its foundation in environmental differences. In the development of **food resources**, climatic problems are important, since large areas of the Third World are subject to low and variable rainfall, while others suffer from too much rain which leaches the nutrients out of the soil and creates the notorious hardpans. Even when crops are successfully grown there is the problem of attack by pests, and following the breakdown of control programmes as a result of war in north-eastern Africa, the FAO reported in 1979 that 50 countries in a belt stretching from western Africa to India were threatened by desert locusts. The problem of crop failure is a constant threat and in the same year, the FAO listed 13 countries (11 in Africa and 2 in Asia) suffering abnormal food shortages. The development of **physical resources** is also a problem. Many countries suffer from shortages, especially of energy, and although these may be made up by the considerable HEP potential in Africa, the costs of development will be enormous. Even where mineral resources are found, extreme climatic conditions make exploitation difficult and expensive. However, limits on the supply of physical resources do not necessarily bar development if the human resources are available, as witnessed by countries such as Japan, Switzerland and Denmark, but, unfortunately, economic and social problems abound.

Social problems

Two groups of social problems can be identified, the first concerned with the size and health of the population, the second with social attitudes and institutions. The underdeveloped countries are currently undergoing a **demographic revolution** as death rates fall as a result of death control by medicine and science. As yet, birth control has not increased to anything like the same extent, and consequently the size of the population is increasing enormously. In Mexico, for example, the crude death rate fell from 26·1% in 1932 to 9·0% in 1976, while the crude birth rate has remained very high at 45% per annum. As a result, total population rose from 18 millions to over 65 millions, with the prospect of 135 millions in the year 2000. There is also a very high dependency rate with up to 46% of the population under the age of 15. Of course, Western Europe and the USA experienced rapid rates of growth in the 19th century, but there it was accompanied by a corresponding economic growth. Equally serious is the problem of ill-health, locked as it is into the circle of poverty. **Ill-health** springs from environmental conditions and poor health-care facilities, but it is basically a function of poverty, especially in relation to the problem of undernourishment, caused by insufficient food, and malnutrition, caused by poor quality food (Chapter 17).

It would be arrogant to suggest that the **social attitudes and institutions** of underdeveloped countries are wrong or somehow inferior to those of industrialized countries, but there is no doubt that many of them make economic growth difficult. In any society there is the vested interest of those with economic and social power who are likely to resist change, and in rigid societies, closely controlled by religion and taboo, this conservatism is reinforced. Decisions are made within a framework of social custom and tradition, and in many peasant societies oppressive forms of land tenure siphon off profits and prevent change. The problem is compounded because poor educational facilities and the resulting illiteracy limit horizons and reinforce traditional practices. In countries attempting to introduce change, literacy is a vital element, if only to enable workers to read the instructions on a machine or a bag of fertilizer.

Economic problems

The economic problems facing the underdeveloped world cannot be seen simply as internal problems for each country but must be related to the development of the world economic system which depends on the collection of resources on a world-wide basis. (Chapter 23). This interdependence is reflected in the UN's concern in declaring the 1970s the Second Development Decade.

A basic problem facing all underdeveloped countries is the **shortage of capital** necessary to provide both the agricultural and industrial capacity to ensure that standards of living rise. This capital is needed not only to build factories but, perhaps even more important, it is needed to provide an **economic infrastructure** of transport networks, power supplies and educational and social facilities. Since this type of investment is capital intensive and slow to show a return, it must be provided by governments. Unfortunately, the tax base on which Third World countries rely is very small and there is a need for foreign aid in the form of grants and loans. In 1971 the UN established a target whereby 0·7% of the GNP of the industrialized countries should be given as official development aid (ODA), but by 1977 this figure was not being met and the industrialized countries were only giving an average 0·3% as they felt the effects of the recession following the rises in the price of oil. At UNCTAD IV in 1976 the situation was improved somewhat when the official debts of the poorest countries were written off, but unfortunately oil price rises have led to a growing volume of commercial debt since that time.

Closely related to the problem of capital shortage is the problem of **commodity prices**. It is an unfortunate fact that most of the underdeveloped countries have at one time been colonies of the developed countries, and it is claimed that although political independence has been granted in recent years, there is still an economic colonialism, or neo-colonialism, which pays low prices for Third World commodities and charges high prices for manufactured goods. However, the price of one commodity has been raised so successfully that a worldwide economic recession is threatened and the prospect of other commodity prices increasing is being strongly resisted by the industrialized nations as unemployment rises and growth slows.

The problem of **markets** is also serious since the size of domestic markets for those countries which are industrializing is small. As a result, there is a need to seek international markets. However, the industrialized countries are reluctant to open their doors to imports and one issue at UNCTAD V in 1979 was the increase in protectionism by the industrialized countries against industrializing countries such as Brazil and South Korea.

Policy problems

Faced with the extremes of economic development which now characterize the world and an ever widening gap between the rich and poor nations, two questions must be posed. Should anything be done to lessen the inequality between rich and poor, and if so, what is the best course of action?

On the one hand it may be argued that the world is characterized by diversity and that great differences in wealth are inevitable given regional differences in resource endowments and the history of human development. Myrdal has also demonstrated that economic development inevitably reinforces regional inequalities. However, it is not necessary to accept such physical and economic determinism, and there are sound moral and practical reasons why the development process should be better arranged. It is morally wrong that two-thirds of the world's population should be living in poverty, and although poverty can be a relative concept, the abject poverty and suffering of millions of people is a fundamental denial of their basic human rights. There are also sound practical reasons why basic inequalities should be reduced. In the first place, the peoples of the Third World represent an enormous potential market and could create a demand-led expansion of economic activity to the advantage of all countries. Second, such inequalities represent a serious political threat since a world of resentful have-nots, rightly or wrongly convinced that they are being exploited for the benefit of a fortunate few, constitute a potential source of conflict. Finally, there is the risk that the existence of large numbers of poverty-stricken and unhealthy people may provide a breeding ground for diseases which would affect us all in a pandemic.

It is generally accepted that the scale of inequality needs to be reduced, but the problem of identifying and implementing a proper course of action will not be easily solved, not least because the problem of underdevelopment varies considerably from country to country.

It can be argued that since the rich countries are industrialized the key to the problem lies in industrialization; many economists have advocated **unbalanced growth** as a solution, in which one sector of the economy is stimulated in the expectation that it will encourage growth in other sectors as linkages develop and further demand is created. However, the production of food is essential if present and projected increases in the population are to be fed and other economists have advocated **balanced growth** as a solution by which the agricultural and industrial sectors of the economy progress together, complementing and supporting each other. Which is the better course is not agreed, but what is agreed is that development need not be capital intensive, and small-scale, labour intensive developments using intermediate technology may be a more appropriate investment than high technology industries using vast amounts of scarce capital and small amounts of plentiful labour.

It is also agreed that economic growth is made very difficult when any benefit is eaten up by unchecked population growth, but the social problems involved in implementing birth control programmes are enormous. It is clear that the path to development requires radical rethinking of social attitudes, values and objectives, and that fundamental changes in institutions will be required. These changes took place in the industrialized countries over a relatively long period but rapid growth is now required if the twin problems of poverty and overpopulation are to be solved in the Third World.

Summary

The world is characterized by extremes of affluence and poverty created by different levels of economic development. Attempts have been made to explain this development with reference to a stages of growth model, and regional differences by a process of cumulative causation. Underdeveloped countries are characterized by a complex interaction of physical, social and economic problems, but the solutions to these problems are not going to be easy to find.

Chapter 27
Rural Settlement

The study of settlements, both rural and urban, has long attracted the attention of geographers, and settlement geography forms an important division of the wider field of human geography. However, it is probably true to say that until recently most interest has been shown by geographers in the study of towns and cities rather than villages and low-order rural settlements. This was no doubt a reflection of the worldwide process of urbanization during the 20th century. But the process of urbanization is also accompanied by rural depopulation. It is now widely appreciated that changes in the economy and employment structure of rural areas, the decline of rural populations and the break-up of the traditional social structure of country areas, together with the growing demands and pressures on the countryside for leisure and recreation, all constitute an important field of investigation for geographers. As a result there has been a recent revival of interest in the geography of the countryside, marked by the publication of a growing number of studies of rural settlement and society.

Early studies of village settlements were very largely concerned with three elements: village site, form and distribution. The term **site** refers to the terrain on which a village has grown up. Village **form** refers to the physical arrangement or pattern of houses and other buildings within a village. A study of village **distribution** is concerned with the spacing and density of rural settlements over a wider area. Inevitably the three elements are interrelated; for example, village form may be influenced by the local site conditions, and the availability of potential sites may influence the regional distribution pattern.

Nucleated and dispersed rural settlement

Before considering the three aspects of village study mentioned above, the point should be made that not all rural settlement is clustered together in the form of nucleated villages or hamlets. In many rural areas the settlement pattern assumes the form of scattered houses, cottages and farms irregularly distributed throughout the countryside. A basic distinction may be drawn, therefore, between clustered or **nucleated settlement** on the

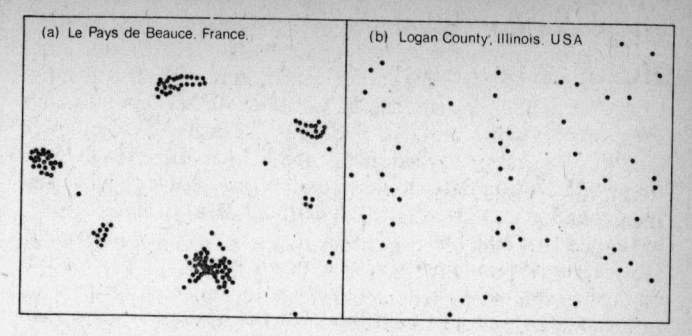

Figure 97. (a) Nucleated and (b) dispersed settlement patterns

one hand, and scattered or **dispersed settlement** on the other. Examples are given in figure 97. The terms nucleated and dispersed are simply descriptions based on subjective evaluations. To add precision to these terms, a measure known as a **coefficient of dispersion** has been devised to measure and express the exact degree of dispersion or nucleation of rural settlement in any area. If the population size of the chief village in a parish or some other small rural unit is known, together with the total population of the parish, then a coefficient of dispersion (C) can be calculated by the following formula:

$$C = \frac{p \times n}{P}$$

in which P is the total population of the parish, p is the population living outside the main village, and n is the number of settlements in the parish. Coefficient values calculated in this way can be used for comparing the relative degree of dispersion of the settlement of a number of parishes.

Village site

Studies of the siting of villages and hamlets are generally based on the assumption that the early settlers in any region made logical evaluations of the physical environment and selected sites for their farms and dwellings in a rational manner. Important considerations were, no doubt, the availability of potential arable or grazing land, a nearby supply of water, and the proximity of building materials and fuel, as well as the need to defend homes and buildings. It is assumed that a combination of these factors explains why the most attractive sites in many areas have been continuously occupied by settlements since very early times. In some cases, later generations have literally built upon the ruins and remains of buildings from earlier generations, so that a 'stratigraphy' of building phases can be identified. Other less attractive sites, or sites which required a more sophisticated technology of land drainage or forest clearance or the sinking of deep wells, were occupied at a later date, or were possibly occupied for a while and then abandoned. J. B. Mitchell in her book, *Historical Geography* has noted that 'the first settlers in a place must often have made false starts and sometimes settled down permanently on a less good site even with a better site nearby, like a picnic party trying first this then that side of a bay, first one side of a hedge then another, and in the end putting up with much that is not ideal rather than move yet once again'.

Despite this reservation, most villages do in fact show a clear response to one or more of the locational influences mentioned above. Thus, **dry-point sites** such as knolls, islands and other elevated locations in areas of swamp and marsh have long proved attractive for settlement sites. Many villages on the Dutch polders and the north German coastlands occupy this type of site. Similarly, well-drained gravel terraces adjacent to major rivers have often been occupied from an early date, as along the Thames valley. Conversely, in areas with restricted water-supply, settlements have grown up around springs and wells and other **wet-point sites** where a good supply of water was regularly available for domestic use as well as for crops and livestock. The spring-line villages at the foot of the chalk and limestone ridges of south-east England illustrate the attraction of this type of site. The need for a site which could be easily defended against attack was also a prime consideration at the time when many villages were founded. **Defensive sites** include the land within a meander loop as well as the more obvious hilltop sites. Considerations of trade and commerce may also have been important for certain villages, hence the attraction of bridging points, river confluence sites, sites at the head of estuaries or the limit of navigation on rivers, as well as gaps and valleys in upland areas.

Village form

Ignoring for the moment the dispersed type of rural settlement illustrated in figure 97b, it is possible to identify a number of distinct forms of nucleated village in the rural landscape of

Western Europe. Certain of the most common village forms are listed below:

1. **Green village** This type of village consists of houses and other buildings, often including the village church, clustered around a small village green or common or other open space.

2. **Street village** This is a linear form of village, sometimes referred to as a shoestring village. Houses are strung out along a routeway which suggests the importance of transportation during the early growth of the village. A similar form of elongated village is found running along the crest of banks and dykes in the English Fens and Dutch polders where poor drainage of the adjacent lands has impeded lateral development of villages.

3. **Cruciform villages** This type of village has grown up at an intersection of routeways, and consists of four lines of buildings radiating out from the intersection. The exact form depends upon the angle of the route intersection and the amount of infilling of buildings which has occurred between the axes.

As well as these basic forms, there are, of course, many composite, intermediate and indeterminate types of layout. It is also interesting to note that the basic European village forms have been duplicated in many parts of the New World where early settlers from Europe attempted to recreate features of their homelands. Along the Atlantic seaboard of the USA, for example, there are numerous small towns and villages which are reminiscent of their British counterparts and have been strongly influenced by European rural traditions. This, however, contrasts strongly with the rural settlements of the western states which were laid out at a later date and were strongly influenced by a system of land holdings imposed by the federal government. Lands west of the Ohio River were divided into a regular grid pattern of townships, sections and quarter-sections before being allocated to settlers. There the villages are monotonously alike and consist of a regular grid pattern of streets laid out on either side of the main street. Such examples serve to make the point that not all villages have evolved gradually over many centuries, but that in many parts of the world modern planned rural settlements also exist. Examples of the latter include the Israeli *kibbutzim* and *moshavim* and the *ujamaa* villages associated with recent rural development programmes in Tanzania.

The distribution of villages

A further aspect of village study is concerned with their spacing in the rural landscape. The distribution of villages and hamlets in any region is influenced by a variety of factors, including patterns of relief, drainage, soils, water-supply, transport and communications, as well as the particular historical development of the region. It should be remembered, too, that the significant factors are those which operated at the time of the establishment and early growth of the rural settlement pattern. Many of these factors are, of course, no longer significant at the present time. For example, with the widespread provision of piped water-supply in most rural areas, there is no longer any reason why villages should be tied to wet-point sites.

The distribution of villages in any area may be described as showing a tendency towards even spacing or towards concentration or clustering, or it may appear to be a random distribution with no clear tendency towards either even spacing or clustering.

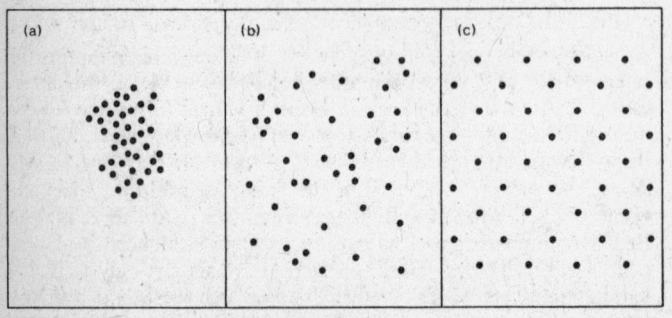

Figure 98. Spatial patterns of village settlements: (a) clustered, (b) random, and (c) evenly-spaced

A basic problem is that of measuring where any particular pattern lies on a scale between these two extreme forms of distribution. The solution to this problem may be found by a technique known as **nearest-neighbour analysis**. This involves calculating a nearest-neighbour index (R_n) by means of the following formula:

$$R_n = 2d \sqrt{\frac{n}{A}}$$

in which A is the size of the area concerned, d is the mean distance between villages, and n is the number of villages in the area. In theory, values for R_n can range from zero, which would signify total concentration, to a maximum value of 2·15 which would be produced by a perfectly uniform distribution of villages in an area. A result of 1·00 would indicate a purely random pattern. Values above and below 1·00 suggest a tendency towards even spacing and clustering respectively.

Rural depopulation

Almost without exception, migration from rural to urban areas is the dominant type of internal migration in the world today. The large-scale movement of population from country to town is a feature of both developed and developing nations. This combined process of rural depopulation and urbanization is primarily a response to economic motives, and can be conveniently explained in terms of the 'push-pull' factors described earlier in Chapter 18. In the rural areas of departing population, the 'push' factors include a reduction in demand for farm labour resulting from increased mechanization of agriculture, lower wages than in the towns, poor housing conditions for many rural families, and a restricted range of social and welfare amenities. In contrast, the 'pull' factors which the urban destinations offer, or are thought to offer, include more varied employment opportunities, higher wages, better schools, shops and entertainment. Many of these urban attractions are, of course, more imagined than real, but that is unimportant. Provided that any potential migrant perceives the city as an attractive destination, then that alone will influence the decision to migrate.

The process of migration from rural areas is age-selective, in that the majority of those who move are young adults. This has two effects; first, it causes an ageing of the population as a progressively higher proportion of elderly people is left in the villages, and second, it produces a gradual reduction in birth rate as the members of the population in the reproductive age groups move to the cities, so that eventually death rate may come to exceed birth rate. In other words, the simple loss of population by migration becomes augmented by what is sometimes termed **biological depopulation**. Declining village populations also create another problem; namely, that of maintaining an adequate level of services and amenities for those who remain. The result is often a closure of village schools, a run-down of rural bus services, and the transfer of many service functions to nearby towns. This makes the village less attractive for many residents, strengthens the 'push' factors, and encourages further outward migration. Rural depopulation and its consequences form a cumulative process.

Urbanization of the countryside

The movement of population between village and town described above is only part of the story. Rural/urban migration is not simply a one-way flow; there also exists a certain amount of return-migration, as former villagers, disenchanted with city life, return to their village or home district. But what is even more important is the movement of urban population into villages adjacent to urban areas, and the growing use of rural areas for leisure and recreation and even for the establishment of second homes.

Commuter villages In recent years transport improvements, such as the building of motorways, together with a continuing rise in the level of private car ownership, have combined to allow city-workers to live at a much greater distance from their place of work. Thus, commuting hinterlands around major cities have been progressively extended, and many city-workers now live in villages and travel into the city for work, shopping and entertainment. A significant number of elderly people also move to the country on retirement.

In these ways the traditional social structure of rural areas is being changed. In most villages within a 50 km radius of a major city there is now a sharp division between the long-established 'native' population born in the vicinity of the village, and a population of 'newcomers' recently arrived in the area whose social and employment ties are still with the town from which they have moved. The division also follows lines of social class and age. The 'native' population tends to be older and usually engaged in working-class rural occupations, while the 'newcomers' consist chiefly of young, affluent, middle-class couples with a higher level of car ownership, better housing and an urban source of income. Many writers have recently suggested that this division of rural society into a two-class structure has destroyed the community spirit of many villages. For the same reason the actual appearance of many villages has also been radically altered, with urban-style housing estates grafted onto a core of centuries-old buildings in the vernacular style. Too often the result is a visual conflict resulting from the unsympathetic scale, style and building materials of the new housing.

Second homes Another form of urban influence in many villages is represented by a growing number of second homes owned by urban families and used on an occasional basis. In some cases these are cottages or former mills and barns which have been converted into a second home for weekend or holiday use; in other instances they consist of purpose-built bungalows, chalets and huts; some surveys even include caravans and houseboats in the category of second homes. Second homes are obviously most numerous in the more affluent countries of the world. In general terms they may be related to national living standards; more specifically, the proportion of families owning a second home may be correlated with factors such as the level of private car ownership, length of paid holidays, or simply the financial ability to purchase a second home for occasional use only. In Sweden and France 20% and 18% respectively of all households enjoy the use of a second home. Latest estimates suggest that about 2·5% of British households own a second home.

Country	Estimated no. of second homes	Date	Source
USA	3,000,000	1970	R. L. Ragatz
France	1,232,000	1968	H. D. Clout
Canada	500,000	1973	W. M. Baker
Sweden	490,000	1971	C. L. Bielckus
Australia	250,000	1973	R. W. Ronertson
UK	200,000	1969	A. W. Rogers
Norway	170,000	1969	C. L. Bielckus
Czechoslovakia	166,000	1971	V. Gardavský

Table 7. Numbers of second homes in selected countries

Second Homes: Curse or Blessing? is the title of a recently published book edited by J. T. Coppock. The title is indicative of the division of opinion which exists about the effects of second homes in rural areas. Some experts have suggested that second homes serve to rejuvenate declining rural areas by creating a demand for services, and by providing rural property owners with the opportunity to sell houses at a price which could not be afforded by local residents. Others have argued that second homes, which usually stand empty and unused for much of the year, deprive needy local residents of valuable housing and undermine the traditional village social structure described earlier.

Recreation in the countryside In recent years there has been a marked increase in the number of town-dwellers visiting rural areas for leisure and recreation. Some engage in outdoor activities such as hiking, climbing, camping and sailing, but most are motorists who simply drive round the countryside. Tourism is now one of the most serious forms of urban encroachment on the countryside. As with second homes, there are both advantages and disadvantages: services such as garages, shops, pubs, hotels and boarding houses benefit from increased trade, but the price that has to be paid includes the presence of camping and caravan sites in areas of scenic beauty, traffic congestion on narrow country lanes, conflicts between farmers and tourists, and problems of litter and pollution.

Given the problems of rural depopulation and urban encroachment on the countryside outlined above, and the serious problems which both processes create, it is not surprising that many governments now regard rural planning as a high priority, demanding as much attention as the more obvious problems of urban planning. In the UK, for example, a policy of concentrating rural population and services in **key villages** has been attempted in many counties, and the establishment of National Parks, Areas of Outstanding Natural Beauty, Nature Reserves and other protected areas is an attempt to deal with the problem of urban visitors to the countryside. The modern approach to rural problems, typified by recent work of the Forestry Commission, involves multipurpose integrated planning which aims to introduce new employment into country areas, stabilize village populations, and provide carefully planned recreational facilities for urban visitors.

Summary

Early studies of rural settlement were almost exclusively concerned with the site, form and distribution of villages. Recently the emphasis has shifted more towards the social aspects of rural settlements, with much attention being given to the processes and problems of rural depopulation and urban encroachment on the countryside in the form of growing numbers of commuters, second home owners and tourists. The aim of rural planning is to resolve the problems caused by these processes.

Chapter 28
Urban Relationships

The study of towns and cities is a long-established field of interest in human geography and as early as 1925, E. W. Burgess presented a model for the social structure of large cities based on his observations of Chicago, while in 1933, W. Christaller formulated his central place theory which is still basic to our understanding of both the spatial and functional relationships of settlements in any region. The use of models and the search for theory was established at an early date in urban geography. Through the years the emphasis in this field of study has constantly shifted: at times it has been the design and morphology of towns and cities which has commanded most attention; at other times the economic functioning of urban settlements. Currently, it would seem that most interest is being shown in the social aspects of towns and cities, especially the problems of urban housing, employment and social welfare. In this first of three chapters on the geography of towns, attention is directed to the relationships that exist between the different orders of settlements found in any region.

Size relationships

It is an observable fact that in any region there are numerous small towns, fewer medium-sized towns, and very few large cities. This fact can be examined more closely: the towns and cities in any region can be arranged in descending order of population size and given a rank number. The largest city is ranked No 1, the second largest No 2, and so on down to the lowest-ranking, smallest town in the region. As early as 1913 it was suggested by F. Auerbach that when these rank numbers are plotted against their respective population sizes a regular relationship can be seen. More recently this same point was restated in more precise terms by G. K. Zipf in what he termed the **rank-size rule**. According to Zipf, 'if all the urban settlements in an area are ranked in descending order of population, the population of the nth town will be $1/n$th that of the largest town'. That is to say, urban population sizes in any region can be arranged in the following series: $1, \frac{1}{2}, \frac{1}{3}, \frac{1}{4}, \ldots, 1/n$. The rank-size rule can also be expressed by means of the following formula:

$$P_n = \frac{P_1}{n}$$

in which P_n is the population of town rank n and P_1 is the population of the largest or primate city. Thus, according to the rule, if the largest city in a region has a population of 750,000 then the fifth-ranking town should have a population of 150,000. The urban rank-size relationship for any country or region is often presented graphically, in which case it is normal to use a logarithmic scale for both axes. This converts a concave curve into a linear or almost linear result.

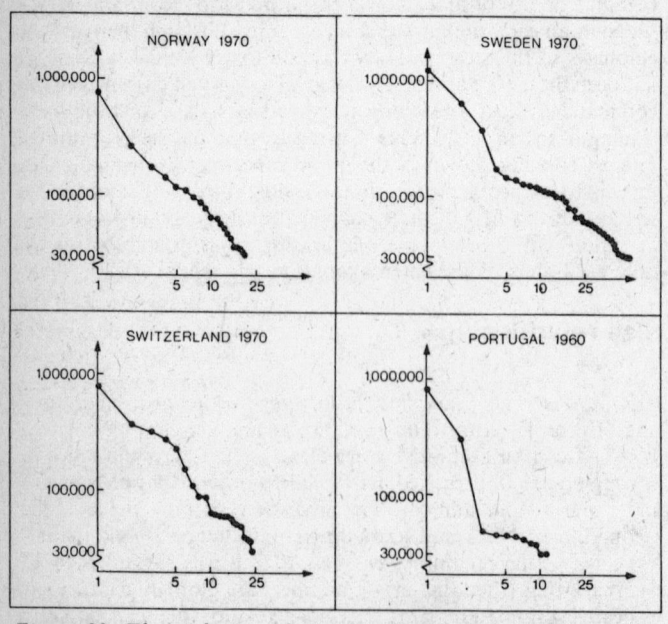

Figure 99. The rank-size relationship for four European countries: (a) Norway, (b) Sweden, (c) Switzerland, and (d) Portugal

It should be noted that the rank-size rule implies a gradual progression or **continuum** of town-sizes from largest to smallest, rather than a **hierarchy** of size categories with groups of towns of similar size. This contradicts the basic idea contained in central place theory which is discussed later in this chapter.

The law of the primate city The largest city in a country or region is referred to as the **primate city**. According to the rank-size rule, the primate city should be twice the size of the second city; that is to say, the populations should be in the ratio of 2:1. However, in many cases the ratio is much higher. For example, in Uruguay the ratio for the primate city (Montevideo) and the second city (Paysandu) is almost 17:1. Such a country or region is described as having a **high level of urban primacy**. The reverse situation, as in Canada where the ratio of Montreal and Toronto is 1·1:1, is referred to as a low level of urban primacy.

In a study entitled *The Law of the Primate City*, published in 1939, M. Jefferson attempted to explain the circumstances under which a high level of primacy might occur. Jefferson argued that once any city had become dominant in a region, 'this fact gives it an impetus to grow that cannot affect any other city, and it draws away from them all in character as well as in size to become the primate city'. More recently A. Linsky sought to identify the common characteristics of a number of countries all with very high levels of urban primacy. He concluded that a high level of primacy tended to be associated with countries which were small in extent, had high population densities, high rates of population growth, low per capita incomes, a high degree of dependence on agricultural exports, and in many cases a former colonial status. Such characteristics are, of course, typical of many developing nations. It seems possible, therefore, that a high level of primacy is associated with a primary stage of economic development. Industrialization and urbanization probably stimulate the growth of lower ranking towns, reduce the level of primacy, and bring the rank-size relationship more in line with the predictions of the rank-size rule.

Functional relationships

The term **central place** is used to describe any settlement which provides one or more services for the surrounding population. These services may be specialized, high-order services requiring a large supporting population, or rudimentary, low-order services able to conduct a profitable business with only a very small supporting population. A theatre and a small general store provide examples of high- and low-order services respectively. The size of population required to support different services is referred to as the **threshold population** for that service. The size of threshold population is greater for high-order services than for low-order services. Table 8 provides an example of threshold populations for a number of British retail stores.

Store	Threshold population
Boots the Chemists	10,000
Mac Fisheries	25,000
Barratts (shoes)	20,000–30,000
Sainsbury	60,000 (for a medium-sized self-service store)
Marks and Spencer	50,000–100,000
John Lewis (a department store)	100,000

Table 8. Estimated threshold populations for selected stores

In the analysis of urban functions it is generally assumed that if a high-order service is present in a given town, then most lower order functions will also be present. Working according to this principle it is possible to select a series of key functions which have a regular widespread distribution and to use them as indicators of settlement status. Figure 100 shows a scheme of this type, proposed by J. A. Everson and B. P. Fitzgerald.

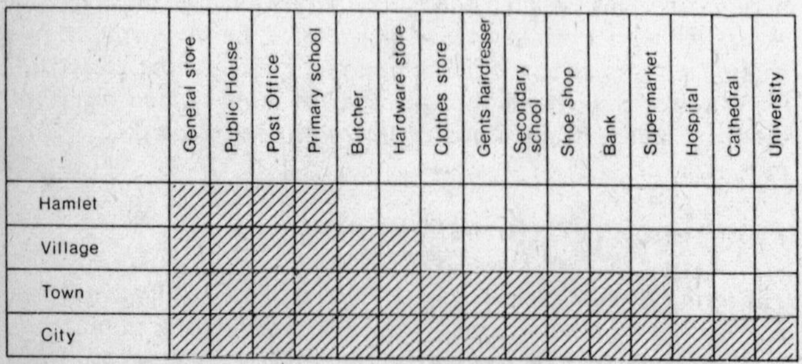

	General store	Public House	Post Office	Primary school	Butcher	Hardware store	Clothes store	Gents hairdresser	Secondary school	Shoe shop	Bank	Supermarket	Hospital	Cathedral	University
Hamlet	▨	▨	▨	▨											
Village	▨	▨	▨	▨	▨	▨									
Town	▨	▨	▨	▨	▨	▨	▨	▨	▨	▨	▨	▨			
City	▨	▨	▨	▨	▨	▨	▨	▨	▨	▨	▨	▨	▨	▨	▨

Figure 100. Settlement status defined by indicator functions

Relationships between function and settlement size In general terms the larger a given settlement, the greater the number of services it will provide. Figure 101 shows the results of a study of four towns in West Cornwall. The number of different functions present in each town has been plotted against its population size, and the 'normal' relationship between urban size and functional importance is revealed.

Sometimes when this exercise is carried out, deviant situations are revealed. Small towns often provide more services than their size would suggest, while other quite large towns contain few services. These anomalies have been commented upon by various writers. For example, it has been suggested that towns with a large number of services in relation to their size are often tourist towns or route centres, providing services not only for their own population but also for a large transient population.

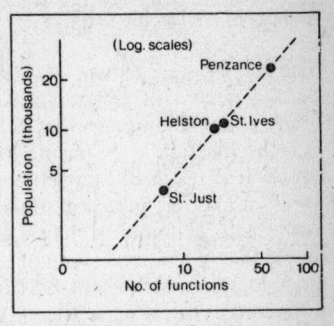

Figure 101. Population sizes and functional importance of four towns in West Cornwall

Conversely, those with a lesser number of services than their size would indicate are frequently dormitory towns situated near to a much larger urban settlement which has impeded their own functional development. Despite these anomalies, there are many empirical studies confirming the hypothesis that larger places provide more functions than smaller places.

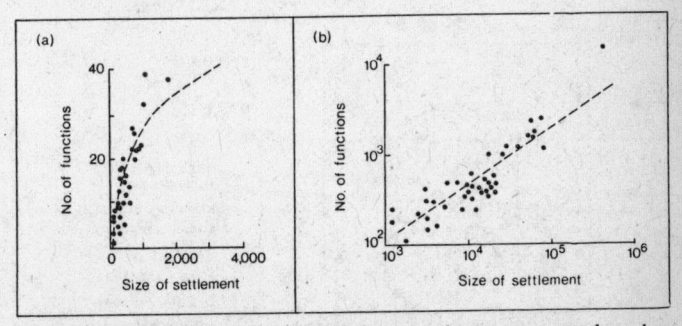

Figure 102. Relationships between functional importance and settlement size in (a) southern Illinois, USA, and (b) southern Sri Lanka. Note that the latter graph uses logarithmic scales

It appears from the curvilinear form of the relationship shown in figure 102a that as towns grow larger they add progressively fewer functions for each additional increment in size. The linear relationship is produced in figures 101 and 102b by the use of logarithmic scales.

Spatial relationships

The spatial arrangement of settlements in the landscape has long been a subject of geographical interest. Implicit in this field of study is the assumption that some sort of order and logic underlies the location and spacing of towns and villages in the landscape. It is assumed that settlements do not grow up in a totally random and haphazard manner and that a measurable degree of order is to be found in their spatial arrangement, even if it is not immediately apparent. One of the earliest attempts to seek order and logic in settlement spacing was W. Christaller's highly influential central place theory of 1933.

Christaller's central place theory Although Christaller's theory emerged from his studies of the settlement pattern of southern Germany, it is in fact largely concerned with the theoretical patterns of settlement which he believed would develop on an **isotropic surface** or idealized landscape consisting of perfectly uniform terrain, climate and soils, and presenting equal ease and opportunity of movement in all directions (page 257).

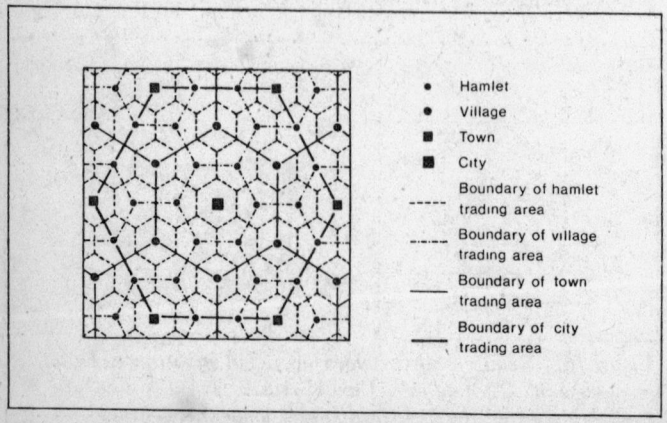

Figure 103. The $k = 3$ *network of settlements and service areas according to Christaller's central place theory*

According to Christaller, in such an area the lowest order of settlements (hamlets) would be perfectly evenly spaced and surrounded by hexagonal service areas or hinterlands. For every six of these lowest order settlements he suggested that there would be a larger and more specialized settlement (village) which in turn would be located at an equal distance from other villages and also surrounded by a larger hexagonal service area. Similarly, larger and more specialized settlements (towns and cities) would also be equally spaced and surrounded by even larger service areas (Fig. 103). Christaller's suggestion was that the smallest centres would be located approximately 7 km apart. The next largest centres were envisaged as serving three times the area and three times the population. It was argued that they would be located at a distance of $(\sqrt{3} \times 7)$ km = 12 km apart. In the same manner the next highest service areas in the hierarchy would be three times larger than those of the preceeding order. This kind of arrangement of settlements and service areas is referred to as a $k = 3$ hierarchy. It is based on what Christaller termed the **marketing principle**; that is to say, the $k = 3$ arrangement tends to develop in those regions where the provision of goods and services constitutes the main influence on settlement patterns. Christaller envisaged that other forms of settlement hierarchy might develop under different circumstances.

Christaller argued that in any region in which transport costs are particularly important a $k = 4$ hierarchy of settlements tends to develop (1, 4, 16, 64, ...) since this maximizes the number of central places on straight-line routes. He referred to this as the **traffic principle**. He also suggested that in regions with a highly

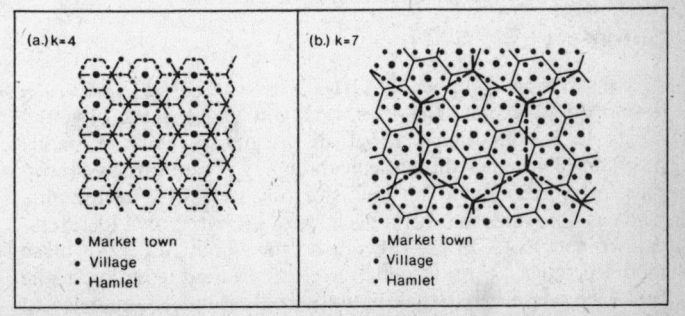

Figure 104. (a) the $k = 4$ *network according to the traffic principle, and (b) the* $k = 7$ *network according to the administrative principle*

developed system of central administration a $k = 7$ hierarchy (1, 7, 49, 343, ...) would tend to emerge. This is the so-called **administrative principle** which maximizes the number of settlements dependent on any one central place, as well as eliminating the shared allegiances of other k-value networks.

In the different settlement hierarchies proposed by Christaller, a consistent k-value is envisaged at all levels of the various systems; that is, the same basic spatial arrangement applies to villages, towns and cities, although the scale of pattern varies at each level. It has often been suggested that arrangements of this type with a fixed k-value show only a poor approximation to reality. In 1940 the economist A. Lösch proposed a modified version of Christaller's central place theory in which different k-values were allowed to co-exist at different levels in any settlement pattern. In Lösch's model which, like Christaller's, also uses hexagonal service areas, the various hexagonal systems, $k = 3$, $k = 4$, $k = 7$ and so on, are superimposed on each other at different levels in the system. The result is a much more complicated theoretical network, but one which, it is suggested, shows a much closer approximation to reality (page 263).

The main problem involved in comparing the central place model with reality is that the conditions of the isotropic surface are never fulfilled. Inevitably the theoretical arrangement of settlements in any region is distorted by the actual geographical conditions of that region. This is not to suggest that central place theory should be dismissed. The models of Christaller and Lösch still provide useful measures against which the real world can be compared. An understanding of the theoretical patterns helps to reveal and clarify the 'special' factors operating in any area.

Summary

A considerable number of models and theories have been developed to explain the sizes, functions and spacing of settlements in the landscape. Much discussion still centres on the question of whether the settlements in any region form a continuum or a hierarchy. The rank-size rule suggests a continuum, whereas Christaller's central place theory is based on a hierarchical arrangement. On the other hand the Löschian central place model produces a result which is closer to the prediction of the rank-size rule. Despite their limitations, these various models and theories are of considerable value in aiding our understanding of actual patterns of settlement in the real world.

Chapter 29
Urban Morphology

The term **urban morphology** refers to the physical arrangement or structure of any town. It is concerned with the patterns of roads, streets, building blocks and individual buildings. The study of urban morphology involves the description, analysis and explanation of the various functions of different city districts, patterns of land use and the variations in building density and building form within city areas.

The complex mosaic of urban land-use in any large town or city is the product of innumerable decisions on the part of residents, workers, planners, architects and companies, as well as local and central government officials. By and large these decisions are made on the basis of economic considerations. For most city residents, for example, the choice of residential location will be based on the cost of housing in different districts and the distance and cost of the journey to work. Similarly, industrial decisions are made on the basis of company profitability. There are certain other influences, such as aesthetic considerations and urban conservation issues, but these are generally far less important than the purely economic factors. The general principle is that 'any urban site will be occupied by the type of land-use which is able to derive the greatest utility or profit from that site and consequently is able to pay the most for it'. The value that is attached to any site is usually related to its nearness or accessibility to the city population as a whole. As an early writer on urban land economics, R. M. Hurd neatly summed up the point with the comment that 'since value depends upon economic rent, and rent on location, and location on convenience, and convenience on nearness, we may eliminate the intermediate steps and say that value depends on nearness'.

Urban bid rents The principle outlined above may be examined more closely by considering the ability of four potential users of urban land to pay rent for sites at varying distances from the city centre. Retail users need the greatest accessibility to the whole urban population, so central locations are essential for most large shops and department stores. Thus, near the city centre, retail use can outbid most other potential uses. However, the

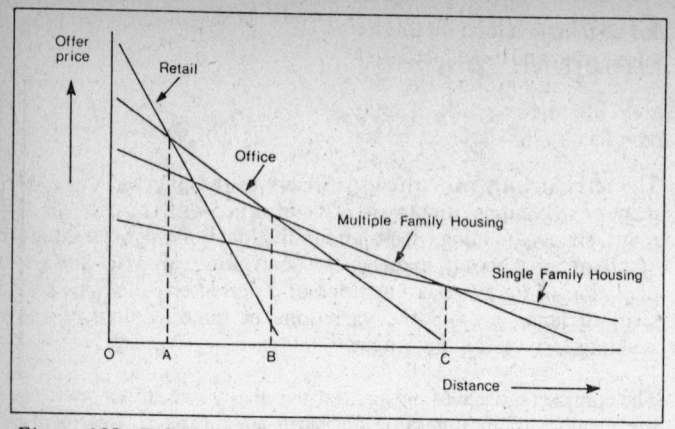

Figure 105. Bid rents in relation to distance from city centre for four users of urban land

readiness to pay high rents for retailing declines very steeply away from the city centre. Office and commercial users also seek central locations, but absolute centrality is less important for them. The bid rent for offices is therefore less high than for retailing at the city centre, but it also declines less steeply away from the centre. Multiple family housing schemes, such as large apartment blocks, give a larger return per unit area than single family housing. Consequently they are able to afford the higher costs of more accessible inner city locations. Single family housing, providing the lowest returns and offering the lowest bid rent of the four selected land uses, is therefore relegated to the least accessible sites around the urban margin. In figure 105 the various bid rents have been superimposed, and the highest bidder at successive distances from the city centre is clearly seen. If the resultant land uses are rotated through 360° around the city centre (O) to produce a two-dimensional diagram, a concentric pattern of land use will result. Both the result and the principles involved are similar to those of the von Thünen model for agricultural land use shown in Chapter 25.

The urban land value surface The over-all pattern of land values in any city is referred to as the urban land value surface. It is essentially a reflection of accessibility within the city area. Thus, land values reach a grand peak at the city centre which is the most accessible district within the whole urban area. Values are also high along both the main radial and circumferential routes in and around the city area. Secondary peaks of high land value also occur at intersections of major routes since they are favoured by a high level of accessibility. Districts located between and distant from main routes form areas of relatively low land values. Since certain districts in any city area are far better served by public transport than others, the urban land value surface usually declines more steeply from the central peak in some directions than in others. Although

Figure 106. Urban land value surface for a large city area

accessibility is the chief influence on urban land values, it is not the only one. For example, in a study of Chicago, M. Yeates demonstrated that land values in that city are greatly influenced not only by distance from the city centre, but also by a number of other factors, including distance from major shopping centres, distance from Lake Michigan, distance from elevated subway lines, as well as purely social factors such as the proportion of non-white population and the population density of any district.

Having considered certain of the underlying influences on patterns of urban land use, attention can now be directed to specific functional areas in the city and particular categories or urban land use. Any large city obviously provides many services and fulfils many functions. Inevitably it is a centre of industry, commerce, transport, retailing, administration, education, entertainment and so on, as well as being the place of residence for a large urban population. While there is a great deal of mixing, nevertheless these different urban functions tend to arrange themselves in a series of distinct land use zones. Three such zones will be discussed in this chapter: first the central business district, second, urban housing areas, and third, industrial zones within the city.

The central business district

The central business district, or CBD, which is sometimes also referred to as the downtown district, urban core or central area, is that part of any city which is concerned with its business and civic life. It is that part of the city which contains the principal shopping streets and main public buildings. It usually includes the city's tallest buildings, its heaviest concentration of cars and pedestrians, and its highest land and property values. For out-of-town people the CBD is synonymous with the city itself.

Delimitation of the CBD In terms of area the CBD is a relatively small part of any town or city – in many cases as little as 5% of the total built-up area. It is normally located at or close to the geographic centre of the urban area, and in many English towns its location corresponds with the historic core from which the settlement has subsequently developed. Many of the CBD characteristics described above can be quantified and mapped, and present possibilities for delimitation. The main problem is that characteristics such as building heights, traffic flows, land values and the presence of certain categories of land use, all have their highest concentration at the core of the CBD and then gradually decline outwards towards an indefinite boundary zone around the edge of the CBD. Precise delimitation is therefore difficult, and different results are obtained according to the criteria used.

During the 1950s important pioneer studies of the problems of CBD delimitation and the internal structure of the CBD were carried out by two American geographers, R. E. Murphy and J. E. Vance Jr., who pointed out that in American cities there is a very sharp decline in land values away from what they termed the **peak land value intersection** located near to the centre of the CBD. They suggested that a line representing 5% of the peak land value corresponded very closely with the edge of the CBD and might be used as a boundary indicator. Figure 107 shows the relationship between the 5% value line and the edge of the CBD in Phoenix, Arizona as defined by land use. The use of a land value

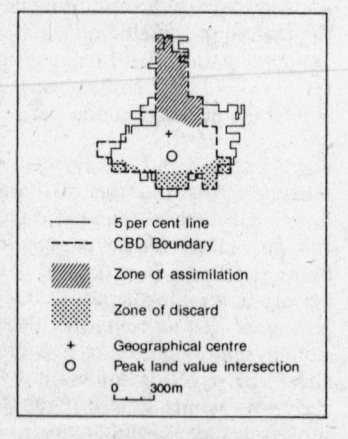

Figure 107. The CBD of Phoenix, Arizona (after Murphy & Vance)

for delimitation has the virtue of objectivity, but the main problem, especially in the case of British towns, is that valuation data are difficult to obtain. Murphy and Vance also drew attention to the fact that the boundary of any CBD is never static. They coined the terms **zone of assimilation** to distinguish an area into which CBD land uses are expanding, and **zone of discard** to mark an area of CBD retreat. The former is often characterized by a spread of shops, offices and hotels into former residential areas, while the latter takes the form of a shabby, deteriorated district with low-grade retail stores and much vacant property. It was also suggested that the peak land value intersection gradually shifts in the same direction as the zone of assimilation.

Land use in the CBD shows a close adjustment to the pattern of land values within the central city and is related to distance from the peak land value intersection. At the heart of the CBD, land and property values are so high that only companies with a large turnover and substantial profits can afford to occupy these most costly and prestigious sites. Thus, large department stores, major chain stores, supermarkets and headquarters offices tend to be found at the core of the CBD. Just beyond this innermost zone are found smaller shops and offices, while the small traders with only modest profits are forced out towards the margin of the CBD where a greater proportion of non-CBD land uses and vacant premises start to appear.

However, this simple relationship between type of land use and distance from the peak land value point is distorted in various ways. For example, businesses which are dependent upon each other for their day-to-day operation often cluster together and form a distinctive enclave within the CBD. For example, a financial district with banks, solicitors' offices, estate agents, stock brokers, accountants, insurance companies and the like, is often evident in many large cities. Another modification of the normal pattern of land use is created by the presence of a large bus or rail station at the edge of the CBD. Transport termini of this type attract hotels, boarding houses, restaurants, cafes, car-hire firms and travel agents, so that the station often becomes the centre of a sub-system of land use within or at the edge of the CBD.

The preceding comments give some brief indication of the type of spatial relationships that exist within the CBD. This part of the city is, of course, subject to constant change and adjustment in response to residential population movements, transport developments, and even changes in shopping habits. In the USA, for example, the CBD of many cities is now badly deteriorated and scarcely used by local residents who prefer to shop in large purpose-built shopping malls in the suburban districts around the edge of the city. The opening of similar shopping centres in Europe, such as the Brent Cross shopping centre in North London, possibly heralds a similar trend, although elsewhere in Europe old city centres, inadequate for modern needs, have been completely redeveloped in order to maintain their traditional status. Examples of the latter process include the Högtorget Centre in Stockholm and the Lijnbaan in Rotterdam.

Urban residential districts

In general terms urban population densities and urban housing densities attain their highest values close to the city centre and decline progressively outwards towards the suburban margin of the built-up area. This relationship between population and housing densities and distance from the city centre is referred to as the urban density gradient. It can be expressed by the following formula:

$$d_x = d_o e^{-bx}$$

in which d_x represents the population density (d) at distance (x) from the city centre, d_o is the central density, e an exponent of distance and b the density gradient or rate of decrease of population density with distance from the city centre, a negative exponential decline. As an explanation of this relationship, it has been suggested that 'the poor live near the city centre on expensive land, consuming little of it, and the rich at the periphery consuming much of it. Since the land consumed by each household increases with distance from the city centre, population densities must drop'. This view corresponds with the ideas of E. W. Burgess on the process of city growth (described later in this chapter). According to Burgess, 'as the city grows outwards from the centre so new houses are built on the periphery. New fashions in housing appear at these points and such houses are desired, and can only be afforded, by the richer elements of the population and they, in consequence, move progressively outward. As this happens the outmoded houses they abandon filter down the income scale. This produces concentric residential zones with increasing income, and by implication increasing social status, from the centre outwards. These are conventionally named working or lower class, middle class and upper class zones.'

It is possible to identify a number of distinct types of urban housing which are found in most large cities and which may be related to the processes described above.

1. Central city housing Although the central city is generally lacking in housing since it is a less profitable use of land than shops and offices, there are nevertheless a few small residential enclaves, usually of prestige status, in the innermost districts of most large cities. The exclusive residences of Mayfair and Belgravia in London provide examples of this type.

2. Inner city housing In many cities the CBD is surrounded by a transitional land-use zone containing many deteriorated slum properties. Beyond this **twilight zone**, as it has been termed by some writers, there are the inner city housing districts. Such areas usually contain a variety of housing types, including large 19th century houses now sub-divided into multi-family units, late-19th century tenement blocks and terraces of small working-class houses. These various types of housing may extend out along the main roads towards the suburbs.

3. Suburban housing Whereas the inner city housing is of 19th century origin, most suburban housing is a product of the 20th century, and is often interpreted as a reaction against the poor, overcrowded conditions of the inner city. Thus, suburban housing is built to a much lower density, is dominated by detached and semi-detached single-family residences with private gardens, and contains a greater amount of public open space. Much suburban building takes the form of monotonously uniform housing estates developed either by private builders or by the municipal authority. **Ribbon development**, consisting of long lines of houses straggling out along main roads, was a common feature of suburban building of the 1920s and 30s.

4. Dormitory towns Around many large cities an attempt has been made to check the suburban invasion of farmland and open space by the creation of a **green belt** within which housing developments are severely restricted. However, with the growth in private car ownership it is now possible for city workers to live in small towns beyond the green belt and to commute into the city each day. Towns of this type which fulfil a residential function for the central city are termed dormitory towns. Examples include the Surrey towns of Dorking, Redhill and Reigate.

Like other types of urban land use, residential areas are subject to constant economic and social change. Once fashionable areas may become progressively down-graded by the sub-division of large houses and their occupation by lower-income groups. This process is known as **filtering-down** and may be illustrated by the Notting Hill district of London. The reverse process, known as **gentrification**, involves districts of former artisan cottages and small houses becoming fashionable and being purchased by middle class families at greatly inflated prices. Parts of the inner London districts of Islington and Chelsea have undergone this gentrification process.

Industry in the city

Compared with the large number of published studies dealing with both the CBD and urban housing, relatively few studies have sought to generalize about the patterns of industrial land use within cities. Most research on industrial location has been concerned with patterns of location at the regional level, rather than the intra-urban scale. Part of the problem lies in the fact that both the type and amount of industry varies widely from city to city. In some cities, manufacturing industry is virtually the *raison d'être* of the city itself, while others are more concerned with other functions such as administration and contain relatively little manufacturing. Under these circumstances it is difficult to find recurrent or even similar spatial arrangements. Nevertheless, despite these problems, it is possible to establish certain general principles about the types of location favoured by different types of industry within any large city.

Industry in the central city Despite the fact that manufacturing makes no contribution to the function of the CBD, it is not unusual to find small workshops and industrial premises scattered throughout the central city. Industry of this type selects a central location for various reasons. For example, it may supply retailers within the CBD with its products, as does the garment industry north of London's Oxford Street, or it may distribute its products over the whole city area, as in the case of Fleet Street newspaper publishing, or it may need to draw highly skilled specialized workers from the whole urban field as does the Hatton Garden jewellery industry. In some instances, centrally located industry is simply a relict feature of an earlier pattern of industrial location.

Industry close to the waterfront, canals and railways Industry concerned with the processing of heavy or bulky imported raw materials is usually located adjacent to port sites, major waterways or rail termini. Examples include grain milling, sugar refining, paper making, metal smelting and cement production. These are often 'nuisance' industries, creating noise, dust, fumes or smoke, and ideally should be sited away from housing as well as close to bulk transport facilities. Public utilities such as gas and power stations often occupy a similar type of location. The Thameside industries of London's East End are of this type.

Industry along radial and ring roads With the growth of road transport for the movement of raw materials and products, many industries have moved away from the congested inner city districts to sites along main roads in and around the city. Decentralization has been encouraged by the use of electrical power, which allows flexibility in the choice of site, and by the presence of a large suburban labour force. The lines of factories along London's North Circular and Great West Roads provide good examples of this type of location.

Industry in the suburbs Manufacturing industry is also found in a variety of other types of suburban location. For example, industries requiring very large amounts of land for assembly or production lines or for storage or disposal of waste products often seek out suburban locations where land is relatively cheap compared with the inner city. In other instances, purpose-built factory units have been provided by the municipal authority in the

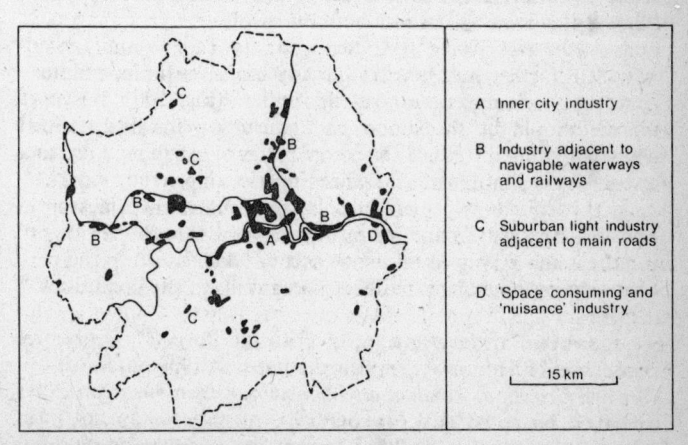

Figure 108. Distribution of manufacturing industry in Greater London (after J. E. Martin)

form of **trading estates** or industrial estates in the outer city. Examples include the Park Royal and Borehamwood Industrial Estates in outer London.

Urban land use models

Attention has so far been directed to specific types of land use – retailing, offices, housing and industry – and the typical locations which they occupy within the city. However, attempts have also been made to formulate **comprehensive models** of urban land use in which the overall pattern of land use is analyzed.

The concentric or zonal theory This is one of the earliest attempts to present a comprehensive model of urban land use. It derives from the work of E. W. Burgess on the social and morphological areas of Chicago, and was first presented in a paper of 1925 entitled *The Growth of the City: An Introduction to a Research Project*. According to Burgess, 'the typical process of the expansion of the city can best be illustrated, perhaps, by a series of concentric circles which may be numbered to designate both the successive zones of urban expansion and the types of areas differentiated in the process of expansion.... Encircling the downtown area there is normally an area of transition which is being invaded by business and light manufacture. A third area is inhabited by the workers in industries who have escaped from the area of deterioration but who desire to live within easy access of their work. Beyond this zone is the residential area of high class apartment buildings or of exclusive 'restricted' districts of single family dwellings. Still further out, beyond the city limits, is the commuters' zone – suburban areas or satellite cities' (Fig. 109). Burgess's scheme should be thought of as a useful **normative model** which attempts to reduce the complexities of urban land use to a series of very simplified, generalized relationships. The model has, in fact, been widely criticized as being anachronistic, lacking in universal application making insufficient reference to the siting of industry, and failing to take into account distortions to the concentric zones caused by radial routes and local site conditions.

The sector theory An early critic of Burgess's concentric model was H. Hoyt who published a paper in 1939 on *The Structure and Growth of Residential Neighbourhoods in American Cities* in which he noted that 'residential rent patterns do not form successive concentric circles.... From the evidence presented it may be concluded that the rent areas in American cities conform

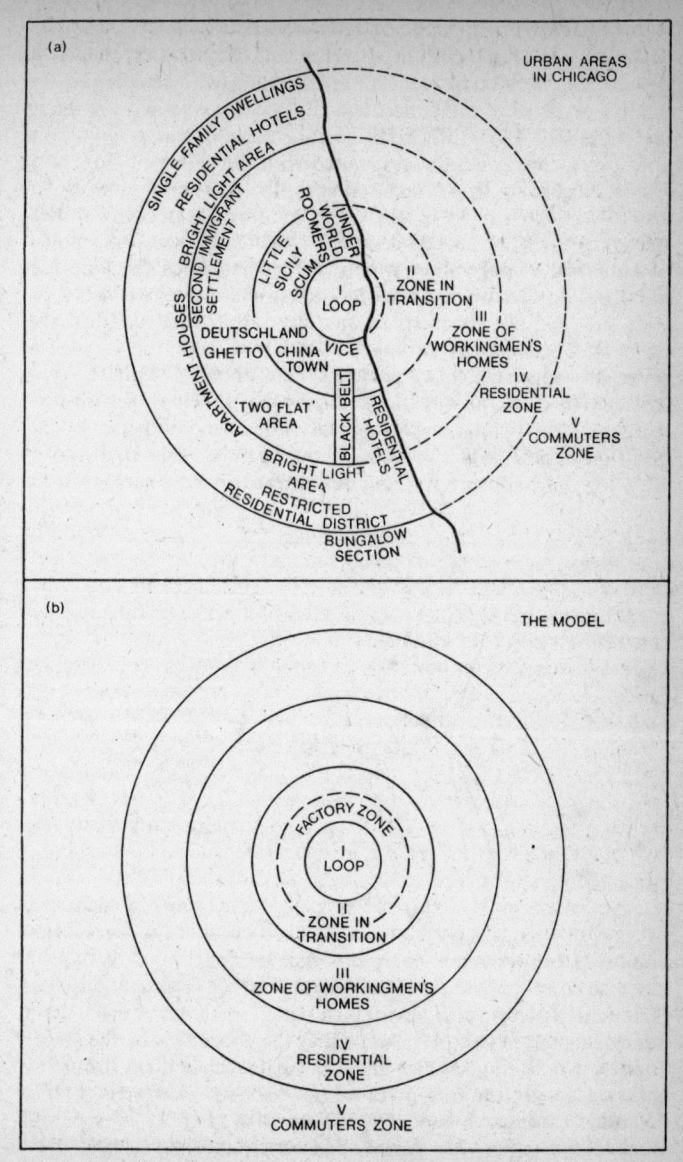

Figure 109. The concentric model of urban land use

to a pattern of sectors rather than concentric circles.' Another American, M. R. Davie, in a paper on *The Pattern of Urban Growth* also noted that 'very often distorting factors so frequently disrupt or obscure the concentric circle pattern so as to make it useless as a tool for study'. The so-called 'sector theory' of urban land use is thus generally associated with the names of Hoyt and Davie. According to the sector theory, the pattern of land use in any city is determined by the directional arrangement of routes radiating out from the city centre. These create a sectoral pattern of land and rental values which in turn influence the land-use pattern. In other words, it is the directional element which controls the land-use contrasts in any city rather than the distance element. The land-use structure comes to assume the form of a series of wedges which widen and spread outwards from the central city in different directions. According to Hoyt, a high-rent residential district in one part of a city will extend outwards by the addition of new belts of housing along its outer edge. In a similar way, low-rent housing will extend outwards in another direction.

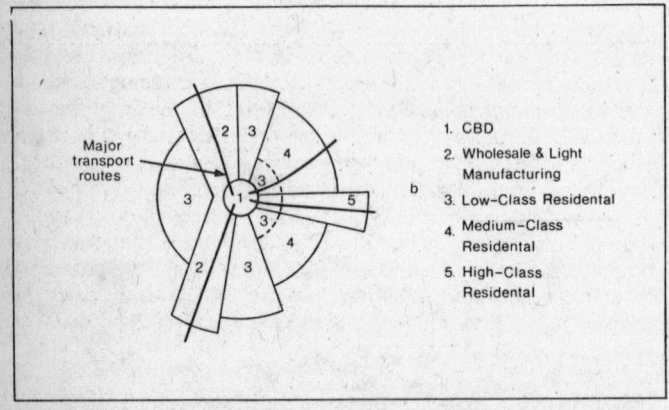

Figure 110. The sector theory of urban land use

The multiple nuclei theory In reality, patterns of urban land use are far more complex than either the concentric or the sector models would suggest. In an attempt to move away from the massive generalizations involved in both, C. D. Harris and E. Ullman proposed a model made up of a number of separate nuclei. In a paper, *The Nature of Cities*, published in 1945, they pointed out that most large towns and cities do not grow from a

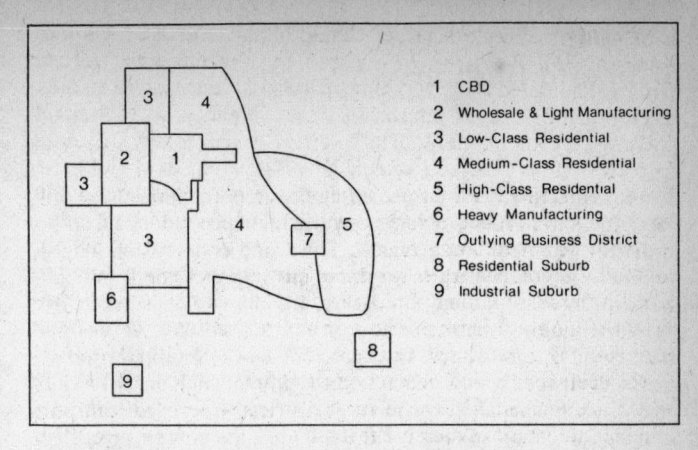

Figure 111. The multiple nuclei theory of urban land use

single centre, but rather are formed by the progressive integration of a number of separate nuclei to form a 'patchwork' of urban land-use zones. The processes which produce this mosaic of land uses are not random. According to Harris and Ullman, the pattern is determined by a number of controls. For example, certain activities require specialized locations within the city, and no others will suffice; many activities tend to cluster together, while others repel each other and tend to remain separate; many activities cannot afford high-rent locations and can never compete with other land uses able to afford such sites. None of these principles were new; all had been discussed by other writers. The contribution of Harris and Ullman was to use these principles to produce a model of urban land use which is more flexible than either the concentric or sector models, and capable of being applied to the land-use pattern of most large cities.

Summary

Patterns of urban morphology are determined chiefly by urban land values which in turn are influenced by accessibility. The concept of urban bid rents clarifies the nature of competition for urban sites. Urban land uses have been studied individually – for example, Murphy and Vance's work on the CBD – but attempts have also been made to formulate comprehensive models of urban land use, notably the concentric, sector and multiple nuclei models.

Chapter 30
City and Region

From comments made in preceding chapters the impression will have been given that any large city has close economic and social ties with its surrounding region. Town and country are, indeed, mutually interdependent. Any large city supplies goods and services to the surrounding population, and many of its workers live in adjacent dormitory towns and 'urbanized' villages. At the same time country areas supply raw materials and agricultural produce to the central city, and depend on the city for high order services which are unavailable in the rural districts. Improved transport and communications mean that these links are now stronger than ever before. A. E. Smailes has remarked that 'to a degree quite unknown in the past the inhabitants of the areas between urban centres look to the towns and are drawn within their spheres of influence'.

The term **urban field** is used to refer to an area which is linked economically and socially to any urban settlement. Other terms are also used in the geographical literature; for example, sphere of influence, zone of influence, catchment area, tributary area, umland and hinterland. They all mean much the same thing, although strictly speaking the term hinterland should be used to refer to the area served by a port. The term **city region** is also used to describe the urban field of a very large urban centre. Both urban fields and city regions should be thought of as **functional regions** characterized by a system of flows and links around the central city (page 205).

Delimitation of urban fields

Many geographers have shown a preoccupation with the problems of delimiting urban fields, and there exists a large amount of published material on this subject. In general terms two basic approaches have been adopted. First, there are empirical studies which seek to measure and analyse the actual links that exist between any town and its surrounding region, and second, there are deductive studies which discuss the size and shape of urban field that ought to exist on the basis of various assumptions and abstract, deductive arguments. The one approach is concerned with reality, the other with theory.

The empirical approach The task of identifying the actual extent of any town's influence on the surrounding area is by no means easy. The normal approach is to select a number of indices which are appropriate to the size of the town in question and reflect its main central place functions. The selected indices must be capable of being expressed cartographically so that a series of overlapping boundary lines may be drawn around the urban centre to indicate the area over which it extends its various influences. An examination of studies of this type will reveal that a number of fairly standard measures are used in such work, together with a wide variety of other indices which often display considerable ingenuity in their selection. Commonly-used measures include school and hospital catchment areas, place of residence of factory and office workers and newspaper circulation areas. Figure 112 shows the urban field of Penzance defined on the basis of a variety of such measures. It will be

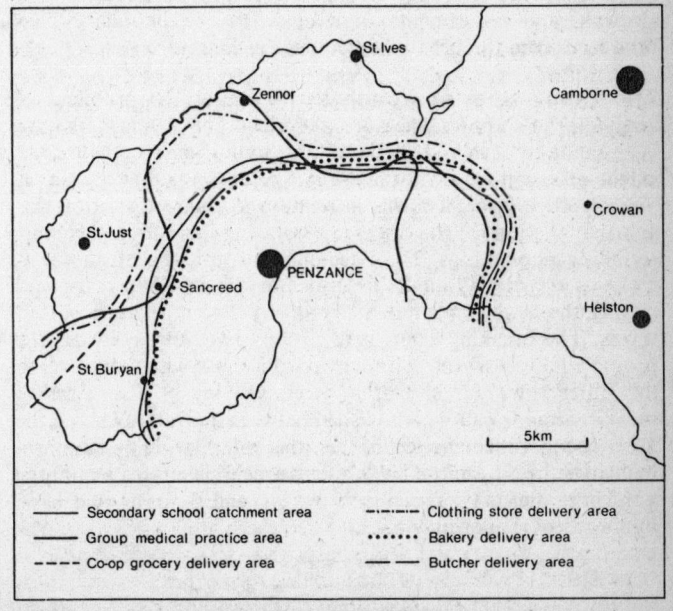

Figure 112. The Penzance urban field defined by various measures

noticed that while there is a general degree of similarity in the results obtained from the different indices, there are nevertheless important discrepancies in detail. This is one of the problems with this type of approach. It is unusual for the boundary lines produced by various indices to correspond exactly. It is normal practice to present the various boundaries collectively rather than to reduce them to a single average or composite line.

The information required for studies of this kind is collected within the town itself, but the approach may be reversed. It is possible to carry out a questionnaire survey among the inhabitants of villages surrounding any town in order to determine the use that they make of the town for different types of services. How frequently is the town visited for various services? What proportion of the village population actually works in the town? What other towns are used for particular services and how often? H. E. Bracey used this type of analysis very effectively in a study of the zones of influences of various towns in Somerset. In the case of the urban field of Penzance, a supplementary survey was carried out in the villages of St. Buryan, Sancreed, St. Just, Zennor and Crowan, and adjustments were made to the boundary lines produced from the urban data sources in Penzance itself.

The theoretical approach Partly due to the problems of applying the empirical measures described above, attempts have been made to develop techniques for establishing the theoretical extent of urban fields on the basis of certain assumptions about the attractive force of towns in relation to their population size and the 'friction' of the distance separating them from their surrounding populations. These techniques are based on the principles of the gravity model described earlier in Chapter 18, and involve the establishment of a **breaking-point** between pairs of towns. The breaking point between any two towns divides the people who will travel to one town from those who will travel to the other town for similar services. Obviously if a series of breaking-points can be established between a given town and the other towns which encircle it, then this will provide a theoretical indication of the central town's urban field. The position of the breaking-point (x) between two towns (i and j) can be calculated by means of the formula

$$d_{jx} = \frac{d_{ij}}{1 + \sqrt{\frac{P_i}{P_j}}}$$

in which P_i and P_j are the populations of the two towns, and d_{jx} is the distance of the breaking point from the smaller town, j.

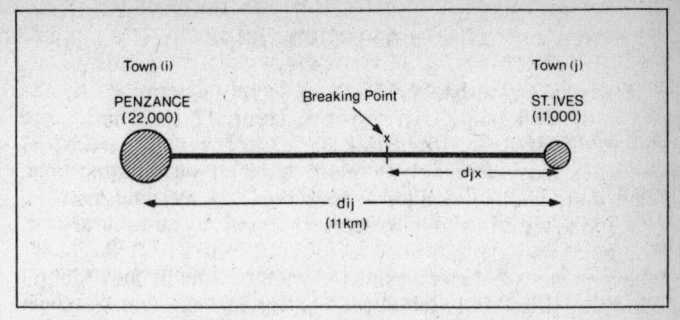

Figure 113. Location of the breaking point between two towns

Taking the example of West Cornwall, the formula may be illustrated by reference to the two towns of Penzance and St. Ives which have populations of 22,000 and 11,000 respectively, and are located 11 km apart. By using these values in the formula it can be calculated that the breaking-point between the two towns should lie at a distance of 4·6 km from St. Ives.

$$d_{jx} = \frac{11}{1 + \sqrt{\frac{22,000}{11,000}}}$$
$$= 4·6 \text{ km}$$

It is important to appreciate that breaking-point theory is based on a number of assumptions which may not be borne out in reality. It is assumed, for example, that the relative attraction of different towns is simply a reflection of their population sizes. This may not be the case: relatively large towns with poor quality retailing facilities may be unattractive to shoppers. On the other hand, it is possible to substitute values other than mere population size into the formula. It is also assumed that the non-urban population will make the choice between alternative destinations in a logical, rational manner, selecting to visit those towns which lie closest in terms of distance or time or cost. Again, this may not be the case. Recent studies have shown that shoppers' perception of distances to different centres may be highly distorted. Distances to unattractive shopping centres tend to be overestimated and distances to prestige stores often underestimated. In any case many urban visitors may be prepared to accept a sub-optimal return for the time and cost of their travel to the city. None of these possibilities are accounted for by breaking-point theory.

The size and shape of urban fields

The size of any urban field is very largely determined by the degree of development of the town as a central place. This is more important than mere population size: large towns of an industrial character may serve only a relatively small surrounding area, while quite small market towns concerned with retailing, distribution and administration may serve a surprisingly large rural area. The point may be well illustrated by the results of P. R. Odell's study of the two Leicestershire towns of Coalville and Melton Mowbray (Fig. 114). Melton Mowbray is an ancient market town and has strong ties with its surrounding rural area, while Coalville is a coalmining town of relatively recent growth and provides few services for its surrounding population. Although the two towns are similar in size, their contrasting functions produce two urban fields which are very different in extent.

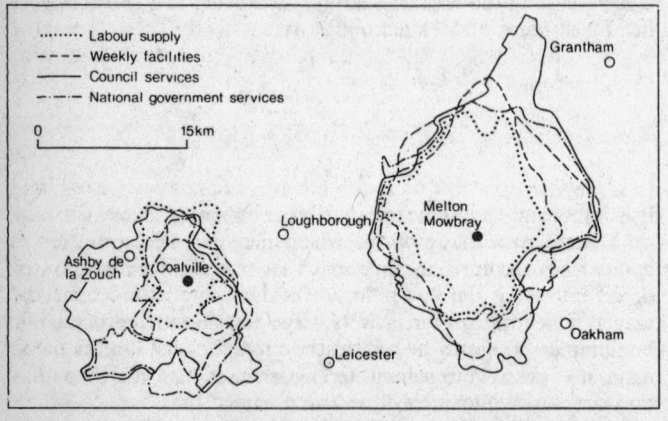

Figure 114. The urban fields of Coalville and Melton Mowbray

The spacing of towns in any region is also important. Where towns are widely spaced, the potential exists for urban fields to encompass a very wide surrounding area. On the other hand, large numbers of closely-packed towns inevitably produce a pattern of small, restricted urban fields. Thus, Norwich, which has no town of comparable size within a radius of 65 km, has a very extensive urban field, while in the West Midlands the close proximity of Wolverhampton, Wednesbury, West Bromwich, Walsall, Dudley, Warley, Stourbridge, Birmingham and other towns, has resulted in a series of small overlapping urban fields, no single one of which dominates the surrounding region in the way that Norwich dominates East Anglia.

Urban fields rarely form symmetrical or circular shapes around central places, but rather take the form of irregular figures, the outermost points of which extend out along main roads, especially those with good public transport services. Conversely, certain physical features, such as rivers and estuaries with few bridging points, may act as barriers and isolate rural areas relatively close to an urban centre. For example, H. Carter has shown that the urban field of Wrexham extends no more than 8 km east of the town where its further growth has been restricted by the course of the River Dee which is crossed by only a single road bridge in the 28 km above Chester. In a similar manner A. R. Smailes has pointed out that the urban field of Middlesbrough is most extensive along the main road east towards Whitby, but is restricted to the south and west by the paucity of bridges across the Rivers Tees and Leven. Areas to the west of the Tees have better connections with Stockton and Darlington than with Middlesbrough.

Relationships between urban fields

In any region in which there is a hierarchy of central places, there is usually a 'nested' arrangement of urban fields. That is to say, small towns providing low-order functions serve the population of a very restricted surrounding area. These small urban fields themselves lie within the larger urban fields of higher-order central places, which in turn form sub-systems within the area served by large regional centres providing the highest order of goods and services. This is the normal arrangement in any region with a well-developed hierarchy of central places.

A point of interest in the type of arrangement described above concerns the relationships that exist between the urban fields of central places of the same order or level of importance. It has been suggested that two situations can be observed. There are either **zones of overlap** which enjoy a duplication of services and in which the population shares its allegiances between two or more towns, or there are **zones of vacuum** where the edges of adjacent urban fields fail to meet and in which the population makes little or no use of urban services. This latter situation is unusual in most developed nations. In the UK, for instance, less than 10% of the total population lives more than one hour's travel by public transport from a city centre. But in the developing nations, with far lower levels of urbanization, and where towns are often much more widely spaced, it is not unusual for areas to lie beyond the sphere of influence of any urban centre and for the population to make little or no use whatsoever of urban services.

So far in this discussion it has been assumed that the spatial extent of any town's influence over its surrounding area can be thought of as a single boundary line. This is, of course, a simplification of reality. Urban influences gradually diminish away from the built-up area of the city, and the margin of any urban field is therefore best regarded as a zone of diminishing influence merging into adjacent urban fields, rather than a precise linear boundary. Indeed, many writers have suggested that the whole area of urban influence, not just the margin of the urban field, can be best analysed in terms of a series of roughly concentric zones of diminishing influence around the central city. For example, A. E. Smailes has proposed that urban fields can be divided into three zones: a **core area** which very largely corresponds with the built-up area of the city and over which the city reigns supreme; an **outer area** in which the city is used for high-order services,

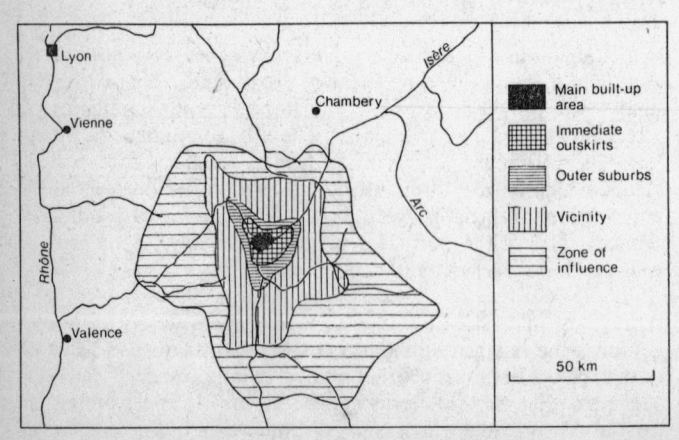

Figure 115. The zones of influence of Grenoble

but other small centres are used for low-order services; and a **fringe area** in which the city is used only infrequently and by a small proportion of the population. On the basis of his study of urban catchment areas in Somerset, H. E. Bracey suggested a similar zonal division, and referred to the **intensive, extensive and fringe areas** of the urban fields in that county. The same concept of zones of declining influence is also implicit in figure 115 which is based on a study by H. Vivian of Grenoble's urban field.

It has frequently been pointed out that since the urban fields of large cities form functional regions, it would be logical for municipal and other local government boundaries to correspond with the approximate extent of at least the major urban fields. In fact, this is rarely the case. In many countries, municipal boundaries were established at an early date and often bear little relationship to contemporary urban fields and city regions. Changes in local government boundaries in England and Wales in 1974 did little to improve this situation. In many cases the area linked to, and served by, a single city is administered by several local authorities.

Summary

Towns and their surrounding areas are mutually interdependent. The term 'urban field' describes the area which is linked economically and socially to any town. Delimitation of urban fields can be based upon various empirical measures, or may involve a theoretical approach using techniques derived from the basic gravity model formula. The size of any urban field is largely determined by the functional importance of the town, while its shape is influenced by the arrangement of local transport routes. Urban fields can be subdivided into a series of roughly concentric zones of diminishing urban influence away from the central city.

Further Reading

General
Bryant, R. H., *Physical Geography Made Simple*, 2nd edn. (W. H. Allen, 1979).

Bowen, D. Q. et. al., *A Concise Physical Geography* (Hulton Educational, 1972).

Haggett, P., *Geography: A Modern Synthesis*, 3rd edn. (Harper & Row, 1979).

Knowles, R. and Wareing, J., *Economic and Social Geography Made Simple*, 3rd edn. (W. H. Allen, 1980).

Meteorology and Climatology
Barry, R. G. and Chorley, R. J., *Atmosphere, Weather and Climate*, 3rd edn. (Methuen, 1976).

Flohn, H., *Climate and Weather* (Weidenfeld & Nicolson, 1969).

Gaskell, T. F. and Morris, M., *World Climate: the Weather, the Environment and Man* (Thames & Hudson, 1979).

Gates, E. S., *Meteorology and Climatology*, 4th edn. (Harrap, 1972).

Sutton, O. G., *Understanding Weather*, 3rd edn. (Pelican, 1969).

Geomorphology
Bradshaw, M. J. et al., *The Earth's Changing Surface* (Hodder & Stoughton, 1978).

Brunsden, D. and Doornkamp, J. C. (eds), *The Unquiet Landscape* (I.P.C. Magazines, 1974).

Gass, I. G. et al., *Understanding the Earth* (Open University, 1971).

Rice, R. J., *Fundamentals of Geomorphology* (Longman, 1977).

Small, R. J., *The Study of Landforms*, 2nd edn. (Cambridge University Press, 1978).

Biogeography
Collinson, A. S., *Introduction to World Vegetation* (George Allen & Unwin, 1977).

Fitzpatrick, E. A., *An Introduction to Soil Science* (Oliver & Boyd, 1974).

Pears, N. V., *Basic Biogeography* (Longman, 1977).

Simmons, S., *Biogeography: Natural and Cultural* (Edward Arnold, 1979).

Tivy, J., *Biogeography: A Study of Plants in the Ecosphere* (Oliver & Boyd, 1971).

Population Geography
Beaujeu-Garnier, J., *Geography of Population*, 2nd edn. (Longman, 1978).
Clarke, J. I., *Population Geography*, 2nd edn. (Pergamon, 1972).
Peterson, W., *Population*, 3rd edn. (Collier Macmillan, 1975).
Trewartha, G. T., *A Geography of Population: World Patterns* (Wiley, 1969).
Zelinsky, W., *A Prologue to Population Geography*, 2nd edn. (Prentice-Hall, 1970).

Economic Geography
Abler, R., Adams, J. S. and Gould, P., *Spatial Organization: The Geographer's View of the World* (Prentice-Hall, 1971).
Estall, R. C. and Buchanan, R. O., *Industrial Activity and Economic Geography*, 3rd edn. (Hutchinson, 1973).
Hodder, B. W., *Economic Development in the Tropics*, 2nd edn. (Methuen, 1973).
Morgan, W. B. and Munton, R. J. C., *Agricultural Geography* (Methuen, 1971).
Robinson, H. and Bemford, C. G., *Geography and Transport* (Macdonald & Evans, 1978).
Simmons, I. G., *The Ecology of Natural Resources* (Arnold, 1974).
Smith, D. M., *Industrial Location: An Economic Geographic Analysis* (Wiley, 1971).
Warren, K., *Mineral Resources* (David & Charles, 1973).

Settlement Geography
Carter, H., *The Study of Urban Geography* (Edward Arnold, 1971).
Chisholm, M., *Rural Settlement and Land Use*, 2nd edn. (Hutchinson, 1968).
Clout, H. D., *Rural Geography: An Introductory Survey* (Pergamon, 1972).
Dwyer, D. J., *The City in the Third World* (Macmillan, 1974).
Everson, J. A. and Fitzgerald, B. P., *Settlement Patterns* (Longman, 1969).
Everson, J. A. and Fitzgerald, B. P., *Inside the City* (Longman, 1972).
Hall, P., *World Cities*, 2nd edn. (Weidenfeld & Nicolson, 1969).
Johnson, J. H., *Urban Geography: An Introductory Analysis*, 2nd edn. (Pergamon, 1972).

Index

abrasion, 94, 104, 112
accelerated erosion, 155
accessibility, 222, 237
adiabatic processes, 20–1
advantage,
 comparative, 232, 255
 secondary, 248
agglomeration, 249
agriculture, 157, 159, 224–35
air mass, 36–7
albedo, 12, 54
allometric growth, 90
alluvial fan, 87
alluvium, 86, 237
altiplanation terrace, 100
anabatic wind, 52
animals, 137, 148–8, 151, 227
anticline, 65
anticyclone, 28, 42–3, 50
asthenosphere, 60–1
atmosphere, 9–17, 21, 152–5
Auerbach, F., 285
autotroph, 128, 131
average expectation of life, 187
azonal soil, 124, 125

barchan dune, 103, 106
barrier beach, 112
base exchange, 118
batholith, 68
beach, 109–12, 156
 raised, 115
behavioural matrix, 259
beneficiation, 238
Bergeron mechanism, 24, 154
berm, 106, 111
biogeography, 128
birth rate,
 controlled, 184
 crude, 182
 in the UK, 185
 standardized, 182
 voluntary, 184
blowout, 106
boreal forest, 144
Borlaug, N., 179
Bracey, H. E., 313
braiding, 84
break-of-bulk point, 218, 248
breaking point, 308

breaking point theory, 308–10
brown earth, 124, 126
Burgess, E. W., 285, 298, 302
Buys Ballot's law, 27

calcifuge, 139
calcimorphic soil, 125
capital
 in agriculture, 230
 in mining, 240
 money, 248
 physical, 248
 shortage, 272
carbon cycle, 133
carnivore, 129
Carter, H., 311
catena, 122
census, 161
central business district, 295–8
 delimitation of, 296
 land use of, 297
 zone of assimilation, 297
 zone of discard, 297
central place, 287
central place theory, 290
centripetal force, 28
channel, 82, 85, 87
chelating agent, 120
chemical weathering, 73
chernozem, 125
chinook wind, 20
Chorley, R. J., 77
choropleth map, 163
Christaller, W., 285, 290
cirque, 94
city region, 306–13
Clarke, J., 185
clay-humus complex, 118, 157
cliff, 112–3
climates, 44–56
 and agriculture, 225
 and industry, 249
 and mining, 237
climatic change, 13, 16, 56
climatic climax, 141
climatic geomorphology, 78
clouds, 21–2
 frontal, 38
 seeding of, 154, 228

coast, 107–16, 156
co-efficient of dispersion, 277
commodity prices, 239, 273
compensation point, 136
competition,
 in agriculture, 231
 in transport, 219
complementarity, 210
compressing flow, 93
concentric theory of urban land use, 302
condensation, 19
conduction, 10, 72
connectivity, 222
continental drift, 60
convection, 10
convergence and divergence, 30
convergence of form, 78
coombe rock, 99
Coppock, J. T., 283
Coriolis force, 26
corrasion, 85
creep, on slopes, 75
crevasses, 93
critical erosion velocity, 86
cumulative causation, 269
current, 15, 109
cuspate bar, 112
cycles of erosion, 79
 hydrological, 14, 81, 92
 nutrient, 132
 phosphorus, 135
 soil, 122
cyclonic flow, 28

Davie, M. R., 304
Davies, J. L., 115
Davis, W. M., 71, 79, 80, 84, 91
de Castro, J., 184
deciduous forest, 143
decision making, 207, 244
 optimising, 208
 satisficing, 208
 sub-optimal, 259
decomposer, 129
deficiency disease, 177
deflation, 103
deforestation, 154
delta, 87, 96
demand,
 agricultural, 224

316

industrial, 255
  minerals, 239, 243
  industry, 255
demographic revolution, 271
demographic transition model, 173–6
demography, 161
deposition, 86–7, 95, 103, 109–12
depression, 40–2
desert,
  climate, 48
  ecosystem, 147–9
  landform, 104
  soil, 125
desilication, 121
description in geography, 202
detritivore, 129
dew, 54
dew point, 20
diastrophism, 61
distance, 192, 211
  absolute, 212
  convenience, 212
  cost, 212
  decay, 211
  economic, 215
  perceived, 215
  relative, 213
  time, 212
divergence, 40
doldrums, 33
dormitory town, 299
dot distribution map, 163
drainage basin, 78, 89, 90
drift, glacial, 96, 101
drumlin, 95
dune, 103, 106
dust bowl, 155
dynamic equilibrium, 89

earthquake, 62
easterlies, 33–4
ecology, 128
economic activity,
  patterns in, 203
  primary, 200, 202
  secondary, 200, 203
  tertiary, 200, 204
  quaternary, 200, 204
economic development, 267
  agricultural, 224
  balanced growth, 274
  unbalanced growth, 274
economic infrastructure, 231, 250, 272
economic man, 258
ecosystem, 128–141
  desert, 148

forest, 143
  grassland, 145
  marine, 149
  modifications, 157
  tundra, 147
ecotone, 146
ecumene, 168
edaphic factor, 138
effective demand, 225
eluviation, 72, 120
energy sources, 236, 247
energy, types of, 9, 10
  river, 82
  ecosystem, 130
environmental control, 135
environmental management, 159
environmental hazard, 226
epeirogenesis, 61, 114
epiphyte, 143
equatorial rain zone, 46
equatorial trough, 48
erosion, 85, 94, 103, 112
esker, 96
eustasy, 114
eutrophication, 157
evaporation, 15, 18–19, 72
evapotranspiration, 15, 120, 138
exchange, system of, 206
exchange pool, 133
explanation in geography, 205
  inductive, 207
  deductive, 207
extending flow, 93

farming types, 233
fault, 66
feedback, 68, 110
ferralsol, 121, 125
fertility, 181–6
filtering-down, 300
firm, geography of the, 249
fjord, 115, 202
firn, (nevé) 92
Flohn, H., 46
flood(s), 105
  control, 159
  plain, 87
flow diagram, 9, 10
fluvioglacial deposit, 95
fog, 22, 38
Föhn wind, 20
folding, 65
food chains, 129
forest, 54, 142, 160
fossil fuel, 133, 205, 243
freeze-thaw action, 98
freight rate, 219

frontier of settlement, 169
front, 33, 38–40
frost hollow, 53

game theory, 260
gangue, 238
gelifraction, 97
geliturbation, 97
general circulation, 13, 31
gentrification, 300
geographical cycle, 79
geographical determinism, 165
geographical possibilism, 165
geomorphology, 59
geostrophic wind, 27, 35
Gilbert, G. K., 88
glacial action, 94–7
glacier, 92
gleying, 121, 126
government policy,
  and agriculture, 232
  and industry, 249
  and minerals, 241
  and transport, 219
graben, 64
grade, 88, 91
graph theory, 222
grassland, 145
gravity model, 191, 211
green belt, 299
greenhouse effect, 13
Green Revolution, 179
ground ice, 92, 97
groynes, 156
grumosol, 125
Gulf Stream, 50

hadley cell, 31
hail, 24
halomorphic soil, 125
halophytes, 137
hanging valley, 113
harmattan wind, 47
Harris, C. D., 304
head, 99
heat island, 56
heliophyte, 136
herbivore, 129
heterotroph, 128, 131
horst, 64
Horton, R. E., 89
Hoyt, H., 302
humidity, 18
Hurd, R. M., 293
hurricane, 42, 226
humus, 117, 144, 145
hydraulic action, 85, 112
hydraulic radius, 82
hydrograph, 81
hydrological cycle, 14, 81, 92

hydromorphic soil, 125
hydrophyte, 137

Ice Age, 16, 57, 100-01
ice-wedge, 99
Industrial Revolution, 153
industrial site, 246
industry, 244-56
 city, in the, 300
 change, 253
 types of, 249, 252
intervening opportunity, 191, 210
igneous rock, 65, 237
infiltration capacity, 155
insolation, 11, 13
intertropical convergence zone, 33, 46
intrazonal soil, 125
inverse distance law, 191, 211
inverted relief, 66-7
iron pan (hard pan), 120, 271
island arc, 63
isobar, 26
isostasy, 61, 97, 114
isotropic surface, 257, 290

Janelle, D., 214
Jefferson, M., 287
jet stream, 29, 47
Johnson, D. W., 115

kames, 96
karst, 68
katabatic wind, 52
kettle-hole, 96
knickpoint, 88
Köppen, W., 44
krill, 151

labour,
 agricultural, 230
 industrial, 247
 in mining, 240
Lamb, H. H., 57
land-and-sea breeze, 53
landslide, 75
land tenure, 229
lapse rate, 13, 20
latent heat, 19
laterite, 121
law of the primate city, 287
leaching, 120, 251
least cost theory, 261
light, 135-6, 226
lightning, 25
limestone relief, 68
lithosphere, 60
location theory, 257-66

agricultural, 257
industrial, 261
loess, 102
Lorenz curve, 164
Lösch, A., 263, 292
low-energy coast, 113-4

malnutrition, 177, 272
Malthus, T. R., 178
 and resources, 242
management, 247
mangrove swamp, 114
mantle, 59
marine ecosystem, 149
market area, 263
markets, 231, 246, 273
mass movement, 74-6, 155
maximum revenue theory, 262
meander, 83
metamorphic rock, 65
migration, 189-93
 chain or stage, 190
 laws of, 190, 198
 net migration balance, 181
 models and theories, 190
Milankovitch curve, 16
Miller, A. A., 44
mineral, 66, 236, 245, 253
misfit stream, 83
Mistral, 48, 226
Mitchell, J. B., 278
Mohorovicic discontinuity, 59
monoculture, 157
monsoon, 34, 46-8
moraine, 95
mor humus, 144
morphometry, 89
mountain,
 barriers, 34, 50
 block, 63
 building, 62
 climates, 52-3
 soil, 125
mortality, 186-89
mortality rate,
 age-specific, 187
 crude, 186
 infant, 187
 standardized, 186
mull humus, 144
multiple nuclei theory, 304
Murphy, R. E., 296
Myrdal, G., 269

natural selection, 140
nature conservation, 159
nearest neighbour

analysis, 163, 280
net reproduction rate, 182
network, 209
 analysis, 222
 connectivity, 222
 effectiveness, 222
 planning, 222
nevé (firn), 92
nitrogen cycle, 133, 157
nivation, 99
nonecumene, 168
nutrient cycle, 132

occlusion, 41
ocean(s), 34, 36, 149
 floor, 63
 current, 13
optimal location, 257, 261
optimum population, 180
ore, 236
ore-dressing, 238
orogenesis, 62
overpopulation, 180, 275
oxygen, 154
outwash plain, 96
overland flow, 72, 76

pampas, 146
parallel retreat, 79
patterned ground, 98
peak land value intersection, 296-7
pediment, 105
pedogenesis, 120
pedology, 117
pelagic zone, 151
Penck, W., 79
peneplain, 80
perception, 215, 281, 309
periglacial processes, 92
permafrost, 51, 98
phosphate, 158
phosphorous cycle, 135
photoperiodism, 136
photosynthesis, 128, 132, 136, 148, 149
physiological drought, 137, 148
pingo, 99
plankton, 128, 150
plate tectonics, 60-2
plucking, 94
podzolization, 120
podzol, 124, 126
point bar, 84
pollution, 56, 152-3
polygon, periglacial, 98-9
population,
 age-structure of, 194
 census, 161
 composition, 194
 concentration, 168

318

data sources, 161
density, 163
distribution, 163-8
  natural increase of, 181
  occupation structure, 199
  optimum population, 180
  pyramid, 195
  register of, 162
  sex-ratio of, 197
  world growth of, 170-72, 271
populations, biotic, 140
Pred, A., 259
precipitation, 22-4, 52
pressure gradient force, 26
pressure release, 73
process-response models, 110
productivity in ecosystems, 130-2
profitability, spatial margins to, 264

radiation, 10
rank-size rule, 285
Ravenstein, E. G., 190, 198
raised beach, 115
recreation, 284
regional differences,
  backwash effect, 269
  spread effect, 270
regional policy, 250
region, 204, 233
  farming, 233-34
  formal, 204
  programming, 205
regolith, 77, 79
relationships, 203, 250
relief, 217
rendzina, 127
resource management, 242
resource process, 205
resources,
  allocation, 206
  demand for, 206
  food, 271
  physical, 160, 236, 271
  non-renewable, 205
  renewable, 205
  supply, 206
ria, 115
ribbon development, 299
rift valley, 64
river, 81-91
roche moutonnée, 94-5
rock type, 65
Rossby wave, 29, 40
Rostow, W., 267
run-off, 76, 155

rural depopulation, 281
rural settlement, 276-84
  nucleated, 276
  dispersed, 277

saltation, 102
salt marsh, 107, 114
sandur, 96
savanna, 147
scarification, 155
Schumm, S. A., 77
sciophyte, 136
sea-floor spreading, 60
sea-level change, 114-5
seasons, 227
second home, 283
sector theory of urban land use, 302
sedimentary rock, 65, 237
seif dune, 103
sere, 140
sierozem, 125
sirocco wind, 48, 226
slope, 71-80, 122
Smailes, A. E., 306, 312
Smith, D. M., 265
smoke, 153
smog, 56
social attitudes and institutions, 224, 228, 272
soil, 15, 117-27, 160, 226
solifluction, 99
solum, 119
species structure, 129
spit, 112
storm surge, 109
storm beach, 111
Stouffer, S., 191
Strahler, A., 89
stratosphere, 13
striation, 94
strip mining, 155, 237
strophic balance, 27
subduction zone, 61
subsidence, 155
succession, 140
sulphur dioxide, 153
swash, 108, 111
syncline, 65
systematic geography, 203
system, 9
  atmosphere-ocean, 15
  cascading, 10
  control, 152
  earth-atmosphere, 9-17
  ecological, 204
  farming, 232
  hydrological, 14, 81
  manufacturing, 244
  open, 71, 88-9
  slope, 71

spatial, 204
transport, 220

technology,
  and agriculture, 228
  and industry, 255
  and mining, 237
  and transport, 214
tectonic force, 62-4, 114
temperature, 12-13
  effect on agriculture, 226
  effect on organisms, 136
terrace, 87
thalweg, 88
theory,
  behavioural, 193, 207, 257, 263
  normative, 207, 257, 302
thermal low, 42, 47
thermal wind, 29
thermocline, 150
threshold population, 287
throughflow, 72, 76
thufur, 98
thunderstorm, 24
tide, 109
till, 95
time factor (historical), 16
  in climate, 14, 56
  on coasts, 107, 114-5
  in glacial landforms, 100-1
  in soils, 122
time-space convergence theory, 214
tolerance range, 135
tor, 69, 100
trace element, 132
trading estate, 302
trade wind, 32
transferability, 211
translocation, 120
transpiration, 15, 136
transport, 209-23
  air, 218
  agriculture and, 231
  costs, 216
  flows, 220
  industry and, 245
  mining and, 238, 240
  network, 220
  ocean, 218
  pipeline, 218
  rail, 217
  road, 217
  route, 220
  system, 220
tree, 142
trophic structure, 129
tropical rain forest, 143

319

summer rain climate, 46
tropopause, 13
tsunami, 63
twilight zone, 299
tundra, 147–8

Ullman, E., 210, 304
underdeveloped countries, 270
undernourishment, 177, 272
underpopulation, 180
unloading, 67
upper air motion, 28–30
urban climate, 55
urbanization, 156
urban settlement,
  bid rent, 293
  continuum, 286
  density gradient, 298
  field, 306–13
  function, 287
  hierarchy, 286
  land-use models, 302–5
  land value surface, 294
  morphology, 293
  residential district, 298–300
  size, 285–7
U-shaped valley, 94

valley profile, 87–9
valley widening, 85
Vance, J. E., Jr., 296
varves, 97
veldt, 146
volcano, 64
village, 276–84
  commuter, 282
  cruciform, 279
  distribution, 280
  form, 278
  green, 279
  key, 284
  site, 277
  street, 279
von Thünen, J. H., 257, 294

waste disposal, 247
water availability, 137, 246
water-layer weathering, 113
watershed management, 159
wave, 107
weathering, 73–4, 120
Weber, A., 261
westerlies, 32, 47, 49
wind action, 102
wind belt, 26–35

xerophytes, 137

yardang, 104

Zipf, G. K., 191, 285
zonal climates, 46
zonal soil, 124
zonal theory of urban land use, 302